SPEAKING FOR
THE PEOPLE

Duke University Press Durham and London 2021

SPEAKING FOR
THE PEOPLE

Native Writing and the Question of Political Form

MARK RIFKIN

Designed by Courtney Leigh Baker and typeset in Garamond
Premier Pro by Westchester Publishing Services

Library of Congress Cataloging-in-Publication Data
Names: Rifkin, Mark, [date] author.
Title: Speaking for the people : Native writing and the question of
political form / Mark Rifkin.
Description: Durham : Duke University Press, 2021.
Identifiers: LCCN 2020049187 (print)
LCCN 2020049188 (ebook)
ISBN 9781478013419 (hardcover)
ISBN 9781478014331 (paperback)
ISBN 9781478021636 (ebook)
Subjects: LCSH: American literature—Indian authors—History
and criticism. | American literature—19th century—History and
criticism. | Politics and literature—United States—History—
19th century. | Indians, Treatment of—United States—History. |
Indians of North America—Government relations. | Indians of
North America—Colonization.
Classification: LCC PS153.152 R56 2021 (print) |
LCC PS153.152 (ebook) | DDC 810.9/897—dc23
LC record available at https://lccn.loc.gov/2020049187
LC ebook record available at https://lccn.loc.gov/2020049188

COVER ART: (*Top to bottom*) William Apess, courtesy Wikimedia
Commons; Zitkala-Ša, courtesy the Library of Congress; Sarah
Winnemucca, courtesy the Nevada Historical Society; Elias
Boudinot, courtesy the Oklahoma Historical Society.

Contents

Acknowledgments

I've been thinking for a long time that I wanted to write about representativity in nineteenth-century Native writing. However, the impetus for this project most directly comes from Dr. Jason Cooke's wonderful dissertation, "Indian Fields: Historicizing Native Space and Sovereignty in the Era of Removal." I served as his advisor, and working with him led me back to this project idea. While my focus on questions of surrogation and the shape of governance differs from his attention to discourses of history and the work of notions of Indianness, his excellent work played a large role in inspiring this study.

Thanks so much to Courtney Berger, Sandra Korn, and everyone at Duke University Press for another wonderful experience. I'd also like to thank the anonymous readers for their incredibly helpful feedback. The research for this project was funded partially by a Faculty Research Grant from UNC Greensboro and completion of the project was made possible by a year of research assignment. Portions of the book were presented at Tufts University, Deakin University, Penn State University, UNC Chapel Hill, Wellesley College, the Native American and Indigenous Studies Association, the Modern Language Association, and C19, and I would like to thank all those who invited me and the organizers of the conferences as well as all those who attended my presentations and provided feedback. Parts of chapter 2 previously were published as "Shadows of Mashantucket: William Apess and the Representation of Pequot Place," *American Literature* 84, no. 4 (2012): 691–714, and parts of chapter 3 previously were published as "Among Ghost Dances: Sarah Winnemucca and the Production of Tribal Identity," *Studies in American Indian Literatures* 31, no. 1–2 (2019): 170–207.

There are numerous folks whose continuing presence in my scholarly world makes this work possible. Among them are Chad Allen, Joanne Barker, Nancy Bentley, Lisa Brooks, David Chang, Eric Chefitz, Pete Coviello, Jean Dennison, Rod Ferguson, Beth Freeman, Ashley Glassburn, Mishuana Goeman, Alyosha Goldstein, Lisa Hall, Grace Hong, Shona Jackson, Daniel Heath Justice, Dana Luciano, Scott Morgensen, Dana Nelson, Rob Nichols, Beth Piatote, Joseph Pierce, Audra Simpson, Kara Thompson, Kiara Vigil, and Priscilla Wald. I would also like to thank those folks at UNC Greensboro who for the past thirteen years have made my everyday life in the academy so much richer. Thanks to Heather Adams, Risa Applegarth, Danielle Bouchard, Sarah Cervenak, Daniel Coleman, Asa Eger, Jen Feather, Tara Green, Gwen Hunnicutt, Janine Jones, Elizabeth Keathley, Karen Kilcup, Derek Krueger, Cybelle McFadden, Christian Moraru, Noelle Morrissette, Jenn Park, Gene Rogers, Scott Romine, María Sánchez, Amy Vines, and Karen Weyler.

In addition to the folks above, there are also those beyond the university who keep reminding me of the inestimable importance of family and friendship. Thanks to Tiffany and Will Allen, Sheila and Alex Avelin, Zivia Avelin, Laura and Jim Baxley, Keith Brand, Craig Bruns, Ali and Adam Cohen, Kevin and Justin Dichter, Lori and Steve Fineman, David Horowitz and Courtney Allison, Steve and Dianne Horowitz, Mike and Rebecca Hardin, Debbie and Andy Johnson, Drew and Elizabeth Johnson, Steven and Erica Johnson, J. J. McArdle, Alicia and Bobby Murray, David Peck and Abby Kornfeld, Stefanie Peck, Toby and Brian Pecker, Sarah Johnson Saunders, Lisa Smith, and Jon Van Gieson.

Erika Lin, you already know. I'm deeply grateful to Neal and Sharon Rifkin and Gail Dichter for being there for whatever shape things take.

To Rich Murray, my love for you is never in question, and the form you give to my life makes everything possible.

In 1978, the Bureau of Indian Affairs developed official criteria and an evaluative process for recognizing Native peoples who currently were not officially acknowledged as such for federal purposes.[1] The guidelines have changed over the years, having been updated most recently in 2015, but a number of elements of the process persist across these alterations, including the need to prove descent from a "historical Indian tribe" (or from "historical tribes that combined"), existence as an "Indian entity," the possession of a "distinct community," and the presence of consistent "political influence or authority" over members.[2] Despite changes in the kinds of evidence used to meet these qualifications, they continue to point toward the need to signify *Indianness* as a discrete kind of bounded difference in order to become legible as an Indigenous people within the legal and administrative networks of settler governance.[3] The presumptive form of such Indigenous collectivity entails having a group of persons who belong exclusively to it (rather than having multiple relations with various "Indian entities"), a clearly delimited landbase to which they have more or less exclusive claim, and a system of governance that has jurisdiction-like extension over this outlined group and place. We might describe this model as the *political form* of the Indian tribe. As Joanne Barker notes, in federal Indian law and policy, "the recognition of Native status and rights is really about the coercion of Native peoples to *recognize themselves* to be under federal power within federal terms," further indicating that the determination of whether an entity fits the model of "Indian tribe" is "most certainly not about who is and is not recognized so much as it is about the ongoing processes of social formation that work to keep Native peoples subjugated to U.S. power."[4] Presenting one's people as organized in ways consistent with the political form of the *Indian tribe*, though, provides the condition of possibility not only for accessing particular legal and material resources (such as having territory put in "trust" and officially made governable under tribal law) but also for being able to speak and advocate for that collectivity in relation to institutional networks for whom that form provides the organizing template for entrée.[5] In this way, the recognition process highlights the intimate imbrication of political form, collective voice/speech, and institutional intelligibility. Moreover, the figure of the "Indian tribe" points to the ways that the effort to represent Indigenous peoples to (settler) political institutions and for political purposes may rely on a depoliticization of peoplehood in two senses: casting the "tribe" as itself a kind of cultural and/or racial entity whose character and boundaries are not the stuff of politics; and treating the dynamics of peoplehood as themselves expressive of a de facto collective unanimity, rather than as subject to politics—in the sense of ongoing negotiation, disagreement, and debate among the people who comprise *the people* (including, possibly, as to where to draw the borders of peoplehood, geographically and demographically).

To seek recognition by settler institutions and publics entails offering a portrait of peoplehood that licenses representative speech in the name of that collectivity.[6] Serving as a political spokesperson requires that one speak in ways that can be heard as *representative*, as indexing a coherent collective entity and doing so in ways that appear to be expressive of that public's sentiments, wants, and needs. Nineteenth-century Native writing by intellectuals from peoples on lands claimed by the United States offers numerous examples of just such a claim, to be speaking in the name of a particular (set of) people(s) in order to pursue recognition of one kind or another.[7] Unlike in the case of the pursuit of federal acknowledgment, though, such texts are neither acts of governance per se (undertaken by constituted authorities operating in their publicly authorized capacities) nor direct engagements with U.S. officials. Rather, these authors present themselves and their accounts as representative in order to engage with settler publics, often seeking to mobilize them to call for changes in existing (Indian) policy. In doing so, though, such texts need to negotiate non-native expectations about what can count as Indigenous peoplehood, including by what process the authors can appear as proper spokespersons who can convey collective dispositions, grievances, and desires.

In characterizing these texts in this way, I mean to invoke existing scholarly and activist conversations about the meaning of the pursuit of settler recognition by Indigenous peoples, and I mean to raise questions about the processes, aims, and struggles collated (and critiqued) as "recognition." The authors considered here—Elias Boudinot, William Apess, Sarah Winnemucca, and Zitkala-Ša—

are writing across a range of circumstances and policy formations (Indian removal in the Southeast, the guardian system in southern New England, the invasive implementation of the reservation system in the West, and the imposition of allotment and boarding school education), and they do so under conditions of extraordinary duress, in the context of active and explicit settler projects of expropriation, intervention, and detribalization that both pressurize their speech and animate it. We can see similar kinds of pressures at work in the present in both the United States and Canada, in the form of increased efforts to repudiate prior official acknowledgments of sovereignty, gain access to Native territories (those recognized as such by the state and not), expand extractive industries on and near Native lands, extend forms of economic extraction, and force Native peoples to organize their governments in ways conducive to such settler initiatives.[8] Turning back to nineteenth-century writings in the current moment, then, serves as a way of lifting off of the particular embroilments of the present (and the specific terms in which they are staged—in law, by activists, and by scholars) in order to explore the intertwined processes of engaging the state's colonial imperatives and of negotiating how to define and organize the form of peoplehood as lived "on the ground."

Looking back to these earlier authors, the contexts out of which their writings emerged, and the aims and implications of the strategies they employed opens possibilities for developing more textured ways of talking about the politics of peoplehood—both toward non-natives and within/among peoples—and the complex and shifting relations between these dynamics. In their efforts to mediate settler frameworks, writings by nineteenth-century Native authors draw attention to the intellectual labor entailed in navigating, inhabiting, and seeking to reorganize non-native networks. Attending to that work of negotiating with settler forms draws attention to the broader question of how Indigenous modes of peoplehood are (re)shaped in their interface with settler ideological and institutional formations. This set of issues lies at the heart of existing discussions around "recognition." *Speaking for the People* argues that these texts' efforts to secure non-native recognition of Indigenous modes of peoplehood, governance, and territoriality illustrate the force and contingency of settler frameworks as well as the struggles involved in narrating Indigenous collectivity under ongoing colonial occupation. In claiming an ability to represent Native peoplehood (to speak *about* by speaking *for*), the writers I discuss all offer portraits of what peoplehood *is*. In doing so, they make choices among a range of potentially disparate, even incommensurate, ways of envisioning indigeneity and Indigenous governance. The choices about how to do so are affected by available non-native ways of understanding Indianness, tribal identity, and what constitutes a "political" claim—particularly one emerging from a group not deemed civilized or fully capable of "political" action. Authors mobilize such templates in order to gain access to and participate as intelligible speakers/claimants within what can be characterized as *settler networks*—media circuits, institutional structures (governmental and not), and discursive formations. The ways they stage the legitimacy of their own entry into and speech within such networks affect how indigeneity will appear within such texts, even as the texts themselves seek to redirect the frameworks they employ to Indigenous ends. Such texts demonstrate the negotiatedness of Native political form as it circulates in settler networks, official and popular. These writings, then, also draw attention to broader questions with regard to how to understand choices of political form and the orientating contexts in which such choices occur, a set of practical, philosophical, and ethical concerns that arise not solely in direct print engagements with non-native publics but also within the extratextual dynamics of Indigenous governance. The matter of how to understand, organize, and experience peoplehood separate from imposed settler forms and interests lies at the heart of contemporary critiques of recognition. While in many ways taking such critiques as my organizing frame of reference, my analysis of how nineteenth-century Native texts sought to stage their own representativity aims to open additional avenues for thinking about how conceptions and experiences of collective identity, voice, and self-determination continually emerge through ongoing processes, in which the form of peoplehood remains an open-ended question.

The approach to nineteenth-century writing that I'm suggesting foregrounds the problems and elisions involved in taking a conception of sovereignty or peoplehood as a given against which to assess Native efforts to grapple with political form. The de facto legal referent for sovereignty lies in a conception of Indigenous governance as centralized and operative over a clearly bounded territory with an easily defined, determinate population. While this paradigm might capture the institutional matrix of constitutional Cherokee nationalism (chapter 1), for instance, it does not well suit relations on and between reservations in southern New England (chapter 2), the geopolitics of prophet movements in the Great Basin (chapter 3), or the workings of and among tiospayes on the Plains (chapter 4). Looking at the varied historical and geopolitical dynamics across the nineteenth century that shape these authors' work underlines that Indigenous political form does not have an archetypical outline, instead taking shape with regard to the particularities of disparate Native peoples' geographies, philosophies, relations with other peoples, and dense entanglements within the colonial frameworks of those who seek to occupy Indigenous lands and to extend authority over Native peoples and territories. What's at stake, though, when a particular model of peoplehood analytically functions as *the Indigenous real*? Such de facto assessment can be seen when Native texts' requests and demands for recognition (and their mobilization of particular kinds of political form in doing so) are viewed as wanting due to either of the following: their difference from what is taken to be the basis for the governance of the people in question at the time the text was written and published ("here's what the *actual* political structure of the Cherokees [or Pequots or Northern Paiutes or Yankton Sioux] was during that period"); or the ways another account of sovereignty is taken to be unimplicated in colonial relations, envisioned as less compromised than the version of political form offered by a given writer ("here's how Native people(s) *actually* are when they're not trying to accommodate non-natives"). In that interpretive mode, a text's particular account of peoplehood—a particular employment of political form—is understood to succeed or fail to the extent that it can be seen as consonant with a given extratextual political formation, itself taken as expressive of real (colonially uncontaminated) Native self-understanding of a people's collective identity, their connections with their lands and waters, and their kinships and diplomacies.

This way of reading—or, more broadly, this way of approaching what constitutes indigeneity—can end up measuring representations of peoplehood in relation to a presumptive Indigenous real that lies elsewhere, such that Native writings (or other articulations of sovereignty and peoplehood) are positioned as properly bearing that real: being seen as either sovereignty-enacting acts of affirmation or expressions of a kind of false consciousness. Put another way, a claim to represent the people gets assessed against another portrayal of peoplehood that conceptually and rhetorically is positioned as representative in ways often not acknowledged as such. Attending to texts that themselves assert their representativity—a common feature of nineteenth-century nongovernmental Native writing—helps highlight the question of how a particular vision/version of indigeneity comes to stand for peoplehood and the intellectual and political import and implications of that metonymic process. In examining the dynamics and struggles around such metonymy within nineteenth-century writing, I hope to generate additional tools for thinking about how such substitutions can be at play in both enacting and refusing recognition, in efforts to address non-native publics and to offer what is envisioned as a more authentic vision of indigeneity that can serve as a model for collective governance beyond the state. What I'm pointing to is the potential for the de facto mobilization of a notion of authenticity against which other formulations of indigeneity come to be delegitimized as *less truly Indigenous*. Such a framing can posit a somewhat idealized, normative model of indigeneity as *the* standard, elevating one version of a people's or set of peoples' governance in a given period in ways that erase extant alternatives as well as the tensions among them and the processes and philosophies at play in navigating those tensions. By contrast, through a turn to the modes and circumstances of articulation for nineteenth-century writing, I seek to highlight the texture, difficulties, and labor of negotiations over political form within situated circumstances of ongoing colonialism.

The Work of Native Writing

When thinking about where to turn for visions of indigeneity and self-determination not constrained by colonial terms and aims, scholars often look to Native literary texts as sites to locate alternatives to dominant non-native form(ul)ations. If settler discourses offer skewed, stereotypical, and just plain vicious accounts of Indigenous people(s), the argument goes, Indigenous literatures can function as a corrective, providing an archive of representations that convey Native realities and philosophies that have been targeted for erasure and destruction within colonial political economy. The precise contours of "the literary" may remain somewhat elliptical, understood as written "stories," acts of imagination, or as operating in a variety of media (many of which historically have not been understood by Euro-Americans as "writing"); but this category provides a way of locating kinds of signification and transmission that operate outside the institutionalized circuits of colonial governance.[9] Even if texts interface with such networks, as in various sorts of petitions and memorials, they are cast as remaining external to the organizing logics of the state with which they engage. This desire for the literary to serve as something of an outside—as an index to a real that is effaced or defaced in non-native narratives (official and otherwise)—positions it as serving a de facto representative function. This representative relation casts the textual as expressive of extratextual dynamics, as providing an emblematizing connection to configurations of actual, genuine Indigenous collective life. Native writings are presented as serving as a conduit to Indigenous modes of worlding that materially exist beyond the text, encapsulating them and providing a textual outline or index of them. Moreover, those worldings enact sovereignty and self-determination otherwise, beyond settler impositions and deformations, or at least beyond the accounts of the real at play in settler narratives. In implicitly positing that Indigenous texts offer a representative account of lived matrices of Native sociality and governance, though, such scholarship tends not to engage the dynamics of that relation. What is the form in which such typicality or exemplarity is staged? How is such a form chosen, what conditions influence that form, and what's at stake in the difference among possible forms? How do the terms of engagement with non-natives, including the pursuit of recognition by them, affect how form is chosen and employed? Moreover, how does the writer manifest that they legitimately can offer such an account, including through the use of a particular form or forms that signifies their ability to speak for a given (set of) people(s)? These questions suggest approaching representativity less as an intrinsic quality (a presumptive relation to the real) than as a set of mediations constantly being renegotiated in the context of varied expectations about and frameworks for conceptualizing what constitutes Indigenous collectivity.

In order to avoid subsuming Indigenous writings within the canons of settler nation-states, Native literary studies has emphasized the connections between such writings and colonially obscured Native social formations as well as the ways such texts articulate Indigenous political distinctiveness as autonomous polities, which cannot be understood as ethnic/racial minorities *within* the settler-state. As Lisa Brooks notes, in Abenaki the "root word *awigha-* denotes 'to draw,' 'to write,' 'to map,'" and "it is no coincidence that the word *awikhigan* came to encompass letters and books or that wampum and writing were used concurrently to bind words to deeds. Transformations occurred when the European system entered Native space." She later adds, "The word *awikhigan* has come to encompass a wide array of texts, and its scope is still expanding. It has proved to be an adaptable instrument."[10] The technologies of what gets referred to as "writing" came to function in ways that played roles similar to those of previous technologies and modes of communication, and this continuity means that there was no fundamental rupture when Native people(s) started employing English and previously alien forms of textual production. The fact that prior to the seventeenth century alphabetic writing and the Euro-American version of the codex were not part of Indigenous systems of knowledge production and record keeping in what is now the United States does not mean that the use of such forms either fundamentally disoriented previous Native self-understandings or marked some sort of drift from a more truly autochthonous, and thus more legitimate, expression of indigeneity. Brooks observes that the "focus on questions of authenticity, and the maintenance of binaries that assume that the adoption of Christianity or literacy is concomitant with a complete loss of Native identity, has obscured the complex ways in which Native communities have adopted and adapted foreign ideas and instruments," adding, "Culture, like anything that is alive and 'engaged,' must grow and change."[11] Part of such change involves the incorporation of once-foreign technologies and practices, and to interpret that process of alteration as inherently declension from a purer, prior state is to cast Indigenous peoples as fundamentally static and unhistorical, in ways that can only envision them vanishing.[12]

Framed in this way, rather than viewing Native-authored texts originally written and published in English as somehow innately compromised or as bearing the marks of translation into an inherently non-native medium, we can read such texts as expressive of collective Indigenous principles, sentiments, and knowledges that defy the givenness of settler mappings, categories, and conceptual paradigms. Such writings may be read as actively seeking to challenge non-native frameworks, especially extant ways of perceiving and engaging *Indianness*. As Daniel Heath Justice insists, "Our literatures are just one more vital way that we have countered those forces of erasure and given shape to our own ways of being in the world," and such forms of Indigenous self-articulation "are in no way determined *by* colonialism. Indigenous texts are by and large responsive, not reactive." He further states, "To argue for and produce Indigenous writing *as such* is necessarily to engage in political struggle and to challenge centuries of representational oppression."[13] The modes of collective expression given voice in and by Native texts contest colonial misconceptions, interested misrepresentations, and erasures. Yet, instead of being simply reactive, they aim to convey versions of Indigenous being and becoming not present in settler-generated texts and archives. Such portrayal of Indigenous realities is, in and of itself, an act of "political struggle": "Given that so much of what people think they know about Indigeneity is self-serving colonial fantasy that justifies and rationalizes the continuing theft of Indigenous lands, violence against Indigenous bodies and relations, marginalization of Indigenous lives, and displacement of Indigenous being, there is a deep and urgent need for more accurate representations."[14] What constitutes this struggle over representation as specifically *political* is the ways settler portrayals play prominent roles in exerting and normalizing colonial authority over Native peoples and lands. Dominant depictions take part in various ways in the foreclosure, (mis)translation, management, and decimation of Native polities. Literature emerges in such arguments as a site for manifesting the existence and vitality of Indigenous lifeworlds. More than making such dynamics visible, though, Native literary texts transmit the idea that those extratextual matrices are political orders, that they were, are, and will continue to be incommensurate with narratives of the settler-state's rightful and commonsensical jurisdiction over spaces and subjects putatively within its borders.[15] As Beth Piatote argues, "Literature illuminates the web of social relations that law seeks to dismantle. . . . Literature challenges law by imagining other plots and other resolutions."[16] As against what she describes as a valuing of Native writing for "its expression of cultural difference," Maureen Konkle insists on the importance of attending to how literary texts illustrate "Native struggles for political autonomy," an emphasis that precludes "the incorporation of the literature into the canon that represents the United States."[17] *Accurate representation*, then, entails addressing webs of social relations that exist outside the terms of settler law, and such webs themselves are expressive of political autonomy.

However, if dominant non-native ideological frameworks and modes of perception contribute to the denial, misconstruction, regulation, and diminution of Indigenous political separateness, engaging across that gulf would involve a negotiation with the settler forms through which indigeneity is (mis)apprehended. The way of approaching Native writing that I've been discussing tends to envision texts as expressive of extratextual formations, as somewhat mimetically bearing the latter in ways that can replace "colonial fantasy" and, instead, convey Indigenous realities that lie beyond state-sanctioned frames of references. The author's choice of political form—how to portray Indigenous collectivities as polities and how to depict the contours and character of that status—appears as more or less given, even automatic, and the extratextual formation to be referenced by a given text often seems singular (implicitly presuming the existence of shared or stable political paradigms among a given people, as well as agreement on the boundaries of peoplehood, both geographic and demographic). From this perspective, Native literature encapsulates lived forms of Native peoplehood, standing in for them in ways that provide a reliable index, that faithfully represent such forms—serving as representative of them. Speaking of contemporary Indigenous struggles with the terms and assumptions at play in settler law, Dale Turner observes that "indigenous peoples must use the normative language of the dominant culture to ultimately defend world views that are embedded in completely different normative frameworks."[18] If Native authors seek to intervene in the normative paradigms guiding non-native opinion, collective action, and government policy so as to make possible acknowledgment of Indigenous political orders in ways other than the normal operation of existing framings of Indianness, wouldn't that effort affect how such authors portray Indigenous political form?

The attempt to persuade non-natives entails textually staging Native political orders in ways that would be intelligible to those publics, even while reorienting and refunctioning settler representations to get them to operate otherwise—to produce changes in extant colonial administration. Brooks asks, "What happens when we put Native space at the center of America rather than merely striving for inclusion of minority viewpoints or viewing Native Americans as a *part* of or on the *periphery* of America? What does the historical landscape look like when viewed through the networks of waterways and kinship in the northeast?"[19] Adopting an analytic framework centered on Native space and Indigenous sociopolitical formations, though, is not the same as reading Native writings as themselves immanently expressive of such networks. If a commitment to engaging and making visible extratextual Native modes of relation, governance, and mapping shapes scholarly efforts, that enframing goal does not necessarily mean that the texts in question will directly reflect such perspectives and practices, even if tracing the texts' varied, complex, and even vexed relation to such networks provides a guiding principle of interpretation.

To the extent that nineteenth-century Native writing aims to address and circulate among non-native publics, to take part in settler networks, the conditions of such participation affect how the texts configure and perform peoplehood. Drawing on the work of Bruno Latour, one might describe the understanding of Native textuality I've been discussing as one in which texts function as *intermediaries* rather than as *mediators*. Latour suggests that an intermediary "is what transports meaning or force without transformation: defining its inputs is enough to define its outputs"; whereas for mediators, "their input is never a good predictor of their output; their specificity has to be taken into account every time. Mediators transform, translate, distort, and modify the meaning of the elements they are supposed to carry."[20] Viewing Native writings as vehicles for the conveyance of extratextual truths/realities suggests that what they do as texts is bear a set of meanings or relations; they transport that content from one site to another. By contrast, treating texts as mediators suggests that they perform important intellectual and perceptual labor, drawing attention to the ways they alter the meaning and shape of Indigenous peoplehood in the process of portraying it.[21] Representation involves transformation, translation, and modification. Latour presents mediators as connecting to each other through "*traceable associations*," links that form a network, but that network is less a noun, a stable configuration or consistent entity, than an ongoing (set of) process(es) of relation, "a string of actions where each participant is treated as a full-blown mediator."[22] In analyzing networks as emerging through processes of linked mediations, Latour aims to move away from accounts of "social" phenomena that posit a "structure" as lying behind them and explaining them. As he suggests, "The presence of the social has to be demonstrated each time anew; it can never be simply postulated. If it has no vehicle to travel, it won't move an inch," and in this way, one needs to illustrate the relations among mediators "through which inertia, durability, asymmetry, extension, domination is produced."[23] If each mediator does not simply bear meanings, frameworks, and forms of force but potentially shifts them, then each mediator does work in *producing* the kinds of regularity often shorthanded through concepts like *system*, *structure*, *logic*, and *grammar*. Moreover, that process of production/performance cannot be explained by reference to a "social" formation that simply lies behind it; instead, whatever networks to which "the social" might refer in a given instance need to be constructed and reconstructed mediator by mediator, in ways that might have a certain consistency but whose consistency needs to be explained and accounted for in terms of the work of mediators, rather than merely assumed as an immanent whole.

Form provides much of the continuity in the ongoing (re)construction of networks, and when attending to nineteenth-century Native writings, we can trace the itinerary of the forms they employ as a way of understanding the network(s) in which they participate and circulate. Latour observes, "As soon as we concentrate on what circulates from site to site, the first type of entities to snap into focus are *forms*," and he defines this term as follows, "a form is simply something which allows something else to be transported from one site to another. Form then becomes one of the most important types of translations," adding, "To provide a piece of information is the action of putting something into a form."[24] Even as mediators potentially alter what they transport, they come into relation through shared form—ways of organizing, shaping, and orienting "information" such that it can be transmitted. Latour suggests that while "there is not 'underlying hidden structure,' this is not to say that there doesn't exist *structuring templates* circulating through channels most easily materialized by techniques—paper techniques and, more generally, intellectual technologies being as important as gears, levers, and chemical bonds."[25] In this vein, one might understand non-native ways of depicting Indigenous peoples as "templates" that help provide structure-effects as they move across multiple sites—legislative statutes, administrative policy and action, judicial decisions, belletristic non-native writings, newspaper accounts, and so on.

The movement of such templates, though, less creates unanimity or homogeneity than opens the potential for various templates—kinds of forms—to proliferate and amplify each other or create feedback. As Caroline Levine argues in her discussion of the relation between aesthetic and social forms, "Occasionally an institution's repetitive patterns align, but more often they work across and athwart one another, generating a landscape of power that is nothing if not messy and uncoordinated." She later notes, "As many different hierarchies simultaneously seek to impose their orders on us, they do not always align, and when they do collide, they are capable of generating more disorder than order," as one often "ends up reversing or subverting the logic of another, generating a political landscape of radical instability and unpredictability."[26]

Considering the dynamics of settler colonialism, therefore, involves attending to interactions among numerous institutions, governmental and otherwise, and those networks as they are constructed and reconstructed through a wide range of mediators circulate a range of forms/templates that may be at odds with each other.[27] The treaty form is the most familiar such template in the nineteenth century, including in its centrality to projects of legally legitimizing removal (as discussed in chapter 1).[28] However, if treaties presume a certain model of Native nationhood (with qualities similar to the conception of the "Indian tribe," discussed earlier with respect to federal acknowledgment), that model was not the only one available in the nineteenth-century United States, or even the only one at play in federal relations with peoples with whom the government had treaties. Other models, within and apart from federal governance, included portraying Native peoples as childish remnant populations in need of superintending care, as in the guardian system in southern New England (chapter 2); dangerous mobile masses prone to violent outbreaks and sway by charismatic leaders, who need to be contained on reservations (chapter 3); and prospective citizens in need of training in civilized modes of home, family, and property, which they will receive through allotment and federally provided schooling (chapter 4). These settler templates for figuring indigeneity sometimes overlap, and even when they do not, other extant models can be cited as a way of seeking to shift the dominant parameters of policy in play in a given time and place. The template of the "Indian tribe" as a coherently bounded and centrally governed entity often serves as the go-to for Native writers across the nineteenth century, since of the legal and political forms circulating in non-native networks (official and popular), this model/form seems most conducive to assertions of collective autonomy in decision-making as well as the preservation of access to and control over the use of lands and waters to which a given (set of) people(s) have longstanding connection. In claiming to speak for a (group of) Native nation(s), an author draws on such available forms, mediating them in ways that enable the text both to plug into existing settler networks (existing processes for generating and circulating information and materializing possibilities among non-natives) and potentially to "transform, translate, distort, and modify" such templates in order to put them to work in moving settler audiences toward altered action.[29]

Scholarly work in Native literary studies has developed rich ways of addressing how Native authors occupy non-native forms so as to move them beyond their initial aims or trajectories, but those accounts tend to focus on what happens in the absence of what might be understood as a specifically *political* idiom or in the context of individualizing accounts of Indianness (versus affirmations of Indigenous collectivity). Discussing Native authors writing in the early twentieth century, Kiara Vigil indicates the importance of considering "how Native speakers, writers, actors, and activists were able to strategically harness the expectations of largely non-Native audiences on behalf of themselves and Indian Country" through a "representational politics [that] revolved around how to retain their own definitions of indigenous sovereignty while fighting for political citizenship that was not about integration but rather a means for tipping the balance of power in their favor." She emphasizes how, in pursuing what sometimes looked like an assimilationist agenda, these intellectuals developed "more tools in their arsenal" to "critique and reshape the nation that continued to threaten indigenous sovereignty." In a related vein, Christopher Pexa explores what he terms "unheroic decolonization," which involves "creating accounts of [Indigenous] life that played up its innocuousness, transparency, and availability to the settler society": "to seem utterly harmless to settler audiences while actually working to decolonize and rebuild Indigenous communities."[30] Such modes of reading underline how Native writers strategically play on non-native genres and expectations in ways that enable their texts both to move public conversations and to preserve Indigenous principles in situations of extreme pressure, surveillance, and intervention. However, if these analyses tend to focus on how Native intellectuals continue to hold onto Indigenous peoplehood amid public discourses that do not acknowledge peoples as polities, similar questions arise about what is entailed in taking up given ways of signifying Indigenous political identity(/ies).

If we don't presume that textual mobilizations of political form simply derive from (function as intermediaries for) extratextual modes of Indigenous governance, we need to develop more tools for talking about the politics of representation through which Native writings depict the shape, substance, and scope of Native politics. How do Native writers make choices about the forms they use to convey peoplehood, how do historically and geographically specific circumstances affect such choices, and what are the situated implications of framing peoplehood in these ways? Mishuana Goeman argues that "Native women's literature presents ways of thinking through the contradictions that arise from the paradoxes and contradictions that colonialism presents and that Native people experience on a daily basis," further indicating that such texts "are not testaments to geographies that are apart from the dominant constructions of space and time, but instead they are explorations of geographies that sit alongside them and engage with them at every scale."[31] In illustrating and navigating such contradictions, offering portrayals of Indigenous geopolitical formations whose terms do not exist apart from the colonial categories and mappings with which such portrayals are engaged, nineteenth-century Native writings might be read less as expressing or enacting an extracolonial sovereignty than as negotiating the possibilities for signifying sovereignty in relation to non-native networks.[32]

In this way, the depiction of political representativity in a text, or a text's explicit claim to be representative, itself enacts a mediation.[33] When speaking of the role of Native literature in challenging settler law, Piatote notes "its power as critique extends from its ability to draw upon the same metaphors, plots, and language that construct the law's rationale and expression."[34] This way of conceptualizing the political work of Native writing differs from an understanding of it as expressive of social forms that lie beyond the scope of non-native law and policy; here the emphasis is on how such writings engage settler templates, "draw[ing] upon" the modes of figuration—the kinds of form—available in extant non-native discourses on Indianness and playing certain familiar ways of portraying Native people(s) against others. We might understand this gambit as a bid for recognition, as an effort to characterize Native social relations in ways conducive to non-native perception and engagement with Native peoples as landed, self-governing polities. Such a translation/transposition of Indigenous being and becoming into non-native templates, though, does involve an effacement or disowning of that which does not fit the form in question—a process that often involves the gendered erasure of women's roles as decision makers and agents for generating political bonds and that tends to substitute more bounded and hierarchical conceptions of political structure for more rhizomatic modes of association.[35] In thinking about how oppressed peoples engage with dominant discourses and institutions, Gayatri Spivak cautions about the consequences of running together two different senses of *representation*—as "proxy" and as "portrait"—in order to suggest that "beyond both is where oppressed subjects speak, act, and know *for themselves.*"[36] Such intellectual practice, she suggests, tends to efface analysis of the "ideological subject-constitution within state formations and systems of political economy" as well as "a critique of the subjectivity of a *collective* agency," the terms by which such subjectivity institutionally is constituted and normalized.[37] The conflation of the two senses of *representation* produces this effect, Spivak argues, because what gets effaced in that fusion is the ways that the potential for someone to serve as the representative for a group depends on an existing portrayal of who/what that group is, a portrayal that is normalized in the attribution of representativity to the spokesperson (in the sense of someone bearing delegated political authority or of an intellectual whose depiction is offered as exemplifying the group). To the extent that the United States determines that the political form/template of the "Indian tribe" (or Native nation) will serve as the one through which Native peoples can be recognized as representing themselves, the kinds of subjectivity expressed by Native participants in U.S. print public spheres will have to reckon with that form.[38] However, while adopting certain limited/limiting ways of portraying peoplehood may be necessary to gain entry to settler networks and as part of addressing settler publics, the use of such formulations does not inherently involve an ideological investment in those forms, especially in contrast to an investment in a vision of peoplehood that is treated as the baseline against which to measure other representations/formulations.

With regard to Native-authored texts, if one focuses on the intellectual labor at play in writing, the *work* of giving rhetorical and narrative shape to Indigenous political form in the context of settler occupation (and in the act of seeking to speak to and move settler publics), the text becomes something other than a conduit—more or less successful, more or less accurate, in conveying a vision of peoplehood that is seen as providing the proper and coherent referent for the text's account. As Chris Andersen has argued, the idea of Indian/Indigenous *difference* tends to posit a determinate set of distinctions between Natives and non-natives, in which the former are measured against a de facto baseline defined in terms of the latter and in which such distinctions provide the basis for determining what constitutes Native authenticity. He suggests, instead, "beginning with the assumption that Indigenous communities are epistemologically *dense* (rather than just *different*)."[39] Indigenous networks are dense, in their multiplicity, internal heterogeneity, historical dynamism, and complex and multivectored engagements with non-natives and other Indigenous people(s). The forms, shape, and pathways of such networks are affected by but not equivalent to those organizing settler networks. Nineteenth-century Native writings that claim a representative voice in speaking to non-natives are affected and marked by Indigenous networks even as they are oriented toward settler ones. I am arguing that these writings should not be read as merely intermediaries for either kind of network. Engaging with the political work these texts do and the stakes of their uses of form involves setting aside a view of them as simply transmitting meanings and relations from elsewhere, or as failing to do so, in favor of attending to the templates they employ and the aims and effects of staging peoplehood in the way each does, at that time, in that conjuncture, for that (set of) people(s).

In this way, drawing attention to these texts' ways of negotiating colonial pressures and expectations reflects back on how we approach the forms of governance "on the ground." If the work these writings perform cannot be understood either as simply an endorsement of the forms they circulate or as a relative deviation from an Indigenous political real, the work of Indigenous governance itself can be rethought as an ongoing set of mediations/negotiations in the context of continuing colonial occupation. How can attending to such texts foreground the complex and contingent character of political form as it circulates within a range of disparate networks and across multiple sites? How can the scene of recognition provide insight about the compromises, torsions, strategies, and difficulties with respect to Indigenous sovereignties as lived—in all their multivalent complexities? What are the affordances and consequences of adopting particular kinds of political form, what possibilities are opened and what effaced, and what principles guide such negotiations, in located circumstances?[40] Rather than seeing Native writings as conveying a vision of nationhood that has been materialized in actual Indigenous governance (whether fully recognized or not by the settler-state), scholars can attend to how Native texts operate as mediators in using settler templates to navigate settler networks, and doing so opens possibilities for foregrounding how the process of choosing a political form through which to give material shape to peoplehood in the world (not simply in writing, but in governance as well) involves complex negotiations and struggles—especially in the context of continuing settler assertions of jurisdiction and underlying sovereignty. Put another way, I seek to explore what happens if we do not read Native texts in English in the nineteenth century as bearing—serving as *intermediaries* for—extratextual political formations, whether those formations are (in Brooks's terms, quoted earlier) "networks of waterways and kinship" that defy state mappings or are state-like apparatuses.[41] Foregrounding such processes of negotiation, conflict, and adjustment with settlers and among Indigenous people(s) draws attention to the kinds of difficult and fraught intellectual and political labor involved in envisioning, protecting, (re)defining, and sustaining Indigenous peoplehood in the midst of occupation—not just in the nineteenth century, but up through the present.

Recognition, Redux

I've been arguing that nineteenth-century Native texts, especially in portraying themselves as offering representative accounts of their people(s), adopt particular kinds of political form in order to frame their concerns in ways legible to non-native audiences. We might characterize such efforts as bids for recognition. I've also suggested that such tensions and negotiations around political form are at play not just in *the depiction* of Indigenous governance but in *the practices* of such governance as well. Turning to current discussions and debates focused on pursuing settler recognition and employing settler forms links the study of these older texts to the exigencies of the present moment (asking what light they can shed on contemporary struggles) while foregrounding the political and intellectual stakes of negotiating with and seeking to disorient settler templates. Recent critiques of recognition as a political goal have illustrated numerous ways that the effort to engage with state-sanctioned paradigms and policies results in not just the deformation of Indigenous goals (their rerouting into projects and formulations counter to what had been sought) but the reinforcement of modes of settler governance, which gain additional legitimacy through apparently consensual Indigenous participation.[42] However, thinking about the ways and ends to which nineteenth-century texts mediate political form in their staging of the terms, content, and contours of Indigenous collectivity and governance opens up questions about what "recognition" entails. To what extent is the mobilization of what might be understood as settler forms equivalent to an identification with them, to an affective investment that normalizes or naturalizes them? Moreover, do all such forms work in concert, as intermediaries in the ongoing production of an organizing settler structure or logic? Might some forms be mobilized against others, or might they be set to work in order to try to shift extant settler networks? In this way, engagement with nineteenth-century writings might offer additional possibilities for conceptualizing how Indigenous peoples negotiate the forms of their self-governance amid ongoing occupation—under conditions of what Jean Dennison has characterized as "colonial entanglement."

The critique of recognition might be understood as having three main lines of analysis: the settler-state extends acknowledgment in ways that confirm its underlying jurisdiction and right to manage Indigenous peoples and territories; the state seeks to interpellate Indigenous people(s) into subjectivities that normalize such jurisdiction, especially through gestures of official acknowledgment; and, as against these gestures, Indigenous peoples need to turn to their own sources of normative authority and social forms instead of accepting those proffered by the state. For example, Glen Coulthard argues that the current "politics of recognition" "seek[s] to 'reconcile' Indigenous assertions of nationhood with settler state sovereignty via the accommodation of Indigenous identity claims in some form of renewed legal and political relationship" with the state (in this case, Canada), but such an apparent embrace of indigeneity "promises to reproduce the very configurations of colonialist, racist, patriarchal state power that Indigenous peoples' demands for recognition have historically sought to transcend." The problem with seeking state acknowledgment comes with the ways it tends to present recognition as a kind of beneficent gift from settlers bestowed upon Native people(s), as well as to require accepting as a given "the background legal, political, and economic framework of the colonial relationship itself."[43] Even as state engagement with Indigenous peoplehood seems as if it will provide access to legally sanctioned kinds of claiming, authority, and autonomy (such as governance over lands the U.S. federal government acknowledges as part of Indian Country), that process also entails forms of categorization that, to use the language of the U.S. acknowledgment guidelines (discussed earlier), make an *Indian entity* legible as such. Speaking of contemporary political struggles for Indigenous self-determination, Leanne Simpson suggests, "The first tenet then of radical resurgent organizing is a refusal of state recognition as an organizing platform and mechanism for dismantling the systems of colonial domination," and similarly, Audra Simpson (no relation) argues, "There is a political alternative to 'recognition,' the much sought-after and presumed 'good' of multicultural politics. This alternative is 'refusal,'" which "raises the question of legitimacy for those who are usually in the position of recognizing: What is their authority to do so? Where does it come from?" Moreover, such a turning away from recognition enacts a "refusal to be enfolded into state logics."[44]

To be recognized by the state, then, is to fit extant state parameters of identification, which themselves take for granted the existence, legitimacy, and jurisdictional dynamics of the state itself. As Joanne Barker observes, "Troubled notions of Native culture and identity attach to Native legal status and rights in ways that force Native peoples to claim the authenticity of a culture and identity that has been defined *for* them." Conversely, Barker adds, "the deployment of recognition" serves as "evidence that the United States has realized itself as a fully democratic, humanist, and civil society, rendering historical violence and fraud against native peoples an unfortunate aberration."[45] Recalling Spivak's formulation discussed in the last section, the ability to be represented *to* the state (to have what are understood on state terms to be political relations with it) hinges on ways of being represented *by* the state (portrayals of what constitutes a political collectivity). In exerting the "subjectivity of a collective agency" within state processes, Native peoples need to inhabit a mode of subjectivity that makes sense within and is generated out of the discursive and institutional dynamics of settler governance, even as that participation can be circulated as evidence of Indigenous assent to such governance.[46]

Foregrounding how processes of institutional interpellation can derail Indigenous political projects and aims, critiques of recognition often go further in suggesting the ways modes of state acknowledgment can engender self-defeating forms of everyday subjectivity. Coulthard argues that "settler-colonial rule is a form of *governmentality*: a relatively diffuse set of governing relations that operate through a circumscribed mode of recognition that structurally ensures continued access to Indigenous peoples' lands and resources by producing neocolonial subjectivities that coopt Indigenous peoples into becoming instruments of their own dispossession." He links the production of forms of legal subjectivity for Indigenous peoples (which confirm the jurisdictional framework that enables settler access to Indigenous "lands and resources") and the internalization of such subjectivities as experiential frames of reference for Native people. Coulthard observes that "the maintenance of settler-state hegemony requires the production of what [Franz Fanon] liked to call 'colonized subjects': namely, the production of the specific modes of colonial thought, desire, and behavior that implicitly or explicitly commit the colonized to the types of practices and subject positions that are required for their continued domination."[47] In this way, while critiques of recognition tend not to use this formulation per se, they can be understood as presenting the attempt to achieve settler acknowledgment as what might be described as "cruel optimism." Lauren Berlant argues, "A relation of cruel optimism exists when something you desire is actually an obstacle to your flourishing," adding, "Optimism is cruel when the object/scene that ignites a sense of possibility actually makes it impossible to attain the expansive transformation for which a person or a people risks striving": "In scenarios of cruel optimism we are forced to suspend ordinary notions of repair and flourishing to ask whether the survival scenarios we attach to those affects weren't the problem in the first place."[48] Pursuing recognition by settlers, such accounts suggest, engenders an attachment to political forms and processes that actively thwart Indigenous flourishing by providing a sense of possibility—for autonomous governance, for defining the polity on (the) people's own terms, for an ability to set independent policy, for extended or renewed connection to and stewardship over particular lands and waters—that is deferred or undone by the very settler forms and processes that Indigenous peoples have taken up to sustain themselves.

More than addressing how Indigenous persons and peoples are called on to occupy particular kinds of legal and administrative identity in order to engage with settler governance, Coulthard suggests that the dynamics of such official networks become part of quotidian Native perceptions and orientations, as the stuff of commonsense self-understanding. He argues that "these images, along with the structural relations with which they are entwined, come to be recognized (or at least endured) as more or less natural" and that "these values eventually 'seep' into the colonized and subtly structure and limit the possibility of their freedom."[49] Beyond setting the terms for public enactments of indigeneity aimed at non-natives or influencing the contours of state-acknowledged Native administrative structures, the forms and frames utilized within settler governance come to shape Indigenous phenomenologies, affecting the character of ordinary "thought, desire, and behavior." They come to function, Coulthard argues, as the naturalized parameters for Indigenous persons in their negotiation of everyday circumstances as well as in the projection of future horizons. The kinds of subjectivity generated in and by settler institutions, then, are envisioned as influencing the lived subjectivity of Indigenous people. Seen in this way, the pursuit of recognition, in the sense of inhabiting and mobilizing settler political templates, is continuous with—and perhaps follows directly from—everyday modes of identification that normalize Natives persons' and peoples' status as "colonized subjects."

However, does drawing on settler forms, such as in nineteenth-century Native writings, necessarily entail this kind of affective attachment? How might attending to the mediations enacted by such texts open room for considering the ways that the taking up of particular political templates for certain purposes is not equivalent to those forms contouring Indigenous psychic life and consciousness more broadly? How might these texts illustrate the ways the taking up of settler forms might function as part of strategies for disjointing networks of colonial governmentality, specifically by playing certain dominant forms against others? Speaking of the workings of U.S. Indian policy, Barker indicates that "Native peoples were coerced to *recognize themselves* to be under federal plenary power and then to mediate their relations with one another through the terms of that subjugation."[50] This redeployment of non-native modes of recognition as the basis for intratribal and intertribal relations involves the kind of internalization Coulthard notes. Such an account, though, can imply that change is unilateral, as if once-alien forms can only have one set of meanings that they inevitably reproduce. At one point, Barker suggests that non-native notions of Indian purity, the need for Native people(s) in seeking modes of state recognition to prove their "aboriginality," "makes it impossible for Native peoples to narrate the historical and social complexities of cultural exchange, change, and transformation—to claim cultures and identities that are conflicted, messy, uneven, modern, technological, mixed."[51] The presence of messy, conflicted, uneven kinds of Native identity (whatever that might mean), though, presumes that change and transformation are not solely assimilatory, that extant Native social processes may be altered without them becoming less Indigenous or simply expressing degrees of colonial subjugation/subjectification along a singular continuum. Recalling Andersen's formulation discussed previously, such changes are part of Indigenous *density*, rather than expressing relative *difference* from a settler norm—or one that marks Indigenous authenticity.

In this vein, the kinds of political forms cited and circulated in what appear as calls for recognition might be functioning as part of Indigenous dynamics of change and transformation (including strategies that seek to produce change and transformation among settler publics). The citation of King Philip as a Native analog for George Washington (chapter 2) or the portrayal of Yankton tiospayes as a site of semianthropological study (chapter 4) may draw on extant settler frames of reference, but that fact does not mean that such frames are inherently continuous with the author's felt sense of being, never mind that of the peoples(s) they depict. In both of these cases, for example, Native writers are seeking to use settler forms as a way of naming kinds of collective relations such that Indigenous peoplehood might be registered by non-native readers (instead of it being seen as either vestigial and in need of ostensibly beneficent white care or as backward and in need of civilized adjustment through forms of domestic engineering).[52] In these instances, the issue is less that Native people feel bound to kinds of identifications that are disabling of their own self-determination than that Native political processes are not intelligible as such due to the imposition of settler legal and administrative frameworks. This point returns to Spivak's discussion of representation in its two senses: "representation as 'speaking for,' as in politics, and representation as 're-presentation,' as in art or philosophy," or proxy versus portrait.[53] She argues that "the staging of the world in representation—its scene of writing" or the dominant, institutionalized mode of portrayal—is not equivalent to the "ground level of consciousness," or everyday kinds of perception and self-understanding.[54] Instead, the need to be intelligible as a political collective to colonial institutions (a need arising both from processes of colonial management and from the colonized's efforts to affect colonial policy and governance) involves a second-order process of translation in which colonized peoples' accounts of themselves (including their governance and territorialities) need to pass through, and be transformed by, the matrix of colonial re-presentation. That translation/deformation may or may not be occurring in the sites of everyday life for the majority of the colonized population and that proxy/portrait nexus that conditions colonial intelligibility may or may not affect the continued existence of subaltern networks.

In many ways, critiques of recognition seek to highlight the power and vitality of Indigenous political formations, principles, practices, and philosophies that cannot be translated into settler terms—to trace the presence of subaltern Indigenous formations and to argue for their significance in projects of resurgence and decolonization. For example, Leanne Simpson emphasizes the importance of turning away "from trying to transform the colonial outside" and, instead, focusing on the "flourishment of the *Indigenous* inside," and that (re)orientation involves "significantly re-investing in our own ways of being: regenerating our political and intellectual traditions; articulating and living our legal systems; language learning; ceremonial and spiritual pursuits; creating and using our artistic and performance-based traditions."[55] Discussing India under colonial rule, Ranajit Guha argues that in accounts of the "politics" of Indian people, "the parameters of Indian politics are assumed to be or enunciated as exclusively or primarily those of the institutions introduced by the British for the government of the country and the corresponding sets of laws, policies, attitudes and other elements," but he insists that "parallel to the domain of elite politics there existed throughout the colonial period another domain of Indian politics in which the principal actors were not the dominant groups of the indigenous society or the colonial authorities but the subaltern classes and groups constituting the mass of the laboring population."[56] We might understand settler colonialism as producing such a dislocation in which only certain modes of governance count as "politics" (i.e., "the Indian tribe") and in which a wide range of extant and ongoing practices, processes, and principles of collective belonging, placemaking, decision-making, and resource distribution do not register as political. Simpson's reference to "the *Indigenous* inside," then, functions as a refusal of the colonial dynamics of intelligibility, instead pointing to subaltern formations that remain as sources for understanding and enacting politics, peoplehood, sovereignty, and self-determination.

However, to the extent that the employment of settler forms is cast as continuous with and expressive of identification with such forms (the pursuit of recognition as indicative of the presence of colonized subjectivities), such analysis brackets the potential for there to be any mediation of settler templates that arises out of connection to Indigenous networks. Looking at nineteenth-century Native writings and their claims to representativity, attending to how they negotiate with political form in light of settler assumptions and expectations, though, highlights the variable ways form can be employed. These texts show the (relative) potential to dislocate form from its dominant trajectories in reproducing, or continually reconstructing, settler aims and geographies— the ways such forms can serve as mediators rather than intermediaries. These writings also further underline that the political form of Indigenous peoplehood itself is variable, shifting, and often contested (a subject of ongoing, complex tensions and negotiations within and among peoples), rather than singular and given. As noted earlier, the treaty serves as the paradigmatic model of

Indigenous political form for much of the nineteenth century, both in terms of federal Indian policy at the time and in scholarship about the period, but there are a wide range of peoples with whom the United States did not negotiate treaties (including across southern New England and through much of the Great Basin), the policy of treaty making officially was brought to an end in 1871, and the modes of policy at play in much of the latter half of the century (especially through and in the wake of allotment) did not conform to the diplomatic principles of sovereign-to-sovereign relation implied by treatying. However, even when actual treaty relations are not present, Native writers mobilize it as a template through which to characterize a (set of) people(s) as having a coherent political character, a determinate landbase, and processes of governance with which the United States must reckon. As Chadwick Allen suggests, Indigenous writers "might *re-recognize*, rather than deconstruct, the authority of particular colonial discourses, such as treaties, for their own gain."[57] At other points, nineteenth-century Native writers cite monarchy, the American Revolution, constitutional structure, and ethnographic conceptions of tribal wholeness as ways of giving form to Indigenous collectivity in ways that aim to refigure extant official and popular portrayals of Indianness so as to engage with settler publics. These varied rhetorical strategies for portraying peoplehood are keyed to extant non-native discourses in order to gain traction within settler networks while also working to "transform, translate, distort, and modify" such networks' habituated modes of operation—the regularities of how they (re)construct Indians as a kind of population as well as the spaces and subjectivities of settlement.[58] In doing so, texts seek to play on contradictions and unevenness within and among settler institutional structures and discursive frames, aiming to emphasize and maneuver the inherent legitimacy crisis that attends settler claims to exert authority over Indigenous peoples and territories.[59] The approaches and forms writers employ do not simply follow from extant practices and principles of governance at play among the people(s) they discuss, and the use of such forms does not inherently bespeak something like an ideological commitment to the terms of their depiction. Writers can employ a range of forms that are in tension with each other (chapter 2) or can subtly illustrate the limits of the templates they employ even as they are mobilizing them (chapter 4).

These writers' efforts, though, put pressure on the distinction between the "colonial outside" and "*Indigenous* inside." If, as Leanne Simpson notes, the aim of turning to the latter is to engender the "flourishment" of Native peoples, the direct assault of settler legal and military force puts the potential for an inside in jeopardy, through removals and other modes of land seizure, programs of extermination for those persons/peoples found outside reservation borders, and projects of detribalization whose horizon is the disintegration of all Indigenous collectivities. While aiming to prevent such colonial violences or trying to respond to them cannot and does not provide the primary horizon for Indigenous being and becoming, attempts to engage with and mobilize settler political forms in order to shift popular sentiments so as to alter the political calculus and trajectory of Indian administration operate as a defense of the *inside* through tactical employment of what might be taken to be outside forms.[60] For example, as I argue in chapter 3, Sarah Winnemucca's portrayal of her family as providing the leadership for an integrated Paiute nation enables her to assert rights to control over their reservation(s), as opposed to being subjected to the virtually limitless discretion of appointed Indian agents, or, as discussed in chapter 4, Zitkala-Ša's assertion of her own representativity as an autoethnographic witness allows her to draw on incipient anthropological notions of "culture" to argue against the supposedly civilizing benefits of allotment and boarding school education. While Native writers might identify with the kinds of political form they circulate (such as in Elias Boudinot's defense of the vision of Cherokee nationality propounded by those, including himself, who signed the treaty that led to the Trail of Tears or, to a lesser extent, Winnemucca's emphasis on the descent of chiefly authority through her family), extant critiques of recognition can presume such attachments in ways that may flatten out the contexts, aims, and labor of engagements with settler networks.

The kinds of questions raised with regard to political representation (in both its senses) by Native writings also come to bear on scenes and dynamics of Indigenous governance, opening onto analyses of the ways political form gets cited, mobilized, and mediated in Indigenous networks. What kinds of proxying are at play in various formations of governance, and what political templates are circulating in the ongoing (re)construction of those modes of governance? Further, how have these networks of Native governance been affected by settler presence, pressures, and interventions? How has the context of ongoing colonialism influenced the ways once-alien kinds of political form have become part of such governance? Particularly, inasmuch as Native peoples sought to find ways to address settler institutionalities, they developed their own structures and processes that could articulate with non-native frameworks, processes that may or may not have been integrated into everyday understandings and enactments of peoplehood (as in Guha's distinction, noted earlier, between "elite politics" and those of subaltern populations). The distinction between inside and outside becomes somewhat murky: the two enter into shifting topological relations whose dynamics (or density) cannot easily be mapped, especially if posed in those terms—inside versus outside or, perhaps, recognition versus refusal.[61]

While critiques of recognition powerfully articulate philosophical principles for good governance and offer vital accounts of relational ethics that are envisioned as creating conditions for Indigenous peoples' flourishing, such analyses sometimes can efface the distinction between normative political theory and a description of political process. What processes are there for negotiating over the political forms and principles that peoples will use in defining themselves and enacting sovereignty and self-determination? What are the situated ethics and difficulties of such ongoing negotiations? In her analysis of contemporary Osage constitutional reform, Dennison argues that attending to colonial entanglement "calls attention to the inherent power dynamics within the ongoing colonial context without erasing the agency" that Native people(s) exert in negotiating that context. She observes that "this approach allows for understanding settler colonial forces as having a varied, dynamic, and uneven impact across space and time" in ways that also "negate the easy divide of colonized and colonizer," adding, "The key is making something out of this structure that does not mirror the oppression of the colonizer."[62] Similarly, addressing efforts to modify current environmental policy within the Cherokee Nation, Clint Carroll explores "indigenous appropriations of state forms in order to counteract ongoing injustices," thereby "illuminat[ing] how indigenous nations have been able to envision the state form for themselves and which attributes of this form have been addressed to account for various indigenous situations and values" in ways that suggest "indigenous state *transformation*." The "state form," as an example of a (once-)settler template, becomes part of Indigenous governance in ways related to ongoing colonial pressures while not entirely reducible to them as an "outside" force. The modifications and mediations of that form arise out of ongoing negotiations, disagreements, debates, and deliberations over the entailments and affordances of particular kinds of political form in their ability to materialize principles, philosophies, ideals, and ethics that are of import to the people(s) in question.[63] Thus, while taking on board the critique of the uncritical adoption of and investments in state forms and institutions, this scholarship also explores the mediations enacted in framing Indigenous governance amid both ongoing colonial superintendence and the presence of varied—sometimes mutually antagonistic—conceptions of collective identity, decision-making, and desirable futures among a given people. In this vein, attending to nineteenth-century Native writers' pursuit of what might be called recognition—or, at least, the mobilization of forms intelligible to non-native publics in the effort to secure greater possibilities for exercising sovereignty and self-determination—opens onto broader consideration of the work performed by citations and circulations of kinds of political form (such as a constitution, chiefdom, or legislative council) within situated contexts of entanglement and continuing settler occupation.

The connection between the choice of political form (whether in published texts or in actual governance) and lived subjectivity, though, remains open, vexed, shifting, and riven with potential discontinuities. For instance, in noting Native people's and peoples' "refusal to be enfolded into state logics," Audra Simpson develops the notion of "feeling citizenships," which "are structured in the present space of intracommunity recognition, affection, and care, outside the logics of colonial and imperial rule"; yet, she also observes that such "intracommunity" modes of relation themselves are crosscut by the legacies of colonial categorizations that have become part of governance structures ("the math [of legal genealogies], the clans, the mess, the misrecognitions, the confusion, and the clarity," or "the calculus of predicaments").[64] Such felt connections, then, are not so much "outside" of colonial rule—in the sense of being beyond it, unaffected by it, or free of its component parts—as operating in ways that do not take the processes for forging networks and modes of regularity at play in settler governance as a (necessary) template. From this perspective, *recognition* and *refusal* might be rethought less in terms of the employment of particular kinds of (political) form—with attendant assumptions about the affective attachments, ideological commitments, and kinds of subjectivity thought necessarily to follow from such usage—than in terms of the orientation or trajectory of such forms' use.[65] Citation of that form allows entry into and/or sustains what sort of networks? What mediations are enacted in the mobilization of that form? Who participates in the process of deciding to employ that form (and the mode of its mediation) in *representing* the people (in both senses—as proxy and portrait)? What relations does the employment of that particular form (seek to) create between networks of governance and everyday modes of interpersonal connection, principles of collectivity, ethics, and aspirations for Indigenous flourishing? When reading nineteenth-century Native texts, then, one might consider the extent to which texts seek to create a sense of accountability to Native people (including how texts relate to available intra-Indigenous networks for producing a sense of political legitimacy), even amid authors' employment of tropes, forms, templates that aim toward modifying and transforming the perceptions of settler publics.

From the perspective of extant ways of critiquing recognition, though, not only can support for certain kinds of political form appear as a mode of cruel optimism, or an expression of colonized subjectivity, but the work of nineteenth-century Indigenous intellectuals in mediating settler templates potentially can be denigrated or dismissed as an expression of some version of false consciousness. While none of the scholars whose work I've addressed make such a move, it might seem to follow from some of their ways of theorizing indigeneity. In highlighting the complexities of how these earlier authors frame peoplehood, I hope both to further texture available ways of talking about the politics of pursuing "recognition" and to expand the resources for addressing the variety of ways Indigenous intellectuals approach and figure the politics of peoplehood. At the same time, I want to hold onto the pressing questions and concerns raised by critiques of recognition in their consideration of the circumstances that will facilitate Indigenous flourishing and resurgence, adding to rather than bracketing their insights. As Goeman argues, "Rather than construct a healthy relationship to land and place, colonial spatial structures inhibit it by constricting Native mobilities and pathologizing mobile Native bodies," and the adoption of such frames for Native governance can enact forms of "self-disciplining" that also "abstract space—decorporealize, commodify, or bureaucratize—when the legal ramifications of land or the political landscape are addressed," a process that helps engender and sustain "asymmetrical relationships" with regard to gender, race, sexuality, and other vectors of identity, status, and individual and collective self-expression.[66] These forms of abstraction tend away from, and often actively disavow, what Coulthard has characterized as "grounded normativity," "the modalities of Indigenous land-connected practices and longstanding experiential knowledge that inform and structure ethical engagements with the world and our relationships with human and nonhuman others over time."[67] This "web of connections," in Leanne Simpson's terms, is "generated in relationship to place" as part of Indigenous *worlds* that themselves rely on everyday modes of relation: "Nishnaabeg life didn't rely on institutionality to hold the structure of life. We relied upon process that created networked relationship."[68] Employing the forms of abstraction Goeman addresses may foreclose engagement with the "modalities" of other place-based knowledges and processes of relation, which become subaltern in the process.[69] Mobilizing such forms with respect to governance also may involve drawing on associated templates with regard to what counts as a political issue and who counts as a political subject, including the installation of heteropatriarchal principles that devalue and deny access to women and that position concerns "regarding children, families, sexual and gender violence, and bodies . . . as less important."[70] Conversely, we also need to address how particular forms and frames that are intelligible to the settler-state may enable the ongoing construction of, in Carroll's terms, "*sovereign landscapes*" that "reconfigure" such forms in the interest of opening them toward other Indigenous principles, philosophies, and ethics—a process that Dennison has characterized as aiming to increase the "future capacities" of Indigenous governance and sociality.[71]

I want to suggest, though, that we understand and trace the implications of mobilizations of political form in ways that are about the situated affordances of a given form (what kinds of linkages among sites and modes of framing does that form put into play in given instances?), rather than treating particular forms as necessarily metonymically signifying colonized (versus self-determined/resurgent) kinds of consciousness and/or as indicating a fully integrated settler "logic" or "system." What I'm asking is, can refusal—the repudiation of settler frameworks operating on their own terms and toward their intended ends—dwell within what may look like the pursuit of recognition? How might the employment of particular forms in what, from one angle, appears to be a bid for legibility also, from another angle, function as a means of capacitating resurgence—such as in the struggle for the acknowledgment of Native sovereignty in New England amid guardianship (chapter 2), the insistence on Paiute rights to reservation lands amid relocation and agents' punishing discretion (chapter 3), and the insistence on the value of Dakota socialities amid allotment and projects of civilization (chapter 4)? How can distinctions be discerned between cruel optimism and tactical or strategic acts of mediation in the service of Indigenous survivance? What practices of reading and interpretation might surface such potentials? Presuming that peoplehood has a clear normative shape and principles that can be contrasted to those at play in settler administration can end up reinstalling a backdoor version of authenticity in ways that deemphasize the difficulties, challenges, and possibilities at play in the active and ongoing negotiation of what form(s) peoplehood will, can, and should take, matters of collective process that lie at the heart of self-determination. My readings of nineteenth-century Native texts, then, work in the interest of opening up a more expansive set of conceptual tools and strategies for addressing the contingencies, tensions, and antagonisms—the political and intellectual labor—at play in negotiations over how to represent peoplehood in the midst of ongoing colonialism.

Organization and Chapters

In turning to nineteenth-century (con)texts, my aim is less to provide lessons that can directly be implemented in contemporary struggles than to draw on historical distance in order to stage what might be described as a politics of reading. If we do not view such writings as simply expressive of an extratextual real but as illustrating complex negotiations over the articulation and form(s) of peoplehood, the process of trying to understand those mediations and their relation to various networks and publics provides something of an intellectual model for approaching the density of shifting Indigenous matrices of governance. The readings seek to illustrate the varied rhetorical negotiations taking place within a set of historical and political contingencies amid a range of possible ways of understanding peoplehood that may not be consistent with each other and that may fit only unevenly within settler frames. The somewhat fine-grained discussion of how writers seek to navigate and negotiate those complexities, multiplicities, and varied sets of demands and needs *is* the point, in that doing so draws attention to the intellectual and political work of self-determination—its messiness and continual unfinishedness. Such dynamics at play in the process of close reading also further suggest the usefulness of literary studies within Indigenous political theory, since careful attention to the multidimensional and situated ways texts make meaning can help amplify the importance of contingency and form to discussions of (contemporary) Indigenous sovereignty and self-determination.

The chapters each address a particular intellectual's engagement with a specific configuration of law and policy that informs how they approach the project of portraying peoplehood and constituting a representative public voice through which to advocate. If we do not take the accounts of Native political form offered in their writings as directly expressive of Indigenous sociopolitical dynamics on the ground, as it were, we can approach these texts as staging versions of collective identity meant to speak to settler publics. This approach seeks neither to endorse their formulations nor to overemphasize their efficacy in altering popular opinion or shifting the terms of settler administration. Rather, in each case, the chapter aims to track the mediations involved in the kinds of political form the authors employ—how they do so and toward what apparent end(s). Such analysis seeks to draw attention to (1) the affordances and constraints at play in the use of given forms within situated and entangled circumstances and (2) the relations envisioned between the authors and the people(s) for whom they position themselves as spokespersons. In all of the chapters, I address the ways these authors' representations of political identity lead to the effacement of other, extant formations of peoplehood. In doing so, though, my aim is to illustrate the variety of ways of envisioning and enacting peoplehood in the context of continuing (and intensifying) settler occupation, the pressures shaping such articulations in specific times and places, and the difficulties and intellectual labor that attend choices around how to conceptualize, characterize, and organize Indigenous governance. I'm particularly concerned with the role of gender in these dynamics, with respect to who constitutes a political subject, what kinds of formations get to count as "politics," and how certain formulations come to be understood as representative. The chapters return to questions about not only how texts address the role of women within their stagings of political identity and leadership but also how these authors' portrayals of the contours and character of peoplehood address issues and relations that might broadly be characterized (within settler discourses) as "domestic" matters.

The first half of the book focuses on Indian relations in the East during the height of the treaty period and the push for removal as a federal policy. I begin with Elias Boudinot and the Cherokee Nation because of their paradigmatic status in talking about nineteenth-century Indian affairs, in the period and largely still in contemporary scholarship. Chapter 1 addresses the struggles around defining Cherokee nationality in the 1830s, illustrating how intellectual citations of political form in relation to settler networks can be disjunct from political processes of decision-making within Indigenous ones. Despite numerous treaties with Native peoples, the federal government in 1830 adopted a policy of seeking to remove all Indian tribes from east of the Mississippi, particularly in the Southeast. In *Letters and Other Papers Relating to Cherokee Affairs* (1837), Boudinot aims to justify the choices made by him and the other members of the Treaty Party, who signed the removal treaty Cherokee officials had rejected. He argues that Cherokee leaders had deceived the Cherokee people about the possibilities for remaining in their traditional homeland, and he offers a vision of Cherokee political identity as based on sustaining the health and welfare of the Cherokee population rather than retaining a specific landbase. He argues for the need to speak to non-native policy aims and frameworks in what he portrays as more realistic terms than elected Cherokee leaders had been offering. In doing so, though, he not only sets aside the processes of governance under the Cherokee Constitution, adopted in 1827, but displaces the ways that government structure itself balanced tensions between a centralized bureaucratic apparatus (largely initiated by and oriented around the interests of an elite) and continuing popular Cherokee commitment to decentralized, older modes of matrilineal-clan and town-based governance. Boudinot offers a heteropatriarchal and elitist account of Cherokee peoplehood that edits out the ongoing role of such tensions and attachments in Cherokee constitutional governance. In the place of an engagement with these dynamics and negotiations, Boudinot substitutes a generic, serialized conception of what it means to be Cherokee—one more consistent with non-native notions of Indianness and Native governance. *Letters* defines Cherokee peoplehood in ways modeled on norms circulating within settler networks and casts endorsement of that conception of nationhood as a sufficient justification for serving as a spokesperson for the Cherokees in interactions with the United States. In Boudinot's text, and the arguments of the Treaty Party, there is no way for nonelite perspectives to matter, and the text turns on substituting a particular kind of intellectual mediation for answerability to the very people in whose name Boudinot speaks. In this way, the text enacts what might be termed a recognition imaginary, in which settler templates provide the normalized background principles through which to define and defend Indigenous peoplehood, as against popular principles ordered around kinship and place—with which Cherokee leaders continued to grapple in ways that Boudinot dismisses as deceit and contradiction.

Chapter 2 turns from the treaty-recognized Cherokees to the peoples in southern New England, who at that point lay outside the reach of federal Indian policy and the treaty system. Despite the federal government's assertion of authority over Indian affairs in the 1780s and early 1790s, states in New England refused to cede such jurisdiction, continuing pre-independence patterns of Indian policy. Prior to the American Revolution, colonial governments in Massachusetts and Connecticut had legally acknowledged Indian reservations, appointing non-native guardians to oversee them. Part of the work facing Native intellectuals in New England was forging ways of portraying Indigenous collectivity that could enable non-natives to see tribes as political entities with the ability and right to govern themselves. In his writings in the late 1820s and 1830s, William Apess (Pequot) seeks to challenge the dominant portrayal of Native peoples in New England as a dependent and disappearing population in need of governmental care. He does not cast himself as having been tasked to speak for a particular political community. Instead, he invokes figures of exemplarity that can stand for Indigenous peoplehood. Those figures do not serve as evidence of Native governance per se: they do not so much *prove* Native sovereignty as *presume* it, rhetorically producing sovereignty as a background against which the foregrounded figure comes into view. In his writings Apess experiments with how to generate a portrait of peoplehood for which political proxying would be appropriate, as opposed to racializing, paternalizing, and corrupt *care* by non-native guardians. Apess draws on various kinds of figuration in an effort to produce metonymic ways of signifying the presence and scope of Indigenous sovereignty and self-determination. In *A Son of the Forest* (1829/1831), he draws on his own life to highlight vicariously the existence of the Pequots as a nation; in *Eulogy on King Philip* (1836), the Wampanoag sachem Metacom serves as a means of registering Native peoples as self-governing political entities on a par with the United States; and in *Indian Nullification* (1835), Apess employs a range of frames (including references to the Cherokee Nation, the Revolutionary War, and chattel slavery) to indicate the violence of the guardian system and to illustrate that the Mashpee (and by extension, other Indigenous groups in New England) need to be engaged as fully self-governing polities. Through these figurations, Apess seeks to generate the potential for political recognition by non-natives, even as the means of doing so tend to reinforce heteropatriarchal conceptions of political order and rule—through axiomatically presuming masculine rule and effacing the labor of women in sustaining both the reservations themselves and kinship relations among them.

The second half of the book examines the work of representation amid the ruins of diplomatic relation (the implementation of the reservation system, the end of treaty making, and the imposition of allotment). Chapter 3 reads Sarah Winnemucca's *Life among the Piutes* (1883) in light of the politics of mobility and prophecy in the Great Basin. In the late 1860s and the late 1880s, prophet-led movements emerged out of visions of Native regeneration dreamed by Northern Paiute men, and these movements can be understood as part and parcel of a broader set of sociospiritual dynamics that were prevalent throughout the Great Basin region during the entire period. Yet, in Winnemucca's narrative, she does not discuss these movements at all. Attending to the historical presence of the Ghost Dances highlights the ways the account of Paiute peoplehood developed within the text relies on effacing and disowning the dispersed networks of sociality, placemaking, and leadership coalesced by these prophetic movements. In contrast, Winnemucca consistently depicts herself as part of an unbroken chiefly line that leads the entire "Paiute nation," in particular offering that political genealogy as validation for her ability as a woman to represent the people in public fora. Positioning herself as an extension of her father, himself cast as the head chief of an integrated tribal entity, she seeks to produce a cohesive sense of Northern Paiute identity that is more consistent with the terms of Indian policy in order to challenge the discretionary powers exerted by agents and to advocate for the preservation of state-recognized Paiute landbases, despite the end of formal treaty making in 1871 and the adoption of increasingly autocratic administrative principles in the federal management of reservations. As against Winnemucca's claims to speak for a unified Paiute polity/public, though, Ghost Dance movements highlight the ways forms of Indigenous peoplehood in the Great Basin in the late nineteenth century did not fit the terms of Indian policy, organized as it was around notions of clearly delineated tribes with discretely demarcated landbases, and tracing Winnemucca's evasion of the Ghost Dance underlines the intellectual labor at play in seeking to engage with non-native popular and political discourses.

In the process of doing so, though, she also must displace prominent regional principles, practices, and geographies that run counter to the administrative and ideological frameworks at play in Indian policy, since such regional formations undermine both her claim to stand for the Paiute people and the presence of a clearly delineated *Paiute people* for whom she could speak.

Chapter 4 takes up the movement in the late nineteenth century away from a diplomatic/military idiom to a proto-anthropological one as the predominant non-native way of portraying Native peoples, addressing the change in kinds of representativity asserted by Indigenous authors. Increasingly, Native peoples were portrayed not as geopolitical entities but as collections of racialized persons who engaged in barbaric "tribal relations" that needed to be eliminated. In response, Native writers begin to work within emergent ethnographic modes of description, casting themselves as informants who can testify to everyday forms of collective practice. In 1900, Zitkala-Ša published a series of three stories in the *Atlantic Monthly* based on her life experience growing up on the Yankton reservation, attending boarding school, and working for Carlisle Industrial School, the most famous of the off-reservation educational institutions. If ethnographies of Native peoples usually involved white narrators' reconstruction, reordering, and elucidation of accounts offered by Indians, whose own testimonies were taken as indicative of prevalent patterns of behavior and belief, Zitkala-Ša occupies that position of representative Native speaker in order to provide her own account. This mode of self-stylization, or positioning herself as representative, enables her lived experience to stand for the existence of a (political) collective. Zitkala-Ša's implicit presentation of herself as spokesperson for the Yankton, and the portrait of their peoplehood that she offers, is not readily marked as a *political* form. Fusing the roles of ethnographic subject and object, she partakes in one of the few possibilities in the period for Native self-representation to non-native publics. She reorients the conceptual resources of ethnography toward highlighting the value of what at the time were termed tribal relations, while analyzing settler policy as itself producing forms of incapacity, rather than remedying those which supposedly arise in the generational transmission of Indianness. She draws on extant popular interest in Indians (such as in Wild West shows) while casting her experience as evidence of the potential value of ordinary Indigenous social formations—what might be described as the site of Indian domesticity, which is cast as in need of reformation in official rhetorics. Yet, even as she draws on extant ethnographic strategies, she subtly illustrates how they recycle stereotypical understandings of Indianness and, thereby, limit possibilities for registering historical and ongoing forms of Indigenous sovereignty and self-determination.

Speaking for the People illustrates how the conditions of settler colonial rule affect how Native intellectuals articulate and employ political form in their writings. Such entanglements mean that nineteenth-century portrayals of indigeneity by Native authors should be treated less as simply or directly expressive of extratextual modes of peoplehood than as negotiating the terms through which indigeneity gains meaning within settler frameworks. In doing so, their writings inhabit, challenge, and refunction non-native discourses in ways that facilitate engagement and advocacy with settler publics, but, reciprocally, such templates also, then, orient the accounts of Indigenous peoplehood offered in their texts. Foregrounding the ways these authors and texts position themselves as representative draws attention to the background assumptions about Native identity and governance that provide the condition of intelligibility for their modes of public speech and engagement. Exploring the potential distinctions/disjunctions between their accounts and extant Indigenous geopolitical formations, though, is less in the interest of underlining the authenticity of the latter against the former than of highlighting the dynamics and politics of mediation. What does inhabiting settler-sanctioned or settler-intelligible political forms *do* in particular historical and political conjunctures? How can we understand that effort as different from identification with settler frames (even if, at times, such identification also is present)? Conversely, how might we understand the possibilities offered by the use of such forms as also having costs? Such costs and erasures, which often are deeply gendered, point back toward the dynamics of force that permeate colonial entanglements, the intellectual labor of figuring out how productively to engage such force, and the ethical complexities and densities of that engagement. While my analysis is focused on nineteenth-century Native authors, I want to suggest that such scenes of writing and representation provide ways of approaching the broader questions of how to conceptualize engagement with settler forms and frames of reference at all levels and how to understand decisions about the shape of Indigenous governance and the flourishing of Native peoples as matters of ongoing deliberation, discussion, and debate—as open-ended processes rather than ready solutions derivable from a set of foundational first principles on which all the people who comprise *the people* might not agree.

1. WHAT'S IN A NATION?

Cherokee Vanguardism in Elias Boudinot's Letters

In December 1835, Elias Boudinot, along with nineteen other Cherokees, signed what would come to be known as the Treaty of New Echota. When ratified by the U.S. Senate the following spring, it made possible the removal of the Cherokee Nation from the Southeast to Indian Territory—an event commonly known as the Trail of Tears. Boudinot and the other signatories were members of what was called the Treaty Party. They were not legally authorized as representatives of the government of the Cherokee Nation, which had rejected the treaty they signed in two prior council meetings over the previous six months.[1] Members of the Treaty Party, though, had served in various official positions over the previous decade, including Major Ridge, John Ridge, and Boudinot himself, who until his resignation in 1832 had been the original and sole editor of the Cherokee national newspaper, *The Cherokee Phoenix* (having gone on two government-initiated trips to raise funds for the nation in 1826 and 1831–1832). Despite flouting the administrative determinations of the Cherokee government, Boudinot published a book-length defense of his decision to sign the treaty—*Letters and Other Papers Relating to Cherokee Affairs: Being a Reply to Sundry Publications Authorized by John Ross* (1837). He frames it as a response to public declarations and accusations by John Ross, the principal chief of the Cherokee Nation—who had been in that position since 1828. In *Letters*, Boudinot argues that the Treaty Party acted in the best interests of the Cherokee Nation and that, as such, they spoke for the Cherokee people. His assertions in this vein open questions about what it means to represent the Cherokee populace and, conversely, how to conceptualize Cherokee nationhood itself.

Given the existence of a Cherokee national government and the fact that Boudinot and the Treaty Party were not serving as agents of it (and were directly flouting its authority), by what logic can he cast their actions as representative? More than adopting an elite perspective with respect to the proper character of Cherokee governance, a perspective largely shared by Cherokee officials and enacted as national policy, the text presents the ability to serve as a proxy for the Cherokee Nation as dependent less on political process (engagement with the desires, opinions, and expressed will of the Cherokee public) than on commitment to a particular form for the nation. Boudinot challenges the wisdom and validity of the Cherokee national government's policy of rejecting U.S. attempts to remove them, but in doing so, *Letters* offers an account of Cherokee identity that largely comports with the existing constitutionally sanctioned political architecture of the nation. The government of the Cherokee Nation in the 1820s and 1830s certainly represented the Cherokee people, in the sense that there was no other political entity popularly authorized to exert jurisdiction over Cherokee territory or to speak for Cherokees in diplomatic engagements with U.S. officials. The profound alterations in Cherokee governance over the prior several decades, though, put pressure on what we might mean by *representation*. The Cherokee Constitution lays out a tripartite framework of governance modeled on that of the United States, with an executive branch, a bicameral legislature, and a court system, and this basic structure remained in place in 1835, although interference by Georgia and the criminalization of Cherokee governance in the state meant that elections had been suspended since 1832 (a point that Boudinot cites as a sign of the questionable legitimacy of Ross's regime). While formally ratified in 1827, this constitutional configuration largely reflected existing institutional processes in the Cherokee Nation, which themselves emerged over the course of the previous decade and which enacted a heterogendered and racialized conception of Cherokee identity and political process—particularly in terms of the displacement of women from the scene of formal political life and the limitation of possibilities for belonging and participation by people of African descent (whether or not they also had Cherokee parents).[2]

That process of centralization over the course of the 1810s and 1820s, though, largely was led by what might be described as an elite.[3] In "On Some Aspects of the Historiography of Colonial India," Ranajit Guha suggests the importance of attending to the "class outlook" of those who generally were responsible for producing the documents of Indian nationalism: "In all writings of this kind the parameters of Indian politics are assumed to be or enunciated as exclusively or primarily those of the institutions introduced by the British for the government of the country."[4] As Cherokee governance took on the form of a state apparatus, those familiar with Euro-American institutions, property, and forms of gendered domesticity—those most conversant with the terms and dynamics of settler networks—come to the fore of Cherokee political life and enact policies that largely seek to reproduce those dynamics within the nation.[5] While not directly seeking the affirmation of the United States in enacting laws and policy, the Cherokee government increasingly adopted institutional norms consistent with those of settler governance.[6] Guha further suggests that "parallel to the domain of elite politics there existed throughout the colonial period another domain of Indian politics in which the principal actors were not the dominant groups ... but the subaltern classes."[7] With respect to the Cherokees, one might understand the vast majority of the nation that did not engage in large-scale farming for the market, did not hold slaves, did not know English, and continued to use towns and clans as meaningful matrices of belonging as subaltern in this way. The constitutional government, though, also represented those outside the elite, in the sense that it spoke in their name and that they participated in elections and such.[8] Cherokee national governance opened avenues for popular assent that worked to legitimize the existence of the institutional structure, but those modes of representation translated subaltern social formations into elite configurations in ways that both limited the potential for alternative principles and practices of relation to signify as expressions of Cherokee nationality (such as webs of connection based on town and clan belonging) and limited participation in political processes (including voting) along lines of both gender and race.[9] Although winnowing possibilities for nonelite formulations of Cherokee collective identity and interests, the Cherokee government maintained strong public support, primarily due to its repeated rejection of U.S. attempts to seize Cherokee lands. The commitment to sustaining the national landbase generated widespread endorsements of the government's legitimacy, even as ordinary Cherokee perspectives on and practices of belonging, decision-making, and landholding often did not conform to the principles undergirding national policy.

What happens, though, in the absence of such political mediation, when intellectuals claim to offer a representative version of Cherokee nationalism shaped by elite principles but absent any process of popular accountability—a vision of Cherokee political identity shorn of the labor of politics? *Letters* seeks to justify the actions of the Treaty Party by virtue of their claim to be acting in the best interests of the Cherokee people. In doing so, the text suggests that Boudinot and the other signatories to the Treaty of New Echota are aware of the threat posed to the existence of the Cherokee Nation by the United States in ways ordinary Cherokees are not, and so they must act in the name of the latter. Boudinot charges national leaders with having misled the Cherokee public about the possibility of remaining in their current location while also continually suggesting that the ignorance of most Cherokees makes them credulous in ways Cherokee officials, particularly John Ross, can exploit. Within this framing, though, no popular resistance to removal ever can be credible or freely chosen, because such a position depends on not having correct information or not correctly interpreting that information. In *Letters*, there is no way for non-elite perspectives to matter, and the text turns on substituting a particular kind of intellectual work for answerability to the very people in whose name Boudinot speaks. Boudinot offers an account of Cherokee peoplehood that treats its form as self-evident in ways that enable him to dismiss all other perspectives and formulations as mere backwardness and ignorance, simultaneously casting Cherokee national leaders' efforts to grapple with popular frameworks and investments as merely obfuscation, deceit, or shameless pandering.

If the use of settler political forms can be seen as expressive of colonized subjectivity within critiques of recognition, Boudinot's ways of formulating Cherokee identity could suggest such an interpellation into settler modes. However, his portrayal of Cherokee statehood is continuous with the institutional structure of Cherokee governance in the period, even as he and the Treaty Party flout the authority of that very government. We might understand Boudinot in *Letters* as enacting a kind of cruel optimism, as discussed in the introduction, in his identification with the perspective/frames of settler authorities, even as he insists on the continued existence of Cherokee nationality (albeit in a form detached from Cherokee territory as such). Rather than seeing his elite vision of Cherokee nationhood (as a liberal republic) as inherently compromised, as necessarily divorced from what otherwise might be cast as the Cherokee real, though, we can focus on how the text substitutes elite intellectual judgment based on settler models for a politics of popular accountability. In doing so, Boudinot makes recognition by non-natives into virtually the sole prism through which to view Cherokee peoplehood and its political form, a vision of Cherokee collective identity that is cast as representative in its expression of civilized principles of reason in ways severed from debate among Cherokee people. Yet, even as Boudinot's text and the actions of the Treaty Party suggest the dangers of substituting intellectuals' public discourse—especially as articulated to non-native publics—for Indigenous peoples' own determinations about their governance, *Letters* also raises questions about the idea of a ready distinction between "the Indigenous inside" and "the colonial outside."[10] The parallels between Boudinot's ways of conceptualizing Cherokee nationhood and those at play in constitutional Cherokee governance suggest how the mediations at work in *Letters*—the text's engagement with settler networks—point back to the mediations, entanglements, and densities of Cherokee politics on the ground. In this vein, we can critique Boudinot's elite commitments and their heteropatriarchal and antidemocratic orientations but not for their failure to mirror a more authentic set of Cherokee principles imagined as existing apart from the context of colonial force. If we see Boudinot's articulations of Cherokee identity and governance as problematic in their endorsement of settler norms, the issue is less a failure to embody values that are truly Cherokee than the ways his formulation of intellectual and political authority renders subaltern nonelite formations, casting them as lacking substance or merely a result of ignorance.

The text's presumption of the Treaty Party's right to surrogate for the Cherokee people inseparably is bound up in an elite orientation that underwrites the idea that familiarity and identification with liberal political economy prequalifies one for setting policy for the nation, absent any meaningful engagement with Cherokee publics.[11] The issue, therefore, is not Boudinot's turn away from Cherokee "culture," an embrace of "progressivism," or some psychological turn (possibly connected to the prior options).[12] Attending to the continuities and disjunctions between Boudinot's formulations and the actions of the Cherokee national government reveals less the former's deviation from a set of authenticating core Cherokee principles than discrepant trajectories in taking up the same political form—the liberal state. Both Boudinot and Cherokee governance employ that template in mediated ways that are directed toward securing Cherokee political autonomy while being shaped by an elite frame of reference. However, constitutionally sanctioned Cherokee officials did so in ways further mediated by popular Cherokee formulations of Cherokee identity, including ongoing connection to their current lands. Boudinot employs the frame of the liberal state absent such relations to a broader Cherokee public. The issue, then, is not so much Boudinot's taking up of this form per se as his use of it in ways that displace any possibility for Cherokee perspectives that do not conform to settler frames. Engaging with Boudinot's text in these ways illustrates possibilities for distinguishing between the use of settler templates and identification with them and for tracing how articulations to non-native publics can help index complex processes of negotiation over the form peoplehood will take within Indigenous governance—what I have characterized as the politics of peoplehood.

Elite Orientations

To speak of the existence of an elite suggests a distinct class whose significant wealth sets them apart from the rest of the populace while also enabling them to take up positions of authority through which they exert control over the lives of the less wealthy majority. While such a dynamic does occur in the Cherokee Nation in the decades leading up to removal, that way of talking about the elite as a political formation does not fully capture the concept's meaning in the colonial context of settlement. Instead, we might conceptualize the elite as, returning to Guha's formulation discussed earlier, those who mobilize a particular "partial view of politics" based on the sociopolitical forms introduced by the colonizer.[13] In this sense, being part of the Cherokee elite would entail having a frame of reference shaped by the terms of settler political institutions and economic processes. As Sara Ahmed observes, an orientation can be described as an effect of a habitual turning in a particular direction: "If such turns are repeated over time, then bodies acquire the very shape of such direction." Moreover, this directionality occurs against a background, which provides "the conditions of emergence of an arrival of something as the thing that it appears to be in the present."[14] An elite orientation, then, could be described as a way of conceiving potentials for social organization and political process in which principles of liberal political economy serve as the background—a habituated turning toward such models.[15] Other ways of formulating collective claims appear unintelligible as such, rendered subaltern in their failure to fit the vision of Cherokee nationality toward which elite discourses and ideologies turn and which they help realize. In *Letters*, familiarity with the dynamics of non-native institutions becomes the basis for declaring the political judgment of Boudinot and the other members of the Treaty Party to be superior to that of other Cherokees. The text indicates that their intimate knowledge of settler social forms and dispositions gives this elite group the right to stand for the Cherokee people, since ordinary Cherokees lack the background understanding that would facilitate reasonable decision-making with respect to the future and welfare of the Cherokee Nation.

Before the early nineteenth century, the Cherokees did not have a centralized structure of governance empowered to legislate for everyone in Cherokee territory. While larger councils were called as necessary, particularly in order to respond to non-native imperatives (including demands for land cessions), ordinary governance largely occurred at the level of autonomous towns, which often met in regional councils, had their own leaders, operated primarily by consensus, and were linked to each other both through regional associations and shared participation in the seven clans that encompassed all Cherokee people.[16] In response to ongoing federal efforts to pressure the Cherokee people into ceding further lands, representatives from the towns created a National Council in the first decade of the nineteenth century, which would address issues of concern to all Cherokees (especially with respect to U.S. needs and demands). In 1809, the Council created the Standing Committee (later to be known as the National Committee), a group of thirteen leaders appointed by the Council to handle issues that arose in between annual Council meetings and whose determinations would be reviewed and approved formally by the Council when next it met.[17] Over the course of the 1820s, there were a series of significant changes to the form of Cherokee governance, including dividing the nation into eight districts (replacing town-based representation), limiting the size of the Council to thirty-two members (four per district), and requiring that all laws have the formal approval of the Committee.[18] These changes reversed the direction of Cherokee governance: from a limited delegation of authority to the Council from the towns and by the Council to the Committee to, instead, a consolidated set of national institutions that bypasses the towns and that centralizes the Committee, which shifts from being an administrative means of engaging with external concerns to the primary initiator of domestic policy for the Cherokee Nation.[19] In that process, Cherokee governance increasingly adopts the structuring templates of Euro-American political economy as the basis for domestic policy. To be clear, that shift has nothing to do with accepting U.S. jurisdiction or with a willingness to cede Cherokee territory. The adoption of an institutionalized national government emerges as part of opposition to U.S. interference in Cherokee affairs and in order to facilitate collective refusal of settler efforts to further constrict the Cherokees' landbase in the Southeast or to push for the wholesale removal of the nation to west of the Mississippi.

In justifying the actions of the Treaty Party, though, Boudinot argues that constitutional Cherokee officials, Ross in particular, had ceased to represent the people due to the fact that such officials had engaged in an ongoing program of deception. Discussing the impeachment in 1834 of three members of the Cherokee legislature for advocating removal (among them Major Ridge and John Ridge), including having authorized themselves to serve as part of a delegation to Washington unlicensed by the Cherokee government and in competition with the official one, Boudinot observes, "It was a most extraordinary spectacle to see a few leading men acting in this extraordinary way, under cover of the *will of the people*, when those people were purposely kept from discussion and truth, by which alone they could be enabled to exercise *their will* to good and beneficial purposes."[20] Ross and those who supported this action appear to be cloaking themselves in their own representative status in order both to disable free discussion and to prevent the actual expression of popular will. Boudinot implies that were the "truth" known, the Cherokee public would choose a different path, one more broadly directed to "good and beneficial purposes" rather than simply being shaped by the partial interests of those serving in positions of authority. According to Boudinot, officials present themselves as the legitimate bearers and interpreters of popular will, but that appearance masks the fact that they only seem to be so due to their having seriously misled the public while seeking to silence those who would convey the "truth." He charges that the "*constituted authorities* of the nation" have created "the illusive appearance of having a vast majority opposed to us" (161). Boudinot further suggests that the image of the Treaty Party as "a small minority opposed to the will of the people" depends entirely on "*[a] want of proper information among the people*," and the absence of such information results from Cherokee officials' decision to withhold it from the people: "They have been taught to feel and expect what *could not* be realized—and what Mr. Ross himself must have known *would not* be realized" (161). Ross's depiction of himself and other Cherokee officials as the proper representatives of the Cherokee Nation, as conveying the disposition of the "vast majority," hinges on their continuing to generate false hope by making promises that they *must have known* could not be fulfilled. Boudinot notes that the opposition to the removal treaty would continue "*as long as they understood you as trying to reinstate them in their country*," further asking, "Is it right to humor this delusion?" (213). Following this logic, if the idea of the Cherokees remaining in their current territory can be nothing but a "delusion," then the promotion of this notion by the "*constituted authorities*" of the nation manufactures and sustains opposition to removal, which allows officials to cast themselves as representing the popular will and to castigate those who signed the treaty. According to Boudinot, the apparent "*will of the people*," in whose name Cherokee officials speak, is an effect produced by the knowingly false claims of officials, while such resistance is cited as if it were a cause of officials' actions. The government's claim to representativity, therefore, cannot be legitimate, because it fundamentally is based on a series of lies. What truly matters in determining the validity of acts of political representation is "what the majority *would do*" if they were aware of "their true situation" (162).

Boudinot understands himself to be in a position to know for certain the value and veracity of the information being presented to the Cherokee people by Ross, a knowledge that allows him to calculate what the Cherokee people "*would do*" and what they would support if they had all the facts. However, what gives him this epistemic advantage relative to the rest of the Cherokee population? Addressing the emergence of the Treaty Party, Boudinot notes, "'What is to be done?' was a national inquiry, after we found that all our efforts to obtain redress from the General Government, *on the land of our fathers*, had been of no avail" (160). He is referring to the refusal of Andrew

Jackson's administration to prevent Georgia's extension of jurisdiction over the Cherokee Nation even after the U.S. Supreme Court found in *Worchester v. Georgia* that Georgia's laws doing so were unconstitutional. Starting in 1827, in the wake of the Cherokees' adoption of a constitution, Georgia began passing a series of laws extending the state's jurisdiction over Cherokee territory. These laws included annexing Cherokee lands to state counties, distributing those lands through a public lottery, refusing to recognize the laws and acts of the Cherokee Nation, and criminalizing the operation of Cherokee governance and efforts to prevent removal.[21] In the wake of the Jackson administration's failure to implement the Court's decision in *Worcester*, Boudinot indicates that "to a portion of the Cherokee people it early became evident that the interest of their countrymen, and the happiness of their posterity, depended upon an entire change of policy. Instead of contending uselessly against superior power, the only course left, was, to yield to circumstances over which they had no control" (160). The oppressive circumstances faced by the Cherokees in light of the federal government's abandonment of them to Georgia's invasion of their territory create conditions in which the need for a "change of policy" becomes "evident." Yet, only "a portion of the Cherokee people" reach this conclusion, despite the supposedly self-apparent *uselessness* of fighting due to the power arrayed against them and their inability to alter the situation. What distinguishes those among the people who see this inevitability from those who do not, those who continue to endorse the old "policy" of the Cherokee government? Later in the text, in a letter addressed to Ross (dated December 4, 1836) in which he reiterates the reasons for his support of the Treaty of New Echota and provides a critique of Ross's administration, Boudinot indicates that "those who have watched attentively the progress of Cherokee controversy from its commencement to the present time[,] those who know what was actually the condition of the Cherokees before the making and publishing [of] the 'instrument' in question," would be able to distinguish the true political condition of the Cherokee Nation from the "impression" that Ross has sought to convey, which is "not in accordance with the facts" and in which he is "clinging only to an empty title" (215). Here Boudinot suggests that there is a determinate perspective from which to view what has happened that will reveal "the facts" of the case. The members of the Treaty Party and John Ross both seem to occupy such a position, with the former deciding to act on that knowledge and the latter choosing to *cling* to an "empty" vision of the nation that continues to support Ross's narrative of his own representativity.

From this perspective, certain Cherokees have a more intimate awareness of the ins and outs of the "Cherokee controversy," such that they would know better the *actual condition* of the Cherokee Nation, and Boudinot presents himself as among those who come to endorse removal on the basis of such information, of which the majority of the Cherokee population supposedly is unaware. He asserts that "a large majority of the Cherokee people would prefer to remove, if the true state of their condition was properly made known to them" (177). Yet, rather than agreeing to removal in order to redress the desperate conditions faced by the Cherokee people (Georgia's passage of laws asserting jurisdiction over Cherokee territory, decisions by the U.S. federal government, aggressions by the Georgia Guard, etc.), those in positions of authority in the Cherokee Nation chose to present a deceptive picture of the actual political options available and the possibilities of success, thereby fabricating a majority whose support of those leaders' representative authority rested on falsehoods. Thus, Boudinot suggests, the Treaty Party needed to step in to represent the majority who could not represent themselves due to the misleading account they were receiving.

Although suggesting that the Cherokee people have been misled, the text also repeatedly articulates the notion that the majority of Cherokees illustrate a pronounced tendency toward such mystification. When describing how Ross had depicted the Treaty Party in the fall of 1835 as a "faction" renewing their "allegiance" to "'the constituted authorities of the nation,'" Boudinot asks with respect to popular understanding of Ross's statement, "What do you suppose would be the understanding of an ignorant, prejudiced Cherokee, from such an explanation as that" (185–186). Boudinot goes on to deride "the reasoning of these deluded people" in their presumption that this putative defeat of the Treaty Party had meant that "the country is now saved" (186). If national leaders have deceived the people, the latter's own *ignorance* and *prejudice* appears as the reason why they would end up believing the claims made to them. "Deluded" here seems to refer less to an action taken against the Cherokee majority than to a state of affairs that results from the majority's own inclinations. In seeking to undermine Ross's claims to represent the will of the majority of the Cherokee people in their opposition to removal, Boudinot later observes of Ross's statements since returning from Washington, D.C., in the wake of the treaty's ratification by Congress, "It is enough to mislead those who have no mind of their own" (221), and previously, the text describes Ross as having "the entire confidence of an ignorant and confiding people" (191). Rather than merely castigating authorities for not providing "*proper information*," Boudinot presents the Cherokee people as largely lacking an ability properly to interpret the information they do receive. Their "reasoning" does not lead them to appropriate conclusions, so Boudinot and the other signatories to the Treaty of

New Echota need to step in to act in the Cherokee population's stead, doing what Cherokee officials like Ross ostensibly should have done given their apparent ability to appreciate the "facts."

The text's account of the Treaty Party's claim to representativity relies on portraying the Cherokee people as in need of elite leadership in order truly to understand the circumstances faced by the nation. In discussing the legitimacy of this de facto act of political surrogation, Boudinot insists, "If one hundred persons are ignorant of their true situation, and are so completely blinded as not to see the destruction that awaits them, we can see strong reasons to justify the action of a minority of fifty persons—to do what the majority *would do* if they understood their condition—to save a *nation* from political thralldom and moral degradation" (162). The text suggests that the Cherokee populace's *ignorance* lies less in a lack of information as such than in an inability to see the import of current circumstances—of perceiving the "true situation." To *understand* here entails drawing on a set of interpretive principles, or an interpretive key, that provides the means through which to process raw information and to make sense of it, to produce lines of analysis that enable substantive judgments about extant probabilities and strategies for ensuring the well-being of the nation.[22] Boudinot indicates that the interpretive framework employed by large swaths of the Cherokee citizenry *blinds* them. Addressing the selection in October 1835 of a delegation to represent the Cherokees in negotiations with federal officials, Boudinot notes that most of those present at the Council incorrectly believed that the delegates so chosen would prevent the cession of Cherokee lands: "Such were the impressions entertained by one class of the Cherokee—but there was another to be satisfied—the intelligence of the country—those who understood the situation of the Cherokees, and foresaw the consequences of persisting to reject the propositions for a treaty, those who believed that a treaty was inevitable, and ought to be made speedily" (189). In favoring the signing of a removal treaty, the members of the Treaty Party possess an "intelligence" that sets them apart as a "class" from the majority of the population, showing a foresight that Boudinot implies lies beyond the capabilities of most ordinary Cherokees. He casts the principles they employ in engaging with the political dynamics and stakes of the situation created by state and federal policy as inherently inadequate to the task of generating true, rational conclusions about the actual conditions they face. Boudinot intimates that in light of these widespread deficiencies, he and others who can see what's happening must act on behalf of the broader Cherokee populace.

Boudinot's assertion of the right to represent the people gains meaning against a set of background presumptions about what kinds of sentiments, principles, and modes of social organization enable expressions of "intelligence" and which can be dismissed as backward because they remain mired in prejudice and ignorance. What prequalifies the Treaty Party to speak for the nation is that, as a "class," they embody the civilizing tendencies that serve as the basis for forms of political engagement, that provide the template for what will constitute political voice. Separate from the question of removal per se, *Letters* implicitly frames perceptual capacity—awareness, sight, understanding—as a function of individual and collective participation in patterns of enlightening cultivation made possible through adoption of the structures of liberal political economy. Although scholars often underline a shift in Boudinot's thinking in the early 1830s as he comes to view removal as the only option for Cherokee survival, his earlier writing illustrates an orientation toward settler-introduced social forms as the means of assessing the nation's welfare and potential.[23] In "An Address to the Whites," delivered as part of his Northeastern fundraising tour in 1826, Boudinot portrays the Cherokees as acquiring the "means of civilization" that would allow them to stand as a nation worthy of U.S. recognition (77).[24] Although certainly shaped by Boudinot's need to ingratiate himself with white audiences and persuade them of Cherokee worth in terms with which they would be familiar, the text offers a vision of Cherokee peoplehood consistent with the tenor and enactments of Cherokee governance over the prior decade, further consolidated in the adoption of the Cherokee Constitution a year later.[25] Among the things "of late occurrence" that could provide evidence of "Indian improvement," Boudinot includes "the organization of a Government" (73–74), referring to the institutionalization of a three-branch system resembling that of the United States and implying that the Cherokees lacked such political order prior to that development. He specifically refers to the members of the National Committee as "men of sound sense and fine talents" (75), alluding to the fact that the Committee largely comprised Cherokees who had adopted bourgeois norms of education, patrilineal inheritance, and participation in capitalist exchange.[26] He earlier observes that the "rise of these people in their movement toward civilization, may be traced as far back as the relinquishment of their towns" (71), thereby casting the forms of sociality, clan networks, and decentralized autonomy that shaped town-based modes of political life as markers of a less-advanced stage of progress that needed to be discarded in order to move "toward civilization." Following Guha's description of the existence of a field of political practice and understanding "parallel to the domain of elite politics" but not encompassed within it, we might describe such investments in towns and clans as an alternative domain of politics rendered subaltern by elite portrayals of it as simply the absence of government.

Moreover, Boudinot presents opposition to the implementation of elite norms and sociopolitical structures as a somewhat senseless negation of improvement by an aggregation of individuals rather than as potentially expressive of modes of collective popular refusal in favor of other principles of Cherokee nationality. Objections to the expansion and institutionalization of liberal political economy in the Cherokee Nation—such as, for example, the prophetic movement against Euro-American social forms in the early 1810s and White Path's Rebellion against the adoption of the Cherokee Constitution in the mid-1820s—appear as mere "individual failings" that throw "obstacles in the path of what Boudinot depicts as an otherwise clearly desirable trajectory toward Cherokee "improvement."[27] He writes, "The adult part of the nation will probably grovel on in ignorance and die in ignorance, without any fair trial upon them, unless the proposed means are carried into effect" (76). The understanding of most Cherokees as enmired in "ignorance"—and, therefore, needing to be led out of their miasma of unknowing by the "informed and judicious"—persists across the events of the late 1820s and 1830s, appearing as a central feature of Boudinot's effort to justify the actions of the Treaty Party in *Letters*.

Boudinot's staging of Cherokee collective identity presents the political form of the state less as expressive of popular desires or assent than as a means of engaging the demands of the U.S. government in informed and judicious ways. Such formulations have little to do with the project of reading Native writing as expressive of popular formations that are nonstatist or antistatist in their orientation. From this perspective, *Letters* might be understood as dissociated from Cherokee identity and as a bid for recognition dislocated from principles internal to Cherokee peoplehood. However, given the parallels between Boudinot's text and the organizing structure of constitutional Cherokee governance and statements by Cherokee officials (particularly John Ross), *Letters* cannot be cast in its elitism as more distanced from the Cherokee Nation than the constitutional government itself. John Ross served as president of the Standing Committee from 1818 until 1828, when he became principal chief of the Cherokee Nation under the Cherokee Constitution—for which he had been the president of the drafting convention.[28] As such, he was intimately involved in the changes to Cherokee governance enacted during this period. Those transformations included the construction of a centralized national governmental apparatus (as discussed earlier) as well as the protection of patriarchal inheritance and belonging to the nation, the limitation of the franchise and governmental service to men, the outlawing of polygamy, the criminalizing of abortion, the creation of a system of legally enforced debts and contracts, the extension of a national tax for which property could be seized if one failed to pay, the outlawing of free Blacks from entering the nation, the setting up of a registry for fugitive slaves (from within and without the nation), the denial of the rights of slaves to sign contracts or hold property, the outlawing of marriage to slaves, the prevention of all business during the Sabbath, and the making of governmental and jury service dependent on belief "in the existence of the Creator."[29] These developments indicate a vision of Cherokee peoplehood oriented toward the kinds of improvement that Boudinot presents as the basis for defending and preserving nationhood.[30]

Moreover, under Ross's leadership, the Cherokee national government sought to suppress the potential for both town-based political formations and challenges to the emerging institutional architecture of the constitutional Cherokee state. These measures included a law that expressly forbid "members of the Committee and Council" from "conven[ing] Councils in their respective districts" and preventing such local councils from "act[ing] officially on any matters of concern to the public affairs of the Nation," as well as the following: removing White Path—an opponent of the civilization program and of further centralization—from the National Council; providing a prescreened list of who could serve as candidates to run as district representatives for the constitutional convention; and criminalizing "unlawful meetings" that seek "to encourage rebellion against the laws and Government of the Cherokee Nation" (which would include opposition to the principles adopted in the newly enacted Constitution).[31] While these laws do not themselves directly address the question of retaining the landbase of the Cherokee Nation, they speak to the template or form for governance at play in national institutions during the period prior to the removal crisis of the mid-1830s.[32]

In addition, Ross's public statements within and outside the nation offer what can be characterized as an elite account of Cherokee nationality. In a memorial to the U.S. Congress in 1829 in the wake of the adoption of the Cherokee Constitution, and Georgia's passage of laws extending jurisdiction over Cherokee territory in response, Ross indicates, "Our improvement has been without a parallel in the history of all Indian nations. Agriculture is every where pursued, and the interests of our citizens are permanent in the soil. We have enjoyed the blessings of Christian instruction; the advantages of education and merit are justly appreciated, a Government of regular law has been adopted, and the nation, under a continuance of the fostering care of the United States, will stand forth as a living testimony, that all Indian nations are not doomed to the fate which has swept many from the face of the earth."[33] The account Ross offers here lines up with Boudinot's emphasis in "An Address to the Whites," for example, on the importance of Cherokees moving beyond popular forms of ignorance, prejudice, and superstition (terms which get repeated in *Letters* in ways discussed earlier). What defines Cherokee peoplehood in the present is the adoption of modes of advancement that will prevent the "doomed" extinction that has befallen other "Indian nations," which implicitly is cast as a result of their failure to implement similar measures. Such sentiments, though, are not solely articulated for non-Cherokee audiences. In his annual message to the Cherokee people in 1828, Ross argues, "By the adoption of the Constitution, our relation to the United States, as recognized by existing Treaties, is not in the least degree affected, but on the contrary, this improvement in our government, is strictly in accordance with the recommendations, views and wishes of the Great Washington . . . and whose policy in regard to Indian civilization has been strictly pursued by the subsequent administrations."[34] While invoking treaties with the United States recognizing Cherokee sovereignty, Ross presents changes in Cherokee governance as part of a process of "improvement" that follows a civilizational trajectory in line with dominant non-native notions of proper social order. Returning to Guha's formulation of elite politics discussed earlier as "assumed to be or enunciated as exclusively or primarily those of the institutions introduced" through colonialism, we can understand Ross as offering an affirmation of Cherokee political separateness that opposes ongoing U.S. projects of dispossession and displacement, but one that figures in terms of background principles of governance drawn from U.S. models.[35] Similarly, in his annual address to the Cherokee people the next year, he describes the Cherokees as "a distinct people" who "have ever exercised" self-rule, which "has been recognized by the Government of the United States, under whose fostering care we have emerged from the darkness of ignorance and superstition to our present degree of advancement in civilized improvement."[36] The U.S. recognition of Cherokee political autonomy seems correlated here to continuing Cherokee "advancement" out of "darkness," a formulation that resonates with Boudinot's depiction of popular attachments as backward and a delusive drag on the future of the Cherokee people.

Furthermore, while *Letters* often characterizes the distinction among Cherokees that enables the Treaty Party to exert superior judgment in terms of "class," alluding to bourgeois markers of proper self-cultivation such as Euro-American-style schooling, the differences and dynamics toward which Boudinot gestures and that are institutionalized as part of Cherokee national governance also are profoundly gendered. In moving away from town-based governance, the centralization of political authority in national institutions diminished the importance of the clans to Cherokee political processes. Or rather, the continued role of clans in everyday social life for the majority of Cherokee people no longer constituted a mode of political relation within institutionalized discourses of Cherokee governance. Cherokee clan belonging was and continues to be matrilineal, and prior to the early nineteenth century, women's councils comprising representatives from each of the seven clans exerted a great deal of influence over leadership and collective decision-making at the town level. However, as Wilma Dunaway notes, "Between 1808 and 1825, elite leaders attempted to break the power of matrilineal clans and of women by instituting a series of laws transforming marriage, property rights, family lineage, and the political rights of women," and in *Cherokee Women*, Theda Perdue observes that the "process toward centralizing and formalizing political power ... [worked] to distance women further from politics."[37] The Cherokee Constitution, in fact, formally limited political participation to "free male citizens."[38] Thus, when *Letters* addresses questions with respect to the "will of the people" and the relation of such sentiments to actions by the "constituted authorities," the text implicitly takes as its frame a conception of Cherokee politics in which women do not exist as public subjects and in which social formations that centered on women no longer constitute the basis for political norms and networks officially recognized as such. In *As We Have Always Done*, Leanne Simpson suggests of the ways Euro-American institutions sought to impose heterogendered forms of social order on Native peoples, "Heteropatriarchy isn't just about exclusion of certain Indigenous bodies, it is about the destruction of the intimate relationships that make up our nations, and the fundamental systems of ethics based on values of individual sovereignty and self-determination."[39] The emergence of elite-led national institutions reorganized the terms of what constituted Cherokee governance in ways that no longer registered prior matrices of relation as political formations, so that more than simply excluding women from political decision-making, the shift away from the clans alters the terms of Cherokee nationhood, of what sovereignty and self-determination *are*. Thus, even as Boudinot challenges claims by national leaders (such as Ross) to speak for the Cherokee people, suggesting that in doing so they simply confirm popular forms of prejudice, the text's vision of elite representation takes shape against a heteropatriarchal background in which the displacement of Cherokee women and the subalternization of the clans serves as one of the central conditions of emergence for the expression of the kinds of civilized supervision and vanguardism that Boudinot endorses.

The question of Boudinot's (claims to) representativity, then, opens out into an analysis of how Cherokee national governance emerges in the interface between U.S. pressures and associated differences among the Cherokee populace that engender varied relations to the political form of the state. The institutional apparatus of Cherokee national governance both works to make Cherokee peoplehood intelligible to the settler-state (so as to prevent dispossession by centralizing collective voice) and instantiates a vision of law and policy oriented by elite frames. As Gayatri Spivak suggests in her discussion of the work of subaltern studies, "A functional change in a sign system is a violent event."[40] Although indicative of the force of colonial intervention, the movement from one system of Cherokee governance (by clans and towns) to another (modeled on the United States) cannot be understood as merely an external imposition nor can its influence be interpreted solely in a negative relation to nonstatist formations. Clint Carroll addresses how in the context of contemporary governance in the Cherokee Nation, a tension arises between relationship-based knowledges and the structure of the state form. While highlighting how "indigenous nations have been able to envision the state form for themselves," he also observes how "the current structure of the Cherokee Nation government, based as it is on rationality, citizen equality, and bureaucratic order, inhibits the influence of 'traditional' sources of authority." Addressing the latter involves "reconfiguring state practices and acknowledging alternative sources of authority," but at the same time, he argues, "discrediting or circumventing indigenous state structures because they do not mirror 'traditional' models may not necessarily result in more freedom for indigenous nations."[41] Even as the state form often translates other political formations into its terms in ways that disfigure them, it also potentially can provide protection for such formations against further colonial intervention, regulation, and disciplining.[42] Thus, while investment in ideologies of statehood clearly respond to settler presence and pressures, that dynamic does not mean they easily can be categorized as external to Native self-articulations, even as the state form bears a range of complex and contested meanings within Native networks that are not easily resolved into a "yes" or "no" with regard to its representativity. Attending to the politics of Boudinot's elitism in his assertions of his own representativity, then, helps foreground the dense set of negotiations at play in Cherokee governance.

The investment of the majority of Cherokees in principles other than those of bourgeois political economy and civilizational uplift signifies in *Letters* as a pervasive ignorance that disqualifies them from proper political subjectivity—speaking rather than solely being spoken for. In this text, "information" entails not just access to data, the putative "facts" of the situation, but the use of a particular interpretive framework for determining what is true, possible, and desirable that itself is oriented around elite principles. The question of determining what counts as a meaningful public position or policy direction, then, depends on already accepting, in Bruno Latour's terms, a set of "felicity conditions" that themselves are dependent on taking certain social dispositions as inherently indicative of the presence of intelligence, perceptiveness, and discernment.[43] Absent those extrapolitical characteristics, individual judgment, consent, and refusal appear as merely the reiteration of prejudice rather than as expressions of popular will on which national acts of governance could be based. Within the normative framework *Letters* articulates, the majority cannot speak in a way that would matter, because they cannot understand the actual political circumstances faced by the Cherokee Nation, as indicated by their lack of awareness of the proper forms of nationality itself.[44] This framing of Cherokee popular sentiment and elite superintendence through notions of "political order," development, improvement, and civilization based on U.S. models might be read as a bid for recognition by non-native publics, one that supports settler narratives of widespread Indian ignorance. Yet, while challenging decisions by Cherokee officials, *Letters* shares much of its organizing conceptual structure with the principles and policies at play in Cherokee constitutional governance. Focusing on how Boudinot stages the terms of his own representativity, and the opacities of what political "representation" means in the context of colonialism, helps draw attention to the complexities and mediations enacted in the Cherokee government's own formulations of representativity and the negotiations among Cherokees over the political form of Cherokee peoplehood in the midst of intensifying settler violence.

Forming the People

If Boudinot's orientation toward liberal political economy also appears immanent within Cherokee national institutions, the difference between using such settler templates and identifying with them (what I have described as a kind of cruel optimism) might be located less in the adherence to a particular political form than in the extent and ways it might be mediated by other forms, principles, and philosophical commitments—in Carroll's terms quoted earlier, the functional possibilities for opening toward "alternative sources of authority." Within *Letters*, popular Cherokee insistence that Cherokee territory is not fungible appears merely as an expression of mass "ignorance," especially in terms of the failure to adopt the framework of U.S. law. By contrast, the Cherokee national government takes up such widely held sentiments, despite uneven popular investment in the administrative apparatus of the nation and the government's support for bourgeois political economy. *Letters* offers a doubleedged critique: leaders who, like the Treaty Party, are among the "intelligence of the country" have not correctly employed civilized norms of interpretation, assessment, and decision-making; and they have not done so because, unlike the Treaty Party, they are humoring forms of popular "delusion" about what's politically possible in the present. Both of these charges hinge on authorities' putative failure, and that of Ross in particular, to follow through on a set of elite principles and perspectives shared with the Treaty Party. *Letters* makes clear that Ross and Boudinot offer discrepant ways of figuring what Cherokee nationality is—seeing it as inhering in a matrix of relations that arise through existing forms of emplacement versus seeing it as the welfare of Cherokee persons as an aggregate population (a collection of persons who could be moved elsewhere and still remain a nation). In *Letters*, Boudinot contends not only that Cherokee nationality can be distinguished from the process of inhabiting a given landbase but also that the continued existence of the nation as such actually requires that they surrender their current lands for territory west of the Mississippi. This argument, though, employs the notion of the nation as an aggregate of (liberal) citizen-subjects that had become increasingly dominant in Cherokee governance over the prior two decades. *Letters* illustrates that what distinguishes Ross and Boudinot's positions is less their ways of conceptualizing the contours and direction of Cherokee nationality than the extent to which their claims to representativity involve engaging with what they both characterize as popular "prejudice." Boudinot's presentation sheds entirely the fierce investment in protecting existing Cherokee lands that sustained popular support for the constitutional government—the ways Cherokee national governance continued to be mediated by alternative formulations of peoplehood so as to generate and maintain popular consent. In this way, *Letters* helps bring into relief the difference between representativity as a unilateral staging of collective identity within and for settler networks versus as a process of negotiation over political form within Native networks.

The text consistently portrays Ross and other officials as fixated on preserving the existing landbase in ways that leave aside the well-being of the persons who make up the nation. Boudinot seeks to distinguish between the citizenry and territory of the Cherokee Nation in order to argue that the preservation of the former as a collective requires surrendering the latter. In a previously unpublished letter responding to charges against him that were printed in the *Cherokee Phoenix* after his resignation as editor, Boudinot lays out this line of argument:

> In one word, I may say that my patriotism consists in the *love of the country*, and *the love of the People*. These are intimately connected, yet they are not altogether inseparable. They are inseparable if the people are made

the first victim, for in that case the country must go also, and there must be an end of the objects of our patriotism. But if the country is lost, is likely to be lost to all human appearance, and the people still exist, may I not, with a patriotism true and commendable, make a *question* for the safety of the remaining object of my affection? (172)

He foregrounds the fact that the loss of the people would mean the loss of the nation, and he indicates that the continuance of the people, even in a different "country," could enable the survival of the nation. The term "people" here refers both to the collective that is the Cherokee Nation and to the persons who comprise the collective. This doubleness allows Boudinot to suggest that if the population of Cherokee persons were to assemble elsewhere with the intent of remaining a Cherokee collective, the national people would remain intact, therefore sustaining the existence of the nation.

The object of his "patriotism"—the Cherokee Nation—does not depend on the inhabitance of a particular "country" or geographic area, but, instead, is (re)constituted through the will of a group of persons, Cherokees, to be a *people*, to continue to exist as a distinct polity (re)made through their membership and collective "affection" for the entity that is the Cherokee Nation. As Bethany Schneider notes, "Boudinot wants to forge, to invent, a people separable from land."[45] *Letters* underlines this point by reprinting the resolutions of the Treaty Party: "Although *we love the land* of our fathers, and should leave the place of our nativity with as much regret as any of our citizens, we consider the lot of the *Exile* immeasurably more to be preferred than a submission to the laws of the States, and thus becoming witnesses of the ruin and degradation of the Cherokee people," adding that this removal is the interest of "regain[ing] their rights as a *distinct community*" (176–177). To be a "*distinct community*," to continue to exist as a nation, entails avoiding being incorporated into the regular jurisdiction of the states that claim the lands of the Cherokee Nation, since doing so would produce "ruin and degradation" that would decimate the lives of Cherokee persons and dissolve the Cherokees as a discrete collective political entity. Simply remaining on the land does not guarantee the continued existence of Cherokee nationality, since the persons of the nation can be eliminated (either murdered or run off as a series of individuals), and even if they could remain it would be in ways that cease to be *national*—that no longer allow for them to have the political, legal form of the nation. Securing Cherokees' "rights" to continue to be "citizens" of the Cherokee Nation, then, provides the justification for the actions of the Treaty Party. They become representative for the nation in choosing the only available option that would allow for the nation to continue as such. Refusing to treat with the United States on the grounds that doing so will preserve the current territory of the nation appears here as an act of national suicide and, therefore, not possibly a true expression of the desire of the people to remain a "People."

In Boudinot's formulation, though, what precisely does maintaining their status as "citizens" mean? One could read this term simply as referring to belonging to the Cherokee Nation. If the nation ceases to be a nation, being swallowed and disintegrated in the extension of the states' jurisdiction over what had been Cherokee lands, then there will be no Cherokee Nation to which they could belong, and they would then cease to be citizens of it. Conversely, as Simpson argues in *As We Have Always Done*, Indigenous bodies themselves can be understood as bearing "political orders," as "centered in our Indigenous presents" in ways that are not dependent on recognition by the settler-state and that enable Native nationhood to function as "a web of connections" or a "hub of . . . networks."[46] While indicating that "Indigenous peoples require a land base," thereby understanding Native nationhoods as "unapologetic[ally] place-based," such networks need not be thought of as locked into a reified geography, especially given ongoing histories of Indigenous mobility and the need to respond to forms of settler colonial dispossession.[47] In this sense, Boudinot's argument might be read as seeing Cherokee bodies as bearing sovereignty and self-determination in their dynamic and ongoing relations with each other, as opposed to a conception of Cherokee being and becoming as locked into a single state-recognized geography and as nonexistent absent continued inhabitance in that specific space. However, in contrast to this nonstatist account of indigeneity as inhering in everyday processes of embodiment and relation, the portrayal of Cherokee identity and belonging in *Letters* takes on a different normative shape, one that aligns national existence with the potential for civilized becoming. In response to Ross's claim "that the Cherokees had not suffered one-half what their country was worth," Boudinot notes, "It is with sincere regret that I notice you say little or nothing about the moral condition of this people" (222), adding that Ross "see[s] them dying a moral death": "When applied to a portion of our people, confined mostly to whites intermarried among us, and the descendants of whites, your account is perfectly correct. . . . But look at the mass—look at the entire population as it now is, and say, can you see any indication of a progressing improvement—anything that can encourage a philanthropist?" (223). Conditions on their current landbase do not allow for "progressing improvement," and the assessment of the Cherokees' situation, including the potential for their "moral death" (distinct from actual death), seems to be shaped by the impossibility for kinds of development that would signify as such to the (white) "philanthropist."

Belonging to the nation, and its continued existence, appears predicated on the potential for kinds of progress that would enable the Cherokee people to live as a nation, rather than, say, as whatever they were prior to "the relinquishment of their towns" (as Boudinot puts it in "An Address to the Whites," quoted earlier). To be a people who are a nation, and thus to be citizens of that nation, then, involves collectively enacting an orientation toward forms of development that accord with the dynamics of liberal political economy. Living in a situation in which individuals cannot take part in such "moral" uplift precludes them, in the text's terms, from being a *distinct community* in a *national* sense. In this vein, Boudinot's patriotism might be described as turning toward a vision or version of the nation in which what makes national belonging meaningful is that it enables individual Cherokee subjects in the aggregate to enact the kinds of "improvement" that, reciprocally, will illustrate to settlers their "rights" to be a nation in the first place. Put another way, in framing his goal as preserving the people as "citizens," given the meanings this term accrues in his writing, Boudinot implicitly aligns Cherokee personhood with a particular mode of living that is intelligible to and valued by non-natives. His arguments about the need to distinguish the "safety" of the people from the attachment to the land gain meaning against that background set of political dispositions—that a political entity is constituted by improving subjects whose existence as a nation is dependent on making such trajectories of improvement possible. The claim to represent the citizenry as such, then, involves guarding against backward modes of attachment that limit the potential for "the mass" to enact this liberal conception of Cherokee national life.

Letters consistently describes Ross's and other leaders' resistance to the loss of their current territory as just such a surrender to the regressive investments of the Cherokee populace in the land. Boudinot charges that "people have become but a mere wreck of what they once were—all their institutions and improvements utterly destroyed," further stating, "The whole of that catastrophe, I mean aside from the mere loss of the soil, a trifle in consideration with other matters, which has overwhelmed and crushed the Cherokees, might have been averted, if Mr. Ross, instead of identifying himself with the contemptible prejudice founded upon the *love of the land*, had met the crisis manfully as it became him to do." Instead, Ross "has dragged an ignorant train, wrought upon by near sighted prejudice and stupid obstinacy, to the last brink of destruction" (198–199). In addition to reducing the "*love of the land*" to a matter of the "loss of the soil," presented as "a trifle" when compared to other unnamed issues faced by the Cherokees, the text casts such attachments to their territory as "contemptible" expressions of "prejudice" that bespeak a stubborn clinging to outmoded notions. Popular connections to the land—understandings of it as the organizing matrix for, in Simpson's terms quoted earlier, the "webs of connection" that constitute the Cherokee people as such—appear as merely expressions of ignorance rather than as political claims.

For Boudinot, the fact that "the mass" of Cherokees, toward whose welfare the text gestures, prioritize continued occupancy of their homeland simply illustrates their backwardness. Within the text's framework, such a set of commitments to ongoing histories of Cherokee placemaking cannot form the background against which to figure Cherokee nationality. For those Cherokees that Boudinot disparages, though, to what extent is remaining a "*distinct community*" an intelligible proposition separate from the network of landed relations from which the Cherokee Nation has emerged as a political entity? From this perspective, what is the nation if it can be severed from this place and still supposedly retain its identity? Early in *Letters*, Boudinot says of the position taken by the Treaty Party, "To advocate a treaty was to declare war against the established habits of thinking peculiar to the aborigines. It was to come in contact with settled prejudices—with the deep rooted attachment to the soil of our forefathers" (160–161). For Boudinot, the nation that is the object of his patriotism has an existence distinguishable from "the established habits of thinking" of the majority of Cherokee people and their "attachment" to their lands. He transposes Cherokee peoplehood into a version of "the people" in which the character of Cherokees' citizenship in the nation can be divorced from their own affective and political formations and in which such formations are translated as *ignorance* and *prejudice* that can be set aside in favor of a *progressive* notion of (privatized) personhood that provides the true basis for national existence—for which the Treaty Party can speak.[48]

Boudinot sketches two strikingly divergent ways of conceptualizing Cherokee collectivity: one based on modes of *improvement*, such that Cherokee social relations increasingly resemble the terms of liberal subjectivity and political economy; and another based on sets of relationships fundamentally shaped by their emplaced relation to each other and their reciprocal role in constituting a sense of place-based collectivity. He aligns the continued existence of the nation as such with the former, and in charging Ross with having wrecked the nation due to "identifying himself" with modes of popular delusion and recalcitrance, the text suggests that Ross has adopted the latter vision of Cherokee peoplehood. The connections to land that Boudinot casts as mere "obstinacy" might be understood as an expression of what Glen Coulthard has referred to as "grounded normativity"—"the modalities of Indigenous land-connected practices and longstanding experiential knowledge that inform and structure ethical engagements with the world and our relationships with human and nonhuman others over time."[49] Presenting Ross and other prominent Cherokee leaders as operating within such normative principles, though, runs against the grain of the history of the Cherokee national government and its increasing commitment to capitalist, heteropatriarchal, and slaveholding norms.[50]

This institutionalized vision of the nation—of what Cherokee peoplehood is and should be and, consequently, what it means to *represent* that nation— runs counter to the everyday principles at play in the lives of most Cherokees. Within the domain of what might be characterized as subaltern politics, towns, clans, and agricultural production largely for subsistence (rather than the market) continued to predominate. As Boudinot indicates, the popular *"love of the land"* circulates within and through "established habits of thinking" and practice, networks for conceptualizing the contours and content of Cherokee identity that differ from the conception of advancement and improvement materialized in Cherokee national governance. Despite national laws and policy to the contrary, land and personal property continued to be transferred largely through matrilineal connections rather than heteropatriarchal inheritance, and town councils persisted through the 1820s and into the 1830s with women participating in significant ways.[51] As Perdue observes in *Cherokee Women*, "Either the Cherokees were exceptionally law-abiding or a dual system of jurisprudence existed in which some people, perhaps most, applied customary methods of social regulation to a traditional code of behavior and others followed the laws of the republic."[52] Similarly, Dunaway indicates, "By 1835, fewer than one-quarter of Cherokee families were undergoing or had made the transition to agrarian capitalism," adding, "Three-fifths of Cherokee families produced about one-third more than they needed for survival while another one-third produced no surpluses at all."[53] The continuing salience of the towns to Cherokee life further is suggested by the transfer of town communities and names to Indian Territory in the wake of removal.[54] At one point Guha characterizes the subaltern classes as "represent[ing] *the demographic difference between the total Indian population and all those whom we have described as the 'elite.'"*[55] In this vein, one might point to the significant demographic distinction between the vast majority of Cherokees and those families who generated significant wealth through capitalist trade, as suggested by the statistics Dunaway cites.

More than merely a statistical distinction, these figures point toward differences in the normative frameworks employed in understanding modes of Cherokee identity. Cherokee residency patterns and agriculture certainly did change over the course of the late eighteenth and early nineteenth century.[56] The distinction to which I'm pointing, though, is not one between the preservation of "tradition," envisioned as an unchanging set of principles/practices, and "progress," imagined as a unilateral adoption of Euro-American lifeways. As Joshua Nelson argues, "Many facets commonly thought part of civilization (like education, worship, and trade) were often already present in some shape in traditional society, or they might be transformed into Cherokee ways of doing things. Cherokee intellectuals were in fact participating in their historical moment in the shaping of civilization and the social and political principled practices that made it up."[57] However, incorporating aspects of Euro-American education and trade within networks of relations in which Cherokee belonging is conceptualized and lived through clans and towns differs markedly from the adoption of a vision of heteropatriarchal, liberal governance, toward which policy enacted by the national government was oriented.[58] We might describe what *both* Boudinot and Ross present as popular attachments and prejudices as instead, in Audra Simpson's terms, "feeling citizenships": "These are alternative citizenships to the state that are structured in the present space of intracommunity recognition, affection, and care, outside the logics of colonial and imperial rule."[59] These continuing modes of recognition and care among Cherokees are at odds with the form of policy adopted by the Cherokee state. Thus, while engaging in an explicitly anticolonial affirmation of the Cherokee people's sovereignty as against settler incursions and interventions, Cherokee national governance institutionalizes a notion of "the people" not dissimilar to the one articulated by Boudinot in *Letters*, in both its contours and the traces of a gap between its terms and popular sentiments (the "darkness" from which Ross suggests Cherokees seek to emerge).[60]

Noting the disjunction between the form of Cherokee peoplehood endorsed within national institutions (as well as in public statements by Ross) and the principles guiding much of everyday life for the majority of Cherokees, though, is not the same as suggesting that the leaders of the Cherokee Nation did not represent the Cherokee people. U.S. officials at various levels as well as articles in the popular press repeatedly sought to present elected Cherokee leaders as a kind of cabal who tyrannically dominated the affairs of the nation, a portrait that Ross consistently and forcefully refuted.[61] As Ross argues in a memorial to Congress in 1829, "The chiefs of our nation are the immediate representatives of the people, by whose voice they are elected; and with equal propriety it may be said, that the people of the United States are afraid of their Representatives in Congress, and other public officers of the Government."[62] In his annual message in 1834, Ross observes with respect to the Cherokee Council, "In the exercise of your representative character, you are required to deliberate upon the affairs of that people, by whose free suffrage you have been elected; and it is to be hoped that whatever measures your wisdom may suggest as expedient to be adopted, will be found to conduce to their welfare and happiness."[63] Rather than suggesting that the national government's claims to be representative were false, that in truth officials were only acting in their own interests or were not actually approved as representatives by the Cherokee people, I am suggesting that the government translated this investment in "welfare and happiness" into an institutionalized form alien to the normative commitments of most Cherokees.

Despite that dynamic, though, national governance still depended on generating forms of popular consent, and much of the support for the government may be understood as deriving from its unflinching rejection of any further cessions of land. Such measures include laws and/or constitutional provisions that deny that emigrants have any claims to land in the Cherokee Nation (including any that would allow them to cede such lands to the United States or sell lands to U.S. citizens), refuse to receive U.S. treaty commissioners to meet with Cherokee officials, assert that the boundaries of the Cherokee Nation will remain inalterable, and criminalize and set a penalty of death for anyone who signs a treaty with the United States to cede Cherokee national territory.[64] In his public statements, Ross echoes this position. In this vein, in a letter to Secretary of War Lewis Cass in early 1833, he states of the Cherokee people that "they are unshaken in their objections to a removal West of the river Mississippi," such that their representatives "can never consent to be the instrument of a suicidal act to our nation's welfare and happiness."[65] Such sentiments appear in several petitions to the Cherokee government drafted by Cherokee women in the late 1810s and early 1820s. They insist that Cherokee officials should "keep your hands off of paper talks" that would cede the nation's territory, arguing that they "do not wish to go to an unknown country" or to cede lands "of which they have been in possession from time immemorial."[66] The petitions, though, do differ in how they frame such claims, registering tensions in Cherokee governance occurring in this period. An 1817 petition indicates that they address the National Council "as mothers" and that to remove "would be like destroying your mothers."[67] A petition from the following year highlights "our common rights" as "the first settlers of this land" and indicts the role of white men married to Cherokee women in inciting the "emigration of our nation" while also indicating that to remove would require "throw[ing] aside the privileges of a civilized life." While arguably oriented in different ways with regard to the changes occurring in Cherokee governance, these petitions point to an investment in remaining on the current Cherokee landbase. As Katy Simpson Smith observes, "Few Cherokees desired Removal, but for women, Removal stripped away their ties to kin, clan, and land, their primary sources of power."[68] Moreover, the various memorials against removal signed by thousands of Cherokees in the late 1820s and over the course of the 1830s indicate the scope of popular opposition to the cession of Cherokee lands.[69] In other words, popular consent to Cherokee national governance largely depended on and took the form of resistance to the cession of Cherokee territory to the United States.[70]

Thus, when Ross and other Cherokee leaders center their policy decisions with respect to the United States on, in Boudinot's terms *"love of the country,"* they are not simply taking a position on where and how best Cherokees might remain a *"distinct community"* in a political sense or expressing their individual *prejudices*, as *Letters* presents it. Rather, they are responding to the ways the Cherokee government itself depended on expressions of popular assent, albeit heavily mediated by the principles and forms of Cherokee national institutions (themselves heterogendered and racializing). Leaders are engaging in a negotiated process of accountability in which the modes of liberal governance endorsed as Cherokee law and policy still need to achieve public legitimacy through manifestations of "mass" consent. Even as evidence suggests that the majority of Cherokees held very different ideas of what constitutes Cherokee peoplehood than those institutionalized by the Cherokee state—a disjunction to which both Boudinot and Ross allude within their rhetoric of Cherokee improvement, advancement, and ignorance—they also appear to have supported the Cherokee government *in that it refused overtures of cession and removal*. Put another way, the government helped to sustain modes of grounded normativity that operated through forms other than those endorsed by Cherokee law and policy, but that very support enabled the government to serve as representative in negotiations with the United States.

The kind of nation and patriotism that Boudinot posits (his account of saving/improving "the people" through removal, as the basis for preserving peoplehood), however, has no relation to this matrix of *attachments* through which the "mass" of Cherokees understood and lived their nationality. Ross and other elite officials may not have endorsed those values and networks of relation either, but if nothing else, they engage the "stupid obstinacy" of such sentiments as the basis of their own claims to representativity. Even as Boudinot argues for the need to sustain Cherokee nationality through removal and, thus, offers an argument for Cherokee sovereignty, he directs it to non-natives—the projected audience for *Letters*—and through a frame of reference centered on settler paradigms. He returns repeatedly to the viability of particular formulations of Cherokee collectivity from the vantage point of the settler-state, assessing how realistic they are in light of white ideas and imperatives. More than pragmatically indicating the value or necessity of a particular political course of action, he actively proclaims the incapacity or perfidy of those expressing countervailing viewpoints/commitments. His claims to speak in the name of the Cherokee people dispense with even the pretense of popular support in favor of the position that what sustains his representativity, and that of the Treaty Party more broadly, is their familiarity and involvement with Euro-American networks. More than navigating processes of entanglement or operating within an overdetermined institutional structure inflected by class, race, and heteropatriarchy, Boudinot orients his vision around Euro-American perceptions and perspectives, mediating them toward the survival of the Cherokee Nation as an aggregate of Cherokee persons but in ways explicitly pitched against the utter valuelessness of popular/subaltern form(ul)ations. Survival appears to depend on the evacuation and denunciation of any other vision of collective flourishing.

From Dissent to Treason

If we read Boudinot and other Native writers for the degree to which their formulations of peoplehood can be seen as transparent (as expressive of extra-textual phenomena on which the text draws), we can end up framing representation as a matter of mimeticism rather than a form of intellectual and political labor that takes part in processes of negotiation and mediation.[71] Turning back to Spivak's discussion of the relation between "portrait" and "proxy," discussed in the introduction, when the two are conflated, "the critique of ideological subject-constitution within state formations and systems of political economy can now be effaced, as can the active theoretical practice of the 'transformation of consciousness.'"[72] The slide between "proxy" and "portrait" in *Letters* allows it to stage a particular intellectual analysis of the situation faced by the Cherokee Nation as *the* political response to that situation. The Cherokee people function as the subject in whose name *Letters* speaks, but the process of constructing such a subject (of generating, in Antonio Gramsci's terms, a "national-popular will") is absent.[73] Boudinot's text illustrates the dangers of substituting a particular intellectual perspective for the dynamics of collective political deliberation and debate: it highlights the problems generated by treating representation as a matter of correct portrayal (adequating an ideal) rather than of vexed relations of proxying under colonially constrained circumstances. The issue is less that Boudinot offers a false or partial account of Cherokee peoplehood than that *Letters* disregards the process of negotiating over the form and direction of the nation, portraying that process as itself contemptible and, therefore, disavowing the *politics* of peoplehood. More than partic-ipating within settler networks, Boudinot envisions the scene of engagement with non-natives as replacing not only the determinations of the constitutional Cherokee government but the dense matrix of mediations through which that government maintains its legitimacy among Cherokee people (even as such governance takes shape around a vision of statehood oriented to U.S. norms). I have argued that reading Boudinot's writing in light of extant Cherokee gov-ernance puts pressure on the distinction between "inside" and "outside" with regard to choices of political form, foregrounding elite continuities between *Letters* and Cherokee national institutions as well as the layered identifications of Cherokee publics in their relation with those institutions. Conversely, *Let-ters* also puts into relief the following: the political limits and consequences of asserting a correct way of portraying peoplehood absent any means of engaging countervailing framings (the notion of either a truly enlightened or a cultur-ally authentic vision against which other models can be deemed compromised, deluded, or failed); and the importance of holding intellectual discourse about Indigenous governance accountable to attend to the difficult mediations at play in enacting such governance (including in relation to colonial administra-tion and exertions of jurisdiction).

Boudinot offers an account of the reasons why the Cherokee government should follow a particular course of action, and he makes what is in many ways a compelling case for the need to endorse removal, as well as foregrounding problems in Ross's communication with the Cherokee public—the lapses in the information Ross conveys. However, this articulation of dissent and the Treaty Party's intellectual assessment of Cherokee political possibilities comes to substitute for the work of politics. As discussed previously, *Letters* does not allow for the possibility of an informed Cherokee popular sentiment that dif-fers from that of Boudinot and the Treaty Party. Rather, to be informed is to follow the line of *improvement*, which under the circumstances of the mid-1830s leads west. In contrast, while endorsing an elite vision of Cherokee na-tionality, government officials also undertake the task of gathering legitimacy through forms of popular affirmation, albeit filtered through mechanisms of governance that themselves remake Cherokee social formations along (racial-ized and heterogendered) liberal terms. What could be taken as a certain eva-siveness in Ross rhetoric, instead, can be read as traces of the process of political mediation in which he's enmeshed—a network of accountability that he man-ages in a skewed fashion but that the Treaty Party and *Letters* evades entirely.

One might wonder why Boudinot and the Treaty Party did not seek to generate popular support for removal, such as by circulating what Boudinot presents as *"proper information"* about the Cherokees' political circumstances. *Letters* does offer extended discussions of Ross's firing of Boudinot from his position as editor of the *Cherokee Phoenix* and of various points at which the members of the Treaty Party thought they had reached an accord with national officials, agreements that Boudinot claims were not kept. While these elements of the text suggest difficulty in reaching the Cherokee population through publication and periods when Boudinot and others might have foregone such communication, believing that a deal was in process with Ross and other Cherokee leaders, they do not fully address the leap in the text from asserting that the Cherokee populace was misinformed to proclaiming the ability to represent the people absent any exercise of popular consent. If the Cherokee national government had ceased to be representative due to what amounts to disseminating disinformation, as Boudinot argues, such actions do not endow the Treaty Party with a representative function. What, then, justifies them taking up that role?

More than offering a sustained denunciation of Ross's leadership and the choices made by Cherokee government officials, *Letters* seeks to justify the actions of the Treaty Party, which extend beyond the signing of the Treaty of New Echota in December 1835. As Andrew Denson observes, "Unable to convince their countrymen that their position was correct, Treaty Party leaders proceeded to negotiate with the United States anyway."[74] After presenting a petition in the spring of 1833 in favor of negotiating a treaty for removal, and failing to gain support for it during the General Council in November of that year, those few men who comprised the nascent Treaty Party organized their own delegation to Washington, D.C. They did so outside the circuits of Cherokee governance, against the wishes of the General Council, and in competition with the nation's authorized delegation. While in Washington, members of this group negotiated a removal treaty, and even though it was rejected by the U.S. Senate, they still brought it before the Cherokee Council in August of 1834, at which point it was rejected by the Cherokee government as well. The Treaty Party then called their own council on November 27. While attended by only eighty-seven people, it still chose a delegation to go to Washington, again in competition with the delegation actually authorized by the Cherokee government. The War Department decided to negotiate with the Treaty Party delegation in early 1835. The document that eventually would become the Treaty of New Echota emerged out of these negotiations. Prior to the fall of 1835, the Treaty Party, therefore, had on multiple occasions ignored the determinations of the General Council, undermined the actions of the authorized delegates, and entered into diplomatic negotiations with the U.S. government. The effects of the ongoing machinations of the Treaty Party can be seen in Ross's repeated need to insist that he and the "authorized delegation of the Cherokee nation" are not "of a party" but, instead, "are the representatives of the nation," as opposed to John Ridge and other "unauthorized individuals" with whom the secretary of war had seen fit to negotiate.[75] The actions of the Treaty Party were flagrantly in violation of Cherokee law. Nelson describes the impeachment of the Ridges and David Vann in 1834 in the following terms: "Politically excommunicated, denied access to any venue for public discourse, and effectively silenced, the frustrated treaty party members were convinced both of the necessity of" a treaty "and of their own superior judgment."[76] However, the impeachment was a direct result of their prior actions, and given the terms of Cherokee law and the seriousness of the implications of their extralegal negotiations with a foreign power, impeachment was little more than a slap on the wrist.[77]

Reappraisals of Boudinot have sought to ameliorate earlier accounts of him as a traitor by challenging the binaries that they suggest tend to animate that judgment of him, instead presenting him as doing critical work within Cherokee nationalism. These scholars note that descriptions of Boudinot's signing of the Treaty of New Echota often present that act as a betrayal of Cherokee nationality due to its refusal of what gets cast as a traditional connection to Cherokee lands and waters. However, as Bethany Schneider suggests, the model of Boudinot as "tragic" or as a "traitor" "lies in its valorization of the individual as existing in subjugation and/or resistance to a largely exterior cultural conflict, which deeply affects and molds the individual but is in essential opposition to him or her," such that the act of treason "is blamed on culture but in the end it belongs to the individual who, however much he may be corrupted or conflicted by culture, is in the final instance not of culture."[78] Schneider questions this vision of culture, indicating its tendency to bracket historical change as well as the political conditions of Indian affairs and the Cherokee Nation in the 1830s.[79] She argues, "The Cherokees undergoing and surviving removal had to enact and reinvent the nation in exactly the treasonous way that Boudinot suggested— they had to salvage and sustain a love of the people when the land had been lost, and discover and reify a passionate love of the new land."[80] In this way, when not read against the background of a somewhat static sense of Cherokee identity, Boudinot's actions and rhetoric become one way of responding to the actual pressures the Cherokees faced in the period. Similarly, Maureen Konkle argues, "What [Boudinot's] writing demonstrates at the very least is that there were and are many perspectives among Native intellectuals and political leaders about how to best deal with the effects of U.S. colonialism."[81] Viewed in this way, Boudinot's discourse, including *Letters*, appears less as a violation of *Cherokeeness* than as an expression of, in his words, "patriotic" opposition to the actions and policy determinations of the Cherokee national government.

Approaching Boudinot as engaged in a project of dissent, such readings suggest, opens the possibility for understanding Cherokee nationalism in more capacious ways. As opposed to viewing it as an expression of an unchanging cultural core, scholars can engage Cherokee sovereignty as a multidimensional field in which criticism of existing authorities plays a vital role. In "Native Critics in the World," Robert Warrior addresses the role of the critic in relation to expressions of anticolonial nationalism. Following in the footsteps of Edward Said, Warrior notes, "The important thing to note in this context is that Said saw criticism as one of the remedies for the excesses of nationalism." With respect to the work of Native intellectuals, he observes that "dissent is perhaps the primary sign of good health in nationalist discourse," further suggesting that criticism "ought to be inclusive of experiences and points of view that are on the margins" and that, at best, it "reflects primary allegiances to its own independence of thought and a willingness to take stands that oppose not just those who hold political power, but also those who wield considerable spiritual power as well."[82] If one reads Boudinot in this way, his rejection of decisions by the Ross administration can be seen as the work of a critical intellectual seeking to temper the "excesses" of national leaders. As Nelson indicates with respect to the removal of Boudinot from the editorship of the *Cherokee Phoenix*, "There is little doubt that the nation controls the press, but lost in the shuffle is the matter of who rightfully controls the nation," adding that such actions on the part of the national government bespeak a commitment to producing "ideological uniformity." Even while noting that Boudinot's political leanings "tended toward the centralization of power," Nelson credits Boudinot with seeking to check potential abuses of power by the Cherokee national government.[83] At one point in *Letters*, Boudinot enjoins, "Think, for a moment, my countrymen, the danger to be apprehended from an overwhelming white population . . . at once overbearing and impudent to those whom, in their sovereign pleasure, they consider as their inferiors" (168). He later amplifies this position, indicating that "our people cannot exist amidst a white population, subject to laws which they have no hand in making, and which they do not understand" (176). He argues here for the impossibility of sustaining Cherokee nationality amid a deluge of settlers and the dismembering power of state "laws." In doing so, he offers a vision of Cherokee collective survival meant to preserve the "people" under circumstances whose implications he suggests Cherokee leaders have not adequately considered.

However, Boudinot's account does not so much stage differences in opinion from the national government or assert a minority perspective as offer what he presents as an authoritative account of Cherokee nationhood, and in doing so, he trades forms of elite judgment based on U.S. sentiment for popular Cherokee political investments. More than opposing those in power, *Letters* in its efforts to exonerate the Treaty Party enacts its own *excesses*. If Boudinot illustrates, in Warrior's terms, an "independence of thought," he also positions his intellectual derivation of Cherokee collective needs and identity—his portrait of Cherokee nationality—as in and of itself sufficient as a basis for political action. In critiquing the effort to evaluate Boudinot's writings against a reified conception of Cherokee "culture," then, critical reappraisals run the risk of overlooking the converse problem: Boudinot's own investment in a particular image of Cherokee well-being and futurity that explicitly is divorced from what he characterizes as the backward delusions of those who disagree with him. Moreover, *Letters* directly articulates the overriding necessity for such a conception of Cherokee nationhood in terms of settler demands. Boudinot keeps insisting that the failure correctly to appreciate non-native ideas, interests, and intentions leads to a skewed image of what Cherokee peoplehood is, should be, and needs to be going forward. While I've addressed Boudinot's elite orientation and the ways it remained disjunct from popular (and subaltern) conceptions of Cherokee peoplehood, here I want to highlight the ways *Letters* repeatedly turns toward the U.S. government as the horizon for validating/confirming its account of Cherokee affairs. As discussed earlier, Boudinot consistently dismisses nonelite Cherokee perspectives as *ignorance, prejudice,* and *delusion,* as lacking the perspicacity and insight of the "most intelligent citizens." Boudinot insists, "The political rights of the Cherokees cannot be restored or secured by a continued *investigation,* or a repetition of the numerous and aggravated *grievances* which they have already laid before the American People" (166). Although the text argues for Cherokees' "political rights" to separateness and autonomy, the focus lies on what "the American People," via their elected officials, will or won't do, rather than on what the Cherokee people want, their relative priorities, their preferred modes of communication with the United States, or what they are willing to sacrifice.

While mediating U.S. removal discourses in the interest of the continued existence of (a particular moveable version of) the Cherokee Nation, *Letters* presents the assessment of U.S. government perspectives made by the members of the Treaty Party as *the* frame for deciding Cherokee national policy. The network toward which Boudinot and the Treaty Party turn and in which their articulations circulate is that of settler political institutions and processes of decision-making. Their way of prioritizing non-native understandings shifts the locus of legitimacy for representing the Cherokee Nation from webs of relation among Cherokee people—or even the institutions of the Cherokee Nation—to the persons and propositions that are most likely to be recognized by the settler-state and settler publics. Describing Boudinot's challenge to the Ross administration's limitation of freedom of the press (in deposing him from the editorship of the *Cherokee Phoenix*), Nelson suggests that Boudinot "searches for a space of participatory deliberation, a place where dissent belongs: a nation of people conversing with rather than controlling each other."[84] Yet rather than arguing for the importance of "participatory deliberation" by Cherokee publics in decisions around removal, *Letters* delinks representativity from any tie to expressions of popular sentiment. The text locates political decision-making among those expressing proper "intelligence" whose judgment can be measured by the extent to which they take their cue from non-native institutions, not other Cherokee people. *Letters* and the actions of the Treaty Party displace the question of *how* a collective Cherokee subject can be constituted, by whom, and for what purposes. I've argued that attending to intellectual labor helps foreground processes of negotiation over political form—the politics of peoplehood—as it operates in differentiable but related ways within settler and Native networks. However, intellectual work cannot substitute for processes of political negotiation. Or, put more plainly, Boudinot's pursuit of recognition (both in terms of the Treaty Party's actions and *Letters*'s appeals to a non-native audience) severs itself from political process, presenting its own legitimacy as predicated on an engagement with non-native frameworks *in contrast to* extant debates among Cherokee people.

We can distinguish between representativity as a depiction of who the people are or should be ("portrait") and representativity as the ideological and institutional means of generating popular assent to governance ("proxy"). With respect to the latter, Boudinot often complains in *Letters* that Ross has secured popular approval by presenting falsities of three different kinds: what is politically possible with respect to Cherokee lands; what the Cherokee government actually has endorsed in terms of powers to negotiate with the United States; and the content of existing negotiations with the United States. As discussed in the first section of this chapter, the text repeatedly indicates that Ross and other leaders have offered an unrealistic account of the likelihood of being able to avoid a removal treaty, thus creating "*a want of proper information among the people*" (161). In addition, though, Boudinot charges that after a meeting between Cherokee officials and members of the Treaty Party in the fall of 1835 in which they agreed to form a single delegation, Ross fudged the terms of that agreement in his public discussion of it. Boudinot asks, "How was the matter explained? Were the congregated Cherokees informed of the unhappy situation of their country and affairs, which has been the cause of their division into parties?" and he then indicates that "Mr. Ross . . . represented us as a faction returning to our allegiance" who would support the actions of "the constituted authorities of the nation to close the difficulties with the United States, by a final adjustment" (185). The instructions from the General Council to this united delegation further obscured the potential for a treaty. Even though "they had signed an instrument of writing conveying" the powers "to dispose of their country . . . the terms to *sell* or *to cede* were not contained in them," such that most people "*never dreamt that the land would be sold*" (188). Boudinot further notes that during the previous winter when Ross was leading the official delegation in Washington, he had "proposed to sell the entire country for the genteel sum of *twenty millions* of dollars," and when that option was rejected by the U.S. government, Ross offered to "refer the matter to the Senate for its award, giving a written obligation to be bound by that award, whatever it might be," which turned out to be five million dollars—the sum that formed the basis for what would become the Treaty of New Echota (190).[85] Ross's public arguments throughout the rest of 1835 against the adoption of a removal treaty, then, can appear hypocritical, at best, and, at worst, as outright pandering at the expense of Cherokee well-being.

Boudinot, though, focuses on what he considers to be the implicit messages conveyed by Ross's statements, instead of addressing the web of political relations in which those statements are enmeshed and that shape their orientation and significance. *Letters* presents Ross's engagement with popular sentiments against removal as evasive and deceptive, playing to mass prejudice rather than doing the hard work of educating the people as to the impossibility of remaining. The "deep rooted attachment for the soil of [their] forefathers," in Boudinot's terms, drives ordinary Cherokee support for the national government (161). While the government enacted laws that sought to extend and legitimize forms of capitalist political economy, heteropatriarchy, and slaveholding among the Cherokees, most Cherokees ignored, bypassed, or struggled against many of those measures (as suggested by White Path's Rebellion, the nonenforcement of the laws in much of the nation, and the continuance of town and clan networks). Where the Cherokee national government had a clear popular mandate, which provided the validation for that government's existence among nonelite Cherokees, was in the refusal to cede more territory to the United States and the preservation of the Cherokee landbase. Boudinot presents the possibility of resisting U.S. imperatives to remove as a topic of debate, in which the "intelligence of the country" immediately would agree on the impossibility of remaining. Yet the legitimacy of policy and government action cannot be reduced to the supposedly inherent merits of a particular argument—a specific portrayal of what the Cherokee government should do or of who the Cherokee people are. Political representation entails some form of popular consent. Even if the potential for expressing and enacting such consent was mediated by the institutions and procedures of Cherokee constitutional governance, largely transposing subaltern political formations into elite terms and limiting participation in ways that were patriarchal and antiblack, Cherokee authorities could not simply disregard popular perspectives in toto and continue to understand themselves as imbued with the will of the people.[86]

What *Letters* depicts as obfuscation, then, might better be characterized as politics. Boudinot and the Treaty Party need not worry about how their formulations of Cherokee nationality and well-being relate to popular Cherokee understandings, since such views are irrelevant in terms of what non-natives will believe and do—which serves as the frame of reference for *Letters*. Cherokee officials such as Ross, though, need to engage with popular perspectives in order to validate their own service as political representatives, and as *Letters* notes, somewhat dismissively, Ross did have "the entire confidence of an ignorant and confiding people" (191). Boudinot depicts such confidence as misplaced and as resulting from the people's failure to appreciate the conditions faced by the Cherokee Nation. We can reverse this charge, though, and see Ross's actions and his rhetorical vacillations as an effort to maintain the popular legitimacy of his administration. In *An Inquiry into Modes of Existence*, Latour suggests, "A *form* is what is maintained through a series of *trans*formations. Suspend the alignment of the transformations and the form vanishes at once," adding, "A form or shape, in this second sense, is always an object (an instrument, a document, an image, an equation) that allows *putting into form*, or *shaping*." With respect to politics in particular, Latour indicates that the transformations and mediation enacted to preserve a sense of political collectivity—to continue to put a collective into form—involve "connect[ing] beings to others so that the collective holds together" in order to "trac[e] an *envelope* that defines, for a time, the 'we'" of the group, creating "a unified representation of th[e] multitude" that can serve as the basis for licensing legislative and administrative action.[87] At any number of points in his engagements with U.S. officials, Ross makes statements such as "The Cherokees have refused and will never voluntarily consent to remove west of the Mississippi," and "The Cherokee people will never consent to sell their freedom—nor dispose of their heritage in the soil."[88] Through the mediations they perform in their negotiations with the

United States, Ross and Cherokee leaders seek to sustain the form of Cherokee nationality. While the effort to do so involves trying to hold onto their current landbase, it more broadly entails maintaining networks of popular assent to government action, a process of avowal by which government action can be affirmed as expressive of a coherent Cherokee "we."

Various decisions and apparent equivocations by the Ross administration that come under fire in *Letters* can be understood in terms of leaders' efforts to preserve such popular support and accountability as the basis of their claim to representativity. This aim leads to Ross's seemingly incongruous proposal in 1834 to "enter into an arrangement on the basis of the Cherokees becoming prospectively citizens of the United States" in exchange for the cession of "a portion of its Territory for the use of Georgia"; this plan also involved enforcement of existing "laws and treaties . . . on the remainder of [the Cherokee Nation's] Territory for a definite period."[89] To some extent, Ross is playing for time until the end of the Jackson administration and the hoped for arrival of someone in the presidency more sympathetic to Cherokee concerns.[90] Yet, he appears to advocate for the dismemberment of the Cherokee Nation *in situ*, which is part of what animates Boudinot's complaints in *Letters* about the prospect of being overwhelmed by white settlers. However, through this maneuver, Ross seeks to remain responsive to what seems like the Cherokee population's own prevailing sense of what defines them as Cherokee. He is working to find a way for them remain in their territory, even if the political shape of that collective dwelling changes. Once the Treaty Party arrives in Washington in winter 1835 and the War Department actively enters into negotiations with them, Ross and the officially authorized delegation do switch tacks to discussing the possibility of removal, leading to the proposal of the sale of Cherokee lands for twenty million dollars and, when that offer is rejected, the proposal of accepting a price that the Senate deems reasonable. After previously asking "upon what terms will the President negotiate for a final termination" of the Cherokee people's "sufferings," observing that many of them have been turned into "homeless wanderers" due to expropriation of their land by whites, Ross indicates that the official Cherokee delegation would be willing "to recommend" a removal treaty on the Senate's terms "for the final determination of our nation," and a month later he reaffirms the delegation's willingness to recommend "to our nation the expediency of closing our unhappy difficulties by a treaty with the United States."[91] In that same message, Ross implores the War Department not to "persist in the unexpected and most extraordinary course which you intimated to us this morning was about to be adopted, that is, of entering into a treaty with John Ridge and others, unauthorized individuals."[92] Although the appearance of the Treaty Party forces Ross's hand, he continues to predicate the actions of the Cherokee government on the expression of popular will, indicating that he will *recommend* the adoption of the treaty but that the delegation cannot, in and of themselves, authorize an agreement—especially one whose terms run so blatantly counter to the expressed sentiments of the vast majority of the Cherokee population.

This articulated intent provides a frame through which to read Ross's communications with the Cherokee people in 1835. In Ross's address to the Cherokee General Council that May, he suggests that "the representatives of the people" should repudiate the actions of "certain unauthorized individuals [who] have entered into certain articles in a treaty formed with the president" and that "should ever any future arrangement take place between the proper authorities of the nation and of the United States Government for the adjustment of existing difficulties, that no arrangement touching those rights & interests will be made without their consent and providing amply for the same."[93] The language here remains somewhat ambiguous, avoiding direct discussion of the offer to the Senate and the Senate's recommendation of five million dollars as the purchase price for Cherokee lands in the east. In *Letters*, Boudinot interprets such vagueness as part of a campaign to mislead the Cherokees, but what I want to highlight here is Ross's indication that any such "adjustment" will be valid only with the approval of representatives chosen by the Cherokee people. His rhetoric indexes a process by which the assent of the Cherokee citizenry becomes manifest, such that governmental actions can be seen as emanating from it—as *representing* the Cherokee people. The mechanisms of such accountability occur through a heteropatriarchal and racializing institutional structure whose background principles are those of an elite commitment to liberal political economy. Yet, while continuing to attend to how those ideological principles and institutional dynamics shape the character of popular engagement and of national governance (rendering subaltern certain Cherokee sociopolitical formations), we also should register the presence of processes of popular consultation and affirmation—a network that generates the terms of political legitimacy for the Cherokee national government.

In *Letters*, Boudinot may gesture toward the welfare of the Cherokee Nation and the existence of the nation as a function of its people, rather than inhabitance on a particular land mass, but the resulting vision of Cherokee collectivity emerges from an intellectual commitment to a particular kind of political form among the members of the Treaty Party, rather than having a means of giving form to popular perspectives—of mediating them into policy that, then, can proxy for the will of a cohesive Cherokee national "we." *Letters* speaks of and for a national collective without having to be transformed by contact with nonelite (or even contravening) viewpoints, investments, and principles. Boudinot claims representativity and insists on the inherent and exclusive legitimacy of his portrayal of Cherokee collective needs without actually going through the process of *forming* a Cherokee political public. That claim to representativity, though, converts dissent into diplomacy, into a self-authorized ability to stand for the Cherokee Nation in negotiations with the United States due to the performance of a version of Cherokee authority pitched for recognition by non-natives. Boudinot and the Treaty Party's alchemical transmutation of their views into those of the Cherokee people absent any mechanism of accountability, then, also turns that dissent, and the justification of it in *Letters*, into treason.

When considering the distinctions between the policy pursued by Ross and the account of Cherokee nationality offered by Boudinot in *Letters*, we might characterize them as arising from the two having different visions for the nation. However, such an explanation overlooks the ways that Ross endorsed the same transformations in Cherokee life that Boudinot did. They both sought to alter patterns of what they characterized as ignorance and backwardness through the implementation of a program of *improvement* that involved the adoption of a modified version of capitalist political economy (where the land is not owned per se) and heteropatriarchal structures of family formation, landholding, and inheritance. That very similarity, then, might provide the basis for an alternative account of the two and their disagreements as expressive of dynamics of dissent within, in Konkle's terms, the "modern Indian nation."[94] From this perspective, Ross and Boudinot offer varied ways of approaching the circumstances of settler intervention and invasion faced by the Cherokee people in the 1830s, with neither of their approaches being more authentically Cherokee. Moreover, such a reading emphasizes the existence of the Cherokees as a polity, with the potential for disagreements among them about the proper direction for the nation—rather than seeing the Cherokees as a cultural entity whose traditions Boudinot has failed to uphold.

However, that story of Cherokee political debate and dissent takes for granted the institutional structure of the nation. Interpreting Ross (and other Cherokee leaders) and Boudinot (and the Treaty Party) as involved in a *patriotic* debate over policy and the best interests of the Cherokee people takes the structure of Cherokee national governance as a set background against which to view intellectual disagreement in ways divorced from the question of how intellectual position taking relates to the political processes of enacting such governance and the attendant negotiations and struggles over the *political form* of Cherokee peoplehood. In its claims to speak for the Cherokee people, to substitute for Cherokee government leaders in engaging with the United States, *Letters* does far more than advocate for a particular viewpoint within Cherokee politics: it extends the Treaty Party's efforts to *enact* a politics of Cherokee nationhood absent any mechanism of popular accountability and in the belief that popular *delusion* actually licenses such intervention/evasion. Their portrayal of Cherokee nationhood stands for the Cherokee people by virtue of the self-declared accuracy of their assessments and value of their (elite) principles and perspectives. While *Letters* both shares the elite orientations at play in Cherokee constitutional governance and mediates non-native discourses in ways that aim toward the survival of the Cherokee Nation, Boudinot figures Cherokee peoplehood in ways that not only remain divorced from processes of reflection and relation among Cherokee publics but actively repudiate such efforts as merely the workings of ignorance and superstition. The "proper information" on which political representations and determinations must depend can only come from those properly educated in the ways of civilized governance and can only be valid when it comports with non-native frames of reference.

Attending to the continuities and distinctions between the vision offered in *Letters* and the workings of the Cherokee national government brings to the fore the intellectual labor involved in seeking to articulate and navigate matters of political form, and it also underlines the limits of treating intellectual labor (including the narration of normative principles for governance and peoplehood) as if it can substitute for political process. The difference is not so much one between engaging with settler networks versus participating within Indigenous ones as, in both relations, between identifying one's portrayal of the people as immanently self-sufficient versus bearing in mind the ongoing densities of negotiation and mediation involved in staging Indigenous political form. How does the nation emerge and function as a political entity within extant social networks, among the Cherokees and in their interface with the settler-state? How does Native intellectual work take part in those processes? As I have suggested, Ross moves within and from the constitutional structure of Cherokee national governance, and that structure as it emerges and is consolidated over the course of the 1810s and 1820s increasingly effaces, marginalizes, and depoliticizes subaltern practices, principles, and modes of association. The terms of peoplehood within constitutional Cherokee institutions are filtered through the template of necessary elite superintendence of the ignorant, beguiled, and obstinate masses. However, the Cherokee national government also creates possibilities for popular consent and understands itself as responsive to popular demands, even while such public participation and voice emerges through the matrix of a heteropatriarchal, slaveholding liberalism. Cherokee statehood, then, is (re)constituted as a form through Native discursive and institutional networks, in which intellectual work participates and circulates but for which it cannot take the place.

Attending to representativity—the claim to express and embody collective voice—brings to the foreground how the act of speaking for the people emerges from and refers back to the mechanisms through which the people are assembled as a unit and the means by which such collective voice is constituted as such. *Letters* asserts the authority of the Treaty Party to stand for the Cherokee Nation in the interest of preserving its existence as a nation, but participation within non-native networks serves as the basis for such surrogation—an awareness of what non-native legislators and officials are prepared to do. As *Letters* illustrates, the normative framework that guides the Treaty Party's relations with the U.S. state is shaped around non-native interests and imperatives, enacting a form of what can be characterized as cruel optimism; the settler government provides the frame of reference for how Boudinot and the Treaty Party envision the conditions of possibility for the well-being of the Cherokee people. In this way, they might be described as turned toward, in Simpson's terms, "the colonial outside," but less as contrasted with a clearly differentiated and delineated "Indigenous inside" than as distinguished from an engagement with broader discussions, debates, and deliberations among Cherokee publics.[95] Recognition by the United States serves not so much as a tactical or strategic aim but as the background against which *Letters*'s account of the Cherokee Nation gains meaning, as the condition for the emergence of the representativity Boudinot asserts. From this perspective, the refusal of removal by the Ross administration appears not as a commitment to "tradition," whatever that might mean, but as part of an effort to secure hegemony for Cherokee constitutional governance, given both widespread popular investments in remaining on their current lands and the ways Cherokee popular support for the national government was conditioned on its ability to mediate relations with the United States to ensure such continued dwelling.

The issue I have sought to underline, then, is not *Letters*'s failure to conform to a particular nonelite account of the content of Cherokee peoplehood or nationality, one more capable of embracing sociopolitical formations rendered subaltern within discourses and projects of improvement and enlightenment. Boudinot's understanding of Cherokee attachments to specific clans, towns, and lands as irrational clinging and "settled prejudices," as "established habits of thinking" that need to be renovated in order to safeguard the Cherokees' existence as a "distinct community," certainly could be offered as part of a program of dissent that seeks to (re)shape the potentials for expressions of Cherokee peoplehood and for the policy of the Cherokee Nation (160–161, 176–177). However, more than laying out a vision of desirable Cherokee futurity and the conditions that will enable it, *Letters* shows how the Treaty Party mobilize tropes of representativity in ways that draw on and participate in settler networks of political relation in order to secure their position as sanctioned mediators. Boudinot draws on the form of the state—in terms of both the institutions of the United States and centralized Cherokee governance (as opposed to, say, consensus-based decision-making in autonomous towns)—so as to assert the Treaty Party's ability to stand for the nation and its citizens. In doing so, *Letters* converts intellectual discourse into political capital, thereby gaining the capacity to remake Cherokee geopolitics absent reference to the sociopolitical networks through which broader Cherokee assent is secured. The text bypasses the processes of negotiation within Cherokee nationhood—the ongoing politics through which peoplehood is (re)fashioned and given shape. In doing so, *Letters* illustrates the limits of seeking to measure Native self-representation against a quasi-authenticating set of core principles, the distinction between engaging with settler frames and identification with them, and the dangers of such engagement—such practices of recognition—when taking a singular vision of people as sufficient absent a robust relation to the multidimensional performances of peoplehood for which intellectuals claim to speak.

2. EXPERIMENTS IN SIGNIFYING SOVEREIGNTY

Exemplarity and the Politics of
Southern New England in William Apess

In the nineteenth century in southern New England, there were no Indian nations. There certainly were Indigenous peoples, including ones who had state-
recognized reserves that extended back into the late seventeenth and early
eighteenth centuries, but "Indian nation" as a political and legal category was
not used to characterize them. These peoples did not have treaties with the
federal government, and the states that claimed authority over them and their
lands—Massachusetts, Connecticut, Rhode Island—refused to acknowledge
law and policy that made Indian affairs a matter of federal governance and diplomacy.[1] Despite the fact that throughout southern New England various laws
from the late seventeenth century onward acknowledged the existence of Indigenous peoples and explicitly set aside and protected reserved landbases for
them, those groups so recognized consistently were placed under the control
of state-appointed non-native superintendents (called guardians or overseers)
who were authorized to make political, economic, and legal decisions about
virtually all aspects of Indian life on reserved lands, including with regard to
the leasing and sale of tribal territories. This colonial regime exerted a more
expansive and harsher form of plenary power than what would be attributed
to Congress at the end of the nineteenth century.[2] Given the proximity of reservations to non-native towns, the high rate of population growth in the region, and the increasingly extractive dynamics of agriculture and commerce,
Native lands became prime sites for settler appropriation, either through theft
of resources such as timber or through outright seizure. The particular shape of
colonial entanglement in southern New England affected strategies both for representing peoplehood to settlers and for organizing on and across reserves in
ways that address the specific modes of inspection, intervention, regulation, and

dispossession to which these peoples were subject. Rather than being characterized as Indian nations, these groups appear in official state discourses largely
as pitiable, if once noble, remnants who need active white guidance to prevent
their total extinction (and/or to facilitate their absorption into the non-native
public). Indigenous sovereignty and political self-determination do not serve,
even nominally, as norms within such policy or in popular depictions of Natives in New England.

Native peoples, though, continued to understand themselves as polities, repudiating state citizenship and insisting on the importance of legal measures
that would keep their severely diminished reservations—or "plantations" as
they tended to be called—intact. If the Cherokee Nation struggled against
federal efforts to remove them, as discussed in chapter 1, they did so within a
discursive and institutional framework in which they were acknowledged by
the United States as having at least attributes of sovereignty (independent self-
government and participation as signatories in the treaty system) and had a
centralized state apparatus that would signify as governance to non-natives.
While the character and actions of the Cherokee national government may
have been subject to negotiation, struggle, and dissent among Cherokees, it
provided a vehicle for contesting U.S. jurisdiction and seeking to preserve
Cherokee lands that would be legible to settlers, garnering popular Cherokee support at least on this basis. The matrix of state policies in southern New
England, though, rendered such a strategy—such means for staging and implementing Native sovereignty—unworkable. Given the devastating effects of
these state formations for Indian affairs, part of the work facing Native intellectuals in New England was forging ways of portraying Indigenous collectivity
that could enable non-natives to see tribes as political entities with the ability
and right to govern themselves.

The writings of William Apess (Mashantucket Pequot) illustrate that project and its difficulties. In experimenting with various ways to represent Native
political identity, he repeatedly returns to a process of metonymic substitution
in which a foregrounded figure comes to embody and textually materialize
what is legally absent—the existence, scope, and normative force of Indigenous
peoples' self-determination.[3] In *A Son of the Forest* (1829/1831), he draws on
his own life to highlight, vicariously, the existence of the Pequots as a nation;
in *Eulogy on King Philip* (1836), the Wampanoag sachem Metacom serves as
a means of registering Native peoples as self-governing political entities on a
par with the United States; and in *Indian Nullification* (1835), Apess employs a
range of frames (including references to the Cherokee Nation, the Revolutionary War, and chattel slavery) to indicate the violence of the guardian system

and to illustrate that the Mashpee, and by extension other Indigenous groups in New England, need to be engaged as sovereign and self-determining. Representativity in these instances inheres less in claims to political delegation—that Apess has been tasked by a political community to speak for it—than in invocations of exemplarity. Rather than focusing on Native polities as such, as Boudinot does for Cherokee nationality and governance, Apess's texts offer representations that center on persons, groups, and events that point toward the continuing existence of Native polities in nineteenth-century New England. The figures he highlights provide a condensed and concretizing way for non-natives to conceptualize Native peoplehood in the region; they function as models through which to envision Natives as self-governing political entities. Apess's life story or King Philip, for example, stands in for ongoing Indigenous sovereignty in southern New England in ways that surrogate for forms of acknowledgment not present in extant law and policy. If settlers have institutionalized practices of colonial "unwitnessing," in Drew Lopenzina's terms, Apess seeks to alter the terms of public visibility and intelligibility by centering images and examples that could be recognized by non-native readers, that could bring peoplehood and governance into focus.[4] Those figures do not serve as evidence of such governance per se: they do not so much *prove* Native sovereignty as *presume* it, rhetorically producing sovereignty as a background against which the foregrounded figure comes into view.[5] While Apess does not appear in his work as an authorized spokesperson for the Mashantucket Pequots or for Native peoples in New England more broadly, the centralized figures in his texts do representative work by serving as proxies for the continued existence of Native polities, despite settlers' declarations of Indians' demise, incompetence, or childlike dependence. These foregrounded images and tropes hold open discursive space for indirectly portraying Native sovereignty, indexing its being and becoming and thus substituting for it without exactly arguing for it or explicitly delineating its contours and properties.

In official and popular accounts, Native peoples were presented as having almost entirely disappeared due to the effects of warfare, expansion of English settlements, inability to adapt to changing circumstances and modern life, and intermarriage with non-natives (particularly African Americans), and the terms of state recognition in New England entailed a subjection to direct non-native oversight that, in the way the policies were outlined, vitiated anything like Native nationhood. Audra Simpson suggests that a "refusal of recognition" expresses a "refusal to be enfolded into state logics," which simultaneously is a "refusal, simply, to disappear," and she earlier argues, "Refusal comes with the requirement of having one's *political* sovereignty acknowledged and upheld, and raises the question of legitimacy for those who are usually in the position of recognizing."[6] Yet, in the absence of pursuit of recognition by the state and tribes' insistence on their historical and ongoing rights to live in and exert authority over their homelands, Native territories would be utterly consumed by settlers, significantly intensifying existing dynamics of impoverishment and scattering peoples across the landscape. One might see parallels here with the difficulties faced by peoples who currently are not federally recognized, who often seek such recognition in order to be able to access the potentials of federal Indian law and policy—particularly having lands that are understood by settler institutions as collectively theirs (put in "trust") and being able to exert legally acknowledged jurisdiction over those lands and their members/citizens. While some peoples in southern New England have gained such recognition over the past forty years, including the Mashantucket Pequots, others throughout southern New England have been denied that status and continue to struggle with the effects of not having the legal tools through which to mark their nationhood.[7]

If Apess's texts can be read as seeking to shift non-native discourses and perceptions, they do not do so by affirming the parameters of existing Indian policy. Instead, they refuse the logics and practices of guardianship, challenge the legitimacy of settler jurisdiction, and insist on the political sovereignty of Native peoples even as they search for means of engaging and reorienting non-native normative frameworks. Discussing the work performed by Native "intellectual labor," Dale Turner insists, *We need to be effective in engaging the existing legal and political discourses of the state*," later indicating, "The project of unpacking and laying bare the meaning and effects of colonialism will open up the physical and intellectual space for Aboriginal voices to participate in the legal and political practices of the state."[8] Apess implicitly engages in such deconstructive practice—stripping away extant official and popular modes of figuring Indianness—while employing multiple ways of signifying Native territoriality, collective identity, and governance that might be more effective in making them legible to non-natives. Recalling Gayatri Spivak's argument (discussed in the introduction) that serving as the representative for a group involves a particular (institutionalized) portrayal of who that group is, we conversely can approach the range of modes of portraying Native people(s) at play in Apess's writing as experiments with how rhetorically to generate a portrait of peoplehood for which political proxying would be appropriate, as opposed to racializing, paternalizing, and corrupt *care* by the guardians.[9] This experimentation and multiplicity shifts the dynamics of accountability; unlike Boudinot, Apess does not claim to serve as the proper voice for a political body nor does he position himself as representative by virtue of his elite difference from and superior judgment to those about whom he speaks. His work can be read as staging possibilities for Native sovereignty, seeking to shift non-native frames of reference away from narratives of Indian dependence, rather than presenting a unilateral account of such sovereignty that casts itself as the only legitimate one. Apess draws on various kinds of figuration in an effort to produce a structuring template or templates, in Bruno Latour's terms, that could metonymically stand for and point toward the existence of Indigenous sovereignty and self-determination[10]—a rhetorical proxy that gestures toward modes of governance without necessarily presuming a set institutional form for them (such as in Boudinot's narration of nationhood in *Letters*). That being said, the engagement with colonial frames can affect the vision offered of Indigenous governance, particularly shifting it into a heteropatriarchal register that tends not only to displace women and women's labor but to sever relations characterized as domestic and familial from the scene of politics.

Apess's process of experimentation, though, produces what can appear as contradictions, inconsistencies, and confusing shifts in his rhetoric, and scholarship on Apess tends to register these tensions within and among his texts as evidence of a conflicted set of ideological commitments. Critics often interpret Apess's use of political idioms and normative frameworks as if they were indicative of his personal investment in them, reading the taking up of a political form as expressive of a kind of consciousness—a lived subjectivity. The proliferation of framings across Apess's writing, though, helps highlight the tactical quality of his employment of these multiple means of figuring indigeneity. Rather than indicating specific changes in Apess's opinions or politics over time, the variability in the ways he seeks to encapsulate or exemplify peoplehood has to do with the dynamics of settler governance and popular discourses in southern New England and seeking to engage with them in ways that can represent Native polities as such—seeking to find ways to signify sovereignty in the absence of legal discourses of Native "nationhood" or of federal treaty making. If the tactical or strategic use of colonial templates, tropes, and frames need not inherently be understood as expressive of a *colonized subjectivity*, shifts among such frames might speak to the absence of a singular set of philosophical or political principles that provides the privileged shape for peoplehood—something like an idealized notion of decolonized subjectivity, envisioned as completely free from and outside of the densities and messiness of ongoing colonial occupation.[11] As Amy Den Ouden and Jean O'Brien suggest, "Strateg[ies] of political engagement with the legal system of a nation-state cannot readily be equated with acquiescence to state power."[12] What emerges from reading across Apess's writings is a sense of negotiation within shifting networks, of ongoing mediation in which the articulation of the form of peoplehood remains an open-ended process.[13] In moving among a range of political framings, his efforts in generating recognition for Native peoples as peoples, instead of as aggregates of racialized dependents, not only require a good deal of intellectual labor, but attending to such labor and the contextual specificity of Apess's uses of political form helps underline the ways such form itself is situated, negotiated, and subject to experimentation, albeit in ways that are not always equally salutary for all Native people.

Mashantucket as Background

Published in 1829 and revised in 1831, *A Son of the Forest* tells the story of Apess's life from his birth through his acquisition of a license to preach as a Methodist minister (after having been rejected by one conference and shifting to a different one). With respect to genre, it could be characterized most easily as a spiritual autobiography, which since the seventeenth century had become the preeminent means of publicly demonstrating one's conversion and found devotion to God within a particular Christian community or organized church.[14] In chronicling the events of Apess's life, the text focuses on his burgeoning faith, the ways in which it was tested through the hardships and challenges that he faced, and his call to preach. Although addressing his identity as Pequot and his relationships with other Mashantucket Pequots, *A Son of the Forest* notably lacks the markers of explicitly *political* identity and antagonism present in contemporaneous public debates over Indian removal in the Southeast, particularly the Cherokees from Georgia (with their history of treaty relations with the U.S. government), in which New England congressmen and activists participated actively as advocates for Native rights (a point on which Apess plays to great effect in *Indian Nullification*, as I'll discuss in the final section). The relative absence of explicit discussion of questions of Pequot territoriality and governance coupled with the narrative's emphasis on Apess's individual experience can make the text seem as if it were largely about the treatment of Native people(s) as racialized (groups of) individuals.[15] However, given the lack of a state-recognized language of diplomatic negotiation through which to indicate Native sovereignty, the text can be interpreted less as lacking a political understanding, or having a merely incipient one, than as seeking to find a language through which to convey a sense of Pequot peoplehood through its depiction of Apess's life. In a discussion of Apess's work with the Mashpee, John J. Kucich suggests that "Apess's configuration of an embodied archive, of histories entrenched in flesh, marks an alternative kind of evidence."[16] In this vein, we might engage his narration of his life as an effort to make manifest ongoing Mashantucket Pequot histories by illustrating how they are "entrenched in flesh," namely his own. His life operates as "an embodied archive" of Pequot presence, serving as a proxy for political identity even in the absence of an account of the workings of Indigenous governance as such.

A Son of the Forest illustrates Apess's awareness of his own status as a spectacle and draws on such non-native interest as a way of refiguring extant popular conceptions of Native identity in New England.[17] As a Native preacher, he appears to many as an aberration. While living with his father for a period in Colrain, Massachusetts, he notes that he "was called to preach the Gospel of our Lord," and although he "was nothing but a poor ignorant Indian," he started "exhorting sinners" in the local Methodist meeting. Soon afterwards, Apess receives permission from a friend to host a meeting at his house, one in which Apess would give "a *sermon* instead of an exhortation," and after this first presentation, Apess "received an invitation to hold a meeting in the same place again," arriving to find "a great concourse of people who had come out to hear the Indian preach" (43–44). Later, when he has begun actively traveling as a preacher (although not yet having an official certificate, or license, from a Methodist conference to serve as such), he notes of his meetings in Albany that "crowds flocked out, some to *hear* the truth and others to *see* the 'Indian'" (51). These moments indicate a keen understanding that being Native makes him seem anomalous as a public speaker.[18] Or, more to the point, his *Indianness* not only marks him as incapable of offering commentary on the Bible but also suggests the inherent oddity of his participation in such civilized activity, as opposed to leading a residually primitive existence in the backwoods of the forest. Apess shows how non-natives perceive him as racialized flesh, as an embodiment of a generic Indianness, and in doing so, he also reframes this perspective.[19] If he is thought to bear Indianness as an innate quality, he makes that attribution into the occasion for addressing the colonial dynamics that shape this impression while refiguring that identification in alternative terms that allow his corporeality to mean otherwise—to circulate differently within settler networks. He insists, "Look, brethren, at the natives of the forest—they come, notwithstanding you call them '*savage*' . . . and will occupy seats in the kingdom of heaven before you" (51). In the place of *savagery*, Apess offers indigeneity, being "native" to "the forest." The text refunctions non-natives' interest in him as an Indian curiosity into an engagement with his embodied—enfleshed—presence as indicative of inherited connections to the land that also bespeak his enmeshment in genealogical matrices that constitute the basis for peoplehood and belonging.

From early in the narrative, Apess turns the meaning of his experience of Indianness outward so as to trace the ways *being* Indian entails participating within Native networks of geopolitical relation. The Pequots, as a distinct group to which Apess belongs, are named while being linked to an icon of the history of English-Native relations in the region. In introducing himself at the outset, Apess presents his paternal grandmother as "attached to the royal family of Philip, king of the Pequot tribe of Indians" (3), and he adds, "As the story of King Philip is perhaps generally known, and consequently of the Pequot tribe, over whom he reigned, it will suffice to say that he was overcome by treachery, and the goodly heritage occupied by this once happy, powerful, yet peaceful people was possessed in the process of time by their avowed enemies, the whites," a process that "violat[ed]" the "inherent rights" of an "oppressed and afflicted nation" (4). Various critics have noted that this claim seems false at two levels: Philip was Wampanoag, not Pequot; and there is little evidence for the idea that Apess's grandmother was descended from him.[20] However, this brief account of Apess's lineage rhetorically condenses a great deal in his personage. His embodied presence points back toward a long line of Native ancestors who have remained part of a "nation" that continues to the present. He presents the story of the family line from which he emerges as one of settler dispossession, which he suggests has shaped the terms of his own life. The text further indicates that Apess's father "was of mixed blood" and that in adulthood "he joined the Pequot tribe, to which he was maternally connected"; Apess's mother is described as "a female of the tribe" (4). Apess's contextualization of his own birth occurs in relation to the connections of his parents to "the tribe," establishing a link between his experience and that of his "nation" that positions the latter as the background against which the former comes into view. In this way, *Indian* bodies appear as embedded within and expressive of Indigenous political orders.[21] This linkage also positions the events in Apess's life as ways of figuring dynamics at play more broadly for Pequot people(hood).

The indication by Apess that he is a "son" of "the forest" resonates with the discussion of his relatives in the narrative—and their association with his tribe and the reservation—while also recycling settler tropes of Indian wildness.[22] The text repeatedly correlates the woods with Apess's sense of himself as a Native person, his relation to other Native people (indicated through kinship terms even when not blood relatives or other Pequots), and his relation to distinctly Indigenous territory. In this way, he develops a prominent feature of non-native narratives of Indians as living in the wilderness into a means of signifying Native geopolitics in southern New England. Figures of the forest serve as part of the metonymic chain through which Apess positions his life experience as a representative way of indexing the survivance of both the Mashan-tucket Pequots and Native peoples in New England more broadly.[23] Toward the beginning of the narrative, Apess's attitude toward the woods appears to indicate his alienation from Pequot peoplehood and his consequent appre-hension of things *Indian*. Very early in his life, Apess is left with his maternal grandparents, and after he suffers a brutal beating at his grandmother's hands, to which I'll return shortly, he is removed at the behest of his uncle to live with white neighbors, the Furmans. Describing the period after he had been sepa-rated from his grandparents and was living with the Furmans, Apess observes, "So completely was I weaned from the interests and affections of my brethren that a mere threat of being sent away among the Indians into the dreary woods had a much better effect in making me obedient to the commands of my su-periors than any corporal punishment," adding, "I had not reason to expect mercy or favor at the hands of those who knew me in no other relation than that of a cast-off member of the tribe." He illustrates this sentiment through an anecdote about the extreme fear he felt when confronted in the "woods" by "white females" whose "complexion[s]" were "as *dark* as that of the natives" (10).[24] In noting that at the time he experienced this terror he perceived himself as "a cast-off member of the tribe," Apess presents the racialized understanding of Native people and Native place (the woods as a site of murderous, savage chaos) as a function of a temporary break in tribal relations. In other words, only when he ceases to believe other Pequots recognize him as one, as part of "the nation" to which his parents belonged (4), do notions of Indianness—of abjectly racialized flesh—rush in to fill the void.

"The forest" only becomes such, as opposed to the specificity of Native terri-torial claims like the Mashantucket reservation, within the context of an appar-ent cessation of tribal relations, with Apess drawing on his own dislocation as a means of figuring more expansive processes of dispossession. Just in the wake of the anecdote about Apess's own apprehensions in the "woods," the text ex-plains, "It may be proper for me here to remark that the great fear I entertained of my brethren was occasioned by the many stories I had heard of their cruelty toward the whites. . . . But the whites did not tell me that they were in a great majority of instances the aggressors—that they had imbrued their hands in the lifeblood of my brethren, driven them from their once peaceful and happy homes" (11).[25] While reiterating the trope of Indian wildness in the wilderness, the narrative turns to Apess's own exposure to such non-native "stories" as a way of challenging their veracity, instead offering an alternative set of meanings borne by the figure of "the forest." Here the text gestures toward ongoing settler violence and the continuing presence of place-based Indigenous peoples, such as the Mashantucket Pequots. In this way, Apess presents his life in ways that allow him to inhabit settler templates for signifying Indianness while mediating and reorienting them so as to point toward unrecognized forms of Native sovereignty.

The narrative's references to the forest allude to the legal conflicts around Native land rights in the period, offering a somewhat imagistic condensation of contemporary struggles. In *The Common Pot*, Lisa Brooks notes "the ironic use of [the narrative's] title in light of the surrounding environment: in Apess's New England, there was little forest that remained." She quotes from Pequot petitions to the state that decry the "destroying of their timber and c[row]ding upon their lands," adding that "the deforestation and dispossession at Mashantucket may have been of one of the reasons that Apess's family was living up north in the backwoods of Colrain, one of the few forested areas remaining in Massachusetts, when Apess was born."[26] In *Tribe, Race, History*, Daniel Mandell observes, "Throughout southern New England, farm communities, after generations of population growth, faced a shortage of pasture- and cropland. Efforts to clear more land for use led to the highest rate of deforestation in the history of the region, creating a shortage of wood but not necessarily more arable land because of the acidity of the soil."[27] The image of the forest, then, speaks broadly to the long-term dynamics of land tenure in southern New England, particularly the implications for Native peoples of Anglo-American population growth and modes of property ownership, commercial agriculture, and logging. This legacy can be seen not only in Pequot complaints from the eighteenth century, but in early-nineteenth-century suits, including one filed in 1817 for the illegal cutting of walnut trees just around the time when Apess returns to Mashantucket after having served in the War of 1812.[28]

As in the text's mobilization of the figure of "the forest," the Mashantucket reservation and Pequot history both are ubiquitous and effaced in the narrative, coming into view often obliquely in ways that gesture toward their unspoken, enframing presence as the condition of possibility for much of the drama of maturation, conversion, and political coming-to-consciousness that occurs in the foreground. The Mashantucket Pequots provide a powerful example of a particularly New England pattern of cycles of acknowledgment and erasure. While under great strain in the early to mid-nineteenth century, the Mashantucket Pequots retained their legal identity as a distinct geopolitical entity, a status that they had held for over a century and a half.[29] First designated by the colony of Connecticut as Pequot land in 1666, Mashantucket was the second reservation created in the wake of the Pequot War for those who would come to be called the "Western" Pequots. In 1637, English forces principally from the

Massachusetts Bay Colony attacked the Pequot village on Mystic River, killing between four hundred and seven hundred people—mostly noncombatants. The next year, the Pequots were declared to be dissolved as a people.[30] Despite this apparent eradication, the colony of Connecticut started officially recognizing a distinctly Pequot place again in the 1650s, establishing a reservation for the Eastern Pequots at Stonington in 1650 and one at Noank on the west side of the Mystic River in 1651. Fifteen years later, additional lands were set aside at Mashantucket, ten kilometers to the north of Noank, partially due to population pressure on the resources at Noank and partially due to increasing settler interference from the town of Groton. In 1714, the legislature eliminated the reservation at Noank, and in 1732, the Connecticut General Assembly effectively cut the lands belonging to Mashantucket in half, leaving the Pequots with use of 989 acres of what at one time had been a three thousand–acre reservation. Roughly another one hundred acres were taken over the next century before the legislature in 1855 mandated the sale of all but 180 acres. By the 1820s and 1830s, the Mashantucket Pequots possessed a legal claim to their, much diminished, reservation, but even when that fact entered public discourse, it did not translate as a federally cognizable matter that should, or could, be the subject of treaty negotiation or of jurisdiction by an "Indian nation."

Like other Native peoples in southern New England, the Mashantucket Pequots in the early nineteenth century were under enormous economic and demographic stress.[31] Participation and mortality during the Seven Years' War and American Revolution had been incredibly high, and over the course of the eighteenth century, encroaching settler presence had made prior subsistence patterns increasingly untenable, leading to growing participation in the market economy (including purchasing food and clothing). The gender imbalance on reservations due to deaths in war was exacerbated greatly by Native men leaving temporarily in search of work, a need also magnified by the claims of local creditors. Not only did the prolonged absence of Native men lead to a relative depopulation of the reservation, which served as occasion for further white encroachment, but it encouraged marriages by Native women to non-natives, particularly Black men. While such patterns of intermarriage may also reflect the continued importance to tribal identity of kinship ties through women, which had been central in shaping patterns of multifamily residency within tribes and creating links among Native peoples from prior to European contact well into the nineteenth century, they helped propel settler discourses of Native disappearance, leading to charges that the residents on reservation were no longer *really* Indian and that reservations simply were serving as spaces of refuge for the most degraded elements of society.[32]

While events during Apess's life take him away from the reservation, the text explicitly and implicitly suggests how such dislocations point toward forms of colonial entanglement that indicate not so much the disappearance of the Pequots as the continuing pressures of expropriation that seek to block the potential for their existence as a people/polity. The text continually demonstrates how Apess's biography illustrates the historical and ongoing force of settlement. In doing so, not only does the text position Apess as something of an exemplary figure, it narrates his embodied experience in ways that trace a negative outline of Pequot nationhood—providing a form for marking what is denied and assaulted through settler political economy in southern New England. After he describes the brutal beating by his maternal grandmother that almost killed him and that led to his residence with the Furmans, he qualifies her actions by offering the following: "But this cruel and unnatural conduct was the effect of some cause. I attribute it in a great measure to the whites, inasmuch as they introduced among my countrymen that bane of comfort and happiness, ardent spirits—seduced them into a love of it and, when under its unhappy influence, wronged them out of their lawful possessions—that land, where reposed the ashes of their sires" (7).[33] Here, he establishes the relation between the current circumstances faced by Native people and the history of tribal land loss. More specifically, his grandmother's drunkenness during the assault is cast as an effect of the introduction of alcohol by settlers, the aim of which, according to Apess, was to defraud Native peoples of their territory. Additionally, he indicates that just prior to the assault, his grandmother had been "out among the whites" (5–6), likely working for them, thereby implicitly situating such service within the context of economies of white exploitation and dispossession. The actions that result in his coming to live among white families until he runs away and volunteers in the War of 1812, then, appear as a function of the long and continuing legacy of non-natives seeking to push Native peoples off of their lands, in ways that also aim to break intergenerational connections that tie them to those territories ("the ashes of their sires").

Moreover, the text insists that the particular incidents and immediate circumstances of Apess's biography need to be situated and interpreted within a frame that can make legible the otherwise invisible *causes* for the occurrences he chronicles. He suggests that in hearing about his grandparents' conduct, readers likely would exclaim, "What savages our grandparents were to treat unoffending, helpless children in this cruel manner" (6–7). As opposed to resting on non-native presumptions of innate Indian savagery (another version of people coming to gawk at the oddity of the Indian preacher), the narrative inhabits and reorients this scene of violence in order to bring into view the background of Indigenous dispossession and deprivation that creates the conditions of possibility for the assault and Apess's attendant dislocation from his tribe. That shift also involves underlining the absence of Native nationhood from the prior way of seeing the scene, highlighting the ways the loss of Pequot "lawful possessions" and the resulting inability to sustain themselves on their lands and need to go "out among the whites" for wage work go missing in the attribution of immanent *Indian* qualities to Native flesh.

Apess further offers his own indenture during his childhood as exemplary of these same dynamics. At the age of eleven, he is transferred from the Furmans to William Hillhouse, the chief justice of the New London County Court, and he describes this process as his having "been *sold*," noting that "after the bargain was made, my consent was to be obtained" (15).[34] Not long afterwards, as a result of Apess's repeated efforts to run away from Judge Hillhouse, his indenture is transferred again, this time to General William Williams. Once again describing this conveyance as a sale, he observes, "If my consent had been solicited as a matter of form, I should not have felt so bad. But to be sold to and treated unkindly by those who had got our fathers' lands for nothing was too much to bear" (16). These moments provide a condensed account of the relation between the nonconsensual seizure and sale of Native territory and the conscription of Native labor through indenture, especially that of Indian children, as part of the broader nexus of Native indebtedness produced by the effects of land loss and the need to rely on English and then U.S. commodities and wages for subsistence.[35] In alluding to this political economy of Indigenous land loss, the narrative presents that continuing pattern of what the text characterizes as fraud, and the making fungible of Native territory and persons, as the background against which the particulars of Apess's life gain meaning. Reciprocally, Apess positions himself and his experience as emblematic of patterns that characterize Native life across New England.

Given that Apess is addressing his time with William Williams in New London, though, these indictments of settler expansion broadly stated have more pointed implications for attending to the Mashantucket Pequots. The Williams family had a long and rich tradition of participation in Pequot affairs, including being sued in the mid-eighteenth century for taking over eighty acres at Mashantucket (a case that eventually led to the official halving of the reservation) and presiding in the late eighteenth century over cases involving Pequots. Further, the William Williams to whom Apess was indentured served as the overseer for Mashantucket for most of the 1810s (starting in 1813), which was just after Apess ran away to join the army, although he certainly would have been aware of Williams's tenure when writing *A Son of the Forest*. Williams was one of two overseers whom the Pequots sought to replace during that time due to their failure adequately to attend to matters at Mashantucket, and he resigned in 1819.[36] Additionally, given that New London itself was built on the site of the Mystic River village destroyed in the 1637 attack, the mention of "our fathers' lands" intimates that Apess's indenture is itself an inheritance of a legacy of displacement and erasure dating back to the Pequot War, and the collectivity suggested by "our" subtly invokes the history of the Pequots as a "nation."[37]

Questions around the visibility of Pequot presence also inflect Apess's discussion of his relationship to Mashantucket. During his description of his childhood after being taken away from his grandparents to live with the Furmans, he does not address his relationship to Pequot people (other than his father) or suggest any connection to the reservation until after he returns from a sojourn in Haudenosaunee territory in the wake of his military service. This absence has led scholars to conclude that he was alienated from Pequot persons and peoplehood in his youth, coming into sustained contact with them only in adulthood.[38] However, his portrayal of his homecoming to the area offers a very different sense of that personal history. When Apess returns to southern Connecticut after his time away, serving in the War of 1812 and doing itinerant labor in its wake, he observes:

> I experienced but very little difficulty on the way, and at last I arrived in safety at the home of my childhood. At first my people looked upon me as one risen from the dead. Not having heard from me since I left home, being more than four years, they thought I must certainly have died, and the days of mourning had almost passed. They were rejoiced to see me once more in the land of the living, and I was equally rejoiced to find all my folks alive. The whites with whom I had been acquainted were also very glad to see me. After I had spent some time with my relations in Groton and visited all my old friends, I concluded to go to work and be steady. (37)

The phrase "home of my childhood" initially would seem to refer to one or all of the white households to which Apess was indentured, since we have not heard of another space that served as "home." Yet he correlates the place of "home" to "my people" and "all my folks." While one may be tempted to see these terms as indicating the Furmans, Apess distinguishes the people to whom he's referring from "the whites with whom [he] had been acquainted," suggesting that such terms of endearment are used with respect to Native people. Moreover, since he describes his time away as "more than four years," rather than the fifteen years since his separation from his grandparents, the passage implies that he regularly spent time with his "people" and "folks" before he ran away from New London to join the army. He presents his "relations in Groton" as those to whom he has gone, and that description, particularly when combined with the phrase "my people" and the use of "home" to index a place occupied by Natives as opposed to whites, strongly conveys the impression that he is speaking of Mashantucket.

While "Groton" officially refers to a town distinct from the reservation, since at least the 1720s the town had claimed preemption rights to the territory of the reservation, linking the two in the minds of many, and up through at least the mid-nineteenth century, both whites and Pequots routinely would speak of those residing at Mashantucket as the Pequots "of Groton."[39] Combined with the earlier reference to his father as having "joined the Pequot tribe" and his later description of himself as going "among my tribe at Groton" (4, 40), the discussion of his return to Connecticut can be understood as illustrating not simply a connection to other Native people in adulthood, but Apess's felt sense of belonging to the Pequot "tribe" throughout his life (or at least substantially preceding his running away), his connection through "relatives" to the Mashantucket reservation, and his sense of the reservation as the "home" of his "people"—a term which itself indexes the tribe rather than merely his blood relations or other Natives.[40]

Prior to this point, though, the text does not offer a robust account of Apess's connection to the reservation as such. This key passage testifying to that ongoing relation appears more than halfway through the narrative; the alternate prism it provides does not fully compensate for the relative absence of the tribe in the text prior to this moment. How can we think about the simultaneous relevance and irrelevance of Mashantucket here? Apess gestures toward the reservation as something of a shadow referent for his discussions of his genealogical relations to the Pequots as a "nation," ongoing Indigenous land loss, the resulting conditions of indenture and labor itinerancy, and Native relations with the "forest." In *Manifest Manners*, Gerald Vizenor explores what he characterizes as the *tribal real*, the persistence of "tribal presence in the very ruins of the representations of invented Indians." Vizenor argues that efforts by Native intellectuals to enter into the "simulations" created by non-native discourses of Indianness carry with them "shadows" that "tease and loosen the bonds of representation in stories." For Vizenor, "shadows are that silence and sense of motion in memories," adding that "the shadows are the silence in heard stories, the silence that bears a referent of tribal memories and experience."[41] As opposed to indicating a lack, "shadows" and "silence" serve as a way of indicating, and theorizing, an active set of "memories" and "experiences" that offer the informing context for what is said/written and that provide an unstated "referent" for the terms and stories which explicitly appear in Native texts. Even as Mashantucket appears only peripherally and somewhat elliptically as a topic in *A Son of the Forest*, it can be understood as the shadow of Apess's invocation of histories of Native dispossession, a silent surround that provides greater specificity and substance to those moments. Or, put another way, Apess positions Mashantucket as such a surround, as the implicit background illustrating a sustained "tribal presence" that is often unacknowledged in settler frames of reference, political discourses, and formulations of a generic Indianness. Positioning his own experience as representative, as a metonymic stand-in for settler violence and Native peoples' survivance across southern New England, he alludes to Indigenous geopolitical formations, the Mashantucket reservation in particular. In doing so, the text can be read as experimenting with the potential for signifying Indigenous political collectivities, searching for a rhetorical form through which to index their existence, even if one that does not appear to be *about* governance as such.

The text's elliptical allusions to Mashantucket point to the reservation's presence and its importance in Apess's formulations of indigeneity, but they do so in ways that reflect the tenuousness and relative invisibility of Pequot peoplehood and placemaking within Euro-American public discourses. As with the discussion of the context for his grandmother's actions, he subtly signals a history that is going unrecognized and suggests that looking for and attending to silences within non-native accounts opens possibilities for engaging with kinds of Native collective experience for which there is not a form legible as such to non-natives. In this way, the narrative stages and challenges the presumption of Native disappearance, suggesting that a lack of explicit reference (such as not mentioning his connections with Pequot people during childhood) should be taken as indicative not of actual absence but of a failure of framing—a faulty set of presumptions about Indianness. The text presents Apess's life as evidencing and providing an embodied archive of such webs of connection. *A Son of the Forest* implies that what is taken by non-natives to be the spectacle of his Indianness actually emerges from and points back toward Indigenous networks of peoplehood and placemaking not visible as such within settler optics. In this way, his fleshly presence becomes a condensed figure for the existence and vitality of those networks, even when they are silent and in shadow.

Given the difficulty of signifying Pequot sovereignty within extant public discourses, the text develops an alternative set of rhetorical strategies for doing so that circulate around elements in Apess's life. As the text does with respect to his connections with the "forest" and with members of his family, the narrative mobilizes his Methodism as a means of delineating the contours of Pequot nationhood. While living with General Williams, Apess is forbidden from attending Methodist camp meetings, which he had begun to do after joining the general's household in New London. In response, Apess remarks, "They had possession of the red man's inheritance and had deprived me of liberty; with this they were satisfied and could do as they pleased; therefore, I thought I could do as I pleased, measurably. I therefore went to hear the *noisy Methodists*" (18). His characterization of his turn to Methodism as a response to the taking of Native lands presents the history of Indian reservations in southern New England, particularly the one with which he is most closely associated, as a crucial informing presence underlying the religious "plot" that occupies much of the narrative's central focus.[42] This enframing of faith as a vehicle of Native identification is inflected later in the narrative by its explicit association with Apess's relatives at Mashantucket. After returning from one of his trips away from the reservation for work, he observes, "When the time for which I was engaged had expired, I went among my tribe at Groton. I lived this winter with my aunt who was comfortably situated. . . . Once in four weeks we had meeting, which was attended by people from Rhode Island and Stonington, and other places and generally lasted three days" (40). Here his paternal great-aunt, Sally George, serves as a vehicle for indicating Pequot sovereignty and Methodist fervor, conjoining Methodism with his relatives at Mashantucket in ways that allow them to cross-reference each other and for both metonymically to index his "tribe" in its survival as a distinct, place-based entity.[43] Another moment that suggests this intimate braiding comes after he is told to stop exhorting until he can formally be licensed: "This unkind treatment, as I regarded it, had nearly provided the ruin of my soul. . . . I viewed myself as an *outcast from society*. . . . I gave way for a little while but soon returned to my *first love*. I went then to my native tribe, where meetings were still kept up" (46). The spiritual crisis that occurs in the wake of being censured and cast out by whites for failing to conform to church rules leads him back to his "native tribe." More than indicating Apess's connection to other Pequots, the passage suggests that they themselves dwell outside "society," in a place apart in which "meetings" have a significance distinct and superior to those that occur among non-natives. While perhaps most directly indicating Apess's Methodist faith, the phrase *"first love"* directly precedes the mention of his tribe, positioning the Pequot people as a potential referent, and the term "returned" connotes a movement in space and a geographic demarcation suggestive of the reservation. Apess's account of his Methodism, then, can be read as itself inhabited by a prior and largely silent association with his people on the reservation, one that provides the informing context through which his faith gains meaning in the text and that, thereby, positions Mashantucket as the background against which the details of his life emerge and achieve significance.

Apess implicitly casts his biography as representative of Native experiences and social formations in southern New England in ways that allow him to function as a metonym for the persistence of Indigenous peoplehood (as against prominent narratives of Indian disappearance and the need for beneficent aid by non-natives). However, the vision of such peoplehood conveyed in *A Son of the Forest* also somewhat displaces the issue of actual governance on reservation in ways that are powerfully gendered. If part of the text's project lies in finding a form through which to convey the geopolitics of Indigenous nationhood, the use of Apess's life (especially the genre of the spiritual autobiography) runs up against the difficulty of conveying Pequot processes of and networks of collective decision-making. Under the guardian system, tribes did not have governing bodies acknowledged as such by the state. Instead, overseers appointed by state officials were the ones given authority to manage natural resources, internal difficulties, and relations with non-native neighbors, serving less as something like a liaison than as an executive with broad discretionary powers (not unlike the Indian agents in the federal system, a dynamic I'll discuss in chapters 3 and 4).[44] The question of how tribes on state-recognized reservations made decisions and distributed resources for themselves, and their principles and priorities in doing so, is deferred and erased within state discourses of Indian administration, even as Native peoples across southern New England continued to petition state officials throughout the nineteenth century on a broad range of issues. *A Son of the Forest* does little to address this issue, in some ways further obscuring matters of governance through its de facto positioning of men's experience as paradigmatic. While many women also left reservations for economic and other reasons, demographic imbalances on reservations largely resulted from men leaving for itinerant work while women remained, keeping up family lands and maintaining local kinship networks. The trajectory of Apess's life in his movement on and off reservation, then, reflects less a pattern for Native people as such than one for Native men. The sociopolitical networks at play on and across the reservation become less visible when men's experiences serve as the means of modeling or marking peoplehood in the region, as the basis on which to seek recognition for Indigenous political identities from non-native publics.

Traces of these issues appear in the narrative's somewhat fleeting reference to Aunt Sally George. As noted earlier, she serves as a way of linking Apess's Methodism back to his relations with other Pequots and connection to Mashantucket. When visiting his aunt, he describes the character of the meetings she holds in ways that emphasize their location outside the circuits of official recognition: "We observed particular forms, although we knew nothing about the dead languages, except that the knowledge thereof was not necessary for us to serve God. We had no house of divine worship, and believing 'that the groves were God's first temples,' thither we would repair when the weather permitted" (40). Here Apess ties Methodism to the forest and his family, offering a concrete image of Pequot locatedness. This brief glimpse of Sally George's role in reservation life, though, raises questions about her position within the tribe. Jack Campisi observes with respect to nineteenth-century Mashantucket politics, "Available evidence indicates that tribal members maintained a council house, met frequently on tribal business, and took an active part in their community affairs," and George is one of the family names of those who centrally took part in council business in the period. Campisi further notes that overseers' reports indicated that women were understood to be the heads of all of the seven major extended family groups.[45] Did Sally George play such a role? Was she serving not simply as a pillar of the community but actually as one of its leaders within an established council structure? Even if she did not occupy that position, she likely had influence and participated in unofficial networks of governance, toward which Apess's anecdote might obliquely gesture but which it does not fully engage and which the narrative has no means of substantively registering. Moreover, the allusion to the presence of "people from Rhode Island and Stonington, and other places" at Sally George's meetings probably refers to Eastern Pequots, Narragansetts, and members of other tribes in the region (40). She certainly seems enmeshed in extended intertribal networks whose maintenance might be characterized as diplomacy. As Mandell suggests, "Indians had forged regional networks in the century before the Revolution. The migration of individuals and families within these networks continued after the war, encouraged in part by regular religious meetings."[46] These fleeting references in his narrative elliptically gesture toward the ways Native peoples themselves were experimenting with political forms and networks on and across reservations in the nineteenth century, in ways that involved elements of earlier social processes but that were not simply continuations of prior patterns. The text's use of Apess's life as the vehicle for conveying Native peoplehood to non-native readers, though, does not provide a ready means of signifying these matrices of ongoing relation, maintained largely by Native women.[47] For example, when discussing the story of Anne Wampy in *The Experiences of Five Christian Indians*, he presents her as poor, illiterate, and only recently converted, but given that she is a signatory to all of the petitions from the Pequots to Connecticut authorities about the overseer, from 1819 through her death, she likely played a significant role in Mashantucket governance, of which Apess would have been aware and which he passes over entirely.[48]

Apess draws on the exoticizing interest in "the Indian" in ways that redirect that spectacularizing enfleshment toward figuring him and his life as exemplary. His embodied experience stands in for the contours and challenges facing Pequot nationhood, metonymically condensing those dynamics and drawing non-native attention toward them. However, the attention he receives is not as a political figure, and he does not appear in *A Son of the Forest* as a delegated representative of the Pequot people. The text, though, does proxy for Pequot presence, their existence as a "tribe," and ongoing territoriality (itself recognized by the state in the form of the reservation), but it does so in a way that gestures toward shadows and silences in settler perceptions, discourses, and institutional frames, experimenting with ways of tracing the effects of colonialism and the persistence of Native peoplehood amid ongoing occupation. Apess seeks to mediate settler networks by turning the terms of his intelligibility—as curiosity and benighted subject of plight—into a vehicle for marking the continued viability of a Pequot public amid intensifying forms of colonial expropriation. Through the account of Apess's life, the narrative traces the political economy of dispossession and impoverishment. The narrative outlines the circumstances of structural violence and entanglement that animate the effort to generate possibilities for recognition that could reconfigure the policies and principles of the guardian system. Speaking to settler publics and seeking to alter the ways they conceive of *Indianness* in New England can be understood as part of an attempt to reorder the politics of settlement, albeit in ways that may tend to efface patterns of leadership on reservation—including the centrality of Native women both as direct participants in governance and in maintaining Native spaces and linking them to each other largely via the work of kinship.

King Philip as Father of the Nation

If Apess's preaching often brought out whites who wanted "to *see* the 'Indian,'" he also would have called forth another image—that of King Philip. Metacom, or King Philip, was the seventeenth-century Wampanoag leader whose resistance to English jurisdictional and property claims helped give rise to the bloodiest conflict in which New Englanders participated until the U.S. Civil War.[49] In 1836 Apess delivers the speech at Boston's Odean Theater that eventually would be published as *Eulogy on King Philip*, and the play *Metamora* frequently was staged at a theater just down the street from him.[50] Commissioned in 1829 by Edwin Forrest, who would become the most famous actor in the

United States (largely due to his repeated performance in the lead role), *Metamora* tells the fictionalized story of King Philip's War, featuring King Philip and ending in his tragic death.[51] By the mid- to late 1830s, the play was one of the most popular entertainments in the country, particularly the Northeast, and it provided an implicit frame through which audience members likely would perceive Apess's presence on stage. Metacom arguably served as the dominant figure of Indianness in the region in the 1820s and 1830s.[52] More than simply providing a convenient or well-known vehicle for talking about the history of New England or the (supposedly ever-dwindling) presence of Natives there, Metacom functioned as a representative symbol of Native pasts and presents. By representative, though, I mean that he stood in for the existence, histories, and identities of Indigenous peoples, operating as a metonymic substitute that condensed the scope and meaning of indigeneity into a concrete personage. In this sense, for non-natives watching Apess, the experience would be almost as much a reanimation of the spirit of King Philip as attending a performance of *Metamora*. In *Eulogy on King Philip*, Apess seizes on this dynamic, that in some sense he would be understood against the background of Metacom and King Philip's War regardless of what he actually said, in order to reorient the cultural and political work of King Philip's status as the exemplary New England Indian.[53]

Apess draws on Metacom's representative status in order to contest the erasure of peoples in southern New England from the geographies of federal Indian policy. Through his depiction of Metacom as a chief executive, Apess presents ongoing Indigenous occupancy in the region as part of a specifically national history, one that both parallels the existence of the United States as a distinct nation and deserves political recognition of the sort elsewhere accorded Indigenous nations through the federal treaty system. This more conventionally political mode of figuration clearly differs from the enfleshed vision of peoplehood embodied by Apess himself in *A Son of the Forest*, but rather than understanding this shift as expressive of something like a growing or altered political consciousness, it can be interpreted as a rhetorical strategy whose form engages with different kinds of public tropes than those in *Son*, suggesting the range and variability of Apess's ways of approaching recognition and of reframing settler expectations. In casting Metacom as the father of a nation, Apess deploys a conception of patriarchal sovereignty that challenges the image of Indians as dependent wards at play in the guardian system, consolidates a vision of Native political existence around a monarchical figure who embodies the authority of autonomous governance on a clearly delimited landbase, and generates a sense of contemporary Indigenous people(s) as lawful inheritors of this domain and as properly ruling over it themselves. However, mobilizing Metacom in this way also both centralizes and masculinizes Indigenous political orders, creating a portrait of Native governance that does not reflect patterns of leadership, decision-making, and resource distribution in either the seventeenth century or the nineteenth century. *Eulogy*, then, engages settler networks of intelligibility at the expense of accounting for prior and continuing regional Algonquian webs of relation.

One might read *Eulogy* as in a sense seeking to set the record straight, to rewrite dominant accounts of New England history in order to insist on the significance of Native people(s) within it, and in this vein, Metacom and King Philip's War provide a powerful means of doing so. Yet, the difficulties faced by the Pequots and other tribes in the period lie less in not being seen as having a history than in being seen as inevitably in a process of decline and disappearance. As Eric Wolfe suggests, "In choosing to memorialize King Philip one hundred sixty years after Philip's death, Apess was presenting himself in the too-familiar guise of the mourning Indian," but in the text's rendering of Metacom and his legacy, "Apess resists the Euroamerican desire to mourn the Indian and redefines his relationship with Philip as melancholia," indicating an ongoing attachment to this supposedly gone past in ways that animate the present.[54] In doing so, *Eulogy* enacts a counterpolitics of commemoration: "Apess challenged the very mode of memory and commemoration by mocking the uses non-Indians made of this genre," thereby "reclaim[ing] New England as an Indian place."[55] Commemoration of a range of historical events in the 1820s and 1830s, including the bicentennial of the founding of the Plymouth Colony and the fiftieth anniversary of the Declaration of Independence, provided a means of publicly staging national history as a site of intense public affect and identification while also extending the duration of that history beyond the American Revolution into the past of English colonial settlement. These dynamics also played out in the genre of what has come to be called "frontier romance," historical fiction set in times and spaces of settler-Native conflict that are presented as firmly belonging to the past, and a number of such popular texts were set in New England.[56] That process of temporal extension also sought to give New England a special role within the United States as the place from which American ideals of liberty and republican community sprang, positioning the Northeast as the origin of the nation despite, for example, the earlier founding of Jamestown in 1607. In the context of such performances of public memory as a means of enabling civic unification and inculcating patriotic structures of feeling, the staging of a commemoration of King Philip taps into that sense of nationalist meaning-making while redirecting it so as to convey a different national ethos than that of filiation to the United States.[57]

From the outset, Apess introduces Metacom by establishing a parallel between him and George Washington. In doing so, the text calls on listeners/readers to understand King Philip as an exemplary figure of nationhood, but of Indigenous nationhood rather than that of the United States. Apess begins by denying that his subject can be compared to the father of the U.S. nation: "I do not arise to spread before you the fame of a noted warrior, whose natural abilities shone line those of the great and mighty Philip of Greece, or of Alexander the Great, or like those of Washington—whose virtues and patience are engraven on the hearts of my audience."[58] Instead, Apess suggests he will "bring before you beings made by the God of Nature," whose "proper virtues remain untold" and whose "noble traits" currently "lie buried in the shades of night" (105). The text casts its aim as revealing that which remains "buried" and hidden from his (non-native) audience. Implying that Philip represents a set of "virtues" distinct from those embodied by Washington, Apess also aligns the former with "nature," with the unadorned land that precedes white occupation, and he further indicates that *Eulogy*, via the figure of Philip, speaks in the name of "beings" whose continuing story otherwise remains "untold." In this way, invoking Metacom becomes a means of marking the existence of a (set of) people(s) whose presence endures in the shadow of the founding of the settler nation. The text lays out this relation in a multivectored passage worth quoting in full:

> But those few remaining descendants who now remain as the monument of the cruelty of those who came to improve our race and correct our errors—and as the immortal Washington lives endeared and engrave on the hearts of every white in America, never to be forgotten in time— even such is the immortal Philip honored, as held in the memory by the degraded but yet grateful descendants who appreciate his character; so will every patriot, especially in this enlightened age, respect the rude yet all-accomplished son of the forest, that died a martyr to his cause, though unsuccessful, yet as glorious as the *American* Revolution. (105)

In something of a reversal of *Eulogy*'s initial demurral, here it forcefully fuses Philip and Washington as condensed sites and symbols of patriotic investment, but for different *causes*.[59]

Apess presents popular sentiments with regard to Washington as a frame through which to understand Philip while simultaneously positioning Philip as a metonymic stand-in through which to frame Native nationhood.[60] Philip gains significance through his being "held in memory" in the present by the "descendants" of those who fought for the same "cause" as Metacom in the seventeenth century. The character of that struggle comes into view through the invocation of Washington, whose place in "the hearts of every white American" speaks to and serves as a symbolic substitute for public feelings about the American Revolution and the existence of the United States as an autonomous nation. Comparing contemporary feelings about Philip and Washington allows Apess to gesture toward Indigenous presentness while giving political form to Native sentiments. He differentiates them from U.S. patriotism, indicating their support for a national *cause* that not only cannot be encompassed within that of the American Revolution but also is a "glorious" cause whose frustration may, in fact, be due to the success of the U.S. bid for independence. This rhetorical maneuver, though, may draw on the popularity throughout the late eighteenth century and first half of the nineteenth century of whites dressing up as Indians in order to stage their claims for land rights, whether in the Boston Tea Party just prior to the Revolutionary War or in struggles against landed elites (which often involve both Indian masquerading and citations of the legacy of the Revolution).[61] Even as Philip and Washington occupy different temporal frames, what links them is that those who bear Washington in their hearts "are in possession of [Philip's] soil" due to the assertion of a "right of conquest." Those in whose "hearts" Philip "yet lives" remain committed to a shadow Indigenous nationalism that lives on amid and despite such conquest, contesting the terms and legitimacy of U.S. nationalism. The figure of Philip provides a means of manifesting contemporary Native structures of feeling and giving them politically intelligible shape for a settler public.

That matrix of surrogation—Philip operating as a vehicle for conveying the "untold" existence of Native sovereignty in New England in the moment of Apess's articulation—plays on the *Metamora* effect of viewing Apess as Philip. If viewers likely would perceive Apess's embodied presence as substituting for the performance of Philip in the popular play, Apess positions himself as one of Philip's "descendants" in order to assert the relevance of Metacom in and for the present.[62] He aims to "melt the prejudice that exists in the hearts" of his listeners by asserting both Philip's goodness and his link to Philip given that "the blood of a denominated savage runs in his veins" (105). The implicit claim by *Eulogy* to speak for Native peoples in New England emerges through the presentation of Apess as himself an inheritor of Philip's vision and struggle. As such, he gives form to the memory of Philip as a way of challenging current settler claims to possession of Indigenous soil, playing with his own ability to signify as representative but in ways that are different from his narration of his own life in *A Son of the Forest*.

To speak as or in the name of Philip is to bear the mantle of his glorious cause. The work of *Eulogy*, then, is less historiographic than hagiographic.

Rather than correcting the historical record, it presents Philip as an inspiring model for emulation. His patriotism to and for a Native nation is bodied forth in the present by Apess and other *descendants* for whom Philip remains in their hearts. Maureen Konkle suggests that "Apess interrupts . . . EuroAmerican History through Native experience, ultimately producing counterhistories that hinge not on Native disappearance, but rather continuity," and she further characterizes *Eulogy* as offering a "necessarily ironic historiography" that aims to "dislodge the foundation of white knowledge . . . in order to open up space for a different history."[63] Even as the text draws on the language of descent, its emphasis lies less in illustrating historical continuity than in employing Philip as a template for signifying forms of Indigenous collectivity that diverge from the presumptions at play in the guardian system. The dislocation in time enables Apess to foreground an image of indigeneity other than extant notions of a decimated, disappearing, and disabled Indianness in need of white benevolent care. *Eulogy* certainly seeks to contest supposed white knowledge of contemporary Natives in southern New England, but it does not so much describe a chain of inheritance as suggest that Metacom animates the present and provides a frame for marking the illegitimacy of settler claims to possession of Native lands.

The double identification of Philip with Washington and Apess himself enables *Eulogy* to present investment in and defense of Indigenous geopolitics as expressive of patriotism while also analogizing such seventeenth-century affects and actions with nineteenth-century responses to continuing settler occupation. Apess observes that something like the Pilgrims landing at Plymouth, "if done now, it would be called an insult, and every white man would be called to go out and act the part of a patriot, to defend their country's rights" (108). By contrast, "when a few red children attempt to defend their rights, they are condemned as savages by those, if possible, who have indulged in wrongs more cruel than the Indians" (110). The movement back and forth across the centuries allows for portraying what is often treated as the moment of American national founding as, in fact, an invasion, while also indicating how Native resistance and patriotism in the present gets miscategorized as indicative of Indian backwardness and savagery, the flip side of discourses of white care for remnant populations in southern New England.[64]

If King Philip serves as a representative Indian for non-natives, Apess draws on such representativity in order to revise extant institutionalized understandings of the character of Native identity(/ies). More than merely a local leader, he was "their king and emperor," deserving of the title "His Majesty" (117). With regard to demands that Metacom appear before the government of Plymouth Colony, *Eulogy* insists, "What an insult this was to His Majesty; an independent chief of a powerful nation should come at the beck and call of his neighbors whenever they pleased to have him do it" (120). These moments highlight Metacom's status as sovereign. The monarchical language underlines that he possesses political authority that separates him from the English colonies as well as from their spurious claims to jurisdiction over his lands. Emphasizing his *independence* in this way reinforces Native *nationality*—that Indigenous peoples rightfully should be understood as sovereign polities instead of as objects of putatively benevolent settler management. In adopting this manner of referring to Metacom, Apess implicitly advances an argument about political scale. Native peoples cannot be subsumed within New England's colonies, and then U.S. states, as a domestic concern. Expanding on the framing analogy with Washington, *Eulogy* insists that Indian affairs are a national matter, a subject of negotiation and policy that properly belongs above the level of colonial/ state governments. As a result of Philip's advisors being tried and executed by Plymouth, he "judg[es] that his white intruders had nothing to do in punishing his people for any crime and that it was in violation of treaties of ancient date," and in response to inquiries from the governor of Plymouth about Philip's displeasure, "The king answered him thus: 'Your governor is but a subject of King Charles of England; I shall not treat with a subject; I shall treat of peace only with a king, my brother'" (122). Apess highlights that the colony's attempt to exert authority over Metacom is an *intrusion* or invasion that violates existing agreements, presented as diplomatic in character. As Konkle suggests, "In his account of King Philip's legal conflicts, Apess elevates those contracts to the status of treaties that unequivocally signify Native sovereignty," which "is significant in light of the conditions faced by many New England tribes . . . who had no or not as many of the formal treaties through which the arguments for Native autonomy and sovereignty were commonly made."[65] These maneuvers on Apess's part position relations with Metacom as offering precedent for engaging with Native peoples in New England as political entities, instead of as racialized dependents to be supervised by non-native guardians. However, perhaps more importantly, Apess's citation of "treaties" and insistence on Philip's position as parallel to that of King Charles, coupled with the earlier connection of Philip with Washington as patriotic leaders of distinct nations, employs Metacom as a metonymic proxy for the nationhood of contemporary peoples.

In this way, *Eulogy* mediates discourses of commemoration in order to reorient them toward marking the evidence of Philip's "cause" in the present. Apess uses Philip's "prophecy" of coming white domination as a temporal pivot to jump from the scene of seventeenth-century warfare to that of the nineteenth-century moment of his speech/writing. He observes,

Our groves and hunting grounds are gone, our dead are dug up, our council fires are put out, a foundation was laid in the first Legislature to enslave our people, by taking from them all rights, which has been strictly adhered to ever since. Look at the disgraceful laws, disfranchising us as citizens. Look at the treaties made by Congress, all broken. Look at the deep-rooted plans laid, when a territory becomes a state, that after so many years the laws shall be extended over the Indians that live within their boundaries. Yea, every charter that has been given was given with the view of driving the Indians out of the states, or dooming them to become chained under desperate laws. (134)

The passage outlines the legal dynamics by which Native sovereignty is effaced and foreclosed. If Philip is "held in memory" by contemporary Natives whose own aspirations lie "buried in the shades of night" (105), that dematerializing denial of Indigenous geopolitics and worldings directly results from ongoing and intensifying settler force, perfidy, and disregard for legal and diplomatic norms. Moreover, in situating the "descendants" of Philip in relation to actions by "Congress" and the question of "treaties," Apess presents Native people(s) in New England as a matter of U.S. national policy, as belonging to Indian affairs as covered under the federal Trade and Intercourse Acts rather than as simply under the ordinary jurisdiction of states like Connecticut and Massachusetts. In this way, Apess repudiates the narratives at play in the guardian system—in Audra Simpson's terms quoted earlier, "refus[ing] to be enfolded into state logics"—while calling on a different set of governmental discourses, those of treaty making and federal policy, as an alternative frame for acknowledging Indigenous sovereignty. Even as he marks for settler listeners/readers the failures of the U.S. government to live up to its promises, his invocation of treaties and federal law shifts the discussion of Native collective identities and placemaking into a different legal and political register, one potentially more conducive to engaging with Indigenous polities as such than the policy architecture at play in southern New England.

The reference here to Native people(s) as "citizens," though, can suggest a frustrated belonging to the United States. Jean O'Brien has suggested that in *Eulogy* Apess "advances a revolutionary idea: that Indians could both exercise self-determination as Indian peoples and become citizens, that is, the notion of dual citizenship." She further argues, "Without an incipient theory of dual citizenship, Apess's oration might seem at odds with itself."[66] However, the meaning of "disfranchising us as citizens" lies in the breaking of treaties and the extension of jurisdiction over Indigenous nations by states. In other words,

Native people(s) are disfranchised from citizenship in their own nation(s), the one(s) for which Philip stands and for which he serves as an expression of patriotism parallel to that felt for Washington by whites—but not by Indians. Allusions to U.S. citizenship serve for Apess as a means of bringing into the present moment the seventeenth-century scene of Metacom's authority, the failure of the English to acknowledge and respect it, and the savagery of attendant colonial violence and disavowal. As the defense of Native lands in the earlier period is cast as expressive of patriotism, *Eulogy* presents current dynamics of settler expropriation and failure to acknowledge Indigenous sovereignty—the stuff of non-native citizenship in the nation-state—as evidence of how "the doctrines of the Pilgrims has [*sic*] grown up with the people" (133). Metacom's struggle in the seventeenth century provides a prism through which to make current practices and privileges of U.S. citizenship visible as modes of colonial invasion, taking U.S. citizenship to task for the ways it normalizes such routine intervention, dispossession, and erasure. Apess charges that in the present generation, "though in words they deny it, yet in the works they approve of the iniquities of their fathers" (115). He further suggests that "it does appear that Indians had rights, and those rights were near and dear to them, as your stores and farms and firesides are to the whites, and their wives and children also" (116). The tranquility of such settler domesticity provides a way not only of marking the importance to Native peoples' of their "rights" but also implicitly of indicating how the (re)production of affectively rich spaces of non-native stability depends on the violation of such rights, on non-natives being "in the possession of [Indigenous] soil, and only by the right of conquest" (105). The denial of legal and political recognition made evident through the story of Philip provides a form through which to narrate contemporary modes of settler jurisdiction and how non-native inhabitance is predicated on a continuance of the "works" of earlier examples of dispossession, despite the effort to "deny" it through discourses of concern and care (such as those that organize and legitimize the guardian system).

With respect to extant rhetorics surrounding white superintendence, the need to save Indians by removing them from the reach of civilization which supposedly threatens to overwhelm and engulf them, Apess suggests that behind such shows of beneficence lies another sentiment. He envisions an imagined statement by the president of the United States, who says, "We want your land for our use to speculate upon; it aids us in paying off our national debt and supporting us in Congress to drive you off." This invented monologue continues, "You see my red children, that our fathers carried on this scheme of getting your lands for our use, and we have now become rich and powerful; and we have a right to do with you just as we please" (135). To belong to the United States here entails being the children of "fathers" who stole Native lands and who have built their homes and families through that process of expropriation. Everything from the quotidian pleasures of the household to the national debt derives from "getting [Native] lands" and contributes to the unceasing goal of "driv[ing them] off." When viewed within a frame of reference centered on Philip, the ordinary "works" of U.S. citizenship, at all scales, come into view as acts of conquest. In this way, Philip serves as a template for marking the Indian problem as national, although less about how the U.S. nation can overcome Native presence than about the problem of failing to recognize Indigenous sovereignties—particularly in southern New England, on the "soil" for which Philip fought. As Apess indicates, "We often hear of the wars breaking out upon the frontiers, and it is because the same spirit reigns there that reigned here in New England; and wherever there are any Indians, that spirit still reigns; and at present, there is no law to stop it" (135). Philip provides a representative means for marking and making visible a "spirit" of conquest that animates everyday settler life and policy in the present, one which affects all "Indians." The repetition of the term "reign" links histories of theft and displacement in New England to actions on "the frontiers" while also troubling the apparent pastness of such struggles "here" (in New England, in the place of Apess's speech-making), further suggesting the need for a transformation of that spirit through "law."

Eulogy, then, subtly calls for modes of legal recognition in New England that could engage with Native peoples' patriotic investment in the *cause* of Indigenous nationhood, as separate from belonging to the United States. The shuttling among time periods mobilizes Metacom as a metonymic vehicle through which to give intelligible form to contemporary Native desires for geopolitical autonomy and self-determination. Apess asks, "What, then, shall we do? Shall we cease crying and say it is all wrong, or shall we bury the hatchet and those unjust laws and Plymouth Rock together and become friends?" (134). He later adds that he has "given historical facts, and an exposition in relation to ancient times, by which we have been enabled to discover the foundation which destroyed our common fathers in their struggle together" (136). He portrays King Philip's War as engendering mutual destruction for settlers and Natives, and he indicates that what would obviate the need for such "struggle," in New England and elsewhere, is removing the "unjust laws" that generate conditions of conflict. To "become friends," though, involves less a merging of interests or identifications, becoming part of a shared national "we," than an acknowledgment of ongoing separateness.[67] There are distinct patriotisms, causes, and lines of descent, and in sketching that distinction, the text employs the figure of Philip to dislodge Indigenous peoples in southern New England from their role as objects of benevolent superintendence and care within the imaginary of the guardian system. Apess works the *Metamora* effect of his own spectacular presence as a speaking/writing subject as a way of drawing attention to the long-term and ongoing colonial entanglements at play in southern New England—the land of Philip—while gesturing toward substantive legal acknowledgment of Indigenous sovereignty as a means of moving toward modes of relation not predicated on violence, deceit, and collective amnesia about the "soil" they all inhabit. Drawing on political idioms familiar to non-native readers—"nation," "patriot," "treaties," "king"—*Eulogy* seeks to give form to Native governance in ways that could move settlers toward recognition of both the existence of such polities and the violence of their ongoing erasure, particularly in New England.

However, in emphasizing Metacom's monarchical stature and the importance of intergenerational inheritance from fathers, Apess constructs a vision of patriarchal sovereignty that may be designed to speak to non-natives but that offers a skewed sense of Native governance, landedness, and relation for both the seventeenth and nineteenth centuries.[68] As discussed in the previous section, Native women played significant roles in governance on reservation in the nineteenth century (even if not officially recognized as such under state laws), as well as doing much of the everyday work of sustaining social relations both within and among reservations. Given that the economies of southern New England led to high rates of male itinerancy in search of wage work, women cultivated and sustained the ties to lands and persons through which peoples were maintained as such. In addition to keeping up kinship ties on state-recognized landbases, Native women often were central in nurturing and promoting webs of connection among tribes across the region through regular religious meetings and annual summer fairs that brought together persons (and relations) from various peoples in ways that worked to preserve a sense of southern New England as an Indigenous space, rather than a series of isolated "remnant" communities.[69] Notably, when speaking of the contemporary moment and its connection to the period in which Philip lived, Apess almost always uses the term "descendants" to refer to Native people(s), while he uses "fathers" to speak to settler legacies and connections across time. This subtle choice might speak to the ways the language of patriarchal leadership does not capture the dynamics of Native social life in the nineteenth century, including at Mashantucket. Yet, in choosing to signify Indigenous sovereignty and landedness through the figure of Philip, and the insistence on his rightful rule over a kingdom, *Eulogy* suggests that the principal way of figuring the geopolitics of Indigenous territoriality is through the alignment of the nation with the male head of state. As in the metonymic expression of feelings for the "cause" of U.S. independence through identification with Washington as the father of the nation, Apess's positioning of Philip in parallel suggests that he functions as the patriarch for the Native nation(s) for which contemporary descendants feel patriotic investment. Moreover, while "descendant" is gender neutral on its face, the term's meaning is influenced by the running references to those who bear ideas and lands transmitted from their settler "fathers," with such a discourse of inheritance itself implicitly gendered given the continuing force of coverture.[70] In many ways, then, Philip provides a way of signifying a kind of patriarchal authority that could constitute a political claim in contrast to the sense of Indians in southern New England as living in feminized enclaves, based on the demographic predominance of women, women's role in leading Native communities, and the legal articulation of Indian reservations as in a state of dependence on white male guardians.

Eulogy implicitly offers a vision of political life and structure as centered on a male executive exerting autonomous political authority over a clearly delimited landbase. As with Washington, Philip serves as a proxy for the nation-state model, in which the American Revolution provides the shape for conceptualizing a kind of Native nationalism that could be recognized as sovereignty-bearing by non-natives. This notion of political form resembles the institutional structure of Cherokee nationalism, as addressed in chapter 1, and like in the Cherokee case, Apess's account of Native governance implicitly disarticulates it from extant sociopolitical formations centered on women (as with the effacement of Cherokee clans and towns) while also displacing women's roles as political actors. In experimenting with ways to signify Native collectivities as polities, *Eulogy* de facto normalizes a heteropatriarchal understanding of what constitutes political identity and subjectivity, individually and collectively. As Leanne Simpson argues, "Heteropatriarchy is a foundational violence and dispossessing force used by the state, replicated by its citizens, and internalized often unwittingly and unknowingly by Indigenous peoples," and she further suggests the force of heteropatriarchy comes from its "direct attack on Indigenous bodies as political orders," including disqualifying women's bodies from serving as representative of Indigenous polities.[71]

Apess's use of this patriarchal imaginary challenges extant accounts of Indians in New England as feminized dependents, but it does so at the expense of an engagement with everyday networks of peoplehood, largely organized and maintained by Native women. In this vein, *Eulogy* enacts what Mishuana

Goeman describes as a process by which "family, clan, and intra and intertribal relationships were reformulated in ways readable to the state," creating forms of "self-disciplining" that occlude Native people's and peoples' "own stories" that might offer different kinds of mappings of peoplehood.[72] If we interpret *Eulogy* as strategically taking up tropes and topoi of sovereignty at play in non-native discourses, that process of rhetorical improvisation does not necessarily mean that we need to read Apess as ideologically committed to such forms (in a relation of *cruel optimism* to them), but, reciprocally, the absence of such investment does not mean that such figurations do not come with their own costs, with intellectual and political consequences for the shape peoplehood takes and for what can count as expressions of indigeneity and self-determination. The disjunction between the patriarchal political templates Apess employs and everyday modes of sociality and governance in southern New England, though, is less a matter of the wrongness or inauthenticity of his account than expressive of negotiations within the situated entanglements of colonial policy in the region, pressures that also bear on and affect the located possibilities for Native sovereignty. Marking this disjunction, then, helps highlight the multi-dimensional politics of such negotiations.

The stakes of Apess's portrayal of Philip and use of him as a means of figuring the contours and character of Native political identity/ies in southern New England can be brought into greater focus through a brief discussion of the significance of Weetamoo. Also known as Namumpum, she was the saunkskwa of Pocasset during the lead-up to what usually is termed King Philip's War. As Lisa Brooks observes in *Our Beloved Kin*, "saunkskwa" "was not simply the word for spouse," as it often was translated in English accounts, "but rather the word for female leader." As Brooks demonstrates, Weetamoo repeatedly was acknowledged prior to the war as having direct authority over Pocasset, by English officials as well as male Native leaders such as Massosoit (Metacom's father, often presented by the English as if he were the leader over all Wampanoag lands/peoples). Brooks illustrates how standard historical accounts of the period not only severely diminish Weetamoo's role in the geopolitical struggles leading up to the war, they collapse Native territorialities and interests into the figure of Philip in ways that facilitate the imposition of a settler framework onto Indigenous networks across New England and beyond: "Although historians have named this conflict 'King Philip's War,' it is better described as a multitribal Indigenous resistance movement during colonial expansion, a complex series of alliances forged by multiple leaders, including Metacom and Weetamoo, to reclaim land and rebalance relations in a shared Algonquian homeland." Such alliances across the Algonquian landscape depended on the maintenance of ties between peoples and territories, creating a complex geography of overlapping matrices of belonging, accountability, and enduring relation. Brooks observes, "Belonging entailed not only residency, but kinship to a particular place and people, of which the *sôgamo* (sagamore or sachem) or *sôgeskwa* (saunkskwa) was the symbolic leader," adding that leaders "were responsible for ensuring distribution of resources within their homelands, and between territories, through a well-established ceremonial and economic system of exchange" in what can be understood as "an Indigenous rhizomatic system of kinship," in contrast to the hierarchical scale structure of authority into which English authorities sought to insert Native polities—a singular Wampanoag kingdom with Philip at its apex.[73] Apess directly recycles this image in his description of Philip's gathering of forces to combat the English: "We find Philip as active as the wind, as dexterous as a giant, firm as the pillows of heaven, and fierce as a lion, a powerful foe to contend with indeed, and as swift as an eagle, gathering together his forces to prepare them for battle. And as it would swell our address too full to mention all the tribes in Philip's train of warriors, suffice it to say that from six to seven were with him at different times" (124). Philip appears as the sole moving force, as the one who is "gathering . . . forces" in response to English encroachments and interventions, and those forces are "his." Even though they belong to different "tribes," they enter the struggle as "Philip's" warriors. The potential distinctions among these peoples and the reasons and relations that shape their participation in the war disappear behind the iconic, epic figure of Philip as a king whose authority extends over "a powerful nation" (120)—one that somehow already encompasses these other "tribes."

This consolidation of Native political authority in the figure of Philip, who can then serve as metonymically representative of Indigenous nationhood in New England, operates within the terms of U.S. discourses and institutions of governance in ways that enable Apess to circulate a vision of Indigenous political autonomy that would signify as such to settler publics. Webs of kinship connection, such as clan and council-based modes of governance largely managed by women in the 1820s and 1830s, do not fit extant settler templates for what constitutes a political entity.[74] In seeking to shift non-native perceptions so as to move listeners/readers toward an acknowledgment of a present tense Native right to "possession of [the] soil" and to self-governance, *Eulogy* draws on and redeploys longstanding settler efforts to reconfigure Indigenous socialities to fit a heterogendered Euro-American framework. Since the mid-seventeenth century, non-natives had been seeking to reformulate Indigenous homemaking, family formation, and governance to fit Anglo models. While the heteronormative ideal of the nuclear family does not become ascendant in the United States until the nineteenth century, the understanding of Indigenous social formations as backward, perverse, confused, and monstrous serves as a running feature of non-native discourses and policy aims.[75] Intervention repeatedly is justified on the basis of needing to instruct Indians on the proper form of domestic life. As O'Brien suggests, "The English 'colonized the family' by mandating marriage form and regulating behavior within families, although throughout southeastern New England . . . Indians continued also to practice customary marriage and at times retained Native marriage rituals and ideals," and Ann Marie Plane observes, "Marriage itself became a metaphor; it spoke not about 'Indian practices' alone but about the entire relationship between the land, the colonizers, and the colonized."[76] While initially targeting behavior in the praying towns, those communities of Native converts to Christianity in seventeenth-century Massachusetts, the attempt to regulate Native family forms—and, through them, modes of land tenure and forms of political authority—extended to colonies intervening in the choice of leaders (based on questions of proper marriage, legitimacy, and lineal inheritance) and creating modes of proprietorship (in which belonging to a given legally recognized tribe, and even control over particular parcels of that tribe's landbase, becomes organized around heteronuclear family units).[77] In addition, since in the late eighteenth and nineteenth centuries legally acknowledged reservations often became sanctuaries for members of other peoples whose land was not so acknowledged (or had ceased to be), and Native women often married non-native men due to the absence of Native men on reservation (as a result of the need to travel for wage work), settler authorities often characterized reservations as having something of a mongrel population in need of racial and familial discipline. In 1849, the guardian for Mashantucket describes the reservation as "extremely hospitable to all vagabonds; receiving, without hesitation, all that come to them, whether white, mulatto, Indian or negro."[78] *Eulogy* implicitly responds to these patterns of official and popular representation—and the settler drive toward familial normalization—with the image of a singular male figure ruling over a well-established kingdom.

Ideologies of patriarchal possession provide the background for Apess's account of Native political identity.[79] Within extant settler networks, forms of social life that highlight reliance on others and that privilege matrices of care and reciprocity signify as feminized dependence, as contrasted with the kinds of self-possessed agency that supposedly qualify one to participate in political life as a full citizen. Thus, when Apess invokes notions of citizenship to characterize Native people(s), he is employing a deeply gendered figuration of personal independence, of patriarchal management, as the basis for self-possession and collective sovereignty.[80] The use of Philip as a surrogate for Native people-hood draws on his status as king/father to stage a vision of Indigenous nation-hood and political subjectivity at odds with the claim that Indians need settler care to survive, a claim offered as a means of legitimizing the forms of colonial regulation and rule that characterized the guardian system. In this way, Apess plays on the *Metamora* effect of his own embodied presence to open possi-bilities for marking prior and ongoing Native sovereignty, using the figure of Philip in an effort to shift non-native perceptions and expectations so as to enable a vision of Indigenous *nationality* (as well as indicating that the status of Native peoples and lands in New England should be a national concern of the United States, not a matter of states' policies). However, this set of maneuvers toward recognition also normalizes a patriarchal conception of politics as part of Apess's entangled engagement with non-native publics, a vision that itself was being imposed on Native communities and with which they continued to struggle in enacting their own internal modes of governance.

Nullification as Negative Space

Up until this point, I've addressed the ways that Apess offers a vision of Native political identity through the development of representative figures (such as himself and King Philip) who can provide metonymic form for conceptualiz-ing Indigenous geopolitics and governance in the absence of the kinds of sover-eignty recognized within the federal treaty system and in the context of some states' institutionalized ideology of benevolent care for vanishing populations. However, in *Indian Nullification of the Unconstitutional Laws of Massachusetts Relative to the Marshpee Tribe; or, The Pretended Riot Explained*, he engages more directly with the issue of political surrogation proper—the dynamics of being selected to speak for a collectivity. Here he presents himself as a represen-tative for the Mashpee in their struggle to be recognized as fully self-governing, to have the ability to exclude whites from claiming resources on their lands, to reclaim their meetinghouse, and to replace the local minister, Phineas Fish (who had been asserting a right to the meetinghouse as part of his ministry). The text itself, though, appears after the Massachusetts legislature acceded to Mashpee demands, at least in part, by formally eliminating the guardianship and making Mashpee into a state district (although still installing a commis-sioner, who formerly had served as an overseer to the tribe).[81] Even as Apess spoke publicly for the Mashpee during the period in which they were pursuing a change in their legal status, in ways the text addresses and to which I'll return shortly, *Indian Nullification* emerges in the wake of that political change. Thus, the text's aims in presenting these events have less to do with the Mashpee struggle per se than with the stakes of their efforts for conceptualizing and addressing the difficulties faced by Native peoples across southern New England. In this way, the Mashpee become an exemplary figure for portraying the political situation of a range of peoples in a similar structural position across the region. More than simply arguing for acknowledgment of Mashpee sovereignty, and by extension that of other peoples as well, Apess stages the difficulty of articulating Indigenous governance and territoriality in the absence of a public discourse through which to do so. *Indian Nullification* draws on a range of different framings through which to try to convey the significance of Mashpee landedness and political autonomy, including comparing their struggle to the Cherokee fight against removal, drawing on the language of enslavement, and invoking the American Revolution and the U.S. Constitution. In employing these multiple and potentially incommensurate frames, the text highlights the difficulty of finding a form that would enable substantive recognition of Indigenous peoplehood and self-determination within and by non-native publics. This very proliferation of approaches, though, has led to some critical efforts to read the text through what are taken as the ideological commitments that these frames supposedly indicate. Apess mobilizes a range of representational strategies in trying to craft an account of Indigenous sovereignty that would be intelligible to settler readers, and rather than treating one or some combination of them as indicative of his philosophical or political orientations, we can read the variability of *Indian Nullification*'s formulations as performatively responding to and illustrating the particular ways extant settler policy in New England works to foreclose Indigenous political orders—a set of difficulties for which the Mashpee serve as a convenient metonymic stand-in.

The question of how to understand the character of Mashpee collectivity appears at the outset and is addressed initially through their ability to select Apess as a spokesperson. A message addressed "To the White People of Massachusetts" begins the text, and it references Apess by describing him as "a brother of our own" who has been "sent" by "the Great Spirit" so "that he might show us all the secret contrivances of the pale faces to deceive and defraud us." They add that due to this activity, "many of our white brethren hate him, and revile him, and say all manner of evil of him, falsely calling him an imposter," and the signatories, presented as "three Selectmen of the Marshpee Tribe," insist that "we love our red brother, the Rev. William Apess, who preaches to us, and have all the confidence in him that we can put in any man."[82] Next is a letter from Benjamin F. Hallett, who is listed as "Counsel for the Marshpee Indians" and who also published a number of articles on the Mashpee case in the *Boston Daily*

Advocate (many of which are interlaced with Apess's commentary throughout *Indian Nullification*). In the letter, Hallett presents the Mashpee leader Daniel Amos as "the first one among them, who conceived the plan of freeing his tribe from slavery" before immediately turning to Apess and indicating, "They invited him to assist them in getting their liberty" (167). Apess's "Introduction" starts the text proper, in which he observes, "It is true that the author of this book is a member of the Marshpee tribe, not by birth but by adoption" (168). Having come to the area in May 1833 as a touring minister and preached to a group of whites in what was meant to be the Mashpee meetinghouse, Apess goes in search of his Native "brethren," "wishing to know more of their grievances, real or supposed," and after having been "requested to hear their whole story and to help them," Apess attends a council in which they explain the difficulties they have had with the state of Massachusetts and local whites. Apess notes, "After listening patiently to the tale of their distresses, I counseled them to apply for redress to the governor and Council. They answered that they had done so, but *had never been able to obtain a hearing*. The white agents had always thrown every obstacle in their way," and he responds that "though I was a stranger among them, I did not doubt but that I might do them some good and be instrumental in procuring the discharge of the overseers and an alternation of the existing laws," should they "give me a right to act in their behalf by adopting me" (173). Readers learn that while Apess cannot claim belonging to Mashpee by birth, he has been chosen by Mashpee people to dwell among them. Not only does that adoption bespeak the capacity of Native peoples to incorporate new members, suggesting that tribal identity remains irreducible to genealogies of reproductive relation, but the selection of Apess occurs in the context and in service of efforts to combat settler deception, fraud, and theft.

The text positions Apess's adoption as itself expressive of the existence of a political entity that can make judgments about membership and that seeks to bolster its ability to advocate for greater self-governance amid the stifling dynamics of non-native oversight. Apess's ability to serve as a representative for the Mashpee with settler publics rests on the existence of an organized Mashpee polity for which he could speak and by whom he could be chosen to do so. Apess reports that local whites keep saying to Mashpees, "'If you will only get rid of Apess, and drive him off the plantation, we will be your friends.' This has been their continued cry since I began to use my poor endeavors to get the Indians righted" (202). Earlier, Apess recounts that during a meeting in July 1833 with Josiah Fiske, a member of the governor's council who had been sent to investigate events in Mashpee, the sheriff of Barnstable County, J. Reed, "questioned him [Apess] as to his right to interfere. He replied that he had obtained it by the adoption of the tribe": "Mr. Reed, if I [Apess switches back and forth between first- and third-person references for himself] correctly understood him, answered that the Indians had no right to do such an act; no power to confer such a privilege. I replied that, if the plantation belonged to them, they undoubtedly had a right to give me leave to dwell upon" (184). These moments highlight the ways *Indian Nullification* weaves together Apess's voice as commentator/narrator, his presence at Mashpee and during the events in question as witness/advocate, and the authority of the Mashpee as a people who rightfully exercise sovereignty over their lands. The text insists that Native peoples' collective legally recognized relation to their lands extends to (other) matters of political authority, including their ability to represent themselves in whatever way they choose as well as their ability to decide who can count as members.[83] Apess further links animosity toward the Mashpee's chosen spokesperson with efforts to dictate the terms of relation between them and non-natives (on what conditions the latter will be "friends," rather than antagonists or enemies). More than simply seeking to justify his own actions, Apess uses his own public articulation to raise the issue of the relation between the terms of acceptable public (self-)presentation and speech for Native peoples and the kind of entity that they are taken to be in administrative, legal, and popular discourses.

Apess also underlines the ways that "white agents" and "existing laws" work to frustrate and foreclose the potential for such political self-articulation, and in this way, the "nullification" in the title refers just as much to the attempted effects of state policy on Native peoples in southern New England as to Mashpee response. The description of the events of the summer of 1833 as a "nullification," though, comes first from newspaper accounts. Locals describe Apess as "the leader of the Nullifiers at Mashpee going about the plantation in full command of all its disposable forest and treasure," and the *Philadelphia Inquirer* claims, "The Indians, inflamed by the appeals of Apes, are now ready for a nullification of all the state laws."[84] In May 1833, the Mashpee declared that they henceforth would govern themselves and would not allow further poaching of resources from their legally recognized reservation: "We as a tribe will rule ourselves, and have the right to do so: for all men are born free and equal, says the Constitution of the country"; "We will not permit any white man to come upon our plantation, to cut or carry off wood or hay, or any other article, without our permission, after the 1st of July next" (175). Created in 1665 by agreement with Wampanoag sachems as a village for Natives who had converted to Christianity, and officially confirmed by the Plymouth General Court in 1685, it had become over the years a refuge for a range of neighboring peoples who either were not acknowledged by the colony-cum-state of Massachusetts or who had lost their lands, due to settler machinations of theft and debt coupled with the civilizing malfeasance of officially appointed agents/ guardians.[85] Apess and Joe Amos, the Mashpee preacher, took the "petition and resolutions" of the Mashpees to the office of the governor in Boston, who recommended delivering them to the secretary of state, which they did, and at the end of June, a convention was organized among the Mashpees "for the purpose of organizing a new government" (178). A public statement was issued by "the National Assembly of the Marshpee Tribe" formally discharging, in Apess's terms, "all the officers appointed by the governor and Council, firmly believing that every one of the existing laws concerning the poor Israelites of Marshpee was founded on wrong and misconception," and July 1 was set as the date at which Mashpee self-governance and control over their landbase would commence (180). On July 4, two brothers, the Sampsons, sought to take away wood from Mashpee land, and they were stopped by Apess and others and asked to unload what they had taken. Apess was arrested for riot and trespass and released on bail, and the governor sent Fiske to investigate/negotiate.

Non-natives' characterization of these actions as "nullification" suggests Indigenous refusal of the existing legal order, but such depiction begs the question of the political status of the agent engaging in such refusal, an issue to which the text devotes a good bit of attention. The use of the term "nullification" hearkens back to resolutions by Virginia and Kentucky in 1798 in the wake of the federal government's passage of the Alien and Sedition Acts, and more recently, it had emerged in the 1832 controversy around whether South Carolina would refuse to obey federal tariff laws.[86] In these instances, though, the prospective nullifier is a state (or states) of the union, acting in ways that may be understood as contrary to federal law or even as unconstitutional but still extending from what otherwise is a legally and politically recognized base of sovereignty. For Apess, though, part of the challenge lies in casting the Mashpee, and other peoples in southern New England, as collective political subjects who rightfully can enact policy. Taking up the term "nullification" itself does part of such work, since it broadly gestures toward a parallel between the Mashpee and the states engaged in practices for which the term was used. However, as a conceptual and administrative framework, guardianship denies the potential for Native people(s) to be fully self-governing, insisting on the need to regulate them for their own welfare. As Donald Nielson notes in his discussion of the situation in Mashpee in the 1830s, the Massachusetts judiciary in 1816, in the case of *Andover v. Canton*, declared that Indians are the "unfortunate children of the public, entitled to protection and support" although "incapable of civilization."[87] In order for the Mashpee to be able to speak for themselves as a political entity, including in rejecting the laws that govern them, there needs to be a public mode of figuration through which they could appear as such an entity. *Indian Nullification*, then, engages in a process of developing such a language, and one of the principal ways it does so, or by which it seeks to clear conceptual and rhetorical space for doing so, is by tracing how extant forms of Indian policy in New England can be understood as less a recognition of Native presence than a negation of Native governance.

Part of the text's strategy lies in illustrating how states, in this case Massachusetts, actively had worked to *nullify* Indigenous sovereignty, to portray Natives as unable to represent themselves and, thus, as needing non-natives to serve as their benefactors. As Konkle suggests, "Apess indicates the political limbo in which the Mashpees found themselves," and Adam Dahl argues that *Indian Nullification* "exposed [the] paternalist principles of the guardianship system as a means of land appropriation and eliminating native conceptions of political peoplehood."[88] More than simply indicating the ill management of the guardian system, including proliferating forms of graft and the routine expropriation of Indigenous resources, Apess explores how existing policy depends on a colonial metalepsis—the confusion of an effect for a cause. Responding to a piece published in the *Barnstable Journal*, reproduced in the text, Apess observes, "The writer here says that the Indians are vile and degraded, and admits that they can be improved. He gives no explanation of the causes of their degradation. If the reader will take the trouble to examine the laws regarding the Marshpees, he will see those causes of the inevitable and melancholy effect and ... will come to the conclusion that any people living under them must necessarily be degraded" (200). If the *degradation* of Native communities serves as the justification for exerting oversight in order to *improve* them, the very legal mechanisms put in place ostensibly to ameliorate such conditions are, in fact, the cause of them. The citation of Native immiseration provides the basis for a regime of putatively benevolent care, but that regime itself produces the conditions it ostensibly aims to address. Moreover, this dynamic has nothing to do with the particular character of the Mashpee or of Indians per se. Instead, it creates the circumstances that get treated as signs of a racialized character—circumstances that would engender similar effects on "any people living" within them. Apess further argues, "The laws were calculated to drive the tribes from their possessions and annihilate them as a people; and I presume they would work the same effect upon any other people," adding the "sorrowful truth" that "heretofore, all legislation regarding the affairs of Indians has had a direct tendency to degrade them, to drive them from their homes, and the graves of their fathers, and to give their lands as a spoil to the general government, or to the several states" (212–213). The text suggests that the laws of the state of Massachusetts illustrate a broader tendency at play in Indian policy as such everywhere in the United States, namely the construction of a situation of apparently apolitical desperation that facilitates the seizure of Indigenous territories and the legal disavowal and material disintegration of Native forms of governance.

More than asserting a particular kind of political subjectivity in whose name Apess or other Mashpees could speak, then, Apess traces the process by which Indigenous peoples in New England come to be figured as lacking any recognizable political identity. One can understand this approach as a response to the employment of the notion of anomaly as a way of characterizing the status of tribes in Massachusetts. This tendency is amply on display in official reports for the state on Indian affairs in both 1849 and 1861, which reflect longstanding patterns in public and political discourse. In the former, the authors of the report, F. W. Bird, Whiting Griswold, and Cyrus Weekes, describe Native peoples in the state as "scattered and poor remains of tribes, who were once numerous and powerful occupants of our hills," noting that "the government of the Commonwealth" has a duty "to preserve their existence . . . and improve their condition." The ongoing history of colonization that generates such dislocations, though, appears as if it were a quality of unresolvedness somehow borne by the tribes themselves. They hold "anomalous meetings" that cannot rightly be described as "municipal"; they live under a "legal condition . . . so anomalous, and so imperfectly defined, that we believe no attempt has ever been made to enforce municipal regulations"; and their legal situation is "singularly anomalous" or "peculiar."[89] If notions of Indigenous sovereignty and self-determination ill fit the terms of law and policy in Massachusetts, the imposition of the latter onto the former does not make Indigenous governance or existence "anomalous." Or, rather, to depict that incommensurability as an *anomaly* or *peculiarity* involves taking the frame of state law as a given from which to assess disruptive Indian presence as an oddity, interpreting it against a normalized background of settler occupation—in which such presence comes into view as incomprehensible aberration.

Similarly, in his 1861 report, John Milton Earle adopts a tone of incredulity when speaking of Indigenous geopolitical formations.[90] With respect to the Gay Head Indians (who call themselves Aquinnah), Earle notes that the existence of the tribe is "remarkable," "by which a community residing in the State, and nominally of the State, and subject to its laws, is yet a sort of *imperium in imperio*, not governed by the laws to which it is nominally subject, but having its own independent law, by which all its internal affairs are regulated." He later notes with respect to the tribes who continue to have state-acknowledged reservations (or "plantations"), "Here are five communities within the State, but not of it, subject to its laws, but having no part in their enactment; within the limits of local municipalities, yet not subject to their jurisdiction; and holding real estate in their own right, yet not suffered to dispose of it, except to each other."[91] These statements suggest that the paradoxes reported—tribes being *in* the state but not *of* it—remain incomprehensible and, thus, politically unsustainable. For Earle, the only thing that enables this precarious situation to continue is state-enacted guardianship: "Had the State omitted its guardianship of the Indians, their property would have been squandered, they would have commingled with the other population of the country, pauperism among them would have greatly increased."[92] As opposed to producing the series of supposed contradictions Earle notes through the illegitimate extension of jurisdiction over Indigenous peoples and their lands, the state saves Indians from utter decimation by maintaining a system of care that extends an otherwise incoherent set of not quite or not fully political arrangements.

The pervasiveness of this way of conceptualizing and articulating Indian affairs puts Apess in the position of needing both to clear away such obfuscating formulations and to develop ways of naming Mashpee presence that could signify as the basis for collective political claims and speech. We might describe this dynamic as a dialectics of refusal and recognition, in which the former seeks to reorganize the terms on which the latter might occur—especially through reorienting dominant frames in ways that might mobilize non-native publics to push for policy changes to what currently functions as Indian law in a given context. *Indian Nullification*, then, engages in the project of, in Turner's terms quoted earlier, "unpacking and laying bare the meaning and effects of colonialism" so as to "open up the physical and intellectual space" for a new mode of engagement with the state. Apess argues that from the seventeenth century to the present "the conduct of the whites toward the Indians has been one continued system of robbery" (214), and he further observes that "it seems to have been usually the object to seat the Indians between two stools, in order that they might fall to the ground, by breaking up their government and forms of society, without giving them any others in their place" (230). The text decries such systemic and sustained theft and the associated strategy of categorizing tribes through figurations of absence and aberration in ways that facilitate the dismantling of their sociopolitical formations, by treating Indigenous peoples as lacking any such regularities. This work of negation, though, does not obviously translate into a means of positively signifying Indigenous principles and practices of governance and territoriality. If Indians are placed "between two stools" so that "they might fall," what remains unclear is how to present them as active political subjects in ways that could resonate with settler publics and, thereby, could put pressure on Massachusetts and other states in New England to alter the terms of Indian policy.

Positioning the Mashpee in metonymic relation to other peoples in the region, as an exemplary instance of more widely applicable structural constraints and possibilities, Apess experiments with ways of capturing Mashpee needs and aims, but that experimentation less suggests a particular set of ideological commitments than illustrates the difficulties of navigating the entangled contradictions produced by settler colonialism. In multiplying potential ways of indexing and legally registering the continued presence of Native people and peoples, the text implicitly indicates how such colonial entanglements have created modes of political density that are registered in this proliferation of forms. In other words, rather than there being a Mashpee polity that has a consistent form that the state of Massachusetts simply has failed to acknowledge, the imposition of particular kinds of recognition through extant Indian policy affects the organization of Indigenous modes of governance, placemaking, and self-articulation, even as those modes do not simply extend the terms or frameworks offered by the state. The accretion of ways of characterizing Mashpee political existence and claims across *Indian Nullification*, then, can be understood as both strategic—seeking to deploy a range of potential forms in the hope that one or more will catch with settler publics in desirable ways—and symptomatic—registering the rendering of Native peoples in New England as legal/political anomaly and the insertion of them into a colonial matrix in which the dynamics of collective self-articulation as well as ordinary world-making are mediated by settler frames, interests, and imperatives.

Apess invokes the Cherokee Nation and its struggle against Georgia and removal in order to recast the terms through which non-natives narrate Native presence in New England. This approach most rhymes with current scholarly formulations of Indigenous sovereignty and nationhood. As discussed in chapter 1, the Cherokees served as a prominent example of Indigenous peoplehood in the period, and the constitutionalization of Cherokee governance and their modes of fighting against Jacksonian-era federal formulations of Indian policy continues to function in somewhat paradigmatic ways in current criticism and historiography.[93] This image of Native nationhood—treaty-recognized, centralized in an institutional apparatus, extending jurisdiction over a clearly delimited citizenry and landbase not shared with other peoples—offers a dominant template for what Native sovereignty is and how it functions as distinct/disjunct from settler management.[94] Although Cherokee nationality involved internal tensions, negotiations, and struggles over its form and legitimacy (in ways analyzed in the previous chapter), the Cherokees provide a powerful and familiar touchstone for *Indian Nullification*'s efforts to congeal a version of Native self-governance intelligible as such to non-natives.

While most of the references to the Cherokees in the text are in material quoted by Apess, his choice and positive endorsement of them indicates his mobilization of these other writers' arguments. The first such mention comes in Apess's citation of a Mashpee petition from May 1833 to the Massachusetts government. In it, they note, "Perhaps you have heard of the oppression of the Cherokees and lamented over them much, and thought the Georgians were hard and cruel creatures," and they ask them, "Did you ever hear of the poor, oppressed and degraded Marshpee Indians in Massachusetts, and lament over them?" This question sets up the assertion, "We will rule over our own tribe" (177).[95] Positioning popular *lamentations* over the *oppression* of the Cherokee people as the background enables the solicitation of sympathy for the Mashpee, who are presented as analogous in ways that also underline their claims to self-rule and the violence of its running foreclosure by the state. Another quote from a Mashpee petition from December 1833 extends this line of thought. Noting the "sympathy for the red men of the Cherokee Nation" expressed by "the white men of Massachusetts," the petition insists, "as it is contended in this State, that our red brethren, the Cherokees, should be an independent people, having the privileges of the white men; we, the red men of the Marshpee tribe, consider it a favorable time to speak" (205). Such public non-native feeling bespeaks a commitment to Cherokee independence, one that opens the potential for engaging political speech by the Mashpee—or by their representative in Apess—that articulates a similar position or desire in relation to Massachusetts (as well as the states in New England more broadly). Less an argument about the structural similarity of the Mashpee and Cherokee situations than an appeal to attach to the former the kinds of sentiments at play with regard to the latter, such calls for popular "lament" and "sympathy" are echoed in the *Boston Daily Advocate* articles by Hallett that Apess cites. Hallett calls on "the honor of the State" and reminds readers of their "bitterness against Georgian violence" (192). He also critiques the "exercise of philanthropy" elsewhere and its poverty "*at home*" (201). While an implicit logical connection underlies this link between the Cherokee Nation and the Mashpee tribe, the exact character of that connection matters less here than the effort to highlight what is presented as an affective incongruity: why do you care about those people (or that people) and not these ones (or this one)? To be unconcerned about the oppression of the Mashpee makes you a hypocrite. Apess's rhetorical gambit in this comparison, then, lies not so much in articulating a particular version of sovereignty as a political framework or norm as in trying to generate the conditions and momentum for Native peoples in New England to circulate widely in nongovernmental networks as bearers of settler sympathy, gambling that such mass identification can engender meaningful forms of legal recognition (whose horizon is Native self-rule but whose precise desired content and contours remain a bit elliptical).[96]

Reciprocally, in employing slavery and the American Revolution as ways of figuring how to understand Mashpee and other Native peoples' struggles, *Indian Nullification* mediates the significance attached to these topics for New England publics, seeking to plug into their affective intensity and reach. At one point, Apess asserts, "We Marshpees account all who opposed our freedom, as Tories, hostile to the Constitution and liberties of the country" (204), and he later states even more forcefully, "I ask the inhabitants of New England generally how their fathers bore laws much less oppressive, when imposed upon them by a foreign government" (211). These allusions to the Revolution, though, point in opposite directions: the first suggests that non-natives are Tories for denying Mashpees the "freedom" promised in the founding of the "country" and the adoption of its "Constitution"; whereas the second, in what might be read as a rehearsal of the rhetorical structure later used in *Eulogy on King Philip*, presents Massachusetts as a "foreign government" denying the rightful political autonomy of Native peoples.[97] These torsions demonstrate the difficulty of trying to signify Indigenous presence, territoriality, and governance—of whatever form—within extant settler processes of political meaning-making, as well as the layered relations of Native peoples to the war for independence and American nationality.[98] Some have interpreted these and similar moments, though, as expressions of Apess's normative commitment to U.S. belonging. David Carlson argues that Apess portrays the Mashpee's struggle "from a perspective that stresses the embeddedness of Indian *individuals* within the legal ideology of the American state," and John Kucich suggests that "Apess acknowledges the legitimacy of the state's power and hence claims a voice within it."[99] This approach treats the modes of representation at play in *Indian Nullification* as transparently referential, as reflective of an investment in dominant frames that the text takes up rather than as a means of mediating those frames so as to coalesce possibilities for collective Native political speech and subjectivity that could function as such while galvanizing non-native support and action. That process generates a series of ideological, conceptual, and rhetorical difficulties, tensions, and contradictions that point to the intellectual labor at play in seeking to negate/refuse/deconstruct institutionalized settler modes of negation.

The text's running description of the Mashpee as enslaved also draws on extant popular investments, palimpsestically constructing a sense of legal and political crisis that licenses Apess's representative appeal and that aims to motivate non-native action. While certainly not a universally held set of commitments in New England, abolition provided a public vocabulary and modes of affective address through which to reorient white understandings of Indian affairs, heightening impressions of existing policy as an immoral system of extraction. In addition to referring to guardians as "masters," the text speaks of Native people(s) as being "held in . . . servitude" and "used . . . more like dogs than human beings," as being sold "for slaves," and as being "enslaved by the laws of Massachusetts."[100] To speak of the Mashpee in these ways is not so much to produce a precise analogy, to suggest a parallel to formal legal enchattelment, as to put the figure of freedom in play as a concept—a template—through which to mark what Mashpees have been denied. Enslavement entails the absence of recognizable political presence, the negation of any possibility of institutionally sanctioned engagement in the system by which one is governed. Conversely, freedom suggests the absence of the modes of domination currently imposed on Native peoples, including their ability to exercise authority over their landbases. Apess charges the "controllers of public affairs" with "holding the rightful lords of the soil in bondage" (205), presenting enslavement as a way of characterizing the forces that prevent Mashpees from collectively governing their territory in the manner they see fit.[101] In mobilizing slavery as a trope for state-sanctioned racialized violence, the text mediates abolitionist sentiment to call forth outrage at the treatment of Mashpees and other Indigenous peoples, but the trajectory of this appeal is not toward expanded participation for Mashpees as regular U.S. citizen-subjects. With respect to the role of abolitionism in Apess's oeuvre, Andy Doolen suggests that "William Lloyd Garrison and a defiant abolitionism offered him a useful model for attacking the racial prejudice that underpinned the state's oppression of nonwhites and the period's racist ideology of white nationalism," further observing that abolitionism "served as a model of political resistance for Apess."[102] Such modeling leads Doolen to characterize Apess, including in *Indian Nullification*, as arguing for U.S. citizenship and "for extending civil liberties" to Native people, such that the Mashpee struggle can be understood as one for "civil rights."[103] This critical framing, though, leaves aside the running emphasis on Mashpee self-governance as an Indigenous polity (including in the ways the text insists on Apess's legitimacy as a spokesperson chosen by the Mashpee), marks state interference in and disavowal of such processes, and calls on the Cherokee example as a prism through which non-natives can understand the stakes of state Indian policy and Mashpee resistance to it. Moreover, the Mashpee and other legally recognized peoples throughout New England actively refused citizenship, indicating that they saw it as a threat to their ability to remain politically distinct entities on their own separate landbases.[104]

In this way, the kinds of political metaphors *Indian Nullification* employs do not necessarily add up to a clear picture of the vision of sovereignty sought by Mashpee people, since the text draws on those metaphors while reorienting them in order to mark and contest the dynamics of state negation. If Apess serves as a surrogate for Mashpee political collectivity, that process of public engagement takes shape against the background of the need to find ways of portraying Mashpee political subjectivity that could register for non-native publics. Prior to Apess's presence among them, though, the Mashpee had been protesting Indian policy in Massachusetts and the actions of the guardians throughout the late eighteenth and early nineteenth centuries. As Mandell observes, "The Mashpee revolt shows continuity rather than change, for its proponents were the children and grandchildren of those who had fought against [Gideon] Hawley and the guardianship, and their goals remained the same."[105] Moreover, as indicated in a statement from the Mashpee council included in *Indian Nullification*, "Our dissatisfaction with the laws and the Overseers was the same as it is now, long before Mr. Apes came among us" (218). Apess's formulations, then, should be cast neither as direct expressions of Mashpee self-understandings nor as an importation of Apess's own ideological leanings into his discussion of the Mashpee case. Rather, *Indian Nullification* stages and engages the difficulty of finding a language for advocacy when negotiating settler networks in which Native political presence is denied outright (cast as collections of vulnerable bodies in need of protection from themselves and others) or is characterized as an unsustainable anomaly. However, Mashpee governance also is not identical across this period. In an 1827 report to the legislature, a committee on Indian affairs in the state notes, "Unable to resolve the disputes with the overseers, the tribal leaders had taken it upon themselves to ignore the trustees and had evolved their own system of tribal management," and in the wake of the formal end of the guardianship in 1834, women ceased to play an official role in Mashpee political institutions, not holding district offices and not voting in local elections.[106] Apess negates existing state frameworks for Indian policy while illustrating the challenges of articulating a positive form for Native political subjectivity amid the conditions created by those frameworks. While the text cannot be treated as simply an extension of Mashpee sociopolitical formations, the tensions present in the text's efforts to navigate settler discourses resonate with the extratextual negotiations over the political form of Mashpee governance, their efforts to navigate the configurations of settler rule that the text chronicles.

Indian Nullification underlines the complications entailed in generating and sustaining, in Latour's terms, felicity conditions through which Indigenous self-governance can be represented as such within and to settler institutions, implicitly casting the Mashpee as exemplary of the challenges that attend this effort to rework settler frameworks across southern New England.[107] Unlike in the case of the Cherokees, in which treaty relations and the attendant legal conception of Indian nationhood provided a form through which to convey and enact Indigenous political identity, Native peoples in Massachusetts, Connecticut, and Rhode Island did not have such a ready template. Even as the institutionalization of nationhood among the Cherokees prevented neither removal nor internal disagreement, it provided a vehicle for engaging with and contesting U.S. policy. As I've argued, the institutional structure of Cherokee nationhood was overdetermined by elite interests and discourses, and while the arguments made by Elias Boudinot and others in the Treaty Party also were elite in character, they were not consistent with the institutional dynamics and modes for legitimizing Cherokee nationhood. The struggles around removal, among Cherokees and with the U.S. government, though, occurred through nationhood as a political *form*. However, in light of the workings of the guardian system and the refusal of states to accept federal jurisdiction over Indian affairs within what they claimed as their borders, this form was not available for use by Native people(s) in New England. Or, put more precisely, nationhood as a particular kind of institutional and discursive form was not intelligible within extant official and popular formulations of Indianness in the region. In order to engage non-natives as part of efforts to contest the terms and effects of the guardian system, Indigenous intellectuals needed to find ways of portraying Native political collectivity and subjectivity such that they could be heard as making claims in the name of polities, rather than as seeking better state-supported care as remnant populations at the mercy of non-native largesse. Apess's writings illustrate the difficulty of and intellectual labor involved in recalibrating how Indigenous peoples enter into settler networks.

Across his texts, he employs metonymic modes of figuration in order to give legible shape to Indigenous identity, governance, and territoriality. In order to do so, he does not so much define what counts as sovereignty, or directly argue for it, as position persons and entities in the foreground that bring with them a background sense of Native geopolitical separateness. In *A Son of the Forest*, Apess's own connection to the Mashantucket reservation and his Pequot relatives—his experiences in the flesh—keep returning as a way of understanding what lies behind the events and commitments in his life that appear to be of greater concern, specifically his conversion and emergence as a preacher. *Eulogy on King Philip* makes Metacom into a vehicle through which to convey Indigenous patriotic commitment to polities that are not the United States, playing on how Apess would have been read as something of a *Metamora* stand-in in ways that redirect attention toward the ongoingness of Native refusals of American belonging. With *Indian Nullification*, he offers his most directly policy-engaged account of Native pasts and presents, mobilizing multiple frames for figuring Mashpee autonomy so as to convey the violence of guardianship and its negation of Native collective agency and self-governance. These examples suggest less a politicizing evolution over time than the range of strategies potentially employed to signify Indigenous presence such that relations with Native peoples could be understood as a matter of political engagement, rather than benevolence or racialized exceptionalism in the face of a legal anomaly. In *Indian Nullification*, Apess does serve as an explicit proxy for the Mashpee, but even there, the emphasis is less on his ability to convey Mashpee complaints, ideas, and interests than on the question of what kind of entity Mashpee is such that he could serve as a spokesperson for them. Within Apess's work, representativity more often involves finding a type that can index Indigenous political existence and its (shifting) contours, centralizing a figure that works to reorient settler expectations and frames of reference. That process entails creating a vehicle through which to generate a sense of Native political orders and to circulate that sense through non-native networks in a way that aims to shift how they operate.[108]

The exigencies of population growth and land seizure in New England produce the need for such translational work, but the transposition of Native sociopolitical formations into formats that could speak to non-native publics also creates displacements that, in particular, have gendered effects. Pressures on Indigenous landbases in the late eighteenth through the mid-nineteenth century in southern New England were immense, largely because of the increasing number of people living in the region due to both natural increase and immigration. Seeking to find ways of persuading non-natives to cease, or even substantively curb, their incursions into Native territories was an urgent concern for Native intellectuals, since the continued existence of the reserved lands was at stake. In engaging this challenge, though, Apess predominantly employs masculinist means of figuring Indigenous political identity, for example foregrounding his own experience of itinerancy and emergence as a preacher and images of sovereign monarchical power with respect to King Philip. While mediating non-native conceptions of what constitutes a polity, Apess's writings generally mobilize dominant heteropatriarchal formulations of public being and political structure in order to gain more expansive recognition of Native socialities and geographies that is not predicated on casting them as vestigial. Except in a few notable instances, such as the depiction of Aunt Sally George in *A Son of the Forest*, his texts either do not substantively engage Native women's presence or cast them as objects of settler maltreatment, as in the case of his maternal grandmother.[109] The networks of kinship, association, care, and governance formed by Native women within and among peoples, from the seventeenth-century setting of *Eulogy* to the present of his writing, receive only peripheral mention, even as those traces point toward crucial dynamics of Indigenous survivance, decision-making, alliance, land use, and self-determination. Apess's experimentation with how to signify something like sovereignty (or a kind of separateness we might mark through the figure of sovereignty) illustrates the difficulties of laboring in the absence of meaningful political recognition, the complexities Native intellectuals navigate in their efforts to engage and redress the colonial expropriations facilitated by that absence, and the (particularly gendered) implications of choosing specific modes and political forms through which to mediate settler entanglements.

3. AMONG GHOST DANCES

Sarah Winnemucca and the Production of Paiute Identity

In the late 1860s and the late 1880s, Ghost Dance movements emerged out of and extended across the Great Basin and into California, the Columbia Plateau, down to the Colorado River, and onto the Plains, emanating from visions of Native regeneration dreamed by Northern Paiute men (Wodziwob of the Walker River Reservation and Wovoka of the Yerington band).[1] The most famous and well documented such prophet movements in the late nineteenth century—the Ghost Dances of 1870 and 1890, as they have come to be known—can be understood, though, as not solely the result of ideologies or principles that derive from a single prophet figure but as part and parcel of a broader set of sociospiritual dynamics that were prevalent throughout the region during the entire period and that were of a piece with a range of other prophet-led movements that preceded and were concurrent with those that come to be labeled as a "Ghost Dance." As Gregory Smoak suggests, "The Ghost Dances were an appeal to spiritual power to overturn a world that was not of their making," but he continues, "The Ghost Dances were not two discrete movements but rather two periods of intense excitement in a continuing pattern of religious practice that stretched throughout the nineteenth century and survives to this day."[2] Yet, in Sarah Winnemucca's *Life among the Piutes* (1883), she does not discuss these movements at all. Not only is this omission quite notable given that the text addresses Northern Paiute politics and history reaching from the 1840s to the 1880s, which includes the widespread response to Wodziwob's visions starting in 1869, but two of the central people in the text were known to be shamans and to have participated in prophet movements (Winnemucca's father and Oytes, both of whom appear as important leaders in the narrative). What's at stake in the text's avoidance of the Ghost Dance and other spiritual formations? How does looking to such movements provide an alternative frame from which to approach the text's account of Paiute identity, governance, and landedness and to interpret the form Paiute peoplehood takes in Winnemucca's narrative?[3]

In the narrative and in her public presentations, Winnemucca consistently presents herself as speaking for the Paiutes, as representing them and their interests to white publics and government officials.[4] While Elias Boudinot claimed to speak in the name of a political entity already recognized by the U.S. government and William Apess sought to generate forms of collective subjectivity in the absence of such recognition, Winnemucca can be understood as drawing on the templates circulated in Indian policy in order to create something of a simulacrum of nationhood for which she could serve as the representative in ways that would enable her campaign of public advocacy. Many scholars have noted that Winnemucca draws on strategies of presentation that would be familiar to white readers in order to promote the interests of the Paiute people.[5] What precisely, though, is the entity in whose name or in whose stead Winnemucca is said to speak?[6] The sense of such a cohesive political entity might instead be understood as an *effect* of the narrative's dynamics, such as portraying the Paiutes as having a principal chief and occupying a clearly delineated landbase. These rhetorical strategies draw on the terms of existing federal Indian policy, including as it had unevenly been applied in the Great Basin. In this way, Winnemucca's claims to representativity can be interpreted less as a relation of surrogation for or delegation from an already existing entity—call it the Paiute people, tribe, or nation—than as a relay within the circuits of policy and practice generated by settler governance. In contrast to Winnemucca's claims to speak for a unified Paiute polity/public, Ghost Dance movements highlight the ways forms of Indigenous peoplehood in the Great Basin in the late nineteenth century did not fit the terms of Indian policy, organized as it was around notions of clearly delineated tribes with discretely demarcated landbases. As Malea Powell argues, "What Winnemucca left out of *Life Among the Piutes* was as important as what she put in," and *Life* can be seen "as more of an extended pamphlet about the claims of the Northern Paiutes than the 'truth' of Winnemucca's life" or, by extension, that of a singular Paiute people.[7] Attending to what *Life* left out, specifically its efforts to avoid and to speak around the sociopolitical implications of the Ghost Dance, emphasizes the constructedness of the account of cohesive Paiute identity that the text offers.[8]

This way of approaching Winnemucca's narrative highlights the difficulties at play in reading the relation between the text's account of Native peoplehood and extratextual Indigenous sociopolitical formations. If Winnemucca can only come into non-native public view as an authorized speaker in her claim to serve as a spokesperson for *the* Paiute people, treated as a singular entity, that depiction of herself enacts a version of Paiute tribal identity that normalizes the terms of settler policy as the basis through which to understand Native peoplehood. Returning to Gayatri Spivak's cautions about sliding two senses of representation into each other, the difference "between a proxy and a portrait," we can see how Winnemucca's positioning of herself as a proxy for what she terms the "Piute nation" depends on a particular way of portraying the geopolitical dynamics at play in the Great Basin—one that effaces the modes of leadership, association, and placemaking out of which Ghost Dance movements emerge and to which they contribute.[9] Approaching her invocation of "the Piute nation" in *Life* as merely referential, as an existing political entity that the text simply cites, ends up obscuring the work Winnemucca's text performs and the politics of the discursive and institutional context in which it does so. She offers a particular staging of Paiute collectivity in order to be able to interface with non-native frameworks (conceptual and political). In doing so, she takes up the terms of federal policy in order to challenge how they have been implemented and to persuade non-native publics of the need for different policy outcomes, enacting what I have referred to as a dialectics of refusal and recognition.

Boudinot and Apess in different ways raise the question of how to represent a people, with regard to who counts as a spokesperson and the ways such representative speech/writing draws on and (re)circulates a particular vision (or set of visions) for how peoplehood works and is internally organized. In both cases, though, the Indigenous polities they invoke clearly exist outside of their discourse—the Cherokee Nation and the Mashantucket and Mashpee tribes. The "Piute nation," though, does not really reference an existing entity. Federal officials had tried to act as if such an entity were present, particularly through the portrayal of Winnemucca's father as the principal chief who could exert authority over all Northern Paiute people in their dispersed, shifting, and flexible bands and family territories. Winnemucca picks up on this project of settler administration and uses it as an organizing structure for her narration of Paiute history, interests, and policy needs. Rather than suggesting that *Life among the Piutes* offers a false account of Indigenous sociopolitical formations across the Great Basin, instead we can explore the text's ways of mediating settler frameworks. In particular, Winnemucca's narrative draws attention to how forms of Indigenous collectivity can be generated through acts of figuration, through efforts to speak in the name of an entity that does not (yet) exist as such. Attending to the intellectual labor of that process highlights the work of generating Indigenous political forms, not solely in terms of describing or reflecting what already is but as the potential to constitute new (kinds of) polities, especially in the midst of ongoing and changing colonial conditions.[10]

Yet, such imagination and invention, even when mobilized in campaigns of advocacy (as Winnemucca does), can efface other formations and networks that do not conform to this vision and that are organized around contrary principles. As discussed in the introduction, the need to constitute an "Indian tribe" in ways that will make Native sociality, territoriality, and governance intelligible as such to the U.S. government often involves reshaping processes of self-identification, placemaking, decision-making, and resource distribution in ways that can generate significant tensions among a people and can threaten the loss of sociopolitical formations, associations, and networks previously understood as vital (such as in the constitutionalization of liberal governance among the Cherokees, as discussed in chapter 1).[11] The narrative distinguishes between the apparent coherence (territorial and political) of the "Piute nation" and the wanderings of other peoples, cast as dangerous to U.S. interests or policy frames—such as the "Columbia River Indians" and the "Bannocks." In this way, Winnemucca reiterates the longstanding association of Native movement with danger and disorder. As Mishuana Goeman suggests, "Rather than construct a healthy relationship to land and place, colonial spatial structures inhibit it by constricting Native mobilities and pathologizing mobile Native bodies."[12] To be outside of the boundaries of legally delimited Indian territory is to be understood as a threat to non-native social, political, and economic formations. This dynamic extends beyond the reservation era of the nineteenth century into the present moment. For example, Nick Estes observes, "'Off the reservation' is an American English idiom that took on murderous meaning with the creation of Indian reservations," adding, "The expression is also current in military and political spheres to describe someone who defies orders, who is unpredictable and therefore ungovernable. Those who 'go off the reservation' are rogues or mavericks in military jargon—the ones who 'cross the wire' of military bases (called 'reservations') or enter hostile territory (called 'Indian Country')."[13] In creating a tribal entity that can serve as a subject for advocacy, Winnemucca engages with this set of settler narratives, seeking to manage and navigate non-native assumptions about Indianness as a mode of barbarous mobility. Tracking the absence of the Ghost Dance in *Life among the Piutes* provides a means of registering the scope, character, and stakes of Winnemucca's construction of a singular Paiute collectivity as well as the possibilities that such an account potentially overwrites.

If one does not assume the existence of a singular political body for which Winnemucca speaks, her speech can be understood as actively working to generate a sense of cohesive Northern Paiute collectivity. Rather than treating the identity of the Paiute tribe, nation, or people as an a priori fact that serves as the background against which we interpret and assess Winnemucca's text, what happens if we approach the narrative as a mediator—as engaged in a process of networking in which the text helps (re)produce the sense of Paiute identity that it cites?[14] From one perspective, Winnemucca's presentation of Paiute identity might be understood as a bid for recognition that reifies the terms of Indian policy, at the expense of the kinds of less rigidly delineated and more porous conceptions of peoplehood at play in prophet movements and associated social forms and mappings. However, we could understand *Life*'s claims to representativity and attendant circumscribed portrayal of Paiute political and territorial identity as part of an effort to navigate the specific entanglements of late-nineteenth-century federal policy. The narrative employs structuring templates that were at play in Indian policy, and through the use of these templates, *Life* seeks to endow Paiute peoplehood with a clearly delineated form. Doing so enables Winnemucca to engage with existing policy frameworks while seeking to shift them in ways that speak to a range of Paiute concerns and constituencies, to engage in what Jean Dennison might term a "politic of contestation" that seeks to increase Paiute "capacities" for autonomous governance.[15]

Understanding the vision of a unified Paiute nation that Winnemucca's narrative offers as a strategic fiction draws attention to the labor Winnemucca performs in negotiating the relationship between settler frameworks and lived formations of indigeneity that do not fit such paradigms. *Life* mobilizes elements already at play in Indian policy to constitute the Paiutes as a specific kind of group, call it a tribe, that functions in particular ways—with a singular leadership on a clearly delineated landbase that is cleanly differentiated from that of other tribes. Winnemucca offers this portrait of Paiute identity and placemaking in order to enable her to advocate for changes in existing federal policy. In the process of doing so, though, she also must displace prominent regional principles, practices, and geographies that run counter to the administrative and ideological frameworks at play in Indian policy, since such regional formations undermine both her claim to stand for the Paiute people and the presence of a clearly delineated *Paiute people* for whom she could speak. Drawing attention to the text's nonengagement with Ghost Dancing underlines the rhetorical processes by which the narrative gives shape to the notion of a Paiute tribe and by which Winnemucca positions herself as the representative for it. By employing definitions of tribal identity at play in Indian law and administration, *Life* seeks to endow Paiute peoplehood with a form recognizable to non-natives that facilitates maneuver within settler networks, but, conversely, working within and through the terms of settler governance in these ways—in order to present herself as a viable spokesperson—also implicitly disowns other extant Indigenous sociopolitical formations, like those associated with Ghost Dancing.

In Search of Chief Winnemucca

Life presents Winnemucca as descended from a chiefly family. During her public addresses in San Francisco and in the Northeast, both just prior to and in the wake of composing the narrative, Winnemucca indicates that she is touring and speaking to white audiences as an expression of her father's aims and status as leader of the Paiute tribe. On May 25, 1883, the *Salem Gazette* reported her as having said during one of her lectures that "I come because my father wished me to tell the true story of my people to the world."[16] A few weeks later, the *Boston Evening Transcript* printed a letter from Elizabeth Peabody, the white philanthropist with whom Winnemucca had developed an incredibly close relationship, and the letter states that Winnemucca "did never assume, but has received, the title of princess and even of Piute queen, in California and Nevada, for she was such in her tribe—daughter of a long line of chiefs, and her immediate father and grandfather very remarkable men."[17] In the "Editor's Preface" to *Life*, Mary Mann, Peabody's sister, refers to the "impulse" for Winnemucca to tell her story as "the dying charge given her by her father, the truly parental chief of his beloved tribe."[18] Moreover, in a speech the previous September in San Francisco, Winnemucca indicated that the "rank" of chief "is inherited from father to son, the oldest son being the chief by law. If he is dead, the one next to him becomes chief; or, if there are no sons, the next male relative; but never a woman."[19] Even as Winnemucca denies her own ability to assume the chieftainship, her lineage legitimizes her as a spokesperson for the Paiutes as a collective, casting her as an appropriate advocate for them with non-native publics.[20] This way of portraying Paiute governance depends on understanding Chief Winnemucca, Sarah's father, as the undisputed leader of a political structure that encompasses Paiutes stretching from what is now southern Nevada up to southeastern Oregon and east into Idaho.[21] Winnemucca's portrayal of her father and her family in these terms helps create the sense of a clear Paiute chain of command that would facilitate diplomatic negotiations, such as those conducted through the federal government's treaty system, while also enabling the narrative to delegitimize other Paiutes who asserted political authority (such as in aligning with the Bannocks in the 1878 war that bears their name). The narrative, though, hints at the existence of other understandings of power at play in the region, such as those associated with medicine people. When seen in terms of these other modes of collectivity and the networks they generate and sustain, Chief Winnemucca appears less as a head of state than as one node among many within what we might understand as the political geographies of Ghost Dancing.

From the beginning, *Life* situates Winnemucca within a line of leaderly succession that licenses her speech as a representative for the Paiute people. In the first paragraph of the narrative, she indicates, "My grandfather was chief of the entire Piute nation" (5), and when her grandfather (Truckee, a name given to him by whites) returns from having fought in the Mexican-American War in California on the side of the United States, he "told my father to take charge of his people and hold the tribe" while Truckee returned to California with about thirty families to work for his "white brothers": "My father took his place as Chief of the Piutes, and had it as long as he lived" (10). Later in the narrative, when Truckee is on his deathbed, "he looked at my father and told him what he must do, as he was to be head chief of the Piute nation" (67).[22] These moments unequivocally present the Paiutes as an integrated political body under a single leader, and they cast that authority as generationally transmitted, such that Winnemucca occupies a privileged position in communicating Paiute interests and aims to non-natives. She appears to readers as, in her own terms, "the chieftain's weary daughter" (12). As such, she provides a vehicle for conveying collective sentiments, particularly in the wake of her father's death a year before the narrative was published.[23] While this vision of inherited authority might give the impression of replicating the kinds of monarchical sovereignty against which the United States fought for independence, the narrative hastens to portray such leadership as more lovingly paternal than oppressively patriarchal. In the chapter concerned with describing traditional Paiute practices and social formations, Winnemucca insists that "the chiefs do not rule like tyrants; they discuss everything with their people, as a father would in his family" (52). Later, when decrying settler efforts to install more tractable Native leaders, she observes, "Sometimes chiefs are chosen by others and set over a tribe. There is no respect felt for such chiefs. That breaks up the family line that is the best thing for Indians," adding, "Their love for their chief holds them together, and helps them to do right. A tribe is a large family" (194). Lineage-based political power does not suppress popular voice but, instead, expresses a broader familial set of relations that characterizes the internal life of the nation. The "family line" of genealogical succession resonates with the fatherly connection the chief bears to the people, and the "love" they have for the chief helps bind them together as a polity. That dynamic legitimizes what otherwise might seem to be a kind of authoritarian, dynastic rule while also casting Winnemucca as something of a mother to the people, presenting her activity in speaking for the Paiute people as an act of love and a fully reciprocated form of maternal concern and care.[24] Moreover, her portrayal of herself as following in her father's line, and as playing a motherly role in the tribal "family," can be understood as partially a response to efforts to discredit her by portraying her as promiscuous. W. V. Rinehart, the agent for the Malheur Reservation whom Winnemucca critiques in her narrative (and elsewhere), circulated stories that Winnemucca had been prostituting herself with members of the U.S. military, a charge published in the *Council Fire* newspaper in May 1883.[25] Her entry into non-native public discourse as a respectable and representative speaker occurs through a gendered figuration of herself as loyal daughter and quasi matriarch within a governing lineage.

In presenting herself as part of the ruling family, Winnemucca invokes a geopolitical entity over which their authority is extended—"the Piute nation"—that supposedly encompasses large swaths of territory in the Great Basin. Quite early in the narrative, she notes, "My people were scattered at that time over nearly all the territory now known as Nevada" (5), and after the establishment of the Malheur Reservation (created by executive order in 1872, although described by Winnemucca as having been established in 1867), Winnemucca observes, "My father did not come in. He sent word by Egan [one of the leaders at Malheur] to me that he would go to Pyramid Lake Reservation to see the rest of our people there" (112).[26] Pyramid Lake was set aside for Paiutes in 1859 in what would become western Nevada, also by executive order.[27] It is in this area that the narrative primarily is set prior to its turn to Malheur (which is accompanied by a six-year jump, from 1869 to 1875, that I will address later). While present at Malheur, Chief Winnemucca remarks with respect to a visit to Pyramid Lake, "I saw a great many of my people. They say they will come here to make homes for themselves" (122). More than simply indicating the scope of Northern Paiute territory, these moments collate these various sites and Paiute groups as part of a shared "nation." The contacts among geographically dispersed Paiutes across this large area, though, occur primarily through Chief Winnemucca and members of his family (including Winnemucca), who appear as surrogates for him or as having authority delegated by him.

Although the narrative highlights the role of deliberation in council as a vital part of Paiute governance (52), in detailing the existence of democratic processes even amid the chief's fatherly guidance, Winnemucca does not discuss any coming together of widely separated Paiutes as a body or a meeting by representatives from groups whose principal dwellings lie far from each other.

What appears here to tie them together as a "people" is their mutual filiation to Chief Winnemucca, and when the narrative refers to them as "my people," it indicates a sense of belonging and relation that appears to be predicated on having a shared "chief." In this way, the text positions Winnemucca's family, particularly her father, as generating a stability of connection among potentially disparate and distant groups. Yet, even as the narrative intimates such networking, the (ongoing re)generation of durable connections among various sites, it displaces that process of connection by speaking as if there were an underlying entity of which the "chief"-dom were merely an expression—an encompassing nation with a structure and solidity that precedes and exceeds the role played by Winnemucca's family. Put another way, the narrative tends to speak of the Paiutes as a political body whose being and becoming gives rise to the Winnemucca family and their capacity to speak for this body, but the text's discussion of the dynamics of such peoplehood, instead, implies that it arises out of relations to the chiefly lineage, as an aggregation of those for whom the "head chief of the Piute nation" claims to speak.

One of the ways the text seeks to manage this representational wobble in the vision of Paiute collectivity it offers is by distinguishing between the "chief" and "sub-chiefs," especially in the sections of the narrative focused on the Malheur Reservation. When discussing her father's warning to the people of the need to flee to the mountains in order to avoid white emigrants while she was still a young child, Winnemucca notes, "The sub-chiefs went everywhere to tell their people what my father had told them to say" (13). As part of the account of Paiute social life prior to sustained contact with whites, the narrative explains, "The sub-chiefs are appointed by the great chief for special duties. There is no quarrelling about that, for neither sub-chief or great chief has any salary" (54). Sub-chiefs clearly exist in a hierarchy with the "great chief," a position occupied by the men of Winnemucca's family: the former serve at the pleasure of the latter, acting as extensions of the chief's authority rather than, say, gaining authority by being chosen as leaders by distinct groups of Paiutes. When the narrative shifts its attention to the Malheur Reservation, it repeatedly refers to Egan and Oytes, the men characterized as leaders of the Paiutes who live there, as "sub-chiefs." However, in addition to the fact that at no point is there any suggestion that either man was appointed by Winnemucca's father, who still functions in this section of the narrative as the "great chief," there is some confusion about these men's status. At one point, while Samuel Parrish (the first Indian agent appointed to Malheur) is promoting life on the reservation, he says, "I want you, chiefs of the Piutes, to ask all your people to come here to make homes for themselves," and while Winnemucca speaks of Egan and Oytes here as "sub-chiefs," Oytes indicates in response to Parrish's request, "I have my men, and our father [Chief] Winnemucca has his," adding, "I and my men have our own work to do,—that is, to hunt for our children" (107). Even as he gestures toward the paternal position of Winnemucca's father, which the narrative consistently correlates to political authority, Oytes insists on the separateness of their groups of "men," rejecting the notion of a singular line of command.[28] That multiplication of kinds of Paiute political identification resonates with Parrish's unqualified pluralization of Paiute leadership ("chiefs of the Piutes"). Thus, even as the narrative consistently casts Winnemucca's family—and her father, in particular—as having an undisputed position of leadership over the Paiutes as a unified polity/people, the text registers tensions in such an account, intimating that political authority may be spread over a wide variety of sites—even having multiple leaders on the same reservation (one chief's "men" at Malheur versus those of another).

The potential absence of a "head chief," though, raises questions about the claim to speak for a cohesive Paiute *nation*, suggesting that the text may participate in the process of generating such an entity rather than simply reflecting its existence and speaking in its name. Scholars have suggested that in the decades prior to sustained contact with non-natives, there was nothing like a Northern Paiute nation, in the sense of having a leadership structure that extended over all Northern Paiute groups or having a clearly delineated territory understood as belonging to such an overarching political body.[29] As Martha C. Knack and Omer C. Stewart argue in their history of the Pyramid Lake Reservation, "The Great Basin, unlike California and many other regions of North America . . . had only a small number of ethnic groups, each using a large territory. These Great Basin ethnic groups were culturally very similar to each other, and none had political organizations of any kind which would have united all members of one group and demarcated them from others. They spoke different, but generally related, languages, and these formed the primary ethnic markers within the region." Western Numic was the language spoken by those groups that come to be known as "Northern Paiutes," but "they called themselves simply 'Numa,' the people; whites called them Paviotsos, or Diggers." The territory used by these groups extended over approximately 78,000 square miles, and while they "considered themselves a distinct ethnic group in contrast to Washos or Shoshones," "there was no single tribal organization which involved all the people of this huge area, nor was there any time during the year when the entire population came together for any purpose."[30] There were over twenty Northern Paiute bands.[31] While distinguished by the particular lands and waters they claimed as their own, the bands did not so much operate as cohesive, discrete geopolitical units as occupy overlapping spheres of use, in which each band recognized the others' rights to control particular areas even as they regularly sought and were given permission to use them as part of subsistence strategies within shifting Great Basin ecologies.

While bands did not operate in isolation, neither did they coalesce into a single, overarching polity. Michael Allen Gualtieri suggests that "these family or 'household' groups were affiliated via a complex web of intersecting consanguineal and affinal relationships, cooperative foraging relationships, and relationships linking particular population clusters—at particular times—to transcendental power (*puha*) itself," including through ceremonies like antelope roundups, to which I will return. He later adds, "These affiliative bands, of course, could continue to coalesce or disperse within their generalized territories on a seasonal or ecological basis . . . *but this does not mean they would lack a sense of 'us.'* The latter perception, indeed, would be augmented by the crucial need for information-exchange among co-residents of marginal zones."[32] Such a sense of collective identity encompassed a group of extended families who understood themselves as having an enduring connection to a specific land-base and/or waters, even as that "us" did not provide sustained parameters for the band members' annual and regional movements. People throughout the Great Basin developed extensive relations of kinship and trade with each other that allowed individuals and families to draw on resources in a range of spaces that were not associated with the band to which they may have belonged.[33] Moreover, as Smoak suggests of Newe peoples, neighbors to the Northern Paiutes who had similar social patterns, "Interaction between family clusters was extensive but informal, and there was no guarantee that the same people would travel, live together, or follow the same leader from year to year," adding, "Modern informants claim that families and individuals often wintered in different camps. Between the family cluster and the larger linguistic community, then, there was no *permanent* social institutions, and ethnic identities did not yet hold the saliency that they would gain by the reservation era."[34] There is debate, then, over whether something like the idea of "chief" makes sense for talking about Northern Paiute groups and modes of authority prior to the mid-nineteenth century, especially given the size of most bands, the variable composition of who was dwelling where during various parts of the year, the ease with which people could change bands (given a range of kinship connections to other groups in the region), and that leadership was a matter of continued popular support rather than institutional investiture or lineage.[35] In this way, we can understand Paiute bands (as well as families and individuals) as complexly networked to each other within shifting and recurrently renewed ties of kinship, trade, and inhabitance but in ways that are not organized around or through a centralized structure of leadership.

Even as Winnemucca's narrative seeks to project a sense of encompassing Paiute political cohesion through the depiction of her family's leadership, the text registers other kinds of authority at play in the Great Basin, which suggest a very different kind of mapping than that of a head chief who can represent a unified nation. Early in the narrative, Chief Winnemucca gathers his people and tells them to retreat to the mountains in response to a dream he had of waves of white settlers. He says, "I dreamt this same thing three nights,—the very same. I saw the greatest emigration that has yet been through our country. I looked North and South and East and West, and saw nothing but dust, and I heard a great weeping. I saw women crying, and I also saw my men shot down by the white people" (14). Years later, Winnemucca's brother Natchez dreams that some Paiutes who are angry at the behavior of Pyramid Lake's agent will, instead of assaulting the agent, attack a place named Deep Wells, killing one man and taking a number of horses (80), and soon thereafter, "everybody ran to him and told him his dream had come true" (83). Additionally, toward the end of the Bannock War, Winnemucca dreams that Egan will be treacherously murdered by the Umatillas on the night that very event occurs; she reminds readers, "Many of my family have seen things in their dreams that were really happening" (184–185). The ability to prophesy in this way, or to receive information about what's occurring elsewhere through visions, seems to run in Winnemucca's family, a link that reinforces their suitability for leadership by suggesting that their authority arises from other-than-human sanction. Toward the beginning of the text, though, we hear of "doctors" and "doctresses" (also known in the text as medicine men) who have the power to call for "a council" and who "can communicate with holy spirits from heaven" (15), and one of them "prophesied" to confirm the truth of Chief Winnemucca's dream (16). These moments suggest that the visionary capabilities illustrated by Winnemucca's family appear more widely among the Paiutes, rather than as a sign of chiefly lineage. Dreaming served as the basis for shamanic power, indicating a spirit entity's endowment of greater than ordinary access to *puha*—the omnipresent forms of energy available in all living things.[36] To be possessed of such increased abilities enabled one to mobilize ambient forms of power to particular ends, especially forms of healing, thereby leading to the figure of the medicine man.[37]

Notably, though, readers do not hear of such figures—doctors and doctresses—after the creation of the Pyramid Lake Reservation, an event that inaugurates an administratively managed relation between the U.S. government and Paiute people(s). One might attribute this silence to the lessening of medicine people's significance over time, except for the fact that those forms of power not only persisted but can be described as intensifying in the ensuing decades. As Smoak argues, popular belief "in the efficacy of shamanism" throughout the region "provided the internal logic of the prophetic religions of the nineteenth century, including both Ghost Dances," adding, "Ghost Dances were a community curing rite that promised the restoration of a world free of disease, death, and spiritual disharmony."[38] The emergence of prophet-led movements that involved thousands of people and spread across the Great Basin and Columbia Plateau, extending at different points into California and onto the Plains, testifies to the continuing importance among the Paiutes and neighboring peoples of puha and those who can wield it. Moreover, U.S. officials understood these networks as a threat to settler governance, suggesting that they generated forms of association antithetical to the aims of federal Indian policy.[39] The absence of further discussion of regular shamanic and spiritually motivated activity later in the narrative, including the fact that the text jumps from 1868 to 1875, skipping over the period of greatest attention to Wodziwob's visions, can be understood as an effort to bypass the kinds of authority generated through these practices in favor of a portrait of Paiute collectivity as organized in ways more amenable to Euro-American political forms.

However, in addition to referencing the Winnemucca family's dreamings, the text also gestures to the importance of puha in securing chiefly status for both Chief Winnemucca and Oytes. Somewhat buried in the chapter on "Domestic and Social Moralities," amid the array of Paiute practices and beliefs discussed, Winnemucca notes, "My people capture antelopes by charming them, but only some of the people are charmers. My father was one of them, and once I went with him on an antelope hunt" (55). While she then devotes three pages to discussing the hunt, she does not explain the significance of antelope charmers among Paiute people(s) in the pre-reservation era. Since antelope were a major source of subsistence and charming was understood as a principal way of gathering enough of them to sustain a band or set of bands for the year, having access to an antelope charmer was of great importance as part of annual food strategies, and being such a charmer granted someone considerable authority within and among bands.[40] Bands, as well as sustained relations among them, could take shape around these figures and the forms of power that they employed. Drawing on the work of Julian Steward, Gualtieri suggests that there was a "sacred basis of political authority," as indicated by the fact that many antelope charmers or shamans were in fact known as "chiefs" of the bands to which they belonged, very much like Chief Winnemucca.[41] This way of mobilizing puha and the kinds of leadership and collectivity that emerged around and through antelope charming are not equivalent to those that gathered around Wodziwob and others who led broader prophet movements, but Sally Zanjani observes that Chief Winnemucca "also prophesied on occasion and related myths to his people that explained their troubles. Some said he could heal bullet wounds. More than fifty years after his death, old men still spoke of his extraordinary shamanistic powers."[42] Moreover, the rituals surrounding the antelope hunt also involved a Round Dance, which throughout the Great Basin served as means of collectively gathering and enacting puha in various annual traditions (including mourning dances among some Paiute groups). Such dances provided the framework, or template, for what would become the central ritual enactment—circle dancing—from which the "Ghost Dance" received its name.[43]

Similarly, with respect to Oytes, Winnemucca casts him as a disruptive influence on the Malheur Reservation while also providing tidbits of information that when attended to point, instead, toward him as imbued with shamanic power. The narrative reports that Winnemucca's father and Egan indicated to Agent Parrish, as evidence that Oytes "is a very bad man," "Our good father, we are afraid of Oytes, because he says he can make us all die here. Last winter we had some kind of sickness, and a great many of our children died. He said it was he who was making us sick" (110–111). In addition, the narrative notes that Oytes claimed to be immune to bullets (115), and at another point, in an effort to heal a Paiute child whom Agent Rinehart had assaulted, Oytes "was laying hands" on the boy (129), echoing the text's earlier description of treatment by Paiute doctors—"Our medicine man cures the sick by laying on of hands" (15). These moments point to Oytes's ability to draw on puha, alternately as a shaman (to heal) and as a witch (to injure). These instances direct attention to the challenge that he poses to the agent's control over the reservation (including his initial refusal to labor and his ongoing relationships with "the Columbia River Indians," to which I'll return in the next section).

These moments, though, can imply less a perverse and malignant willfulness, as the narrative indicates in its running insistence on Oytes's *badness*, than an alternative source of authority. Accounts at the time routinely characterized Oytes as a "Dreamer," meaning that he specifically was linked to the followers of the prophet Smohalla and to the dissemination of the Ghost Dance more broadly.[44] Smohalla was a mid-nineteenth-century leader of Wanapum descent who had been a medicine man, eventually gathering a group of followers that at the height of his influence numbered in the thousands—many living with him in an off-reservation area just south of the Columbia River. At one point,

Smohalla died, visited the spirit world, and returned with a prophecy that, in the words of the local Indian commissioner at the time, "a new god is coming to their rescue; that all the Indians who have died heretofore, and who shall die hereafter, are to be resurrected; that as they will then be very numerous and powerful, they will be able to conquer the whites."[45] He called for a return to older ways and a renunciation of white technologies and practices, including the signing of treaties and the acceptance of government-demarcated reservation lands. The text's depiction of Oytes, as well as of Chief Winnemucca, raises the issue of the role of puha in Paiute sociopolitical formations, modes of leadership, and participation in networks sustained through prophecy while offering a significantly truncated account of those aspects of Paiute life.

How do we understand what seems like a disjunction between the narrative's account of Paiute political identity as integrated across the region and what appear to be longstanding decentralized Paiute sociopolitical dynamics? As Zanjani notes, "None of the children of Winnemucca became shamans, nor did they follow the Ghost Dance messiahs and the Dreamer chiefs who rose from the agonies of a desperate people. When others flocked to hear Wodziwob preach the new Ghost Dance religion at Walker Reservation in 1870, they stood aside."[46] More than simply indicating Winnemucca's lack of response to the messages being offered by various prophets in the period, the choice not to discuss such movements within the narrative and their connection to extant Paiute social roles, forms of authority, and modes of interband relation registers the narrative's effort to offer an account of Paiute leadership consistent with the patterns at play in Indian administration.[47] How does the narrative's depiction of Paiute peoplehood and leadership take part in extant networks of settler policy and publicity, which themselves mediate relations in the region?

More than indicating her father's prominence among the Paiutes, Winnemucca's text repeatedly illustrates how U.S. officials, civilian and military, treat her father as the preeminent leader of the Paiutes as a polity. Although, notably, they often do so when insisting on the importance of bringing him back to state-managed spaces when he has refused to stay within their boundaries. While Winnemucca is at Pyramid Lake, a military officer who had arrived to investigate tensions between the agent and the Paiutes there, receives a message from Fort McDermitt: "'I have got a letter from the commanding officer at the Fort asking me if your father is here with you.' Brother [Natchez] told him he had not been with us for a long time. I was crying, and I told him father had not been in since the soldiers killed my little brother."[48] The officer, then, states, "You and your brother shall go with me, and we will get your father here. If he will come in he will be cared for by the officers of the army. The commanding officer says you are to go with me to Camp McDermitt, and you can get your father and all your people to come into the army post, where you can be fed" (85). Natchez succeeds in bringing Chief Winnemucca to the camp, along with "four hundred and ninety of my people" (103). Later in the narrative, when Winnemucca is working as the translator at Malheur, her father again is sought, this time by Agent Rinehart (spelled "Reinhard" in the text), who attempts on a number of occasions over the course of the 1870s and early 1880s to convince Chief Winnemucca to live on the Malheur Reservation.[49] Once the Bannock War has commenced, Winnemucca receives another request to retrieve her father from a Captain Bernard when she begins working for the army as a scout: "'Now Sarah,' he said, 'if you will go to your father, tell him and his people that they shall be taken care of and be fed. Get all the well-disposed of your people to come near the troops, where they can be safe'" (154). These moments illustrate the ways that Chief Winnemucca serves as an important political figure in the eyes of various U.S. officials, as someone whose whereabouts need to be ascertained and who needs to be brought into spaces more directly regulated by the government (reservations and forts) in order to assert and maintain settler control in the region.

However, Chief Winnemucca's authority—leadership of "his people"— also appears here as partial, as applying only to a limited group of Paiutes who join him in his off-reservation occupancy and movements. Winnemucca points toward the encompassing character of Chief Winnemucca's power as projected by U.S. officials even as, in doing so, she indirectly intimates the limits of that power. Such officials seek to draw on Winnemucca's father in order to generate a sense of coherent Paiute identity over which U.S. authority can be exercised through him, positioning him as a metonym whose compliance can signify and enact the bringing to order of Paiute populations. Reciprocally, Winnemucca cites the Indian service's and the army's use of her father to these ends in ways that reaffirm his role as "head chief of the Piute nation" and, thus, her own legitimacy as the advocate for the Paiute people—as their representative in interactions with non-native publics. Considering the various ways that the U.S. government positions Chief Winnemucca as the representative for a cohesive Paiute political entity, we might understand that process as seeking to generate a *form* for Paiute peoplehood(s) more conducive to implementing the discursive and institutional technologies of U.S. Indian policy. We might approach the notion of "head chief" as a template drawn from encounters with other peoples and earlier processes of settler colonial management that is materialized in the case of the Paiutes through the techniques of settler administration (such as orders from fort commanders and regulations issued by Indian agents). The implementation and circulation of this template by U.S. civil and military actors seeks to structure the geopolitical dynamics of the Great Basin in ways that facilitate settlement, including clearing land for white farming and ranching and constructing a transportation infrastructure across Native lands by way of the railroad.

This dynamic of using Chief Winnemucca to figure Paiute collectivity appears repeatedly in agents' and military officers' accounts of events from the 1860s to the 1880s as well as in the popular press. As Zanjani notes, "Long before Sarah could be accused of aggrandizing her family's position at the expense of the headmen of other bands, white men had started to recognize Winnemucca as a leader and show their preference for dealing with a hierarchical authority—a chief—instead of the assorted headmen of many fluid bands."[50] The desire on the part of various settlers, including Indian agents and military officers, for such a centralized figure as a focus for projects of administrative control can be understood in relation to the massive influx of settler population and economies into the Great Basin from the 1860s onward. While Northern Paiute bands did not have sustained contact with whites until the 1840s, their territories were crossed by travelers heading to California, and the discovery of gold and silver in western Nevada in 1859 led to a rush, exacerbated by the construction of the Central Pacific Railroad (which illegally claimed part of the Pyramid Lake Reservation).[51] As early as 1864, newspapers in Nevada and California were presenting Winnemucca's father as the leader of a cohesive Paiute nation, describing him as "the High Old Chief of all the Pi-utes" and as "emperor," characterizing his family (including Winnemucca) as "royal."[52] Such accounts also appear in eastern newspapers, such as the *New York Times* and the *Washington Post*, in the late 1870s and early 1880s, prior to Winnemucca's extended lecture tour in the Northeast, which began in the spring of 1883.[53] This coverage indicates that the perception of Winnemucca's chiefly lineage—and the accompanying sense of Paiute political unity—well preceded the publication of *Life* and was a longstanding part of non-native public discourse surrounding Indian affairs in the Great Basin. The value for U.S. policy of projecting such a unifying figure appears in the invocations of Winnemucca's father's status in the reports by various agents and superintendents from the early 1860s onward. As with the references to retrieving Chief Winnemucca from off-reservation spaces in *Life*, these moments suggest both the political objectives at play in channeling authority over Paiute people into a single figure and the countervailing tendencies at play among Paiute people(s) that make such a consolidation administratively desirable. In one of the earliest such reports, Agent Dodge indicates in 1859 that "the Piute nation numbers some 6000 souls. . . . Wun-a-Muc-a (The Giver) is the head chief of the nation. He generally stays on Smoke Creek: near Honey Lake," and a report in 1861 from Nevada describes him as "the most important chief or captain in the Pah-Ute tribe."[54]

In many ways, "Winnemucca" comes to function as a public and administrative trope—a form—through which to coalesce a range of different visions and versions of authority among Paiute groups, thereby (re)constructing and (re)circulating the image of a unified Paiute collectivity over which such power could be exerted. General O. O. Howard served in the Great Basin in the 1880s and led U.S. forces in the Bannock War, also playing a key role in advocating for the removal of Paiutes from Malheur to Yakima Reservation in that war's wake.[55] He, therefore, would have had occasion to have significant knowledge of Paiute political structure. When discussing leadership among the Paiutes in his memoir *Famous Indian Chiefs I Have Known*, though, Howard conflates Sarah's grandfather and father into something of a Winnemucca amalgam. Devoting an entire chapter to "Winnemucca," he observes, "Chief Winnemucca, who was born and lived the most of his life beside Pyramid Lake, Nevada, had a thinking mind and a large, warm heart. He was chief of an Indian nation called the 'Piutes,' and before any white men came over the Rocky Mountains to disturb them, there were several thousand Indians, to whom he was like a father," adding that "his eldest son" would "be Chief Winnemucca after him." However, he then notes that, after encounter with white soldiers, "from that time Winnemucca was called Captain Truckee."[56] There is no other evidence of Sarah Winnemucca's grandfather, known as "Truckee" in her narrative and elsewhere, as having gone by the name "Winnemucca," and this slippage from her father to her grandfather suggests the idea of Paiute political authority as a matter of lineal succession. This intergenerational merger creates the impression that there's always a "Winnemucca" in charge of the *Paiute nation*, contributing to the sense that Sarah Winnemucca's father was the reigning such ruler from the early 1860s to his death in 1882. That process of condensing Paiute leadership through what might be termed the Winnemucca-function, though, does not represent a post hoc phenomenon from decades after the events chronicled but rather is an extension of tendencies at play throughout the period covered by *Life*. A petition from citizens in the vicinity of the Pyramid Lake Reservation and published in the *Humboldt Register* in May 1867 charges that "Old Winnemucca, the late Chief of the Piutes, has turned traitor to his tribe, deserted his Country and joined the hostile Indians of the North," and in response, they resolve "that Captain Sou [a band leader residing at Pyramid Lake] be nominated and chosen Chief of the friendly Piutes to be known by the title of 'Winnemucca.'"[57] Even while casting Chief Winnemucca as a "traitor," they suggest that he has abdicated his proper role as leader of "the tribe," and thus another "Winnemucca" must be chosen to replace him.

The reference to him as "Old Winnemucca" points to another source of confusion/conflation through which the singularity of Paiute leadership, and by extension of Paiute peoplehood, is produced within non-native discourses and institutional frameworks. Throughout the 1860s and into the early 1870s, Chief Winnemucca, Sarah Winnemucca's father, often was confused with a Paiute leader named Numaga who was known as "Young Winnemucca" and was Chief Winnemucca's nephew. Most of the meetings between white leaders and "Winnemucca" before and in the immediate wake of the Pyramid Lake War of 1860 actually were with Numaga, but regularly have been misattributed to Chief Winnemucca. As Gualtieri explains, Numaga became widely known for leading Paiute resistance during the Pyramid Lake War and for signing an agreement with local settlers in the Honey Lake region after the war's close (a document that often gets referred to as a treaty even though it had no official legal status): "All through the many years of *Numaga*'s attempt to work with the Whites (viz. 1857–1859) *Poito* [Chief Winnemucca] seems to have kept his band away from the settlers and remained distrustful of the newcomers' intentions. During those years, too, White chroniclers came to simply call *Numaga* by a foreshortened form of his name—'Winnemucca.' . . . 'Winnemucca,' then, rapidly was acquiring a reputation as a 'friend' to the Whites," which "seems to have led to the misidentification of *Numaga*'s peace-keeping effort with *Poito* himself."[58] This routine misattribution consolidated the settler perception of Chief Winnemucca as serving a diplomatic role in engagements with non-natives, helping position him as an authority figure for the Paiutes writ large. His movements beyond the Pyramid Lake Reservation from the early 1860s onward, particularly his relationships with groups in Oregon and Idaho, then, appear to testify to his powerful influence among geographically dispersed Paiute bands as well as, reciprocally, to their mutual belonging to a shared Paiute political entity, as evidenced by their connections to Chief Winnemucca.

Life among the Piutes draws on this administrative and popular narrative of Chief Winnemucca's ubiquitous authority across Paiute space in order to position the text as a mode of diplomatic engagement. In this way, we might characterize *Life* as enacting a treaty imaginary—conveying the sense that Winnemucca's writing itself surrogates for the absent scene of formal negotiation. While demonstrating how Paiute life and political possibilities are entangled with the structures and dynamics of settler colonial policy, then, the text also employs the conceits at play in Indian administration (such as Chief

Winnemucca's ostensible centrality to what is taken to be the Paiute nation) in order to mediate the terms of such policy, redirecting it to alternate ends that challenge ongoing state violence against Paiute people(s). U.S. treaty making with Native peoples officially ended in 1871, and the Northern Paiutes did not have any formal treaties with the federal government.[59] However, amid what Nancy Bentley has described as "the ruins of an absent diplomatic public," Winnemucca seeks to generate the sense of a treaty relationship, with her family serving as diplomatic mediators.[60] In *Life*, she references a "treaty giving the Pyramid Lake Reservation to my people" (73), and in her previous speeches and engagements, she spoke of the Pyramid Lake and Malheur Reservations as resulting from treaties.[61] Although not accurate, as both reservations were created by presidential executive order, such claims create the sense of an ongoing process of political relation and negotiation that obtains between the Paiutes as a nation and the U.S. government. The narrative elsewhere draws on this sense of a history of entering into agreements with U.S. officials for which the terms are unclear or are not honored. At one point, Winnemucca quotes Jim, a "sub-chief" from Pyramid Lake, as saying, "I am going to quit signing any paper, for I don't know what I have been signing all these twenty-two years" (95), and toward the end of the narrative, Winnemucca asserts, "My people have been signing papers for the last twenty-three years. They don't know what they sign" (242). As Michelle Kohler suggests, "Winnemucca directs her critique at documents that make promises for future action but also . . . at documents whose ostensible function is to represent reality."[62] These moments in the narrative implicitly employ the figure of the treaty as ideally an expression of informed consent to shared terms and a promise of ongoing relation of peace and friendship between political actors, while also highlighting the failures of U.S. Indian policy to act honorably or in the spirit of the agreements into which the settler-state and Native nations have entered.

Invoking a legacy of treaty making and treaty violation—or at least one of Paiutes signing documents whose terms are deceptive in ways that gesture toward histories of treaty manipulation by the United States—allows Winnemucca to position the narrative as an effort to engage in a good faith process of negotiation. In this vein, Elizabeth Peabody sent a copy of a newspaper review of *Life* to all the Republicans in Congress, implicitly presenting the narrative as an expression of Paiute political will.[63] This impression strongly is aided by the inclusion at the end of the text proper (just prior to the appendix of letters of support for Winnemucca) of a petition directed to "the Honorable Congress of the United States" whose aim is to restore the Malheur Reservation to "the tribe of Piute Indians," including allowing for the return of those Paiutes who had been removed to Yakima (247). Winnemucca had been gathering signatures for the petition at her numerous speaking engagements. She actually submitted that petition to Congress and testified before the Senate Subcommittee on Indian Affairs during the first session of 1884.[64] Moreover, in the narrative, she describes the request to travel to Washington, D.C., that she, her father, and her brother received from a U.S. official in the wake of the Bannock War. In Nevada, she gets a telegram from "a man named Hayworth [J. M. Haworth], saying, 'Sarah, the President wants you and your father and brother Natchez and any other chiefs, four in number, to go to Washington with me'" (217). A special agent from the Department of the Interior who had been sent to investigate "unrest" among the Paiutes, Haworth brought them to Washington.[65] In her discussion of their time there, Winnemucca indicates that when meeting with various officials she and those with her advocated for the return of the noncombatant Paiutes who had been removed to the Yakima Reservation.[66] This part of the narrative underlines her and her family's role as officially recognized representatives authorized to speak for the Paiutes. In response to a later report that they were "a *self-constituted* delegation," Winnemucca insists, "We did not come of ourselves; we were sent for" (220–221), refusing the idea that they merely had positioned themselves as spokespersons for Paiute collective interests.

Her role as a legitimate representative for the Paiutes is further confirmed both before and after this section in the narrative. Just prior to the onset of the Bannock War, Egan and others request that she "go right on to Washington, and have a talk with our Great Father in Washington" about Paiute concerns related to the Malheur Reservation (146), and at the very end of the narrative (just prior to the petition), she indicates, "I visited my people once more at Pyramid Lake Reservation, and they urged me again to come to the East and talk for them, and so I have come" (246), even though there is no substantive discussion of Pyramid Lake after the text shifts setting to Malheur and it does not feature prominently in her public advocacy. Together, these aspects of *Life* and her public activities while touring the Northeast work to convey the sense of Winnemucca as someone authorized on both sides to serve as an official mediator between Paiutes and the U.S. government, seeking to give a diplomatic cast and force to the proposals offered in the text for addressing the settler-orchestrated expulsions and deprivations experienced by Paiute people(s).

In order to engage in negotiation with the United States, including for the return of Paiutes from Yakima, there needs to be a negotiator who is understood as legitimate. Legitimacy in that relation, though, is a function not solely of Native political philosophies and processes but of what will be understood by settlers as a viable and valid entity with whom to negotiate. In this way, *Life* coalesces a sense of Winnemucca as a representative figure, via her "chiefly" lineage, in ways that position her to perform this semiofficial role while also working to generate a sense of the "Piute nation" as a proper partner for such federal diplomacy. Goeman argues that "the literary . . . tenders an avenue for the 'imaginative' creation of new possibilities, which must happen through imaginative modes precisely because the 'real' of settler colonial society is built on the violent erasures of alternative modes of mapping and geographic understandings."[67] Yet, *Life* testifies to the ways that Indigenous struggles to create new possibilities for Native people(s) through acts of writing also involved the mobilization of non-native "modes of understanding"—such as the existence of centralized "chiefly" leadership over a clearly delimited group—as part of seeking to maneuver within existing policy entanglements. Here, non-native recognition of Winnemucca's capacity to operate as a leader serves as a prerequisite in the text's attempt to leverage Indian policy through public appeal—an appeal modeled on the forms of the treaty system.

While citing the forms of treaty making in ways that seek to consolidate and amplify the significance of the narrative and Winnemucca's appeals more broadly, the effort to present the text and Winnemucca herself as representative relies on generating a sense of coherent Paiute identity and leadership through the invocation of her "chiefly" lineage. The narrative aims to generate just such a sense of centralization through its repeated characterization of her father as the leader of a singular Paiute people, including the characterization of other leaders as "sub-chiefs" and running suggestions that they were appointed by members of her family to these roles. That process of situating her family, particularly her father, in a position of supposedly uncontested authority over the Paiutes as a unified collectivity, though, does not originate in Winnemucca's narrative. Instead, it was part and parcel of governmental, media, and popular discourses in the Great Basin and beyond from at least the early 1860s onward. *Life* mobilizes this story of the political status of Winnemucca's family in ways that enable Winnemucca, and the text itself, to appear as representative—as embodying the collective will of the Paiute people. As Carolyn Sorisio observes in "Sarah Winnemucca, Translation, and US Colonialism and Imperialism," "Winnemucca seems to have promoted her (and her family's) representative status to create an autonomous, if not sovereign, place for Northern Paiutes within the U.S."[68] An article printed in the *Washington Post* during Winnemucca's trip to Washington in 1880 notes, "The objects of the visit of this delegation, as stated by Sarah, is to secure recognition and aid by the Government similar to that enjoyed by other nations. She says the Piutes desire opportunities for moral and intellectual advancement, together with more substantial aid."[69]

Her efforts "to secure recognition and aid" from settler officials and publics require that the Paiutes signify as like "other [Native] nations," a project facilitated by her running invocation of her family's leadership of what she terms the "Piute nation." In making this claim, she recirculates the centralizing template used by federal policy to try to simplify Native sociopolitical formations and to expedite the process of securing consent to Indigenous land loss (having a singular leader of a large group decreases the number of signatories while increasing the jurisdictional scope and significance of their assent). In doing so, though, the text occludes other formations of leadership and identification at play in the region throughout the time period it covers. The powerful influence of forms of shamanic power and prophecies appears fleetingly in the text, more as an indication of semiethnological detail or of the moral bankruptcy of particular figures (such as Oytes's use of witchcraft). Attending to Ghost Dance traces in the text, though, helps bring to the fore the constructedness—administrative and textual—of accounts of unified Paiute nationality and the presence of other forms of peoplehood, ones that need to be effaced if "Paiute" is to emerge as a coherent object of public policy and advocacy within the terms of extant Indian administration.

Separating the Good from the Bad

If the Paiutes live on distinct reservations separated by dozens to hundreds of miles, what enables us to understand them as a singular entity in whose name Winnemucca can speak? Distinguishing between the Paiute *nation* and other peoples gives greater definition to this sense of discrete nationality, generating a sense of its boundedness. More specifically, drawing lines of demarcation that separate Paiutes from other Native groups presents Paiute identity as self-contained and, thus, as juridically differentiable within the terms of Indian law and policy. As opposed to being included within a generic Indianness, understood administratively and popularly as given to unpredictable and savage violence, Paiutes appear in Winnemucca's narrative as peaceful, law abiding, and willing to participate in civilizing processes. In portraying them in these ways, the text explicitly differentiates them from those it labels as "bad Indians," particularly the Columbia River Indians and the Bannocks. By seeking clearly to delineate the Paiutes from neighboring groups, the narrative not only generates a kind of political subjectivity for which Winnemucca can serve as the representative but aims to exonerate those who belong to this category from the critique and censure directed against those other groups, particularly due to their supposed wandering and aggressive tendencies. However, this manner of consolidating a sense of Paiute identity and innocence severs longstanding relationships among groups in the region, creating an atomizing portrait of tribal belonging that effaces complex and shifting cartographies of kinship, alliance, and affiliation. In doing so, Winnemucca's narrative displaces what we might term Ghost Dance geographies and networks, the webs of connection among persons and groups that gain strength through prophet-led movements—Indigenous matrices of engagement that in many ways precede the late nineteenth century but that such movements help further catalyze and extend. While registering traces of these patterns of relation, *Life among the Piutes* also suggests the ways that claims to representativity entail breaking up such networks in order to circulate the kind of tribal identity privileged within settler governance. In this way, the text's strategic engagement with Indian policy does not so much place the Paiutes within Native space, in Lisa Brooks's terms, as work (at least rhetorically) to disaggregate such space.[70]

Much of the political work of the narrative lies in its efforts to persuade white readers of Paiutes' capacity for civilization. The text's account of Paiutes' civilizedness often comes in the form of an inversion of non-native tropes of Indian savagery. For instance, during the discussion of the Bannock War, Winnemucca notes that as she, her sister-in-law, and the military are in pursuit of Bannock forces, she found that "they had left a scalp behind them. It was the first scalp I had seen in my life, for my people never scalped any one. The Bannocks had left it there" (172). She refuses the image of a generic Native penchant for egregious violence, as represented by the popular image of Indian scalping, instead insisting that the Paiutes had no such practice and were utterly unfamiliar with this mode of assault and the tendencies that it signified to whites. In fact, she suggests that Euro-Americans themselves are the ones with deep-seated and longstanding propensities for brutality. When speaking early in the narrative of her grandfather's relation with whites, she observes, "Then my people were less barbarous then they are nowadays" (10), intimating that the sustained contact with whites that ensued after this point in time actually has engendered previously unknown forms of barbarism. Furthermore, in the wake of her brother Natchez's arrest and transportation to Alcatraz for critiquing the Pyramid Lake agent, Winnemucca notes, "Since the war of 1860 there have been one hundred and three of my people murdered, and our reservations taken from us; and yet we, who are called blood-seeking savages, are keeping our promises to the government" (89), and when she and Natchez are asked by the military to find their father and bring him in to Camp McDermitt, she indicates, "The white settlers are talking very badly through the whole country, and they have sent for Gen. Crook to come and kill all the Indians that are not on some reservation"

(99). Not only have the whites engaged in a campaign of theft, assault, and murder for which Paiutes have not retaliated and have, instead, kept faith with the U.S. government, but claims about their supposed "blood-seeking" *savagery* have been used to justify calls for wholesale slaughter of Native people(s). These moments speak to the pattern in *Life*, in Malea Powell's terms, of using "the tropes and figures of 'savagery' and 'civilization' . . . to authenticate and authorize herself," "representing herself as a *civilized Indian woman*" in order to appeal to a non-native readership.[71] Also, as Cari Carpenter observes in *Seeing Red*, Winnemucca's repetition of these tropes "serves to trouble that very distinction between civilized and savage. It is through the rearticulation of the original—the dominant discourse—that she exposes it as a fabrication."[72]

However, if Winnemucca illustrates the ways figurations of Indian savagery circulate within popular and administrative discourses, the challenge she offers to that template involves less a wholesale reimagining of Indianness than a carving out of an exception for (the) Paiutes. In the mention of scalping, for example, she does not so much disabuse white readers of the idea that scalping is a paradigmatic expression of Indian viciousness as insist on Paiute innocence, placing the blame for the practice on the Bannocks. She clearly objects to the wholesale designation of "Indians" as targets of military aggression. Yet, rather than suggesting that the category of the Indian leads to false depictions and understandings of all the peoples caught within it, Winnemucca seeks to exempt Paiutes from such assumptions. The text's repeated underlining of the actions, or lack thereof, of "my people" implicitly casts the Paiutes as free from typical Indian inclinations toward cruelty and carnage. This comparative claim of relative blamelessness resonates with and implicitly builds on existing ways of narrating Paiute bands within U.S. administrative and military accounts. In *Famous Chiefs I Have Known*, General Howard indicates that "seventy years ago the Piutes were a peace-loving and contented people," adding that they "never appeared to be as shrewd and smart as the Snake Indians" and that "they were not warlike."[73] Similarly, reports from the Nevada superintendency during the 1860s and 1870s consistently present the Paiutes as peaceable and interested in maintaining amicable relations with whites, often contrasting them with the other nearby peoples. The annual report for 1864 observes, "I have had the honor to state that during the last year we have had entire peace with the Indians that rightly belong in this Territory. Some hostile tribes from Oregon and Idaho have come into our Territory on the north, and committed thefts and some murders," and the report for 1866 indicates, "There are no Indians within this superintendency who have been so much benefited by their intercourse with the whites as the Pi-Utes."[74] With respect to the Paiute reservations in Nevada during the Bannock War, the superintendent reports, "It was a trying period to the force in charge of the Pah-Ute Reservations, and nothing but the kindly relations existing between us enabled me to restrain the few unsteady ones from participating in the depredations and extending the theater of war."[75] Winnemucca's narrative builds on this pattern, differentiating the Paiutes by citing the exemplary nature of their behavior relative to that illustrated by neighboring peoples.

In addition to highlighting their civilizedness, the text maintains a sense of Paiute pacifism by clearly distinguishing them from those groups understood as threats by U.S. officials. In particular, *Life* takes care to mark this tribal difference with respect to the Columbia River Indians and the Bannocks. The former appear in the narrative once it has shifted focus from the Pyramid Lake Reservation in Nevada to the Malheur Reservation in Oregon. In discussing Oytes's refusal to follow the orders of Agent Parrish, Winnemucca presents his continuing relationship with the Columbia River Indians as proof of his profligacy. After proclaiming, "I am not going to work" (107), Oytes announces that he and his men will go live with the Columbia River Indians (113). Although Winnemucca notes that "they came to trade with my people every summer," Egan declares them to be "bad Indians," and Parrish says that they "were always making trouble, and it was best that they should never come to the reservation at all" (110). Such "trouble" apparently includes their failure to remain within the spaces sanctioned as *Indian* through the reservation system. Repudiating this group allows Winnemucca both to clarify/construct the boundaries of Paiute identity and to underline Paiutes' *goodness* in their relative acceptance of the terms of U.S. policy.

If distancing Paiutes from the Columbia River Indians seeks to ensure the reputation of the former, the text's efforts to prevent the conflation of Paiutes with the Bannocks are even more pressing. Given the recent hostilities between U.S. military forces and Native groups who had come to be known as "Bannocks" as well as the subsequent removal of the residents of Malheur to the Yakima Reservation, one of the text's chief aims is to enable the return of those Paiutes by establishing their innocence. While the narrative reflects the fact that there were Paiutes from the Malheur Reservation who joined with the Bannocks, Winnemucca tends to localize that dynamic in order to preserve a distinction between the groups. She insists, "It was Oytes who first carried some of my people over to the Bannocks" (189). Moreover, while other evidence suggests the prominence of Egan and his band in the conflict, especially after the death of the Bannock leader Buffalo Horn in battle, *Life* repeatedly highlights Oytes's centrality to the war.[76] Linking participation in the war to the forms of aberrance and animosity previously attributed to Oytes allows the narrative to present Paiute presence among the combatants as anomalous. Toward the end of the narrative, Winnemucca asserts, "I have given up those who were bad" (218). The narrative does indicate that the Bannocks were responding to sexual assaults by whites, at least in their movement from the Fort Hall area to the Malheur Reservation (139), and this explanation for the conflict takes part in a broader pattern in the text of understanding forms of what otherwise appear to be unreasonable expressions of Native aggression as direct reactions to white gendered violence, or the ways that settlement itself functions as gendered violence.[77] Apart from this fairly brief, if telling reference, though, Winnemucca casts the Bannocks as engaging in inappropriate violence. Separating the good Indians from the bad ones in this way maintains the integrity of the Paiutes as both a distinct collective and one worthy of public *pleading* in their interests.[78]

More than simply outlining differences among tribes so as to facilitate advocacy, *Life* helps generate a sense of Paiute national coherence by implicitly mobilizing existing administrative templates for understanding Native collective identity. The narrative treats the Columbia River Indians and the Bannocks as discrete groups, and to the extent that they appear as tribes or tribe-like entities, Winnemucca can defend the Paiutes from association with them by highlighting the distinctiveness of Paiute tribal identity. The Columbia River Indians and the Bannocks, though, were not so much longstanding ethnic or political units as complex and shifting networks where belonging had more to do with shared principles (including prophetic affiliations) than genealogical connections or generationally enduring ties to particular territories. While "the Columbia River Indians" often indicated the followers of the prophet Smohalla who had gathered in the area of Priest Rapids just south of the Columbia River in the mid-nineteenth century, the name also served as something of a catchall for the various bands in that vicinity who refused to live on reservations.[79] The annual report from the Oregon superintendency for 1870 notes "the existence among the Indians of Oregon of a peculiar religion, called 'Smokeller,' or Dreamers, the chief doctrine of which is, that the 'red man is again to rule the country,'" indicating that this doctrine "sometimes leads to rebellion against lawful authority."[80] This description suggests a direct relation between the visions of Smohalla (as well as those who follow him) and *rebellion* against U.S. Indian policy. However, other reports suggest a broader field of reference. One annual report from Oregon speaks of "tribes not under the supervision of agents" who "consist of scattered bands along the Columbia River" and who "are scattered over so vast a country that it would be impossible to gather them together for a treaty," and another report suggests, "There are several bands of Indians living on the

Columbia River, all of whom have been parties to treaties, but have refused to comply with treaty stipulations, and who, under the ruling of Commissioner Parker, last June, have thereby forfeited all right and interest in and to lands and annuities per treaty."[81] In his official report on the Bannock War, General Howard recounts, "I was looking for the first disturbance among the Columbia renegades, who were greatly dissatisfied because of the requirements of the Indian Bureau, that they should go to the Yakima, the Umatilla, or other Indian reservations, . . . [which] would result in taking them from their present homes, if their ranges in nomadic life can be called homes."[82] These examples point to the ways that the phrase "Columbia River Indians" less indexed a determinate group than provided a means of collating a range of people(s) whose principal unifying characteristic, in the phrase's various iterations, lay in their refusal to conform to settler-sanctioned procedures, identifications, and mappings.

They rejected the authority of agents and other government officials, the reservation topographies of Indian policy, and the insistence on their belonging to particular federally recognized tribal entities. Andrew Fisher notes, "In the 1870s, roughly a third of the people assigned to the four southern [Columbia] Plateau reservations (Warm Springs, Yakama, Umatilla, Nez Perce) had either refused to settle there or stayed only part of the year," later adding, "These 'renegades' never abandoned their ancestral village sites, cemeteries, and fishing stations along the Columbia River."[83] The notion of *the Columbia River Indians*, then, offered a way of speaking in toto about a range of groups (themselves composed of an assortment of persons and bands from peoples across the region) as if they could be treated as a kind of unit, when the category actually was defined by their negative relation to the terms of Indian administration—their supposed scatteredness, nomadism, recalcitrance, and opposition to white governance.[84]

The "Bannocks" encompasses an even wider array of groups over a much broader territorial range. The term "Bannock" most directly refers to a Northern Paiute dialect, and it was used to encompass Paiute-speaking and Shoshone-speaking mounted bands from the Great Basin who increasingly took part in buffalo hunts to the east during the first half of the nineteenth century. As Smoak notes, "All the Indian peoples who lived in southern Idaho at the time of white contact spoke a dialect of either or both Shoshone and Paiute, two closely related languages," and "among themselves, the various Paiute, Bannock, and Shoshone speakers called themselves Numu, Neme, or Newe, meaning simply 'the people.'" In the wake of the acquisition of horses, Paiute speakers migrated to the upper Snake River Plain "where they adopted the horse-bison economy then developing among the local Shoshone speakers and became an integrated minority within the larger group. It was this bilingual community that became the mixed bands of the treaty era and the Bannocks of the reservation period." The Bannocks come to be associated with the Fort Hall Reservation in what is now southeastern Idaho. Created by executive order in 1867, the reservation served as the principal state-recognized space for the Bannocks in the wake of the Fort Bridger Treaty of 1868, even as those bands known as Bannocks continued to spend most of their time off reservation.[85] However, the term was used more broadly by U.S. officials to include a range of mounted bands across the northern Great Basin and western Columbia Plateau. They are described as "rang[ing] the extreme southeastern part of Oregon, the northern part of Nevada, and southwestern Idaho."[86]

These groups, though, also were folded into the category of "Snakes," for which "Bannocks" was often used as a substitute. As Susan Jane Stowell notes, "Snake" is "a term . . . white trappers and explorers used to refer to Indians they encountered in areas anywhere from the western Plateau to southeastern Oregon and portions of western Nevada."[87] Those peoples loosely called Snakes are, in the words of one official, "a numerous race, divided into various subtribes or bands, and extending over a very large extent of country; but their general characteristics are the same. Their language differs in its dialects, but its groundwork is the same. They are a nomadic people, ranging from Nevada and Utah to Oregon, Idaho, Washington, and Montana, often under different names." He adds, "These Indians are now beyond the reach of the Indian bureau, and probably will never come until its control," further suggesting that "it is utterly impossible to *treat* with them, and it is fearfully expensive, saying nothing of the loss of life, to fight them."[88] Here we see, again, a process of collecting a range of persons and bands into a category that then functions as it if it were referential, as if it simply indicated a particular group or determinate set of groups rather than a kind of relation to U.S. policy. What marks the Bannocks/Snakes as such seems to be that they are "beyond the reach of the Indian bureau," that they do not choose to remain on reservation, and that they occupy spaces to which U.S. officials do not deem them properly to belong. In distancing the Paiutes from *Bannocks* and *Columbia River Indians*, Winnemucca seeks to cast the former as more amenable to U.S. aims and imperatives—as *good* and, thus, as not in need of military discipline and retributory displacement from their lands. In doing so, the text employs strategies of naming and description consistent with those at play in Indian administration in order to mark distinctions among these supposed tribes.

U.S. officials speak of "the Columbia River Indians" and the "Bannocks" as if they were clearly defined tribal entities, but instead, we might understand them as principally marked in non-native accounts by their rejection of settler frameworks. This perspective resonates with Audra Simpson's foregrounding of refusal as an alternative to recognition, suggesting that such refusal "comes with the requirement of having one's *political* sovereignty acknowledged and upheld, and raises the question of legitimacy for those who are usually in the position of recognizing: What is their authority to do so? Where does it come from?"[89] As discussed in the introduction, Simpson highlights the ways that the expectation that Native political forms should fit neatly in nondisruptive ways within settler jurisdictional structures normalizes such structures and displaces the colonial violence enacted through their ongoing imposition. In this way, the people(s) that come to appear in non-native narratives as the Columbia River Indians and the Bannocks might be characterized as engaged in a project of refusal. As Goeman asks, quoting Irene Watson, "Are we free to roam?": "Do I remain the unsettled native, left to unsettle the settled spaces of empire?"[90] Or in Nick Estes's terms, "Natives off the reservation are the unfinished business of settler colonialism—the ones who refused to disappear, refused to sell their lands, and refused to quit being Indians."[91] The practices, porousness, and mobilities of these groups in the nineteenth-century Great Basin contest the geographies of containment imposed through federal practices of categorization and the understanding of each such named tribe as properly belonging to a specific reservation space.

The pursuit of non-native recognition in Winnemucca's narrative, though, sets her at odds with such refusals. She seeks to produce a portrait of the "Piute nation" in and through her claims to representative status that can differentiate that entity and its people from those other groups, who are deemed threatening, blameworthy, and in need of discipline/chastisement by non-native officials. Yet, Simpson also suggests that acts of Indigenous refusal occur in the context of "operating in the teeth of Empire, in the face of state aggression," further referring to Native peoples as existing under settler rule "in states of strangulation," and she asks, "How does one assert sovereignty and independence when some of the power to define that sovereignty is bestowed by a foreign power?"[92] This question brings us back to the entanglements of empire. In this vein, Winnemucca's differentiation of "Paiutes" from "Columbia River Indians" and "Bannocks"—her positioning of herself as the spokesperson for the good against the bad—can be seen as employing settler-defined notions of Native identity and sovereignty in trying to redress the kinds of colonial strangulation at play in the Great Basin. Within regional networks, "Paiute," "Columbia River Indian," and "Bannock" do not function as discrete categories, and the kinds of refusal that get attached to the latter two in settler narratives and that make them targets of state aggression and discipline also characterize actions by some of those labeled as Paiutes. Thus, as part of advocating for "the Piute nation" with non-native publics, Winnemucca generates a version of Paiute nationality that can be disaggregated from extant regional modes of relation, placemaking, and belonging so as to create an innocence-making distance.

That differentiation further can be understood as part of an effort to extricate Paiutes from what can be characterized as the Ghost Dance geographies and networks in which they were enmeshed. Connections among peoples throughout the Great Basin and onto the Columbia Plateau were mediated by prophet movements and conducted in relation to shamanic phenomena of various sorts, and *Life* largely does not engage those relations. The reason for this apparent lapse on the part of the text may have to do with the ways such interactions were noted by the U.S. government and seen as a potentially dangerous source of insurgency, from which Winnemucca wants to distinguish "the Piute nation."

If Winnemucca's father functions in the narrative as a means of projecting the coherence of Paiute identity via his representative status as the "head chief," he also provides one of the most consistent sites of ongoing connection between those groups who appear in non-native accounts as Paiutes and those categorized as Bannocks. One of the earliest reports from the Nevada superintendency mentions a meeting "with Winnemucka and his people, and also some Bannacks who were visiting them at the time," adding, "The Bannacks have returned to their own country, accompanied by old Winnemucka, who intends spending the summer with them and returning to his tribe in autumn."[93] Such presence was not unusual given the kinship relations among the various bands.[94] These connections, though, also may have had to do with Chief Winnemucca's regionally well-known status as an antelope charmer, and that shamanic role may have enabled him to build a relationship with Pasheco, a prophet figure who emerged among the Bannocks in the late 1850s. Pasheco was credited by U.S. officials with organizing an attack on the Mormon mission at Lemhi, in what is now Idaho, and with promoting disruption of patterns of white settlement.[95] Pasheco may have been in attendance at the conference among Native leaders that preceded the Pyramid Lake War in 1860, and in 1863, the local agent asked Chief Winnemucca to visit Pasheco in order to convince him to let settlers on their way to California pass through his territory undisturbed as well as to talk him down from a broader campaign to eliminate white presence in the area.[96] Chief Winnemucca's primary residence at that point was in the vicinity of the Pyramid Lake Reservation in western Nevada. The fact that he was seen as a useful envoy to someone whose base of operations lay hundreds of miles away suggests the likely presence of sustained relations among members of those bands achieved through regular travel, including by Chief Winnemucca. In addition, his prominence as a wielder of puha facilitated connections with others similarly endowed, even when the forms of power they expressed may have differed. Such linkages, though, do not follow patterns of tribal affiliation or territory as they were understood within U.S. policy discourses.[97]

While such connections preceded the Ghost Dance of 1870, the movement arising from Wodziwob's visions seems to have consolidated, intensified, and extended those networks of relation. An 1873 article in the *Idaho Statesman* suggested that Chief Winnemucca "had reportedly turned to the Ghost Dance religion, sending runners to the various tribes to tell of his prophecy that one day Indian warriors would rise from their graves and collect on the plain in a powerful army that would wipe out the white man."[98] By 1871, U.S. officials had started to register the presence of the Ghost Dance and its spread across the region. The agent at Pyramid Lake reported that April that Wodziwob's influence was increasing: "They got impressed with the idea that 'God was coming' and are very susceptible of religious things, and very serious even in their monotonous dance, modifying it very much. Their criers go about the circular camp crying 'God is coming.'"[99] Moreover, a few years later, Agent Rinehart speaks of dances, or "fandangos" as they were called, occurring on the Malheur Reservation several times a year.[100] In his autobiographical recollection of events from this period in *My Life and Experiences*, General Howard observes, "A favorite idea, similar to the 'Messiah craze,' carried by these Dreamers from tribe to tribe all through the Northwest country, was that there would soon be a resurrection of Indians. All the whites were to be killed and the Indians' wrongs would then be righted." He adds with respect to the fact that some Paiutes joined with Bannocks during the Bannock War, "It was while these Pi-Utes were in a state of unrest and extreme discontent that the Bannock messengers had come among them. The outbreak seemed so extensive that the old *tooats* suddenly had a new inspiration to the effect that the time was at hand for the great long-promised resurrection of Indians. This news was carried from tribe to tribe."[101] Bannocks certainly were followers and transmitters of the Ghost Dance movement, spreading it eastward from where it began on the Walker River Reservation in southwestern Nevada, and performing related dances during the war.[102]

The tendency of U.S. officials, civilian and military, to use the term "Dreamer" to refer to adherents of the movement that followed from Wodziwob's visions and the one connected to Smohalla suggests that the two energized each other and expanded the reach of both. In his report following the war, Howard indicates, "Their spirit prophets, for example, Oytes, of the Malheurs, prophesied that the time had come when the Indians were to destroy the whites and recover their country," and Rinehart notes in a letter sent in March 1874 with respect to Paiutes at Malheur, "They all held to that particular religious creed called 'Dreamers' and practiced all the peculiar rites of that strange belief—such as drumming and dancing, bowing and making strange signs."[103] In addition, when the Bannock forces were being pursued by the U.S. army, there was some suspicion that they were seeking to make their way north to join with Smohalla's followers at Priest Rapids.[104] Prophecy in various forms, then, can be understood as mediating relations across the region, facilitating and helping sustain connections among bands and peoples whose primary dwelling places were far from each other. However, as I have been suggesting, such webs of relation do not so much arise purely in response to the Ghost Dance and other vision complexes as build on prior seasonal periodicities, kinship patterns, and ritual conjunctures, which do not fit well within the tribal mappings of Indian policy.

In avoiding discussion of Ghost Dancing and the Native sociospatial networks that animate it and that it further enables, Winnemucca's narrative seeks to generate a sense of Paiute separateness that can justify advocacy for the return of Malheur residents from their exile to the Yakima Reservation. They had been forcibly relocated to Yakima—about four hundred miles from Malheur—as punishment for having participated in the Bannock War, even those who had been noncombatants unassociated with Bannock forces.[105] The petition with which the narrative closes requests "the Honorable Congress of the United States to restore to them said Malheur Reservation," adding, "And especially do we petition for the return of that portion of the tribe arbitrarily removed from the Malheur Reservation, after the Bannock war, to the Yakima Reservation on Columbia River, in which removal families were ruthlessly separated" (247). Presenting the Paiutes who had resided at the Malheur Reservation as having been intimately enmeshed in wide-ranging relations that encompassed the Bannocks and the Columbia River Indians, therefore, would undermine an argument for their right to return to their former federally recognized lands. In her engagements with the press, Winnemucca consistently sought to distance Paiutes from the conflict, insisting in November 1879 that "my people last year did not at all want to go to war, but the Bannacks made all the trouble for them."[106] Such claims seek to counter the charges of general Paiute engagement as hostiles in the war, a narrative principally circulated by General Howard, who in his official report indicates that "all the Malheur Indians" joined Bannock forces.[107]

As against a sense of prophet-animated fluidity among populations and territories in the region, *Life* posits a clear distinction between those few who were guilty of collaborating with insurgents and those innocents who wrongly had been removed to what the text terms "some foreign country" (204). Winnemucca insists, "My people have not done anything, and why should they be sent away from their own country? If there are any to be sent away, let it be Oytes and his few men" (203). Later, when meeting in Washington, D.C., with Secretary of the Interior Carl Schurz, she notes, "I have come to plead for my poor people who are dying off with broken hearts, because they are separated from their children and husbands and wives and sons," and in response to the charge that "they are bad people" who "have killed and scalped many innocent people," she retorts. "Not so; my people who are over there at Yakima did not do so any more than you have scalped people. There are only a few who went with the Bannocks who did wrong," further declaring, "I have not come to plead for the bad ones" (218). While recycling the trope of "bad" Indians from earlier in the narrative, this moment suggests the political ecology in which such a figuration gains meaning and force. To the extent that the Paiutes blend into other peoples, that they are indistinguishable as a unit from those groups that have resisted U.S. policy and administrative mappings, they become legitimately subject to disciplinary action. More than punishment for actual engagement in the war, the removal to Yakima can be justified as preemptive, as seeking to thwart a more general outbreak that would destabilize patterns of white settlement throughout the Great Basin and the Pacific Northwest. In a letter explaining his argument for the removal of all those associated with the Malheur Reservation, including Leggins's band, which was associated with Chief Winnemucca and had aided the military during the war, Howard asserts, "The return of Leggins or indeed of any of the Piutes to the Malheur reservation would have, inevitably resulted in war."[108] In this context, Winnemucca's insistence on the coherence of her "people" and on their separateness from the combatants works as a kind of institutional prophylaxis, creating a sense of tribal identity that can insulate them from charges of an ingrained inclination toward violence.

If they both are a distinct group and are not inherently *bad*, unlike the Bannocks and Columbia River Indians, then the actions of Oytes and those who went with him can be understood as exceptional—an aberrant "few" whose choices do not reflect true *Paiute* principles and tendencies. After her return to the Yakima Reservation from Washington, D.C., Winnemucca reports an accusation launched by one of the displaced Paiutes (Paddy) against Oytes: "You were first on your horse when the Bannocks came. You got us all into trouble, and only for you we had been in our own country. You are the cause of all our suffering" (237). Although I will address the politics of reservation claims and residence in the next section, this moment suggests the ways the narrative correlates Paiute distinctiveness with having their "own country" from which they wrongly have been removed due to the inappropriate conflation of them with the Bannocks. In fact, Winnemucca emphasizes how persuasive her in-person recounting of these dynamics has been in her ability to secure written permission from Secretary Schurz for Paiutes to leave Yakima, even while noting that this promise was never officially promulgated and, thus, did not produce the return it appears to enable.[109]

Disassociating Paiutes from prophet movements allows the narrative to reproduce-with-a-difference non-native accounts of the relation between prophecy and insurgency. The text's earlier implicit characterization of Oytes as a witch, in the complaints of his making people ill, dovetails with Winnemucca's depiction of his participation in the Bannock War in ways that indirectly cite and confirm official narratives of Ghost Dancing as a threat to social order in the region. However, by localizing the disruptive effects of puha-related practices around Oytes, *Life* circumscribes and contains them. In doing so, the text mediates the picture of Paiute peoplehood circulating in official and popular discourses, helping coalesce a sense of general Paiute rectitude that would exempt them from intensified state supervision and would validate their return to their "country"—cast here as the Malheur Reservation. As Andrew McClure observes, "Part of the reason for Winnemucca's success as a voice and representative of the Paiutes, then, was that the whites perceived her as a 'civilized Indian,' an 'Indian Princess' who could act like them."[110] Part of being "like them" entails putative Paiute refusal to participate in the kinds of *savage* activities that the narrative associates with other Native peoples, such as the Bannocks and Columbia River Indians. More than just inverting the civilized/barbaric dichotomy in order to underline vicious and violent patterns of white behavior, Winnemucca draws on this binary to set the Paiutes apart from other Native groups, ones whose participation in prophet movements marked them as particular objects of settler suspicion, supervision, and suppression. The narrative's assertion of Winnemucca's ability to speak for a coherent Paiute people, then, takes part in an effort to clarify the sense of Paiute identity so as to differentiate it from the networks of puha-animated and prophet-mediated relation among people(s) throughout the region. In this way, *Life* implicitly takes up the discourse of Ghost Dancing–as–threat promulgated by civilian and military authorities but redeploys it in ways that exceptionalize such elements in Paiute sociality and, thus, help to coalesce a sense of the Paiutes as properly civilized partners for legal recognition and diplomatic negotiation.

Claiming the Reservation

Indigenous prophet movements in the Great Basin in the late nineteenth century often rejected U.S. policy mappings that sought to locate peoples on particular reservations as their exclusive space of occupancy. Or rather, such movements challenged the sense of determinate and easily delineated peoplehood—forms of tribal identity—on which such administrative cartographies depended. In order to assert that a given people should contain themselves within the boundaries of a given reservation (even when multiple peoples were placed on the same reservation), officials needed to claim relative coherence for that people, treating those who repudiated such processes of settler definition as dangerous renegades in need of military chastisement. While prophet movements rarely motivated violence against whites in the absence of other subsistence-based factors (such as conditions of starvation on reservation and denial of access to areas from which food resources previously had been garnered), prominent settler narratives about such movements' disruptive tendencies were not wrong. These movements did contest the legitimacy of Indian policy geographies and the processes of tribal nomination on which such political topographies relied. From this perspective, we might approach Winnemucca's narrative as participating in this federally sanctioned project of *misnaming*, by which multilayered matrices of peoplehood are carved up so as more easily to fit into the tribal mold of Indian policy frameworks. However, if *Life* contributes to this tendency toward consolidation at play in state initiatives, its maneuvers in this vein can be understood as an effort to secure stable landbases for those who were known as Northern Paiutes in official accounts. In speaking as the representative for "the Piute nation," Winnemucca argues for the need to maintain, restore, and increase Paiute reservations, conveying the sense of a distinct polity whose territoriality must be acknowledged by the federal government. Although in many ways taking up the orienting parameters of settler policy, the narrative mediates them in its appeal for public intervention. Through its portrait of life on Paiute reservations, particularly Pyramid Lake and Malheur, the text contests the almost unlimited discretion exercised by Indian agents while also challenging the regulations enacted to control Native labor and residency.

Winnemucca addresses the question of control over state-sanctioned reservations in terms of the longer history of settler dispossession, staging Native inhabitance in and authority over such spaces as a function of Indigenous peoples' inherent rights to their own territories. During the text's discussion of the Paiutes' exile to Yakima, she provides an encompassing critique of the force of displacement that has attended white presence, of which the removal from the area around Malheur is just the latest example. She declares,

> Oh, for shame! You who are educated by a Christian government in the art of war; the practice of whose professions makes you natural enemies of the savages, so called by you. Yes, you, who call yourselves the great civilization; you who have knelt upon Plymouth Rock, covenanting with God to make this land the home of the free and the brave. Ah, then you rise from your bended knees and seizing the welcoming hands of those who are the owners of this land, which you are not, your carbines rise upon the bleak shore, and your so-called civilization sweeps inland from the ocean wave; but, oh, my God! leaving its pathway marked by crimson lines of blood and strewed by the bones of two races, the inheritor and the invader. (207)

Official U.S. action against the Paiutes appears not as a function of hostile activities on their part (which Winnemucca consistently denies) but as due to a drive toward conquest borne from at least Anglo arrival at Plymouth and carried forth across the continent. The supposed march of civilization here becomes a trail of blood marked by the production of white freedom through genocidal violence.[111] In this process, the true "owners of this land" are replaced by a "race" of "invader[s]" whose residence on Indigenous territories is made possible by recourse to sustained campaigns of unprovoked military assault. Winnemucca presents Paiute attachments to their reservations, and efforts to regulate Paiute sociality on them, in light of this history of aggression and annexation.

Egan serves as the vehicle through which the narrative offers its most forceful articulations of Paiute connections to reservation lands. Agent Rinehart claims with respect to the Malheur Reservation that "nothing here is yours. It is all the government's," to which Egan responds, "We want to know how the government came by this land" (133). He further remarks, "His white children have come and have taken all our mountains, and all our valleys, and all our rivers; and now, because he has given us this little place without our asking him for it, he sends you here to tell us to go away" (134). The narrative here contests the claim by the United States of an underlying jurisdiction that gives the federal government ultimate authority to do what it will with respect to Native lands. Egan's question foregrounds the legitimacy crisis faced by settler rule in its assertion of the de facto domesticity of Indigenous territories, highlighting the absence of consent to such U.S. superintendence. The reservation functions as a bulwark against white incursions—a "little place" that can be theirs in the face of non-native occupation of much of the rest of their homeland.[112] Egan underlines enduring collective Paiute relations with particular lands and waters through the use of "our," suggesting a political entity with whose histories and articulations the United States should engage. The Paiute people may not have asked to be placed within the constricted boundaries of the reservation, but Winnemucca suggests that it represents the remainder of a larger area over which the Paiutes have exerted control that wrongfully has been taken from them largely without meaningful input on their part, or at least under circumstances of escalating duress.

The text further presents the reservation as a kind of space whose insulation from white encroachment is necessary for Paiute survival. Speaking earlier in the narrative to Samuel Parrish, the first agent at Malheur, Egan and Leggins insist, "Tell our Big Father that we don't want to give up any of our reservation. We want it all. The Pyramid Lake Reservation is too small for us all, and the white people have already taken all the best part of it. We cannot all live there, and in the case they take it all we can have this to live on," adding, "There are a great many of our people, and we do not want to give up any of our land. Another thing, we do not want to have white people near us" (115–116). *Life* connects Pyramid Lake and Malheur as part of a continuum of Paiute placemaking, indicating that overcrowding and white incursions at one have required movement to the other. Both locations are part of "our land," and Malheur operates as something of a supplement to Pyramid Lake by providing a backup in case those lands in their entirety are seized by whites (or given to them by the government).[113] Malheur also appears as distant from white presence in ways that create something of a buffer zone that the text suggests better can enable Paiute flourishing. Despite the fact that there's no evidence Egan and those under his leadership ever had any sustained relationship to the Pyramid Lake Reservation, his portrayal as part of a singular Paiute "our" helps coalesce the sense that the Paiutes are a singular "nation" with its own landbase that has been severely diminished through settlement and settler violence. The attribution of such collective ownership to a definite political entity—call it a tribe—facilitates the text's efforts to critique ongoing processes of dispossession and removal and to cast state-recognized reservations as sites of Native sovereignty. To the extent that the Paiutes constitute a *nation* extending over much of Nevada and into southeastern Oregon, Winnemucca can present the reservations associated with Paiute groups as part of a unified homeland that has been carved up as a result of ongoing and escalating settler incursions. Her arguments about protecting Paiute reservations gain force as an extension of her representative status as a proper negotiator for the Paiute people, envisioned as a cohesive polity.

In this way, Winnemucca mediates the role of the reservation in U.S. policy imaginaries, shifting away from prominent popular and administrative accounts of these lands as indicative of U.S. largesse and toward a conceptualization of them as the result of ongoing diplomatic engagements with Native peoples. As a kind of bureaucratic form through which to address Native peoplehood and territoriality, the reservation does not inherently represent Indigenous sovereignty and self-determination. From the 1850s onward, lands reserved for Native inhabitance—by treaty, executive order, or other means—increasingly were portrayed in official discourses and within non-native publics as gifts from the federal government. With the end of treaty making in 1871, that depiction of U.S. administrative modes of acknowledging Native lands gains greater scope and momentum, particularly because the principal legal mechanism for such acknowledgment changes from a constitutionally recognized diplomatic instrument/process to unilateral action by the federal executive branch.[114] *Life*, though, takes up the reservation as a bureaucratic form in Indian law and policy in ways that seek to imbue it with other meanings. Winnemucca aims to (re)orient the public sense of what a reservation is away from understandings of it as a site of unrestrained governmental discretion.

The narrative challenges the portrayal of Paiute reservations as a gift from the U.S. government, which would put residence there at the pleasure of the Indian agent who serves as the embodiment of the government's munificence, authority, and regulation.[115] In addition to characterizing U.S.-Paiute relations as having been conducted through treaties in both her narrative and public speeches (in ways discussed earlier), she emphasizes the unreasonableness of various agents' claims to exert virtually unlimited power over what happens at Pyramid Lake and Malheur. In addition to noting Rinehart's assertion that "nothing here is yours" (133), the text chronicles the discrepancy between his understanding of his authority and that of the previous agent, Parrish. After Rinehart insists, "This land which you are living on is government land," Egan responds, "we don't want the Big Father in Washington fool with us. He sends one man to say one thing and another to say something else. The man who just left us told us the land was ours, and what we do on it was ours" (124). This moment underlines the abrupt, incoherent changes in policy formulations that can arise from changes in agents when they are treated as if they, as avatars of federal will, single-handedly can determine the character of Native residence on reservation. Earlier, with respect to Pyramid Lake, Winnemucca notes that "there were thirteen agents there in the course of twenty-three years" (73), further chronicling one agent's exile of her brother Natchez for refusing to lie about getting rations they had not received and another's assertion, in the face of a refusal by reservation residents to turn over one-third of the grain they produce, that "if you won't do what the government orders, you must leave the reservation" (88, 95). Such a claim, repeated by various agents in the text, casts the reservation as a space conditioned by obedience to U.S. rules and mandates. The agent's license to assert control over all aspects of life on the reservation follows from the vision of it as an expression of settler charity—an altruism whose terms remain set by the donor rather than the reservation being governed by an inherent set of Native rights predicated on prior possession and self-governance. Moreover, even while casting Rinehart as despicable when compared with Parrish, the narrative implicitly raises questions about the latter in his claim that "the government is good to you" since "it gives you land for nothing" (107). By emphasizing the reservations' status as manifestations of the geopolitical identity of the Paiute nation, Winnemucca aims to modify the vision of Native land as government gift. She inhabits the policy architecture of Indian administration, centered as it was on reservation geographies, in order to resignify its organizing parameters.

In this vein, within the narrative, Native people's (and peoples') decisions to leave reservations indicate less an innate, savage inclination toward wandering than protest over poor treatment by U.S. officials and the violation of the promises made upon the drawing of reservation boundaries in the first place. Winnemucca exposes corrupt practices by agents who siphon off resources meant for Paiute people. For example, not only did the agents at Pyramid Lake fail to prevent white encroachments ("Since the railroad ran through in 1867, the white people have taken all the best part of the reservation" while "using the ditch which my people made to irrigate their land" [76–77]), they profit from leasing reservations lands to white herders: "This is the way all the Indian agents get rich. The first thing they do is start a store; the next thing is to take in cattle men, and cattle men pay the agent one dollar a head" (86). Reservation residents further were charged for the goods which they used, including rations (125). However, that issue arose only when rations actually were provided. At many points, Winnemucca notes the starving conditions of people on Paiute reservations due to the government's failure to feed them. In response to the Pyramid Lake agent's provision of "one ton of flour" to a group of Shoshones in order to impress a visiting colonel, Winnemucca exclaims, "You come up here to show off before this man. Go and bring some flour to my people on Humboldt River, who are starving, the people over whom you are agent" (87). With respect to the Malheur Reservation, residents report to her just prior to the Bannock War that Rinehart "has not given us anything to eat; he is not issuing rations to us as father Parrish used to do" (137), and later, Egan asks,

"What does that praying agent mean by not giving us our rations? What does he say about giving rations, anyhow; or, what does he say about giving us some of the wheat which we raised last year?" (141). These forms of exploitation and deprivation motivate flight from the reservations in search of less oversight and better conditions, including procuring basic sustenance. At one point, Chief Winnemucca explains to an army officer stationed in the vicinity of Malheur, "I have a reservation at my birth place called Pyramid Lake. For so many years not one of the agents ever gave me or my people an old rag. I am just from there. My people have nothing to live on there" (121–122).[116] While Chief Winnemucca's choice not to stay at either the Pyramid Lake or Malheur Reservations appears as a problem in need of resolution for a number of U.S. officials in the narrative, in ways discussed earlier, the text suggests that at least part of the reason for his movement lies in government malfeasance, especially in terms of the failure to provide the most basic necessities for those who have been administratively circumscribed within reservation boundaries.

These charges in the text resonate with explanations offered by Indian agents in Nevada, Oregon, and Idaho for the presence of Native people(s) off reservation over the course of the period covered by Winnemucca's narrative. While insisting that Paiutes "will not work for what they think the government owes them," officials in the Nevada superintendency also indicate that there is "no evidence of any attempt to render these reserves habitable or to develop their agricultural resources," and the absence of such resources contributes to forms of Native resistance based on lack of access to subsistence.[117] One agent notes, "No sooner were these supplies in the hands of the Indians, and the fear of starvation removed, than we heard no more of outbreaks," and that same report further suggests, "The meager amount of funds at our disposal required that the utmost economy be maintained in the issue of supplies even upon the reservations; thus a strict injunction was laid to issue supplies only to working Indians and their families."[118] As Rinehart suggests in one of his annual reports, the insistence that Native people on reservation work in order to receive rations (which he notes was legislated by Congress in 1875) may contribute to "the gradual and steady breaking down of tribal relations, and the decline of despotic authority in chiefs" and an attendant increase in "individual responsibility." That federal policy, though, also helps promote habitual movement beyond reservation boundaries, such as noted by agents in Nevada and Idaho: "This going abroad is inevitable, and must necessarily continue unless the Government exercises more generosity toward these Indians"; "I am not at all astonished at the action of my predecessors, in giving to the Indians long permits of absence from the reservation, having been obliged to do precisely as they did, viz, push the Indians out on fishing and hunting excursions for purposes of economy."[119] Moreover, even as U.S. officials cast the Bannocks as savage combatants in need of punishment, the account by the commissioner of Indian Affairs of the 1878 outbreak sets it against a background of deprivation, stating that "the small quantity of supplies furnished to the Bannocks by the government, have forced these Indians to continue their nomadic life to the present time" and that "it is not possible for them to settle upon the reservation which has been set apart for them until such a time as sufficient funds are appropriated by Congress to subsist them while doing the first year's farm work."[120] The agents often express frustration over Indigenous mobilities and animosities, but they also routinely justify such actions and affects in terms of the paucity of resources provided by Congress. These moments in agents' reports suggest that were Native people(s) to receive adequate provisions, they would consent to remain on government-outlined Indian lands. While Winnemucca consistently challenges the legitimacy of the agent system and the integrity of those serving in this role, *Life* largely echoes agents' ways of explaining the choice by some Paiutes to live off reservation or to live on reservation only a portion of the year, contesting not so much reservation geographies as the ways they are managed and funded.

The text's portrayal of flight from the reservation as a function of U.S. failure to provide adequate goods and to engage with resident Natives in nonexploitative ways also implicitly distinguishes the actions of those who refuse such conditions from others whose ingrained tendencies simply make them "bad Indians." Winnemucca's ability to rationalize Paiute behavior that seems antagonistic to the United States—short of participation in what officially is characterized as Native warfare (such as the decision by some Paiutes to join the Bannocks)—is dependent on making Paiute actions intelligible within the terms of Indian policy. In this vein, Winnemucca's presentation of herself as a representative spokesperson for the "Piute nation" facilitates her ability to position her account of Paiute resistance to reservation residence as definitive. She appears to offer the real reasons why Paiutes do not conform to administrative expectations of Indian docility, as opposed to narratives of ever-simmering insurgent intent such as in General Howard's argument for removing all of the Paiutes associated with Malheur to Yakima. Winnemucca's positioning of herself as the one to speak for the Paiute people helps render more persuasive her explanation of Paiutes' noncompliance with the terms of Indian policy. Reciprocally, her ability to offer an explanation that reaffirms the overall reasonableness of the reservation system (although not the actions of Indian agents) helps underwrite her status as a viable mediator with the U.S. government—as opposed to those "bad Indians" who lie beyond the sphere of civilized conduct and diplomacy.

Agents' reports, though, suggest a range of reasons why Native people(s) might refuse reservation residence that are less easily justified to non-native publics. While conveyed in dismissive and racializing ways, these characterizations of Indians' supposed tendencies toward wandering and factionalism provide traces of regional patterns of Indigenous refusal of the imperatives toward centralization, categorization, and containment that animate Indian policy (as well as that provide the institutional template for Winnemucca's articulations of Paiute nationality and reservation-based territoriality). Rinehart's reports from Malheur attribute resistance to residing on reservation to ingrained inclinations, characterizing groups of Indians living off reservation as "wild, roving, half-starved bands" who dwell "far back in the mountains" and as "renegades and stragglers" who cannot "be induced to change their roaming habits."[121] However, he also suggests that they desire to be "away from the influence of the whites" in "summer resorts in the mountains," which they use for "hunting and fishing," and in the wake of the Bannock War, he observes, "Winnemucca's people deserted Pyramid Lake Reservation for this, and soon abandoned it for a worthless life of independent vagabondage around frontier military posts and border towns."[122] These moments gesture toward why groups of Native people would choose to remain off reservation for extended periods, if not stay away entirely. Not only did agents fail to provide enough provisions to sustain large reservation populations, but Paiutes maintained ongoing relationships with other locations from which they derived subsistence and which they understood to be home sites of various kinds.

Yet since these are not locations of permanent settlements, the United States understands such enduring relationships and the kinship connections through which others gain access to these areas as merely "roving" and "roaming" over an otherwise undifferentiated landscape. As Elizabeth Povinelli suggests with respect to state understandings of nonsedentary modes of Indigenous placemaking, "It is only now emerging how deeply the liberal capitalist state has itself been defined in opposition to Western constructions of 'hunter-gatherers'—the arch[e]typical primitive—and therefore how difficult it is legally and economically for that state to make a fair assessment of . . . claims to traditional lands."[123] The matrices of seasonal inhabitance and movement and the shifting social networks through which variously constituted Paiute groups understand legitimate claims to place, then, appear in officials' accounts as the lack of a sustained or sustainable relation to reservation geographies. The Malheur Reservation itself was created as a space in which "to locate all the roving and straggling bands in Eastern and Southeastern Oregon," even as earlier reports suggest that flight from reservation residence may arise from "their desire to return to their old haunts." In the Nevada superintendency, agents often complained of the "unrestrained permission of the companies for the Indians to ride at their pleasure upon the railroads of the State," such that Paiutes and others could evade agents' authority while also "congregat[ing] along the line of the railroad."[124] When viewed from this perspective, reservations appear less as expressions of Indigenous landedness than as the imposition of non-native mappings onto existing social cartographies in ways that, at least in the context of the Great Basin, tend to create an impression of tribal geopolitical cohesion that does not fit extant mutable patterns of association and inhabitance.[125]

Although these dispersed and shifting patterns of leadership, movement (seasonal and otherwise), and coalescence as bands do not arise as a result of prophet movements, such movements worked through and at times helped catalyze these dynamics. As Goeman suggests, "Unlike the maps that designate Indian land as existing only in certain places, wherever we went there were Natives and Native space, and if there weren't, we carved them out," challenging the idea that Native place could or can be confined to those lands legally acknowledged by the United States as Indian Country. The shifting formations of placemaking and political relation at play in prophet movements, which appear in official U.S. accounts as aimless and barbaric nomadism, are part of such processes of creating Native space. Goeman further argues that "colonial spatial construction is not unidirectional, and Native people have mediated these spatial constructions with the best tools at their disposal—storytelling, writing, and sense of place."[126] However, if the storytelling at play in Native-authored texts mediated the colonial mappings of the reservation system, it did not always do so in ways that refused such administrative geographies, instead strategically inhabiting them in ways that also could efface other kinds of Native spatialities. In this vein, Winnemucca's choice in her narrative to avoid sustained engagement with the Ghost Dance and similar prophetic phenomena can be interpreted as related to the text's investment in downplaying the prominence of those modes of Indigenous networking, which run counter to Indian policy aims and the reservation topographies emphasized in *Life*.

Attending to prophet movements and their sociopolitical itineraries would involve addressing the regularity of Native withdrawal from reservations due to their circumscription of extant Native forms of collectivity and placemaking, as opposed to portraying reservation spaces as the baseline of Indigenous territoriality from which absence needs to be explained in negative terms—as a result of sustained deprivation or bad decisions by agents. Winnemucca's narration of

Paiute relations to their reservations, then, can be understood as taking part in what Scott L. Pratt has characterized, with respect to accounts of Lakota Ghost Dancing, as "ontological reduction." Pratt suggests that non-native characterizations of the 1890 Ghost Dance tend to seek to explain away its meanings to participants on the Plains by offering "naturalist" explanations that cast their involvement as merely a reaction to settler violence.[127] Smoak offers a similar rejoinder to such causal narratives: "On one level they [Ghost Dances] represented a culturally consistent appeal to a supernatural power aimed at restoring the flow of that power toward native people. But on another they were a vehicle for the expression of meaningful social identities."[128] The kinds of geopolitical formations and shifting modes of Indigenous self-identification and group belonging at play in prophet movements in the Great Basin take part in a broader set of social patterns that lead various groups of Paiutes to choose primarily to reside off reservation, and those patterns precede and exceed the tribal mappings implemented through Indian policy and the jurisdictional imperatives that animate them.

Winnemucca's focus on asserting Paiute authority over their reservations, though, works to preserve a landbase for (the) Paiute people. Her articulations of her own representativity position her as a spokesperson for the Northern Paiutes, presented as a coherent polity, and in this role, she can deploy the topos of the reservation—a staple within U.S. Indian policy discourses of the late nineteenth century—as a way of figuring ongoing Paiute territoriality while also insisting on the ethical responsibility of the U.S. government legally to acknowledge the Paiutes as a landed polity and their right to self-governance over such spaces. As the culmination of her speaking tour of the Northeast, Winnemucca appeared before Congress in April 1884, and her primary aim in her testimony was to secure a reservation at Fort McDermitt (which was created in July 1889), partially to replace the Malheur Reservation (since it had been returned to the public lands by presidential executive order in 1882) and partially to secure lands nearer where her father had resided for years prior to his death in 1882.[129] Through this effort, she seeks to address the ongoing displacement of Paiute people, including the seizure of their lands by non-natives on existing reservations like Pyramid Lake. As reported by the *Boston Globe* in March 1883 during her Northeastern tour, Winnemucca had "come to Boston to raise money for the purpose of purchasing land and locating her people where they cannot be removed at the whim of every new administration."[130] Reservations, then, function as the means through which to render Paiute territoriality intelligible to the U.S. government, with Winnemucca translating Paiute place-making into the bureaucratic form of the reservation. In *Life among the Piutes* and her public appearances, Winnemucca cites the reservation as the principal vehicle through which to assert and secure U.S. recognition for Native territories and political identities. In doing so, she seeks to participate within the networks of Indian policy, rather than having Paiutes be dismissed or disciplined as "bad Indians" whose wandering and violent propensities indicate the impossibility of any kind of diplomatic, reciprocal relation between them and the settler-state.

In mediating the frames and imperatives of Indian policy, Winnemucca argues for forms of government-recognized Paiute landedness separated from oversight by Indian agents, and her endorsement of allotment is in the service of such liberation from U.S. bureaucratic oversight. As Beth Piatote observes in "The Indian/Agent Aporia," "'Indian' had come to mean a subject administratively and legally devoid of agency and anomalously positioned in relationship to the American state and its values."[131] The kinds of on-reservation deprivations Winnemucca addresses are presented as a result of the official dynamics of subjection/abjection operative in the Indian agency system. In *Life*, she insists "there is no law with agents. The few good ones cannot do good enough to make it worth while to keep up that system" (178), later adding, "I beseech of you, hear our pitiful cry to you, sweep away the agency system; give us homes to live in, for God's sake and for humanity's sake" (243). Winnemucca illustrates the extremity of officials' misconduct in her much-circulated and reprinted letter to the commissioner of Indian Affairs, where she asks, "What is the object of the Government in regard to Indians? Is it enough that we are at peace? Remove all the Indians from the military posts and place them on reservations such as the Truckee and Walker River reservations (as they were conducted), and it will require a greater military force stationed around to keep them within the limits than it now does to keep them in subjection."[132] The desire to be free of agent interference, graft, incompetence, and retribution motivates the argument for allotment, since having reservations overseen by agents suggests not so much protected inhabitance as the absence of "homes to live in," given the virtually unlimited discretion exercised by officials in deciding who could remain on reservation and under what terms. The petition that closes *Life*, which Winnemucca had been circulating in her public appearances, indicates the desirability of the Paiutes receiving "lands in severalty without losing tribal relations . . . where their citizenship implied in this distribution of land, will defend them from the encroachments of white settlers" (247). In contrast to the detribalizing privatization envisioned by the federal policy of allotment as adopted in the Dawes Act of 1887 and the statutes that followed, Winnemucca presents "severalty" as a means for Paiutes to exercise forms of collective authority—to maintain "tribal relations"—while also possessing kinds of legal status, including U.S. citizenship, that would prevent the routine violences and dislocations that accompany Indian policy as it had been implemented in the Great Basin.[133]

Through the push for allotment in *Life* and her public efforts, then, Winnemucca seeks not the obliteration of Paiute peoplehood but, instead, to sustain Paiute *tribal relations*. In making this argument, she presents Paiute reservations as indexing the geopolitical cohesion of the Paiute people. Official and popular non-native narratives of reservations as resulting from U.S. largesse cast these spaces less as Native national homelands than as gifts by a civilized benefactor to benighted peoples, largely in order to prevent their further wandering in ways that would disrupt white settlement. As against this image of legally recognized Native lands, which licenses U.S. claims to the right to regulate all conduct on such lands, Winnemucca insists that the Pyramid Lake and Malheur Reservations, in particular, have been carved out of the pre-contact territories of "the Piute nation." As such, Paiutes should exercise full sovereign authority over them. By presenting herself as the spokesperson for this political entity, which includes but also exceeds the reservations per se, Winnemucca generates a sense of coherent Paiute collective identity that provides the basis for Paiute territoriality. In this way, she draws on the reservation as a form within Indian policy in order to contest the notion that the United States possesses an underlying jurisdiction that allows the government to create and eliminate enclosed Indian spaces at will and to move populations among those sites as it sees fit. Winnemucca's implicit portrayal of Paiute geographies as expressive of an integrated national landbase also works as a way of refuting proliferating depictions of Native peoples as merely roaming across the landscape in ways divorced from meaningful placemaking.

However, *Life*'s presentation of reservations as a significant horizon of Paiute political aspiration runs counter to other evidence from the period that suggests the ongoing refusal by numerous Paiute persons and groups to remain on reservation. While Winnemucca often represents evidence of such trajectories as due to agents' misconduct, and by extension the deplorable dynamics of the agency system as a whole, Paiutes' choices to reside off reservation may be understood as expressive of shifting modes of association, placemaking, leadership, and memory that do not conform to the bounded vision of geopolitical identity at play in federal policy's conception of the Indian tribe. Instead, the social patterns sustained off reservation by groups of Paiutes—groups whose composition keeps changing and whose relation to particular spaces does not take the form of a centralized exertion of jurisdiction—is consistent with the expressions of Indigenous peoplehood within nineteenth-century prophet movements. Conversely, such movements in the Great Basin can be understood as oriented by longstanding regional formations of Native peoplehood that operate in ways irreducible to the reservation-based mappings of indigeneity employed in Indian policy, on which Winnemucca draws in advocating for Paiutes within non-native public discourses.

Winnemucca's narrative does not engage with Ghost Dancing, and arguably, it cannot do so within the ways it frames Paiute identity, territory, and governance. Ghost Dancing draws on conceptions of power (puha), shifting forms of collective identification, and patterns of placemaking that do not align with a conception of the Paiute people as a unified entity with a singular leadership that can easily be differentiated from surrounding peoples. Or, rather, Ghost Dancing takes part in, and circulates through, extant modes of Indigenous networking in the Great Basin, sociopolitical matrices that also supported earlier and other contemporaneous prophet movements that do not result from Wodziwob's vision and its specific dissemination. These geographies are expressive of forms of indigeneity that do not fit easily into mappings organized around Indian tribes, envisioned as discretely insulated from each other in terms of their spheres of governance and bounded territories. However, official discourses of Indian policy, as well as popular accounts, cast deviations from this cartography of tribal separateness as expressive of savage tendencies toward nomadism and/or projects of antisettler warfare. In many ways, *Life among the Piutes* reiterates these ways of framing Native collective identity and territoriality. Winnemucca's account of "the Piute nation" presents it as having a centralized leadership (based in her family) that extends over Paiute communities reaching from mid-Nevada up into eastern Oregon and western Idaho, as clearly distinguishable from other peoples who are viewed as problems by U.S. officials (particularly the Columbia River Indians and the Bannocks), and as possessing an integrated landbase from which federally acknowledged reservations can be carved and over which the Paiute people can exert clear political authority.

Life bends around the presence of the Ghost Dance in the period Winnemucca addresses while also registering traces of such prophet movements and the regional social, spatial, and spiritual processes in which they were enmeshed. Foregrounding that simultaneous absence and somewhat haunting presence in the narrative draws attention to the particular ways Winnemucca formulates the terms of Paiute nationhood, displacing the question of accuracy/authenticity with an attention to the stakes of Winnemucca's use of political form. In positioning herself as a proper representative for *the* Paiute people, she discursively constitutes the entity for which she putatively speaks. Winnemucca's presentation of her chiefly lineage as authorizing her public speech in the Paiutes' name takes part in a project of depicting the Paiutes as a cohesive political identity whose existence as such precedes white intervention, and that portrayal functions in the interest of advocating for Paiutes as a political body—for the protection of extant reservation boundaries, for diplomatic engagement with them by the federal government, for the return of Paiutes from Yakima, and for the dismantling of the agency system. Put another way, the kinds of public advocacy in which Winnemucca is engaged may necessitate the depiction of Paiutes in this way—in the form of the Indian tribe—in order to gain access to the limited and diminishing forms of (geo)political recognition for Native peoples offered by the federal government in the late nineteenth century. *Life* takes up the modes of Indigenous peoplehood circulating within federal policy, seeking to activate the potentials of such framings and to deploy them toward policy ends at odds with existing administrative procedures and determinations (including soliciting support from non-native publics). Thus, if we treat Winnemucca's account as providing a window onto, in Lisa Brooks's terms, Indigenous "political systems, relationships, and epistemologies," we can miss the intellectual and political work performed by the narrative in navigating, mediating, and mobilizing the formulations at play in Indian policy.[134] Attending to the absent presence in the narrative of the Ghost Dance, and related movements and social patterns in the Great Basin, allows us better to see the text's efforts to refunction and reorient extant federal templates while also underlining the limits, erasures, and costs of available official and popular discourses of Indianness and tribal identity.

4. THE NATIVE INFORMANT SPEAKS

*The Politics of Ethnographic Subjectivity
in Zitkala-Ša's Autobiographical Stories*

What is the legal and political status of Native peoples at the end of the nineteenth century? Put another way, what kind of entity are Native peoples in U.S. law and policy in this period? The end of treaty making in 1871 raises fundamental questions about how to regard indigeneity and Indigenous polities. The seminal Supreme Court decision in *U.S. v. Kagama* (1886) turns on these questions, while largely deferring them.[1] The case addresses the murder of one resident of the Hoopa Valley Reservation in California by another resident and whether this crime can be tried as such by federal authorities and courts under the Major Crimes Act, passed the previous year, which made various acts committed by *Indians* against other *Indians* (including murder, rape, and larceny) a matter of U.S. federal jurisdiction. The Court finds that law to be constitutional, indicating that the federal government can exert authority over actions that occur on reservation by members of the people whose reservation it is. The questions forwarded by the U.S. Circuit Court, on which the case is decided, include the following: "Whether the courts of the United States have jurisdiction or authority to try and punish an Indian belonging to an Indian tribe for committing the crime of murder upon another Indian belonging to the same Indian tribe, both sustaining usual tribal relations."[2] In seeking to establish what manner of legal object a "tribe" might be and what sort of connection "tribal relations" could constitute, the decision distinguishes both from the category of "nation," instead presenting Native peoples as "communities dependent on the United States."[3] The Court held, "They were, and always have been, regarded as having a semi-independent position when they preserved their tribal relations; not as States, not as nations, not as possessed of the full attributes of sovereignty, but as a separate people with the power of regulating their internal and social relations, and thus far not brought under the laws of the Union nor of the State within whose limits they resided."[4] "Tribal relations" involve having a "separate" existence with its own "internal and social relations" that, by virtue of being *tribal,* cannot be understood as "sovereignty"—as having an autonomous political existence not always-already (potentially) subordinated to the jurisdiction and governance of the settler-state. Indians, therefore, have distinct collectivities, but those collectivities cannot be "nations" due to their tribe-ness, which is to say their *Indianness.*

While *Kagama* somewhat circularly evades questions as to what particular "relations" constitute an entity as a "tribe" and why Native peoples should be understood as such, the notion of a tribe as a not-quite-political social body circulated widely in nineteenth-century ethnological discourses that themselves rather quickly became mainstay elements of Indian law and policy. The previous chapter addressed the ways that Sarah Winnemucca sought to consolidate Paiute affiliations, alliances, and geographies into an image of tribal coherence in order to generate (or, perhaps, simulate) the potential for diplomatic engagement with the U.S. government, crafting the impression of a singular polity for which she could serve as the representative in interactions with U.S. officials and appeals to non-native publics. However, over the 1870s and into the 1880s, the treaty-imaginary—in which the concept of the tribe served as a mode of figuring Native polities as coherent, centralized (semi-)sovereigns with whom the United States could negotiate—further attenuated. In its place, a vision of Native peoples as developmentally stunted residues of an earlier stage in human history rose to prominence as a central template for indigeneity within non-native networks, popular and official. Lewis Henry Morgan's *Ancient Society* (1877) both provides a powerful example of this understanding and itself offered an intellectual model that heavily influenced later government initiatives as well as provided a framework for what would by the early twentieth century emerge as the discipline of anthropology.[5] In it, Morgan draws a bright line between what he terms "social organization" and "political organization," the latter referring to a nation or state. He insists that to the extent that Native peoples can be understood as having governments, they are of a "purely personal character," since they depend on "gentes" or extended kinship networks. This kind of social structure illustrates a stage in human history he characterizes as "barbarism": "It follows that the history and experience of the American Indian tribes represent, more or less nearly, the history and experience of our own remote ancestors when in corresponding conditions." [6] Thus, tribal relations cannot be "political" in character; instead, they illustrate a kind of social cohesion that will evolve into civilization when the familial and the governmental are completely sundered—as principally illustrated for Morgan by the heteromonogamous nuclear family unit and the advent of private property. Put in Gayatri Spivak's terms, the *portrait* here allows for no process of political *proxying*, since the entity in question is envisioned as simply not political in character.

Thus, from this perspective, Indianness can be defined as participation in a particular kind of antiquated social form, one from which Indian people might be freed and, thereby, transformed into something else. As mobilized within Indian administration, the ethnological account of Native peoples as holdovers from an earlier point in human development articulates with the narration of them as "wards" of the government (a point reiterated in *Kagama*).[7] This depiction enables the portrayal of settler colonial exertions of jurisdiction and efforts to reorganize the quotidian dynamics of Indigenous lifeworlds as beneficent acts of civilizational pedagogy. As Commissioner of Indian Affairs Thomas J. Morgan suggests in his 1889 report on government-mandated projects of Indian education, "Owing to the peculiar surroundings of the mass of Indian children, they are homeless and ignorant of those simplest arts that make home possible," earlier indicating that "the chief thing in all education is the development of character, the formation of manhood and womanhood" in ways that break "the shackles of [the Indian's] tribal provincialism." Perhaps most arresting is his assertion, "They must stand or fall as men and women, not Indians."[8] Through training Native people(s) in the process of *making home* and attendant performances of proper "manhood and womanhood," state-backed institutions and programs can dissolve tribal relations such that those who once participated in them are, then, "not Indians." Indianness and tribalism codefine each other in a catachrestic tautology whereby the one apparently explains the existence of the other: to be Indian is to partake in tribal relations, and to partake in tribal relations makes one an Indian.

This ethnological catch-22 allows Native nations to be cast as other than true political entities—and, thus, as only "semi-independent" and axiomatically superintended by settler governance—due to their Indianness while also envisioning Indianness as if it referred to a kind of engrained inheritance produced through a particular matrix of backward *social relations* that constitutes the tribe as such. The dominant policy imperatives of the late nineteenth century, allotment and the boarding school system, rely for their justification on this biopolitical feedback loop—on "tribal relations" as a *form*, in Latour's terms—in which procreation and social reproduction operate in and through each other.[9] Intensifying colonial invasion in the form of breaking up Native landbases into privately held plots appears as promotion of the health and welfare of this population through processes of de-Indianization, such as displacing extant forms of Indigenous governance, criminalizing Native practices (including ritual dances, use of medicine men, and polygamy), and requiring Native children to attend government-sponsored schools.

However, the displacement of Native peoples in time through an ethnological imaginary also increasingly involved chronicling the specific practices and social dynamics at play in particular tribes, both to capture them before they vanished and to facilitate more targeted and effective detribalizing initiatives. That ethnographic strategy of close observation and description emerges out of an ethnological framework and participates in state projects, but it also opens possibilities for signifying Native collectivity in ways that exceed discourses of the Indian tribe.[10] Within ethnographic processes, usually a white researcher would develop a relation with an Indigenous person or persons who would then serve as a native informant, providing entrée to the people in question and often translating for the researcher. Through this connection, the informant serves as representative in two ways: as a spokesperson for the group; and as typifying the group or, at least, as indicating what is typical for that group. This version of representativity differs greatly from the forms of political surrogation I've discussed in previous chapters. By contrast, the native informant participates within a synecdochic logic whereby that person embodies and/or points to what is taken to be expressive of the beliefs, perspectives, and lifeways of the tribe as a whole, which that person knows as a member of the tribe.[11] The representativity attributed to the native informant is licensed by and reinforces the sense of the integrity of the tribe as a social unit. While often used in ways that presented Native peoples as exotics for non-native readerly consumption or that reaffirmed impressions of Indians' regressive tendencies, and the attendant need for civilizing improvement, emergent forms of ethnographic writing offered an incipiently "cultural" template of tribal identity that had the potential to interrupt ethnology's developmental temporality by focusing on the immanent processes that produce a sense of collective identity. While "culture" does not emerge as a widely used nonhierarchical way of characterizing social difference until the 1920s and 1930s, modes of ethnographic representation that gain prominence in the 1880s and 1890s provide a set of forms that Native writers could employ in figuring Indigenous peoplehood, although a version of it that not directly index political sovereignty as such.[12]

Zitkala-Ša's writings not only illustrate the possibilities of mobilizing culture as a template through which to signify peoplehood and sovereignty, they also thematize the limits of that mode. In 1900, Gertrude Simmons, who used the Lakota pen name Zitkala-Ša, serially published three stories in the *Atlantic*

Monthly modeled closely on her life, including growing up on the Yankton Reservation, her attendance at White's Manual Institute (an Indian boarding school in Indiana), and her time working for the Carlisle Industrial Indian School (the most famous of the off-reservation boarding schools).[13] Written in the first person, these pieces offer an observational account of daily life among the Yankton people, which, when the speaker leaves for boarding school, becomes a firsthand description of the system of Indian education and its implications for Native survivance, as well as an exploration of the effects of federal imperatives on everyday forms of Yankton experience and self-understanding.[14] If ethnographies of Native peoples usually involved white narrators' reconstruction, reordering, and elucidation of accounts offered by Indians, whose own testimonies were taken as indicative of prevalent patterns of behavior and belief, Zitkala-Ša occupies that position of representative Native speaker in order to provide her own account. She positions herself as representative in the ways her lived experience can stand for the existence of a (political) collective. This mode of self-stylization resembles Apess's efforts to draw on his spectacular status as an Indian preacher to draw attention to the existence of vital forms of Indigenous peoplehood in southern New England (discussed in chapter 2). However, while Apess does so in order to signify the Pequots as a "nation," or to mobilize King Philip to index the potential for "patriotism" to Native polities, Zitkala-Ša's implicit presentation of herself as spokesperson for the Yankton and the portrait of their peoplehood that she offers is not readily marked as a *political* form.

Fusing the roles of ethnographic subject and object, she partakes in one of the few possibilities in the period for Native self-representation to non-native publics. Reading these stories as experiments with ethnographic subjectivity—with ethnographic *form*—foregrounds the ways apparently nonpolitical modes of representation might be mediated toward the project of political surrogation, toward providing a background for non-native readers through which they might understand "tribal relations" as other than exoticized, noble, or barbarous difference. Zitkala-Ša reorients the conceptual resources of ethnography toward highlighting the value of what were termed tribal relations, illustrating their social and political density, while analyzing settler policy as itself producing forms of incapacity rather than remedying those that supposedly arise in the generational transmission of Indianness.[15] Her staging of her own ethnographic representativity provides an account of Yankton sociality in other than ethnological terms, in which the very "domestic" dynamics targeted for elimination as backward and immiserating appear actually as providing sustaining cohesion and inculcating desirable ways of being. Many critics rightly have noted the problems of invoking "culture" given the ways it tends to displace engagement with Indigenous peoples sovereignty as polities.[16] But Zitkala-Ša's positioning of herself as a native informant allows for her to offer an account of Yankton worldmaking in which she can illustrate the workings of Indigenous political orders even if not presented in a manifestly political idiom. Moreover, her focus on what would likely be considered domestic scenes and interactions highlights the ways those matrices of relation play central roles in the ongoing (re)production of peoplehood, offering a different vision of the gendered dynamics of Indigenous governance than the variously configured emphases on patriarchy as an organizing principle in Boudinot, Apess, and Winnemucca. Zitkala-Ša also explores the ways non-native conventions for narrating Native collectivity fail in their attempt to reflect Indigenous socialities and self-understandings. In this way, she employs an ethnographic frame while also suggesting its limits, in what might be understood as a self-conscious foregrounding of the costs of mediation and the dynamics of struggling with the (im)possibilities such entanglement produces. In this way, her life-writings might be read as illustrating the simultaneous pursuit and rejection of recognition, or the ways that the former does not necessarily entail an acceptance of its terms.

Reproducing Native Life

The three stories based on Zitkala-Ša's life that eventually would open *American Indian Stories* (1921)—"Impressions of an Indian Childhood," "The School Days of an Indian Girl," and "An Indian Teacher among Indians"—originally were published in successive issues of the *Atlantic Monthly* in the first months of 1900.[17] As one of the highest of high-culture magazines in the period, it could feature these pieces as examples of "literary quality," given the *Atlantic*'s contemporaneous publication of pieces by Edith Wharton, William Dean Howells, and Henry James.[18] Zitkala-Ša's stories implicitly could signify for readers as a response to the policy question posed by Senator Henry Dawes (sponsor of the General Allotment Act) four issues prior, in August 1899, "Have We Failed the Indian?"[19] These stories also could be read as a flipped-over version of the kinds of "ethnographer gone savage" pieces published in other high-quality magazines, such as Frank Hamilton Cushing's accounts of Zuni in *Harper's* and *The Century*.[20] As Tadeusz Lewandowski suggests, "Even the *Atlantic Monthly*'s cultured subscribers, many of whom were perhaps sympathetic to the idea of Indian domestication, had for decades been exposed to harrowing fictitious accounts of 'red savagery,'" even in the very issues in which Zitkala-Ša's stories appeared.[21] Prior to the full flowering of the culture concept in the first decades of the twentieth century, descriptive techniques arose for characterizing forms of collective social difference. These were largely employed by non-natives who sought to describe and categorize the lifeways of Native peoples, protoethnographers who were not university trained, came from all sorts of backgrounds, and wrote in forms other than the scholarly monograph.[22] Zitkala-Ša participates within this ethnographic public sphere in ways that play on its modes of representativity in order to present herself as an authorized speaker while positioning her experience as indicative of both the integrity of a Yankton lifeworld and the violence at play in continuing state efforts to decimate it.

The stories register the continuing government assault on Indigenous modes of collectivity, territoriality, and governance by offering an intimate account of Yankton domesticity as well as a participant-observer rendering of the boarding school process. In *Mohawk Interruptus*, Audra Simpson observes, "We must be mindful . . . that in its theoretical and analytic guises 'culture' is defined in anthropological terms most consistently by its proximity to difference, not its sovereignty, its right to govern, to own, or to labor."[23] In the late nineteenth century, protoanthropological portrayals of what later would come to be understood as "culture" do engage in such depoliticizing work, translating Indigenous peoples as Indian tribes whose internal dynamics need to be distinguished from the political relations of nationhood. While acknowledging this historical itinerary for self-consciously cultural analysis, including as it comes to be adopted as a central part of Indian policy in the reorganization era and afterward, we can approach the ethnographic dimensions in Zitkala-Ša's writing as means of recasting dominant non-native notions of "tribal relations" in order to convey Yankton peoplehood as a vital matrix and to register the force of intensifying settler interventions.[24] As Beth Piatote demonstrates in *Domestic Subjects*, in the wake of the end of treaty making and the onset of the allotment era, "Indian economies, lands, kinship systems, languages, cultural practices, and family relations—in short, all that constituted the Indian home—became the primary site of struggle. The battle, although not the stakes, moved from the indigenous homeland, what I call the tribal-national domestic, to the familial space of the Indian home, or the intimate domestic."[25] The autobiographical stories offer a first-person, ethnographically inflected account of the process of Yankton social reproduction and its interruption by the biopolitical logics and imperatives animating Indian policy. In doing so, Zitkala-Ša foregrounds the "intimate domestic" in ways that draw on its role in extant imaginaries of the Indian tribe, reorienting the focus from chronicling and/or replacing exotic, premodern practices to highlighting the political work performed by such settler framings of Native peoplehood—including their impact on "the tribal-national domestic."

Rather than substituting culture for sovereignty, Zitkala-Ša bookends the first of the stories with explicit attention to how the narrator's early childhood and expressed desire to attend boarding school occur in the context of a history of settler invasion and Yankton dispossession.[26] In the second paragraph, the narrator says of her mother, "Often she was silent and sad," and her mother responds to the narrator's questions by insisting, "Hush; my little daughter must never talk about my tears."[27] Almost immediately thereafter, though, the mother indicates her concern that "the paleface" will "take away from us the river we drink," which leads her to recount the reasons for the deaths of the narrator's father, uncle, and sister: "We were once very happy. But the paleface has stolen our lands and driven us hither. Having defrauded us of our land, the paleface forced us away"; "We traveled many days and nights; not in the grand, happy way that we moved camp when I was a little girl, but we were driven, my child, driven like a herd of buffalo" (69–70).[28] The scene of ordinary Native life appears punctuated by its relation to projects of land seizure and removal. Implicitly, the text suggests that the description of Indian domesticity it has begun to offer, and will elaborate over the course of the story, remains entangled with the ongoing effects of non-native expropriation and the process of seeking to render impossible Indigenous existence (losing "the river we drink" and being further driven on to mass death).

In introducing this element of Yankton history at the outset, Zitkala-Ša complicates the somewhat generic vision for which the story primes readers. The title "Impressions of an Indian Childhood" suggests that the narrative readers encounter will be a relatively typical one, using the indefinite article—"an"—to signal both singularity (this child, rather than that one) and a certain interchangeable seriality (one Indian childhood is much like any other). Once readers learn in the second paragraph that the "impressions" offered will be in the first person ("my mother came to draw water" [68]), this sense of synecdochic substitutability positions the speaker as herself representative, as the particular featured case of the broader "Indian" type. Given these dynamics, the text's fairly quick turn to discussion of the theft of Native lands, and the role fraud and force play in that process, presents such occurrences as themselves also typical, as common parts of an Indian childhood in the late nineteenth century. Moreover, after detailing her childhood activities and her becoming interested in boarding school education in the East (through an attraction to "red apples"), the narrator reveals her mother's reasons for assenting to this wish: "She will need an education when she is grown, for then there will be fewer real Dakotas, and many more palefaces. This tearing her away, so young, from her mother is necessary, if I would have her an educated woman. The palefaces, who owe us a large debt for stolen lands, have begun to pay a tardy justice in offering some education to our children" (86).[29] Zitkala-Ša casts Native participation in the project of Indian education as itself a response to ongoing dispossession. It appears as "tardy" and insufficient recompense for the seizure of Native lands but also as a means of preparing children to live in a world where settler invasion continues, even as the mechanisms of such education themselves reproduce the violence of displacement ("tearing her away"). The descriptive strategies the stories employ, then, less substitute for engagement with the existence of Native political orders than mark the transposition of sovereignty into an ethnographic idiom in ways consistent with public articulations of Indianness in the period.

In this way, Zitkala-Ša alludes to Yankton history as the contextual surround for the events that occupy the foreground of the stories, including growing settler interference in everyday Yankton life.[30] The Yanktons are one of the peoples of the Oceti Sakowin, or Seven Council Fires (commonly referred to as "Sioux"). They and the Yanktonai historically have occupied a geographic middle position between the more eastern Dakota peoples (Mdwekanton, Sisseton, Wahpekute, and Wahpeton) and their western allies, the Teton or Lakota, and prior to sustained settler presence near their lands starting in the 1850s, their territory lay between the upper Des Moines and Missouri River valleys, approximately 13.5 million acres with the north bank of the Missouri River most consistently serving as a sustained residential site. In 1858 in a treaty for which the leader Struck by the Ree served as the principal signatory, the Yanktons officially ceded almost 11.2 million acres, previously having ceded approximately 2.2 million acres in 1830 in a treaty conducted at Prairie du Chien. Despite the fact that many Yanktons raised questions about the signatories' authority to represent the people in this way, the treaty was ratified by the Senate, and as far as the U.S. government was concerned, from that point on the Yankton Reservation consisted of an area covering about 430,000 acres. Zitkala-Ša's story gestures to this loss and attendant efforts to circumscribe Yanktons within the limits of the reservation, especially given rapid increase in the surrounding white population.[31]

Consistent with the broader operation of the Indian service (as discussed in chapter 3), the agents assigned to the reservation exerted enormous authority over the lives of Yankton people.[32] The power they exercised included regulating travel outside the reservation through the issuing of passes, the provision of rations (which given the limited options for other forms of subsistence provided much of the Yanktons' diet and which were restricted as punishment for failing to fulfill the agent's orders as well as due to shifting federal budget allocations), the distribution of plots of land to families for farming (before the enactment of the General Allotment Act), and the management of Native governance. In this vein, an Indian police force was organized in mid-1882 in order to enforce compliance with the agent's directives and Bureau of Indian Affairs (BIA) policies, and in 1885, the agent instituted what was intended to be a wholesale reorganization of leadership: "From the eight bands of Indians, two from each were selected by me last winter, constituting what is known as a board of advisers. The object was to keep the agent advised of all irregularities, violations of the rules of the agency disposing of issue goods and stock, of plural marriages, crimes, and offenses, and to aid in bringing in children to school."[33] Those chosen for this board were "men well advanced in civilization," in explicit contrast to those regarded as chiefs and in order to eliminate the latter. In that same year, an Indian court was established, in which three Yankton judges chosen by the agent would oversee cases of those charged with violating the rules set by the agent.[34] Agents also routinely recommended removing the Yanktons to Indian Territory or reducing the size of the reservation, claiming that it encompassed far more land than could be put to productive use by the Yanktons (meaning for agriculture or grazing).[35] The threat of removal and/or further dispossession, then, remained an ever-present concern in the decades just prior to the stories' publication, which saw the sale of approximately 200,000 acres as "surplus" lands in 1893 under the terms of the Dawes Act.[36]

While Zitkala-Ša draws on and responds to the specific dynamics of Yankton history and Indian policy administration on the Yankton Reservation, within state discourses Yankton identity remains a subset of an encompassing, generic Indianness, and this biopolitical conception of tribal relations—as the generational transmission of a set of immanent proclivities—provides the discursive and political background for Zitkala-Ša's employment of ethnographic techniques. Within Indian policy formulations in the late nineteenth century, as discussed earlier, a *tribe* is decisively not a *nation*, thereby licensing the treatment of Indians as a kind of population broken into separate tribal units rather than as a series of autonomous polities with whom the United States has longstanding, constitutionally mandated diplomatic relations. These groups are seen as constituted through social relations that (re)produce Indianness as an ensemble of individual and collective tendencies. In this frame, the racial as biological inheritance is not separated from the social as a set of learned behaviors, beliefs, and attitudes.[37] Rather, they circuit into each other within a Lamarckian feedback loop. In *The Biopolitics of Feeling*, Kyla Schuller argues that understandings of racialization in the nineteenth-century United States tended less toward notions of inherently fixed types of persons than toward a vision of differential collective capacities for impressibility—for being affected by one's surroundings in ways that could engender positive development within an evolutionary hierarchy: "Impressibility indexed the agential responsiveness of the nervous system to external stimuli, the results of which over time would metonymically transform the body as a whole." In contrast to a genetic determinist conception of bodily inheritance, which emerges in the early twentieth century and is purely a matter of procreative transmission of innate and unchangeable germinal materials, an ideology of impressibility links capacities for civilized comportment (including those transmitted biologically to one's children) to actions taken during one's lifetime. Within this Lamarckian imaginary, "the habits of civilization were thought to impress on physicality and transmit across time as physical inheritance." Thus, as Schuller observes, "a childhood spent barefoot in a Plains tipi impressed savage propensities on the body and mind that the child would never unlearn and would transmit to offspring, whereas the customs of leather shoes, wool and cotton clothing, and stick-frame house served as both the cause and effect of civilization," and she characterizes efforts in the period to produce such change for otherwise stunted/backward populations, such as in Indian policy, as "biophilanthropy." Race and social relations are co-constitutive rather than opposed (as later formulations of "culture" and cultural construction might suggest).[38]

From this perspective, if *Indian* operates as a racial designation, it does not so much indicate a stable kind of body reproductively transmitted across generations as index a kind of biosocial assemblage in which the continuity of Indianness as a physical type (including inborn abilities and inclinations) depends on the matrix of tribalism to sustain it.[39] In *Native Acts*, Joanne Barker describes contemporary processes by which the U.S. government recognizes Native peoples as dependent on identifying "Native traditions" that "have been fixed in an authentic past and then used as the measure of a cultural-as-racial authenticity in the present."[40] The nineteenth-century biopolitics of Indianness to which Zitkala-Ša responds can be understood as generating this "cultural-as-racial" matrix, in which the kind of social dynamics that would come to be characterized in anthropological discourse as "culture" provide the horizon for defining the character and contours of Indian as a "racial" category.[41] In Indian policy and reform discourses, then, to break up tribal relations ("cultural" forms) is to transform Indianness into something else, and the understanding of Indianness as a set of heritable biosocial patterns oriented toward barbarous ends disqualifies it from serving as the basis for a political formation. In his annual report for 1881, the Yankton agent remarks, "We are inclined to bridge the centuries between barbarism and civilization, not giving proper credit for the efforts required to throw off the customs, habits, and teachings handed down by tradition and story from generation to generation, and take up those of another race only acquired after long persistent effort and self-denial." The annual report five years later suggests, "As they become identified with the soil, which yields its fruits in return for labor, and more especially as they . . . begin to realize the comforts and blessings of home life, do they lose their individuality as Indians and pass into a higher existence."[42] "Customs" and "habits" are generationally iterated in ways that produce the specificity of Indians as a "race," and to engage in private property holding is to undertake forms of "home life" that result in the loss of such (racial) Indianness. In these moments, we also can see how ethnographic elaboration of the principles and practices shaping everyday Indian domestic life ("the intimate domestic" in Piatote's terms)—homemaking, family formation, land use, child-rearing and education, ordinary kinds of interpersonal association—becomes crucial to the project of breaking up the tribal matrix by specifying those quotidian modes that engender Indianness, such that they can be targeted for alteration.[43]

In her stories, though, Zitkala-Ša inhabits the ethnographic imaginary in ways that foreground the very sites seen as necessary objects of state intervention in order to recast them as engaging in positive Yankton worldmaking, drawing on her status as native informant in order to do so. At several points in "Impressions of an Indian Childhood," she portrays herself as engaging in sustained observation of other Yankton people around her, their behaviors, and the routines of everyday life. When sent by her mother "to invite the neighboring old men and women to eat supper with us," she notes that, upon her return to her home, "I told my mother almost the exact words of the answers to my invitation," and in response, her mother asks, "What were they doing when you entered their tepee?," which, she indicates, "taught me to remember all I saw at a single glance. Often I told my mother my impressions without being questioned" (71). Later, she notes that she intently watched her mother in ways that provided "practical observation lessons in the art of beadwork" (74). Of her time playing with children her age, she indicates, "I remember well how we used to exchange our necklaces, beaded belts, and sometimes even our moccasins. We pretended to offer them as gifts to one another. We delighted in impersonating our own mothers. We talked of things we had heard them say in their conversations. We imitated their various manners, even to the inflection of their voices" (75). In these moments, Zitkala-Ša presents herself as routinely engaged in witnessing and remembering others' words and actions, as in fact being trained to do so as part of an ordinary Yankton upbringing. More than simply describing occurrences and patterns from her childhood, she underlines that she learned to notice and recall what others do, and that set of acquired capacities provides the basis for the account offered to readers. The text reflexively positions the narrator as engaged in an (auto-)ethnographic project with respect to her people, as gathering information on tribal relations through observation and reporting it in a published narrative. The sites and scenes of Yankton social reproduction appear as an affectively rich and fulfilling series of interactions with others. She and other children are well cared-for and well prepared for life in the community, and such development is made possible through careful attention to the daily patterns of the adults around them. More specifically, in foregrounding her and other children's engagements with their mothers, not only does the text emphasize the domestic character of the relations it addresses, it inhabits the recursive fusion of biological and social reproduction occurring within biopolitical discourses of tribalism and Indianness in ways that stage the scene of generational transmission in other than racializing terms.[44] In this way, Zitkala-Ša's experience comes to stand as representative for quotidian forms of healthful, stimulating, educational, and interpersonally rewarding sociality on the reservation.[45]

These "impressions" of ordinary life growing up on the reservation—of being individually impressed through the matrix of tribal relations—directly contrast the oft-circulated vision of Indian existence as pathological and debilitating, most forcefully and repeatedly offered in official accounts.[46] The annual report from the Yankton agent, across multiple agents, consistently portrays life on the reservation as debased. Constantly describing Yankton living conditions as dirty and disgusting, agents note the failure of civilization policy yet to alter the dynamics of Indian domesticity: "Twenty-five years of well-directed effort with the large provision made for them under the treaty ought to find these Indians living in comfortable houses" with "all the other comforts that characterize the white man's house"; however, "in place of this the Indians have only poor houses, dirt roofs, earth floors[,] . . . little furniture of any kind—and are but little more civilized in their mode of living than when they were in savage life."[47] This fact leads to incredulity at Yankton resistance to sending their children to government-sanctioned boarding schools "when it is considered that the children are taken from a filthy, degraded life, poorly fed and shabbily clothed, and placed in a boarding school, where they are well clothed and fed, with comfortable beds to sleep in."[48] Filthy and polluted households prevent them from accessing the material comforts of civilized homemaking, which themselves bespeak an entire way of life that engenders the capacity for personal growth and collective betterment Indians also are lacking in their current state. As one agent suggests, "Education cuts the cord which binds them to a pagan life," thereby enabling "an elevated humanity in place of abject degradation," and as noted in another report, "Farming, a home, the accumulation of property, a higher social and political status, a feeling of manhood, a consciousness that they have the capacity to do and act for themselves, freed from tribal dictation, will wean them from those old customs which have served to keep them in their normal condition."[49] The use of metaphors related to birth and the biology of childcare (of *cutting the cord* and *weaning*) to refer to Yankton social relations—their "pagan life" and dependence on "tribal dictation"—further indicates the ways that (racial) reproduction and tribal relations are fused as interanimating coproducers of an axiomatically degraded and degrading Indianness that itself needs to be eliminated through domestic (re)training and (re)organization.

The potential for life for Yankton people itself appears to depend on such a transformation. The extraordinary mortality rates on the reservation since its creation in 1859 saw the population fall from 2,600 to 1,716 by 1891.[50] In response, agents continually cite traditional Yankton modes of living as responsible for that decline. One agent indicates, "It has been observed that deaths occur mostly among those who pay little attention to the laws of health; and those who practice agricultural pursuits and observe sanitary rules enjoy better health than their less attentive neighbors." Another report explains, "Owing to exposure, poor houses, and a stupid indifference to the laws of health, there are more pulmonary diseases among them than are found in the same latitude among the whites."[51] The failure to adopt "agricultural pursuits," and the attendant structure of privatized heteronuclear domesticity, results in increased Yankton death. Indian modes of social reproduction violate "the laws of health," illustrating "a stupid indifference" that directly contributes to growing rates of incapacitation and demise. Thus, tribalism appears not simply as a backward set of social relations but as directly contributing to morbidity, as constitutively unhealthful. In the context of this official way of framing Native peoplehood, Zitkala-Ša's depiction of her childhood practices and relationships on the reservation as joyful, edifying, and sustaining draws on the techniques and growing prominence of ethnographic writing to provide an alternative account of what the tribal is—one that seeks to reorient the racializing transposition of indigeneity into Indianness.[52]

In these three stories, the narrator's authority to speak about matters on reservation arises from her having experienced them, which distinguishes her texts from much other ethnographic writing at the time. Ethnography largely arose out of engagements with Native peoples and was promoted by the U.S. Bureau of Ethnology (which became the Bureau of American Ethnology in 1897), but it extended beyond government-authorized studies, increasingly becoming a prominent mode for describing forms of social coherence and difference in the late nineteenth century. As Michael Elliott suggests, it provided a set of rhetorical strategies and generic conventions for conveying "a kind of group-based identity not determined by biological heredity." Yet to be contained in the disciplinary domain of anthropology, with its credentialing protocols, "it could provide textual forums in which American Indians could represent their experiences."[53] At the turn of the twentieth century, Native authorship of ethnographies was infrequent, but not unheard of, such as in the work of Francis La Flesche (Omaha), in his collaborations with Alice Fletcher as well as his own single-authored texts.[54] Although Native participants were crucial to ethnographic endeavors, serving, as Margaret Bruchac notes, "as guides, interpreters, artisans, procurers, and translators," they usually were "classified as 'informants' rather than 'intellectuals,' and the bulk of their writings (when they were preserved) were subsumed into the archives of the scholars that studied them," with them being understood "as informants, not theorists."[55] However, by positioning her experience as providing the basis for her descriptions of Yankton life on reservation and the boarding school system, particularly by having a narrator who speaks in the first person without any textual markers that the stories themselves are fiction, she implicitly presents herself as a representative speaker for the Yanktons.

In this way, Zitkala-Ša plays the role of native informant, and viewing her from this perspective brings to the fore a series of questions about how she comes to stand for the Yankton people and the political work at play in doing so in this manner in the context of settler policy's ongoing assault on, in Piatote's terms, "the tribal-national domestic" through the reorganization of "the intimate domestic." Often in scholarship on Zitkala-Ša, *autobiography* and *culture* serve as tropes to index a kind of personal experience outside settler ideologies from which she can refuse them, or those same tropes indicate her enmeshedness in processes of settlement, such that she appears as if she is somehow between Indian and white social formations.[56] Attending to the ways Zitkala-Ša's texts deploy an ethnographic imaginary, though, foregrounds the frameworks available in the period for signifying Indigenous collectivity, their relation to the apparatus of Indian policy, and the stakes of how she negotiates those frameworks and seeks to participate within non-native networks. Spivak warns of the dangers of treating the speech of the native informant as an expression of "concrete experience," thereby "considering the 'native' as the object for enthusiastic information-retrieval and thus denying its own 'worlding.'"[57] If Native peoples are *worlded* through state-circulated discourses, then speaking within and through such discourses does not provide unmediated access to a tribal real outside of settler frameworks.[58]

Zitkala-Ša's portrayal of her childhood and young adulthood on reservation, as well as her time attending and working at Indian boarding schools, gains meaning within an extant set of representational conventions in which Native peoplehood appears as Indianness (rather than, say, nationhood). Thus, her account neither expresses a vision of Yankton identity (individual or collective) that lies outside of the history of settlement nor does it indicate how such a putatively unspoiled identity has been contaminated through settler colonialism. The experience she presents as authorizing her to speak as the native informant, which also provides the content of the ethnographic narrative she offers, itself is shaped in its articulation by the discourses of Indianness and tribalness that predominate in official and popular modes of engaging Indigenous peoples in the late nineteenth century. Her ethnographic staging of her own seemingly representative selfhood can be read less as a means of speaking for herself in ways that take her beyond non-native frameworks (or that indicate how Gertrude Simmons's sense of herself in life was affected by such frameworks) than as indexing the extant conditions of possibility for presenting Native peoplehood to non-native publics. In this way, Zitkala-Ša's detailing of Yankton social relations can be seen as drawing on ethnographic form to register and value Indigenous peoplehood in the absence of a public discourse of diplomacy or of Indigenous political sovereignty.

Her ethnographic transposition of Yankton sociopolitical dynamics appears in the scenes she chooses to feature in illustrating the narrator's acquisition of competence as a participant in ordinary interpersonal relations. As noted earlier, "Impressions of an Indian Childhood" bookends the story of the narrator's life before boarding school with discussion of the ongoing history of Yankton dispossession and settler invasion, gesturing toward the geopolitics of Yankton peoplehood as the frame in which the text's account of quotidian lifeways is situated.[59] In addition to this explicit engagement with struggles over Yankton occupancy and self-governance, the story stages the narrator's process of coming to understand community norms in ways that allude to practices targeted for elimination by the agent—particularly various kinds of visiting and gathering—due to their promotion of kinds of relationships that are seen as retarding possibilities for progress from Indianness to citizenship. After telling readers about how she learned to observe and remember what others were doing when she entered their tepees, she describes the event to which they were being invited, an ordinary evening gathering in her mother's home in order to eat together and share stories. She describes the dinner, noting her eagerness for "the old people" to "tell an Iktomi story" and her "increasing interest" in the tale being told by one of the old women. During one such evening, the narrator notes tattoos on two of the people present, a "blue star" on "the brow of an old warrior" and "two parallel lines on the chin of one of the old women," and when she asks the women about "the meaning of the blue lines," she is told that they are "secret signs" that cannot be discussed with the child (72). Critics have addressed the importance of the secrecy surrounding the markings, especially the fact that their significance is not revealed to the reader.[60] Of equal importance here, though, is the accumulation of detail about the gathering, which the story presents as a routine feature of daily camp life. Her mother's tepee serves as a site where a range of people living in the camp, likely members of the same tiospaye, come together on a regular basis to have food in common and to converse with each other.[61]

As opposed to the nuclear family households that Indian policy sought to produce, each with its own private land that provides the basis for subsistence (either by growing crops or selling them), Zitkala-Ša indicates the presence of an extended set of relationships that constitutes the everyday matrix of Yankton sociality. This network facilitates the sharing of resources in ways that challenge ideologies of individualist productivity and ownership as the proper basis for social life. This ethos emerges again in the story's discussion of the narrator's efforts to show hospitality to a visitor. When an "old grandfather" arrives at her mother's home unexpectedly while her mother is out, she decides "to play the part of a generous host," offering him her version of coffee and lunch—grounds in cold water and unleavened bread in a bowl (78). Zitkala-Ša emphasizes that the guest and her mother, when she returns, do not chastise or embarrass her for her failed efforts, instead suggesting that the guest had followed "the law of our custom [that] had compelled him to partake of my insipid hospitality" and that they "treated my best judgment, poor as it was, with the utmost respect" (79). Yet, while conveying the character of Yankton custom in ways that highlight its generosity and that work against accounts of Indian savagery, the anecdote also subtly underlines movement among home spaces as a regular and valued part of Yankton collective practice.

Such interactions on and off reservation were a major source of concern to agents due to the ways they facilitated forms of identification, leadership, and resource sharing that ran counter to the project of breaking up tribal relations, both before and after the passage of the Dawes Act. Ongoing networks of labor and sharing of food resources countered agents' attempts to engender de-Indianizing modes of private property holding. As one agent insists, "Individual possession of land and means will cultivate a feeling of pride and self-respect, will powerfully stimulate all to work, and help break up that tribal bondage which now tends to destroy all individuality of character," and after almost a decade of such efforts, another indicates, "Successful farming requires isolation, and their habits and disposition lead them into gangs."[62] That same year, when Gertrude Simmons was living on the reservation after having attended White's Manual Institute for a three-year period, the agent further observes, "One of the prime objects of the Government in the management of Indians, and to make them self-supporting, is to break up the old tribal relations and effectually destroy tribal authority over them as it now exists on most of the reservations through chiefs," additionally asserting, "Before any Indian can be made a good farmer he must become individualized, and this involves complete segregation from the mass."[63] More than simply inculcating nuclear family structures of household formation and food production, the effort to prevent Yanktons from congregating works toward "destroy[ing] tribal authority."[64] Everyday relations among Yankton people, then, help sustain a matrix of "tribal relations" that itself supports a system of governance that contests the legitimacy of settler rule.

If the "management" of Native peoples requires understanding them as a "mass" of undifferentiated Indians whose ability to support themselves depends on the elimination of tribal identity, Zitkala-Ša's discussion of ongoing, intimate engagements among Yanktons in ways that exceed the nuclear family unit not only chronicles forms of everyday practice and the transmission of community knowledge, it gestures toward the means of sustaining the infrastructure of tribal sociality in ways that have direct consequences for preserving Yankton modes of self-governance at all levels. Although the autobiographical stories avoid depictions of chiefs and of what might be understood by non-native readers as political process, they highlight quotidian details that suggest the existence of intricate webs of interaction and care, presenting them as capacious, wholesome, and sustaining rather than as stultifying and incapacitating. In another scene of hospitality, Zitkala-Ša describes a time when she and her mother were on their way to "a public feast" sponsored by relatives of "a strong young brave, who had just returned from his first battle," and they are running late because her mother is "busy broiling a wild duck" for a woman in the camp who is "lying very ill" (79–80). While the emphasis in this part of the story (and on which critics have focused) is on a plum bush from which her mother tells Zitkala-Ša not to eat, the narrator referring to it as "forbidden fruit" (80), the enframing situation intimates that such feasts are a somewhat regular event, so much so that the feast itself does not merit extended descrip-tion, while also implicitly linking this public celebration to the provision of resources to those who are in difficulty. Agents repeatedly complained about such gatherings—often referred to as "dances"—suggesting that they contrib-uted to public immorality (at one point referring to them as "carnivals of vice") while thwarting endeavors to instill capitalist values of private ownership.[65] In an annual report in 1887, one agent observes, "Horses, work-cattle, farming implements, and clothing are too often at these dances, generously offered up upon the altar of an old Indian custom, which is utterly at variance with the civilizing influences of successful farming," indicating the need to replace the "gregarious habits" of "the Indians" with "the more enjoyable blessings of home and family": "That cohesion, which is bred of idleness, of a common history, a common purpose, and a common interest, and unites the Indians in a com-mon destiny, must be broken up before dancing will cease."[66] By normalizing the presence of such events, suggesting the innocence of their purpose and the upstanding character of those who attend them, Zitkala-Ša draws on what she depicts as her firsthand knowledge to refute official claims of depravity but also to sketch the dynamics of Indigenous *commonness* in ways that run counter to extant administrative and popular narratives of tribal lifeworlds as expressive of and contributing to Indians' (racial) incapacity.

In this way, emergent forms of ethnography shape these stories less in terms of the presence of effusive descriptions of the activities addressed than in a con-cern with recounting ordinary features of everyday Indianness. In conveying such situations in ways that suggest they are from her personal experience, Zitkala-Ša presents herself as a representative figure whose account of Yankton sociality is authorized for non-native readers as legitimate and accurate on that basis. Only a couple months after the publication of the three stories in the *Atlantic*, she actually is featured in an article in *Outlook* magazine that focuses on a small cadre of Native intellectuals, titled "The Representative Indian."[67] In implicitly positioning her experience as synecdochic for not just Yanktons but Native people(s) more broadly, Zitkala-Ša mediates emergent ethnographic conventions and publication networks in order to refigure the account of tribal relations offered within dominant non-native discourses. As opposed to produc-ing an inherently backward Indianness, understood biopolitically as a recur-sive fusion of immanent tendencies and learned practices, tribal sociality in the stories is portrayed as engendering sustained dynamics of hospitality and care through extended networks of support and resource distribution. In doing so, Zitkala-Ša also illustrates the presence of multilayered modes of Yankton pedagogy through which children are introduced to collective practices of reflection, consideration, artistry, and storytelling. She intimates a connection between learned practices of observation and forms of ethnographic documentation while presenting tribal communality as inculcating viable and valuable lifeways (rather than, say, barbarous customs destined to be supplanted by Euro-civilization). Even though these pieces tend not to foreground questions of political sovereignty and the representative subjectivity of the narrator differs markedly from the kinds of national identification at play in the writers discussed in previous chapters, the stories gesture toward the ongoing politics of Yankton dispossession. The texts offer an account of the entangled density of Indian lifeways, occurring as they are in the midst of a policy of escalating colonial intervention meant to decimate them. In this way, Zitkala-Ša's "impressions" draw on ethnographic form to offer a vision of Indigenous sociality that provides a counterweight to arguments about the need to eliminate forms of tribal cohesion.

Indians in the Wild

Although ethnographic writing in the 1890s described the dynamics of Indian life in ways that contrast greatly with the armchair ethnological theorizing that had predominated prior to the emergence of the participant-observer model in the 1880s (in the work of Lewis Henry Morgan, for example), such writing remained caught within the orbit of an ethnological imagination of human development. As Elliott suggests, while "the ethnographic texts produced during this period could also employ the realist detachment of professional observation to document tribal life in a way not wholly conforming with a narrative of unavoidable vanishing," they also tended to consign Native people(s) "to an imagined past unconnected to the actual lives of Indians living in the United States. The ahistorical temporal frame of these works left writers and readers ill-prepared to explain how Native peoples might continue"—as dynamically engaging with and adapting to changing conditions in the present.[68] Ethnography, then, often inclines toward a rendering of Indigenous sociopolitical formations as if they were "static museum objects," which also involved making determinations about what practices they observed could count as "authentic" expressions of tribal identity.[69] These reifying tendencies largely treated the peoples described as if they existed apart from the history of settlement, in something of an immanent developmental trajectory relatively divorced from interactions with non-native persons and institutions.[70] However, the articulation of Indigenous separateness in ethnological-cum-ethnographic work, even when envisioned in implicitly anachronizing ways, still raised the ire of prominent administrators in the Indian service who claimed that such efforts to chronicle tribal life stunted the process of detribalization and assimilation of Indians to U.S. citizenship.[71] In this way, ethnographic documentation was seen as having a similarly pernicious effect on the transformation of Indians—and on popular non-native understanding of and support for that process—as Wild West shows. The latter featured Native people dressing and acting in the barbarous ways that allotment and the boarding schools aimed to eliminate.[72] Rather than seeking to diffuse this comparison by distinguishing (proto-)anthropological representation from mass spectacle, we can understand the two as linked in ways that shape how Zitkala-Ša employs figures of *wildness* in her stories. She uses the term "wild" and related tropes to signify forms of Indian difference from white norms and illustrate the violence of settler impositions, particularly through the boarding school system. The stories seek to mediate whites' exoticizing interest in things Indian, turning it into support for Indigenous modes of sociospatiality. The stories draw on popular investments in ethnographic display to present in positive terms the very kinds of tribal relations targeted for eradication as part of the biopolitical project of eliminating Indianness. Zitkala-Ša uses versions of wildness as a way of characterizing Indigenous identity, experiences, and peoplehood, but at the same time, she also subtly suggests the ways such figures, in their dependence on spectacular prefabricated types, can overwrite contemporary Indigenous experiences. Zitkala-Ša positions herself as representative of an Indian kind of wildness worthy of non-native respect while also sketching the limits of the very ethnographic imaginary on which she draws.

' In the late nineteenth century, "wild" was the premier term to mark forms of specifically Indian difference, including the kinds of group dynamics on reservation that ethnography sought to capture. When Francis La Flesche—himself a Native ethnographer—sought to publish his memoir of his time in an on-reservation boarding school (*The Middle Five*), the manuscript was rejected by Doubleday for the reason that "it does not seem to us that the school life should necessarily be excluded, but certainly the burden should be thrown upon the other *wilder* existence"; after it was published, a review in one of Carlisle's newspapers, the *Red Man and Helper*, praises the book for the fact that "there is scarcely a hint of the wild life in this little book; not even the Indian names are used; so that the novelty seekers and those who turn to it hoping for something of aboriginal strangeness are likely to be disappointed."[73] The "strangeness" of Indigenous sociality—the tribal relations that sustain the generational transmission of racial Indianness—can be condensed as "wild"-ness, in contrast to the civilized comportment of citizens. Zitkala-Ša draws on such popular associations, declaring early in the first story that she "was a wild little girl" exercising a "wild freedom" in which she "was as free as the wind that blew my hair" and "no less spirited than a bounding deer" (68). If wildness designates the parts of Indian life that would have been understood as the proper object of ethnographic discourse (and which supposedly were lacking in La Flesche's memoir), the text plays on this set of non-native expectations and desires to assure readers at the outset that they will be getting the kind of portrait of tribalness that they crave and that the narrator will provide entrée to this otherwise alien world. As Ron Carpenter suggests, the text's use of such tropes "initially reconfirms Indian stereotypes."[74]

Zitkala-Ša, though, reorients wild from signaling an ethnological lag—a thrilling difference from white norms in its savage backwardness—to expressing both a sense of "freedom" and a connection to the landscape. After she decides to go east with the missionaries to attend boarding school, the narrator observes, "I was as frightened and bewildered as the captured young of a wild creature" (86), and once she actually enters the school, she insists that "my spirit tore itself in struggling for its lost freedom" and that such struggle was, in fact, "useless" (89). Furthermore, as part of the "iron routine" of the daily schedule at school, she and the other students are awakened "at half-past six in the cold winter mornings. From happy dreams of Western rolling lands and unlassoed freedom we tumbled out upon chilly bare floors back again into a paleface day" (95–96). Native students appear here as domesticated animals ("only one of many little animals driven by a herder" [91]), alluding to the conception of Native peoples as less advanced along an evolutionary timeline as well as to the institutional matrix of allotment by which Indians were supposed to gain independence and manhood through privatized Euro-American-style farming. In addition to offering extended descriptions of the force of school discipline (including the cutting of her hair, corporal punishment for minor infractions, the unceasing and grinding routine of the school day itself, and the poor conditions that contribute to high student mortality rates), the stories inhabit the potentials of wildness to index collective ways of being that lie outside settler frameworks, refusing the ideology of improvement animating Indian policy. If the practices Zitkala-Ša depicts in the first story strain against description of them as "wild," in ways I'll return to later in this section, wildness and associated images of unconstrained movement provide a means of portraying strategies of detribalization (particularly those at play in the boarding school system) as a form of assaultive bondage. The ethnological frisson for readers of seeing Indians in their "wilder existence" gets directed in the stories into an ethnographic focus on the Yankton everyday, a portrait which to some extent thwarts settler longings for Native peoples to appear as vestigial oddities while also providing the kinds of details of tribal life that could at least partially gratify non-native yearnings to consume Indianness.[75] In the latter stories, figures of wildness refer back to the earlier portrayal of the reservation, offering a nonethnological vision of Native sociality, but they do so in a condensed way that capitalizes on the attractions of Indianness for non-native readers.

Implicitly characterizing Yankton social patterns as expressions of wildness mobilizes non-natives' interest in tribalism (as racial alterity) in order to depict the imposition of allotment-era imperatives as a denial of Indian "freedom." This narrative strategy plays on white hunger for something beyond what increasingly was envisioned as an alienating modernity, a craving to which ethnography speaks.[76] As Ryan Burt argues, Zitkala-Ša shows a "nuanced sensitivity for the type of salve the figure of the 'primitive,' and indeed the 'primitive child,' offered an *Atlantic* reader, registering antimodern anxiety and desire for the 'barbarian virtues.'" In this way, the stories can be read "as literary performance, as a type of 'Playing Indian,' wherein Zitkala-Ša draws on her understanding of the allure of antimodern primitivism for her middle-class readership."[77] Crucially, though, this performance is conducted within an ethnographic idiom or frame that allows Zitkala-Ša to position herself as the native informant who can convey the truth of Indigenous being. In doing so, what she presents as her own experiences can serve as a representative account of tribal relations and the effects of Indian policy on them. If her narrative does not exactly bear the imprimatur of scientific investigation, she cites the emerging conventions of ethnographic discourse, such that her use of tropes of wildness functions as more than simply a romantic primitivist reversal of ethnological narratives of Indian archaism. Put another way, if she is "playing Indian," she is doing so in ways that present her narration of the ordinary dynamics of Yankton sociality *and* of the everyday violence of the boarding school as synecdochic, as standing in for larger patterns that allow them to be grasped in their wholeness. Zitkala-Ša is speaking for the Yanktons as a representative figure, although in ways that do not translate as diplomacy, and the texts indicate the presence and desirability of Indigenous place-based collectivity, albeit in ways that cannot register sovereignty as such.[78] In playing the role of "wild" Indian, Zitkala-Ša gestures toward the matrix of social relations thought to generate and reproduce Indians, casting that matrix as producing a tribal form of freedom that cannot be understood merely as a precursor to Euro-American modes of development.[79] Her use of figures of wildness, then, might be described as mobilizing an ethnographic imagination in order to disrupt an ethnological one—to mark the brutalizing effects of civilizational teleology when employed to dismantle Native lifeworlds.

Moreover, the stories play on the presumptive wildness of Native peoples to allude to forms of Indian territoriality, currently under assault due to the allotment policy. Zitkala-Ša laments the loss of her "unlassoed freedom," but that freedom itself depends on access to and occupancy of "Western rolling lands" (95–96). If she chafes against being "driven by a herder" (91), the implicit contrast she offers is with unhindered movement across a terrain, a capacious relation to place threatened by the process of domestication for Euro-American agriculture. Later in "School Days" when she returns to the Yankton Reservation after three years at White's Manual Institute, she says, "I roamed again in the Western country through four strange summers" (97), and during her time there, her mother suggests that she should "be content to roam over the prairies and find my living upon wild roots" (101). Using "roam" to index collective placemaking does not provide a particularly apt depiction of historical dynamics of Yankton residency (except perhaps with respect to annual patterns of hunting, themselves disrupted by the establishment of the reservation in the wake of the treaty of 1858). However, this terminology echoes government accounts of Native landholding, such as in the claim in *U.S. v. Kagama* that the United States has "recognized in the Indians a possessory right to the soil over which they roamed and hunted and established occasional villages" or the assurance in an annual report from the Yankton agent that "nothing more completely tames an Indian, nor is more effectual in weaning him from a disposition to roam, than the civilizing influences of a house."[80] The repetition of tropes of wildness, such as *roaming*, less provides verisimilar ethnographic detail as such than engages in what might be characterized as ethnographic mediation. Zitkala-Ša takes up settler figurations of Indian incapacity—the supposed failure to create true homes and polities—and remakes them as expressions of collective tribal relations to the land, which are being broken up through the imposition of private property holding (and the attendant loss of parts of the reservation). Toward the end of the third story, the narrator remarks, "Like a slender tree, I had been uprooted from my mother, nature, and God. I was shorn of my branches," adding, "Now a cold bare pole I seemed to be, planted in a strange earth" (112). Shifting from animal to vegetation, Zitkala-Ša further underlines a connection to place rent by the imperatives of settler policy, an *uprooting* and transplantation that seeks to extract her (and other Indians) from the (tribal) networks of relation that provide the basis for their "wild" freedom. These apparently individual articulations of desire for and loss of wildness subtly convey a sense of collectivity, though, by virtue of the narrator's implicit citation of ethnographic form in ways that position her as a representative informant.

Even while drawing on the truth-effects of ethnographic discourse in order to suggest possibilities for valuing the tribe as a kind of social form (as opposed to viewing it biopolitically as a medium for reproducing racialized Indianness), Zitkala-Ša gestures toward kinds of popular spectacle in ways that suggest the limits of wildness as a means of characterizing contemporary Indigenous sociality. By the late 1890s, no use of "wild" in reference to Native peoples could escape the connotative orbit of Buffalo Bill's Wild West show. As Joy Kasson suggests, "Buffalo Bill was arguably the most famous American of his time," and from 1883 to 1916, his Wild West show was one of the most popular mass entertainments and served as a principal enframing background against which people across the United States came to view Native people(s).[81] The show contained numerous restagings of events from the Indian Wars as well as examples of Indian prowess in riding and related "traditional" activities, enacted by Native performers.[82] Not only would Zitkala-Ša have been aware of such shows by virtue of their fame, she attended at least one performance of Buffalo Bill's show (as part of a Carlisle school trip, no less). In addition, while she was living in Boston attending music conservatory, after leaving her position as a teacher and recruiter at Carlisle (at which she worked for about two years), she was photographed by Gertrude Käsebier, who previously had gained notoriety for photographing a series of Native performers from the show.[83] Käsebier played an important part in advancing Zitkala-Ša's writing career, as the person who introduced her to the man—Edgar Chamberlin—in whose house she composed the stories published in the *Atlantic* and who would promote her work to the magazine's editor.[84] Given that relation, Zitkala-Ša certainly would have an awareness of Käsebier's other work and would have understood how her own entry into non-native networks of mass circulation occurred in the wake and through the prism of an imaginary shaped by the Wild West show.

Yet, if the stories' employment of figures of wildness invokes such spectacle, that fact would not have made the texts' account seem inherently less ethnographic or realist. In fact, that allusive relation could amplify the texts' claims to realness. William Cody continually staged and advertised the show as expressive of the reality of the West and the Indian Wars, including in his casting of former Native combatants such as Sitting Bull and prisoners from Pine Ridge who were being held by the government in the wake of the Wounded Knee massacre. Furthermore, while forms of ethnological and ethnographic exhibition in the late nineteenth century might have sought to depict themselves as scientific endeavors, in contrast to popular entertainments, they shared methods of presentation, locations, and attendees, including at the various fin-de-siècle fairs meant to illustrate the achievements of Euro-civilization. The World's

Columbian Exposition in Chicago in 1893 offers a particularly rich example of this confluence. Although excluded from the exposition as such, the Wild West show rented a space just across from the entrance to the fair for its entire duration.[85] The show likely would have been experienced by exposition-goers as more or less an extension of the sanctioned exhibits. The exposition itself included the Midway Plaisance, which was filled with a range of exhibits presented as intriguing in their exoticism, including of peoples from around the world, and the "Anthropological Building" contained exhibits of mannequins staged to look like scenes from Indian life with a small group of actual Native people living in a model village just outside. In this way, "the various commercial displays of exotic people along the Midway Plaisance as well as the academic displays around the Anthropological Building made anthropology at the fair seem more like a creation of [P. T.] Barnum than [Frederick Ward] Putnam," according to the head of the Peabody Museum at Harvard who served as the director of the exposition's department of anthropology.[86] The staging of ethnographic detail—of scenes of Native life—occurs in conjunction with the Wild West show, speaking to many of the same viewer interests and putting the two on what might be understood as an ethnographic spectrum.

Similarly, forms of writing that understood themselves to be high cultural and realist in character drew on the forms of exhibition at work in popular entertainments, such as the Wild West show, from which such writing sought to distinguish itself. In *Frantic Panoramas*, Nancy Bentley demonstrates how in the late nineteenth century "the novel is . . . made over into a space of instruction through display, a new kind of public space," adding that "under the pressure of the rivalry, realist fiction begins to resemble the world of spectacle it opposes. But the resemblance is not simply a risk to high culture fiction, it is also that fiction's precondition."[87] The novelistic attention to everyday details that is meant to indicate careful observation and a realist appreciation of forms of group difference, what Elliott refers to as "the techniques and idiom of ethnography," makes use of the types of display popularized through mass entertainments.[88] The ethnographic, then, operates as a mode across seemingly disparate social spheres—the spectacular, scientific, and literary—in ways that also facilitates their cross-referencing of each other.

Zitkala-Ša's implicit allusion to Wild West shows and the vision of Native people(s) they offer, then, actually can amplify readers' sense of the ethnographic realness of her stories. In fact, such shows could glamorize tribal relations in ways that made reformers deeply uncomfortable. The stories play on this disjunction between public presentations of Indians in their *wildness* and the civilizing/detribalizing imperatives of Indian policy. For example, decrying the Office of Indian Affairs' initial plan for the Columbian Exposition, Colonel Richard Henry Pratt, the founder and head of Carlisle, insisted that "the ethnologists were the most insidious and active enemies of Carlisle's purposes." He refused to have Carlisle "subordinated . . . to them": "The exhibit contrived by the two government bureaus [the Office of Indian Affairs and the Bureau of American Ethnology] was calculated to keep the nation's attention and the Indian's energies fixed upon his valueless past, through the spectacular aboriginal housing, dressing, and curio employments it instituted."[89] In celebrating the potential freedoms of "aboriginal" life, especially as contrasted with the violent constraints of allotment and the boarding school system, Zitkala-Ša implies that the kinds of tribal domesticities she portrays enable and express a spectacular kind of liberatory and emplaced wildness that is neither "valueless" nor merely a thing of the past—a desirable form of tribal life for which her narration of her personal experience stands as a representative case study.

The stories' use of figures of wildness, though, is somewhat double-edged, gesturing toward forms of mass spectacle that provide means for valuing Indian difference (even in deeply exoticizing ways) while also implying the failure of spectacular-cum-ethnographic modes of observation in engaging the sociopolitical dynamics of contemporary Native life. In particular, tropes of wildness signal the circulation of the Indian as a type, and Zitkala-Ša explores how the use of that typology as a prism through which to understand Native people(s) can obscure as much as it illuminates. When she shifts her focus from Yankton people to addressing the boarding school experience, she intimates how nonnative interest in tribal relations, on which she plays in the first story, often arises in the context of an enfreakment of Indianness as both oddity to be consumed and barbarous alienness to be carefully managed. As opposed to emphasizing her own practices of observation as she had previously, Zitkala-Ša indicates in "The School Days of an Indian Girl" how she becomes the observed. When she gets on the train to leave for the school, "fair women, with tottering babies on each arm, stopped their haste and scrutinized the children of absent mothers. Large men, with heavy bundles in their hands, halted near by, and riveted their glassy blue eyes upon us." While in response she "sank deep into the corner of my seat, for I resented being watched," the white children's "mothers, instead of reproving such rude curiosity, looked closely at me, and attracted their children's further notice to my blanket. This embarrassed me, and kept me constantly on the verge of tears" (87). The narrator appears as an object of curiosity, a kind of sideshow attraction at which spectators might come to gawk. Similarly, in the third story, "An Indian Teacher among Indians," after she has completed her secondary education, attended college for a year, and then gone to teach in an "Eastern Indian school" (which serves as a stand-in for Carlisle), she notes, "I was watched by those around me" (106). When white supporters come to view the students at the school, "countrymen with sunburnt cheeks and clumsy feet, forgot their relative social ranks in an ignorant curiosity," arriving to witness scenes of Indian education "from morning till evening" and to be "astounded at seeing the children of savage warriors so docile and industrious" (112).[90] These moments illustrate how Native people's Indianness becomes spectacularized within everyday interactions in non-native spaces, of which the boarding school is one. Susan Bernardin argues that Zitkala-Ša "offers an unsettling ethnographic portrait of Euro-American reform culture."[91] However, one might say that these texts sketch the complicity between the kind of interest in the lives of Indians that gives rise to ethnographic documentation and the kinds of objectifying "curiosity" displayed in scenes of white watching. The stories imply that such invasive spectacularization (in ways that resonate with attendance at Wild West shows) deeply informs non-native ethnographic observation and narration, helping contribute to the sense of Native people(s) as disruptive oddities that need to be made into "docile and industrious" subjects.

Furthermore, even when portraying Native life on reservation, Zitkala-Ša's use of "wild" to characterize social interactions appears inapt in ways that seem tactical on the author's part. Put more precisely, she employs such figures in ways that seem somewhat out of step with the other narrative information she has provided. She depicts herself as a "wild little girl" exercising her "wild freedom" in "Impressions," and in "School Days," she offers a retrospective vision of herself as previously partaking in undomesticated roaming. Yet, these images do not fit the discussion of daily practices that she gives readers in "Impressions," which as discussed earlier focus on her learning how to observe and remember, to engage properly in various social occasions, to develop particular skills (such as beading), and to perform hospitality. As Lewandowski observes, "Gertrude is anything but 'wild.' She emulates the cultural accomplishments of her mother, a caregiver and beadwork artist who teaches the values of modesty, self-discipline, and respect for elders and their traditions—a radical departure from white stereotypes," and Ron Carpenter argues that Zitkala-Ša "lures her readers" by "initially presenting herself as a simple Indian, consistent with primitivist stereotypes," even as that presentation is inconsistent with the ways her mother and other adults are depicted.[92] While the stories may lure in readers through stereotypical visions of Indian wildness or play on such notions of Indianness in order to cast tribal relations as a mode of "freedom," the disjunction between such figurations and the more detailed discussion of ordinary elements of reservation life in "Impressions" intimates the incapacity of tropes of wildness to provide much traction in conveying the specifics of the Yankton everyday.

The ways wildness appears as an inapposite ensemble of metaphors here, then, can be thought of as an understated strategy for registering, in Spivak's terms quoted earlier, the ways Native people(s) enter non-native public discourse through settler "worldings." There is no access to the Yankton intimate domestic within ethnographic discourse that does not pass through (biopolitical) discourses of Indianness and their mass dissemination via spectacular performances of "wild"-ness. If Zitkala-Ša positions herself as a native informant whose experience can provide entrée to the hidden realities of authentic Indianness, she also gestures toward how that speaking subjectivity as the representative Indian is conditioned on inhabiting settler frames of figuration that make her intelligible to non-native readers. In other words, the ill fit between her running characterization of herself as "wild" (and the loss of such wildness through boarding school education) and the dynamics of quotidian Yankton sociality she presents can be read as self-reflexively signaling the process of transposition through which her narration must pass in order to enter the non-native print public sphere. In this way, the stories point toward subaltern modes of indigeneity—formations and dynamics of Yankton life that do not fit extant ethnographic framings—as well as Zitkala-Ša's role in seeking to interpellate those dynamics within settler templates for non-native circulation and engagement. Bentley suggests, "Performative modes of expression were not an expedient strategy of 'playing Indian.' . . . Rather, these forms of Native publicity represent an effort at post-diplomatic expressivity, an attempt at world building that looked to the mass communicability of Native styles and signifiers as the materials for securing greater recognition and protection for Native societies."[93] In participating within patterns of "mass communicability," such as employing spectacular figurations of Native wildness, the texts also intimate the ways popular discourses of Indianness help contour the ethnographic imagination through which she gains expression in print as a speaking subject.[94]

Zitkala-Ša both uses tropes of wildness and renders them odd, mobilizing them while also implying their failure to explain forms of everyday interaction. When she returns to the reservation after three years at boarding school, she says of herself, "Even nature seemed to have no place for me. I was neither a wee girl nor a tall one; neither a wild Indian nor a tame one" (97). Just prior to this moment, though, she observes, "My brother [Dawée], being almost ten years my senior, did not quite understand my feelings" (97).[95] Readers know from "Impressions" that Dawée already had completed "three years' education in the East" well before the narrator contemplates leaving for boarding school

(83), so how is it that he cannot "understand [her] feelings"? Is the implication that he already has become "tame" and, therefore, cannot grasp the narrator's sensation of in-betweenness? However, he and the other Native young people to whom the narrator compares herself have gone through the same amount of schooling. She notes, "They had gone three years to school in the East, and had become civilized" (99). Even as Zitkala-Ša allows readers to suppose that the narrator occupies something of a limbo state in which her loss of wildness has not led to a comfortable embrace of civilization, the story introduces elements that suggest that the difference between "wild" and "tame" lies in something other than the shift from the reservation to the school or the imposition of non-native life patterns on Native people(s). The narrator says of some "jolly young people" who pass by her mother's house on their way to a gathering, "They were no more young braves in blankets and eagle plumes, nor Indian maids with prettily painted cheeks" (99). Although indicating something like a picture of them before their time in boarding school, and lamenting the change to what they are now, this image seems to recycle popular notions of Indianness of the kind that would be available in "newspaper photographs, dime novels, and Wild West shows."[96]

While one might interpret this moment as indicative of a weakness in Zitkala-Ša's writing, drawing on stereotypical imagery instead of offering a more grounded depiction of extant Yankton social dynamics, the tinniness of this description could be read as meant to draw attention, albeit somewhat subtly, to the inefficacy of such metaphors—the ways they are imported into the situation in ways that have little to do with the specific place, persons, or relations at issue. To the extent that this scene is meant to reflect the narrator's sense of things, the use of fairly clichéd language here may indicate not so much the narrator's positioning between *tameness* and *wildness* (a kind of representative irresolution produced by state-sanctioned Indian education) as the ways she has learned to adopt this (spectacularizing) frame during her boarding school experience. From this perspective, her performance of wildness since returning to the reservation—including stealing Dawée's horse and riding him until he's foaming at the mouth, and throwing away her school shoes (98–99)—can be seen as adopting a vision of Indianness present in settler formulations while reversing its valences, celebrating barbarous freedom rather than viewing it as a sign of racial backwardness. Similarly, the stories' use of "wild" as a way of describing her pre–boarding school life and loss of freedom in the school might be understood as retrospective, a way of characterizing those social dynamics that has been acquired through increased exposure to non-native visions of Indianness and that is projected backward as a way of characterizing the narrator's past.

To the extent that the stories draw on ethnographic discourse in staging Yankton sociality and the assault on it within federal policy, Zitkala-Ša functions as a native informant whose firsthand experience provides the guarantee of the truth of what is narrated. In this vein, figures of wildness allow her to signify the distinctions between tribal relations and settler norms, thereby indexing forms of Indian difference (and the targeting of them for elimination) while casting such difference as precious in its preservation of modes of freedom as well as undomesticated connection to the landscape. When condensed as "wild," the details of quotidian Yankton life that Zitkala-Ša presents are endowed with value for readers, or at least, the supersession of Yankton tribal relations by civilized manners appears as a violent, even cruel, imposition. Such tropes, though, also point toward the connections in the period between ethnographic description and the spectacularization of Native people(s) in mass entertainments. Wild West shows and ethnography appealed to viewers/readers in similar ways and mobilized kinds of display that resonated with each other. Thus, in using the term "wild" and associated kinds of imagery, Zitkala-Ša mediates these popular forms to direct reader attention and interest to Yankton sociality and to highlight the calamitous effects of federal intervention. Such allusions work to heighten support for Indigenous social formations.

Yet, while readers initially encounter figures of wildness as expressive of everyday Indian life, such figurations come under increasing (if still subtle) pressure over the course of the stories, suggesting a kind of strain in employing this template and introducing implicit questions about its aptness for characterizing Native lifeworlds. The stories seem to use tropes of wildness referentially as a shorthand for Yankton social relations that exceed the terms of U.S. policy imperatives, in ways that readers could engage as straight-forwardly descriptive. Zitkala-Ša, though, also introduces elements that implicitly convey a disjunction between the spectacular-ethnographic connotations associated with wildness and the situations or relations discussed. In this way, she both plays the role of native informant and undercuts it, enacting a representativity that allows her to speak for the Yanktons (in a nondiplomatic mode) while gesturing toward the discursive limitations of ethnographic form. Through their invocations of wildness, Zitkala-Ša's stories indicate how the ethnographic imaginary was not just scientifically oriented but inflected by contemporary mass spectacle in ways that help depict Native people(s) as vitally present in the current moment. Reciprocally, in their disconnection from the relations being described, such figures of wildness intimate broader questions about the capacities of ethnographic representation and representativity as a mode through which to signify Indigenous peoplehood to non-native publics.

Falling into the Everyday

Discussing the presentation of ethnographic exhibits during the Colombian Exposition and similar fairs, Lee Baker characterizes this process as "choreographing the minstrelsy of the real."[97] In this vein, we can approach Zitkala-Ša's performance of ethnographic subjectivity as a mode of playing Indian, staging a performance as the native informant in which she offers a version of her own experience that mediates non-native conceptions of Indian wildness in order to generate possibilities for signifying and valuing Indigenous collectivity in ways at odds with the racializing imaginary of Indian policy. Zitkala-Ša draws on ethnographic strategies to contest the biopolitical account of tribal relations as merely the means for reproducing an Indianness understood as backward and in need of evolutionary advancement. The stories, though, also indirectly signal the limits of this mode of public intervention, suggesting that it implicitly posits an absolute distinction between Indianness and whiteness in which expressions of wildness provide the condition of possibility for authenticating indigeneity as such.[98] In Spivak's terms discussed earlier, treating Native texts as merely transcriptions of "concrete experience" ignores the "worlding" enacted by settler colonialism, and as discussed in the introduction, Spivak further cautions against ignoring the relation between "two different senses of representation"—speaking for a collective and portraying that collective (including the ways it discursively is constituted as a collective, and by whom)—in order "to say that beyond both is where oppressed subjects speak, act, and know *for themselves*."[99] Such conflation and elision enacts a "nostalgia for lost origins" that effaces the ideological and institutional dynamics that shape the intelligibility of the colonized's self-representation under colonialism as well as the multivectored effects of such dynamics on the colonized themselves.[100] In contrast to the call for an authentic speaking subject who can testify to her experience (particularly of a supposedly disappearing way of life), the call for some version of the native informant, Spivak gestures toward the necessity for and difficulty of constructing "a history that can attend to the details of the putting together of a continuous-seeming self for everyday life" for nonelite persons living under colonialism.[101] Zitkala-Ša plays on and subtly critiques non-native desires for a version of Indianness that can be treated as such a lost origin—as noble yet tragically vanishing due to white intervention. As scholars have noted, one of the most prominent motifs in Zitkala-Ša's series of autobiographical stories is the expulsion from Eden, signaled through her repetition of the figure of red apples.[102] Like with her use of figures of wildness, even as she employs this metaphor of the Fall she suggests the ways it fails to address ordinary life on the reservation, both before and after her enrollment in non-native schooling. Through indirectly suggesting the inability of non-native metaphors to encompass these dynamics of the Yankton everyday, the stories gesture toward the limits of an ethnographic frame—the authenticity-generating function of what would become the culture concept—in addressing Indigenous processes for living peoplehood amid intensifying occupation.

While previously having noted the "forbidden fruit" of a plum bush, which was not to be eaten because its "roots are wrapped around an Indian's skeleton" (80), the final section of "Impressions" introduces the biblical motif of temptation and fall.[103] Titled "Big Red Apples," it begins with a discussion by the narrator's mother of the aims of the "two paleface missionaries" who had been in their village: "She told me, after I had teased much, that they had come to take away Indian boys and girls to the East" (83). The narrator notes her friend Judéwin's intense desire to go with them, based on having heard of "the great tree where grew red, red apples" and of "how we could reach out our hands to pick all the red apples we could eat" (84); the narrator asserts that she is "going East" because she "like[s] big red apples, and . . . want[s] to ride on the iron horse" (85). Although the state to which Zitkala-Ša went for school actually did have apples growing there, this "trope serves as a reminder of Zitkala-Sa's fall from Indian paradise."[104] Before the end of "Impressions," when she has gotten on the train that will take her away to the boarding school, she notes, "I felt suddenly weak, as if I might fall limp to the ground. I was in the hands of strangers whom my mother did not fully trust. I no longer felt free to be myself, or to voice my own feelings" (86). By the close of the first story, readers already have a sense of Zitkala-Ša as having lost something fundamental, as having sacrificed her well-being (physical and emotional) through her pursuit of the apples. She has been tempted, and in giving in to that temptation, she has gained not so much the knowledge of the difference between good and evil as that between Indianness and civilization. The next story begins with the section "The Land of Red Apples," which as discussed earlier chronicles the invasive, exoticizing, and embarrassing stares she receives from whites on the way to the school—indicating a process by which she comes to know herself as a spectacle of wildness, as an *Indian*. Moreover, she is debarred from returning to her former innocent state, as her pleas to be reunited with her family go ignored by those around her (89). This sense of exile persists even when she returns to the reservation. She finds herself unable to join in with the other young people and to communicate in substantive ways with her mother (99); she later describes herself as having given her mother up for "the white man's papers," as having been "uprooted from my mother, nature, and God" (112). One might read Zitkala-Ša as mobilizing missionary discourse, including the biblical stories she is taught in boarding school, in order to recast detribalization (the attempt to remake Native people as "men and women, not Indians") as loss, as the gaining of a supposed knowledge that actually destroys rather than saves or uplifts.[105]

However, to the extent that the effectiveness of this figuration depends on viewing her as expelled from "Indian paradise," the metaphor of the Fall appears ill suited from the outset.[106] Life among the Yanktons before she leaves for the boarding school certainly is not an ahistorical utopia. While the narrator may possess a generically imagined childhood innocence, she already is aware of settler presence and power. As discussed previously, early in "Impressions," her mother tells the narrator of their people's dispossession and removal, as well as the resulting deaths of members of her family. Also, readers know that Dawée has attended boarding school (83), and presumably he is not the only one the narrator knows who has done so. In other words, there is no completely atraumatic space of undisturbed wholeness at any point in the stories that could serve as a referent for Eden, thus making the allusion somewhat empty or, perhaps, catachrestic.[107] Moreover, given that Zitkala-Ša does not mention any awareness of the Bible or of Christian teachings prior to the description of learning about the devil once she is in boarding school (94), to which I will return shortly, the allusion to the Fall through the figure of the apples would itself be retrospective, characterizing earlier events through the prism of a mode of interpretation based on what was learned after those events have occurred. Seen in this way, the depiction of the narrator's longing to attend the boarding school as the Fall says something not so much about the decision itself as about how that decision comes to be understood within a frame of reference that arises through boarding school education. As with her later nostalgia over the ways Yankton young people were no more "braves in blankets" and "Indian maids with prettily painted cheeks" (99), assessing persons on the reservation against what seem to be stereotypical images of wild Indianness, the invocation of the biblical story of Adam and Eve and their punishment for giving in to temptation appears as if it provides an explanation or meaningful analysis of events, only to be undercut by its failure to fit the situation described. Or rather, Zitkala-Ša gives readers enough information for this metaphor to seem imposed, even forced, if one does not already presume that Indianness lies on the other side of history—as a prelapsarian paradise of romantic primitivism.

In this way, she might be said to be drawing attention to the conditions of possibility through which Indianness, and Indian wildness, come to signify as such within non-native networks in the late nineteenth century. In order for the metaphor to make sense, one needs already to have adopted a vision of tribal relations as an insulated world apart from settler political economy as well as historical change in toto. The stories, therefore, offer a double irony in inverting the terms of missionization/civilization (boarding school as a fall from grace instead of ascent into Euro-American progress) while then also intimating that the terms of that first irony misconstrue Yankton sociality by casting it as outside of history.

"School Days" goes even further in suggesting the inapplicability of settler-derived frames in representing ordinary Yankton understandings. When teachers introduce Zitkala-Ša to the idea of the devil, she indicates, "I never knew there was an insolent chieftain among the bad spirits . . . until I heard this white man's legend from a paleface woman," and when this figure invades her dreams, she imagines herself as "in my mother's cottage" when her mother is being visited by another "Indian woman" (94). The devil rushes into the house, "look[ing] exactly like the picture I had seen of him in the white man's papers," although she notes that "he did not know the Indian language." Her mother and the other woman take no notice of him, but just as he is about to snatch up the narrator, "my mother awoke from her quiet indifference, and lifted me on her lap. Whereupon the devil vanished, and I was awake" (95). While this passage might be read as indicative of the failure of her boarding school experience fully to crowd out the narrator's emotional investments in her people and life on the reservation, it also can be seen as illustrating how the devil—and by extension the Christian-civilizational interpretive nexus and pedagogical program in which he is inscribed—does not provide a means of engaging the Yankton intimate domestic. Not only do the mother and the other woman fail to register the significance of the devil, he disappears once they move into action. Furthermore, her mother's action itself does not seem to have a great deal of urgency about it, just a quotidian gesture of connection. This figure from "the white man's papers" is out of place, ineffectual, and fleeting when confronted with the details of everyday Native life on reservation. Similarly, when Zitkala-Ša returns home after her first three-year stint at school, her mother seeks to ameliorate her unhappiness by asking her to read from "an Indian Bible," also described here as "the white man's papers," and she refuses to do so, since the book "afforded me no help" and "was a perfect delusion to my mother" (99). This scene could indicate the narrator's growing distance from her mother due to her schooling. Yet, in doing so, it also presents the Bible as profoundly unhelpful in mediating any aspect of that relationship, further suggesting how inapposite a biblical metaphor would be in seeking to portray her relation to the reservation, to her mother, or her mother's thoughts and everyday sentiments—especially given that such figures are "a perfect delusion" to her mother. From this perspective, the stories seem increasingly to cast the image of the red apples and the allusion to the Fall as obscuring more than they illuminate.

The stories' subtle undermining of the use of the Fall as a means of characterizing the narrator's relation to the boarding school, to her people, and to the reservation in the wake of attending school is part of a broader strategy of Zitkala-Ša's in which she worries the very frames that she employs. The repetition of the phrase "white man's papers" throughout the stories gestures toward more than English literacy per se, instead bespeaking particular kinds of interpretive and explanatory frameworks meant to guide approaches to and understandings of Native life. In this vein, ethnographic realness in the late nineteenth century entails the portrayal of Indianness in ways that fit settler expectations of wildness. Even as those non-natives engaged in projects of ethnographic description increasingly distinguished their accounts from explicit narratives of evolutionary development, they continued to characterize their engagements with Native peoples in terms of "salvage," understanding Indigenous languages, practices, stories, and objects as endangered and in the process of being lost or contaminated through exposure to Euro-American civilization and the force of industrial modernity.[108] From this perspective, the failure of Native people(s) to enact forms of indigeneity recognized as such by non-natives becomes the occasion for settler narratives of declension, of ceasing to be authentically Indian.[109] Such a vision, though, cannot capture the changes in Native life brought about by settler colonial interventions, including allotment, except to cast such change as either a rise into civilization or a fall from a previously pristine tribality. Thus, while drawing on the Bible through the figure of the red apples certainly is not in itself a mode of ethnographic representation, I want to suggest that in alluding to the Fall as a way of portraying entry into the boarding school system Zitkala-Ša both enacts and ironizes the conception of contact with non-native persons, institutions, and material culture as a loss of (an ethnographically conceived) real Indianness.

At several points, the stories link the question of faith to the broader imperatives of Indian policy in ways that intimate such an additional turn in Zitkala-Ša's use of the biblical metaphor. While discussing the failure of the boarding school staff to attend meaningfully to the children's health, she asserts, "I blamed the hard-working, well-meaning ignorant woman who was inculcating in our hearts her superstitious ideas" (97), and when contemplating her return to Carlisle after a trip to the reservation, she observes, "I slowly comprehended that the large army of white teachers in Indian schools had a larger missionary creed than I suspected," namely their own professional "self-preservation" (111).

These moments present participation in projects of detribalization and the management of Native peoples in the idiom of missionization and Christian belief, suggesting that the stories' earlier use of Christian narrative can be read less as a useful way of framing Native experience than as expressive of how non-native framings obscure engagement with everyday Native circumstances.

The stories give readers glimpses of life on the reservation that neither fit a conception of Indian authenticity organized around spectacular wildness nor express the sense of a loss of tribal purity through a putative fall into civilization. Through her portrayal of her mother and brother, Zitkala-Ša gestures toward, in Spivak's terms quoted earlier, "the details of the putting together of a continuous-seeming self for everyday life" amid the pressures of the allotment era. In this way, the stories engage what we might characterize, following Chris Andersen, as the densities of Indigenous (or specifically Yankton) experience in the period. In the place of a declension narrative in which Native identity inheres only in its static and reified distinction from white social forms, and in which exposure to the latter dooms the former, the stories subtly illustrate entangled experiences of indigeneity under intensifying occupation that exceed the terms of extant ethnographic imaginaries. In "Impressions," she observes that her mother has "take[n] a farther step from her native way of living. First it was a change from the buffalo skin to the white man's canvas that covered our wigwam. Now she had given up her wigwam of slender poles, to live, a foreigner, in a home of clumsy logs" (83–84). Zitkala-Ša describes these actions as a response to Dawée's return from school "in the East"; rather than indicating that Dawée convinced her mother to do so, though, she notes that "his coming back influenced my mother" (83). At one level this anecdote implies a fall away from a prior Indian authenticity, becoming a "foreigner," but at another level, that assessment is the narrator's, not her mother's. If her mother is "influenced" by Dawée's return, the choice appears to be her mother's, for reasons that are not clearly articulated. This sense of agency and opacity is developed further in the final story, when Zitkala-Ša observes, "My mother had never gone to school, and though she meant always to give up her own customs for such of the white man's ways as pleased her, she made only compromises" (108). Despite having remained on the reservation and not having passed through the boarding school system, her mother could still find value in some of "the white man's ways" and could decide to adopt them to "please" herself, while others she does not adopt. The story somewhat obliquely points toward Native people's capacity to engage with such changes in ways that follow their own inclinations, which remain irreducible to non-native interests, imperatives, or frameworks. Moreover, although in some ways connoting a mediation between otherwise antithetical positions, the use of the term "compromise" here more strongly implies her mother's employment of principles (which remain unenumerated) that guide her choices.

The stories also point toward the ways such change was occurring in the context of colonial force. While on the reservation as part of a trip to recruit students for Carlisle, Zitkala-Ša is sitting with her mother one night, and she notes, "We were facing the river, as we talked about the shrinking limits of the village. She told me about the poverty-stricken white settlers, who lived in caves dug in the long ravines of the high hills across the river." These people "had rushed hither to make claims on those wild lands," and as Zitkala-Ša looks out in the night, she "saw more and more twinkling lights here and there, scattered all along the wide black margin of the river," all of which are white homes (110).[110] This scene indexes the profound effects of allotment-era policy on the Yankton Reservation, which included the privatization of Yankton lands, the loss of "surplus" territory, the ongoing assault on Indigenous modes of self-governance and everyday association, and the use of starvation as a tactic for producing Native compliance. Various agents since at least the early 1870s had attempted to section off parts of the reservation into parcels of land that would be held as private property by individual families (even though they did not legally have the power to do so).[111] The passage of the Dawes Act in 1887 made that goal an official statutory aim of federal Indian law and policy, with allocations based largely around nuclear family units.[112] That process was completed in less than three years.[113] In March 1893, an agreement was forwarded to Washington, D.C., that purported to indicate Yankton assent to the sale of the remaining, or "surplus," lands of the reservation, despite significant evidence of fraud in both the information provided to signatories and the forging of Yanktons' signatures to the agreement.[114] Over the course of the 1880s, as noted earlier, agents also imposed on the Yanktons a tribal police system, a governing council consisting of two representatives chosen by the agent from each of the eight bands, and an Indian court with justices selected by the agent.[115] Such changes were instituted despite the fact that previous agents had indicated the absence of conflict on the reservation and with other peoples, even given that the Yanktons, in the agents' terms, were "without laws."[116] The explicit aim of these impositions, and of allotment itself, was to break up Yankton "tribal relations."[117] In response to opposition to allotment in 1887, the agent asserts, "Indians must not be allowed to assert an authority in conflict with the Government. . . . The Government being supreme, its laws the highest authority in the land, neither traditions, customs, or theories based on falsehood must be permitted to stand in the way of executing that authority."[118] Moreover, rations routinely were withheld as punishment for failure to obey the agent's directives.[119] Zitkala-Ša's references to her "mother's stories of the encroaching frontier settlers" (111), then, signal both the conditions of ongoing violence under which Yankton people are forced to live and the ways everyday life on the reservation involves less questions of purity and authenticity (and their loss) than the process of negotiating forms of peoplehood within the context of settler colonial occupation.

Thus, over the course of the stories, the image of the Fall appears less and less relevant as a way of understanding the choices and lifeworld of Yankton people in the present, further intimating the limits of ethnographic framings that rely on ahistoricizing conceptions of indigeneity. Through discussion of the difficulties faced by her brother, Zitkala-Ša addresses how non-native institutions regulate the potentials for Indigenous self-expression and public critique. When visiting her mother, she learns that her brother Dawée has been fired from his position on the reservation: "Washington sent a white son to take your brother's pen from him" due to his attempt "to secure justice for our tribe in a small matter." Her mother observes that this situation illustrates that "the Indian cannot complain to the Great Father in Washington without suffering outrage for it here" (109). The power of this anecdote turns not at all on the sense of decline from some prior, more authentic version of Yankton identity. Nor does it contribute to an exoticizing portrait of Indian difference. Rather, the kind of tribal relations that come into view, for which Zitkala-Ša serves as the trusted vehicle, involve the ubiquity of government regulation of ordinary life in legally recognized Native space.

Perhaps more significant even than the rebuke Dawée receives for attempting to address corruption in the administration of Indian affairs, though, is the ways such retribution speaks to the entrenched pattern of stymying Indigenous efforts to adapt to the circumstances created by settler invention. Dawée's acquisition of English literacy, participation within the bureaucracy of Indian policy, and use of that bureaucracy to Native ends ("to secure justice for our tribe") illustrates an attempt to turn the circumstances created through allotment-era interventions toward possibilities for generating Yankton collective well-being. In *Speaking of Indians* (1944), Yankton intellectual Ella Deloria speaks to the "decades of paternalism and protection" that Native peoples have endured under federal Indian policy, observing, "In the old days the Indians had dignity and pride. They still do. . . . I am optimistic enough to think they would respond, especially if they are told to go ahead *in their own way*—that too is important—and if a chance is given them to do this without a kind of stifling oversight."[120] The "outrage" of Dawée's dismissal functions as part of this broader pattern of "oversight," and in this vignette, Zitkala-Ša gestures toward the potential for Native people(s) to "go ahead *in their own way*" even amid settler impositions—a process of seeking to exert self-determination that continually is thwarted at micro and macro scales.[121]

Yet even as this description of Dawée's situation indexes the prevalence of forms of unchecked discretion at play in the execution of U.S. settler rule, this anecdote and the story's portrayal of Zitkala-Ša's mother's everyday choices suggest the enactment of modes of Indigenous survivance—the refusal to perform properly the roles and subjectivities scripted for Native people(s).[122] In this vein, agents' reports contain a number of examples of Yanktons rejecting allotment geographies, in terms of both outright repudiation and inhabitation of them in ways that disorient the detribalizing aims of the policy. In the first year after the passage of the Dawes Act and the attempt to implement it on the Yankton Reservation, the chiefs of the bands make their disgust with the law clear. The agent notes, "The surveyors were twice driven from the field by Indians who were sent out for this purpose by some of the old chiefs and those who were affiliated with them in their opposition," adding, "The presence of the military from Fort Randall, 15 miles distant, became a necessity."[123] After the land had been apportioned and certificates of allotment had been issued, Yanktons continued to undermine the privatizing aims of the policy, as "many of them continue the practice of gathering in large numbers or bands when plowing, planting, harvesting, thrashing, etc." In addition, relations of hospitality persist, "assist[ing] their less thrifty neighbors and relations," with the agent noting that each person "will divide his last morsel with his neighbor, however thriftless and improvident the latter may be."[124] Family members continued to grow crops on each other's allotments that would be shared among them; many people did not reside on their allotments year-round, instead living in villages during the winter, "varying the monotony by recounting their past deeds of valor in war, by dancing, often by pastimes calculated to retard the efforts made for their advancement," a pattern that the agent further characterizes as a "nomadic habit—a relic of their ancient custom" that leads Yanktons to "make but little progress in civilization or material prosperity."[125] Zitkala-Ša gestures toward such dynamics in the fact that after she already had described her mother as giving up a "wigwam" for a log cabin (83–84), she later describes herself as looking from her mother's "wigwam" at settlers along the river (110), suggesting that her mother does not live all the time on her own allotment (presumably the plot of land on which the cabin is built). These forms of adaptation and opposition, though, do not fit the narrative of tragic declension from a more authentic state of proper Indianness that provides the background for ethnographic narration.

Even as the narrator's ability to be seen as a credible representor of the reservation turns in many ways on being seen as representative, as the native informant who can convey the ethnographic truths of Indian life, Zitkala-Ša toward the end of the final story becomes more direct in her refusal to play this role. In raising questions about the efficacy and terms of her portrayal of Yankton socialities to non-natives, she sketches the limits of the very ethnographic frame that licenses her speech, within which the notion of a fall from authentic Indianness could appear as a meaningful assessment rather than merely another colonial projection. In a section titled "Retrospection," she states, "At last, one weary day in the schoolroom, a new idea presented itself to me. It was a new way of solving the problem of my inner self. I liked it. Thus I resigned my position as teacher" (112). This revelation is followed by the description, discussed earlier, of the "many specimens of civilized peoples" who would come to visit "the Indian school" and gawk at the students (112). In this way, her "new idea" can be understood as a response to and rejection of the desire of non-natives to observe and come to know Indians in their exotic aberrance.

Whatever her "new way" is, it dispenses with an ethnographic imaginary organized around producing Native difference for settler consumption, even as Zitkala-Ša's stories rely on this very gambit to dislodge a racializing conception of Native backwardness—a notion of Indianness that gets cited in order to justify federal intervention into the *tribal relations* that supposedly reproduce such tendencies. Notably, though, she does not indicate what this shifted sense of "self" might be. In contrast to the elaboration of Yankton sociality in "Impressions" and the figurations of wildness sprinkled throughout the first two stories, she does not provide a way of characterizing "the problem of [her] inner self" or the *solution* to this problem. Instead, readers are offered simply the fact that she "liked" the solution she has found. One might suggest that the refusal to narrate Yankton identity in ways that make it intelligible to non-natives *is* the solution and that the problem she's faced is one created by Indian law and policy—namely, the need to represent indigeneity in ways conditioned by settler frames. Her silence here might be understood as marking a refusal of that forced colonial relation and the terms in which it is enacted.[126] The text here jettisons the ethnographic impulse entirely by foregoing any attempt to convey *Indian* experience to non-natives, particularly inasmuch as doing so entails inserting it into a declension narrative in which it can only be understood as a process of becoming less authentically Native—as a fall from real Indianness or Indian realness.

Over the course of the stories, Zitkala-Ša illustrates the problems posed by extant ethnographic framings for engaging the Indigenous everyday, particularly as lived on reservation amid the impositions and interventions of the allotment era. The stories increasingly reveal the problems of conventionalized ways of figuring Indianness. Yet, they draw on ethnographic expectations and conventions in order to stage a vision of Native collectivity that challenges dominant notions of Indian barbarism and that privileges the very kinds of "social relations" targeted for elimination under Indian policy. Given the predominance in the period of ethnological understandings of Native people(s) as residues of an earlier period in human evolution, Zitkala-Ša's emphasis on quotidian Yankton practices and modes of self-understanding works to indicate the viability and vitality of Native formations of peoplehood. She focuses on patterns of care, education, and hospitality, offering a portrait of Yankton lifeways and worldmaking as capacious and sustaining for those who dwell within them. This vision of indigeneity as actually lived contrasts sharply with proliferating accounts—popular and governmental—of Native peoples as lacking family, governance, and the capacity to adapt to change. Within this biopolitical conception of Indianness, Native people(s) possess ingrained inclinations that point away from civilization and human progress, and such orientations toward regressive stasis are envisioned as generationally inherited through "tribal relations." Within this Lamarckian loop, Indian raciality consists not simply in the procreative transmission of physical characteristics or inborn proclivities but in the traits acquired through Native "social organization" and passed on to children in ways that make such (in)capacities more or less immutable in a recursive cycle of reproduction. As against this vision of embedded inertia, Zitkala-Ša draws on the discursive resources of emergent templates of ethnographic description in order to offer a vision of Indian difference in which it is not evolutionarily dead-ended but, instead, is rich in affective and ethical possibilities that contribute to dynamic and self-sustaining forms of social order.

Part of this rhetorical gambit lies in Zitkala-Ša's positioning of herself as a native informant who can provide a representative account. Even though she speaks of her own life, albeit slightly fictionalized and channeled through an unnamed narrator, she casts the events and perspectives conveyed in somewhat genericizing terms (such as the use of "an Indian" in the titles of all three stories) that present them less as indicative of individual specificity than as illustrative of kinds of collective experience, both on reservation and in Indian boarding schools. As in ethnographic texts produced by non-natives, she suggests that observed behavior and practices can be interpreted as expressive of broader social patterns that speak to forms of communal identity. Such accounts are made possible through a given writer's engagements with Native persons who can testify to the regularity, rather than idiosyncrasy, of such patterns, and in this case, Zitkala-Ša serves as both knowledgeable insider and ethnographer. As opposed to more explicitly political modes of representativity, such as in the negotiations that were part of the treaty system (as cited by both Boudinot and Winnemucca), this way of speaking for a people does not foreground political identity as such. Instead, the sense of collectivity emerges in terms of lived, quotidian formations that eventually would come to be labeled as "culture," in ways that also would come to be distinguished from governance per se. Taking up this form of public speech, then, may seem to translate Yankton sociality in ways that divorce it from questions of sovereignty. However, Zitkala-Ša foregrounds the politics of Yankton dispossession (such as the "debt for stolen lands" [86]) as a way of framing her description of her childhood and the meaning of her entry into the boarding school system. In addition, the absence in the stories of a more directly diplomatic mode of portraying Indigenous collectivity can be understood as a function of changes in U.S. policy and public discourses in the late nineteenth century. As indicated by reports from the agents to the reservation, Yankton peoplehood appears within federal policy and the administration of Indian affairs less as a geopolitical matrix than as a set of vestigial inclinations that need to be managed, disciplined, dismantled, and replaced in order to dispel the Yanktons' Indianness so as to ready them for entry into U.S. citizenship and to ready their lands for privatization (with the "surplus" to be occupied by settlers). In this context, emergent modes of ethnographic subjectivity, including the representativity of the informant, offer the potential to signify Indigenous peoplehood as something other than a dangerous, debilitating, barbarizing anachronism, instead casting it as having inherent, immanent value.

Positioning herself as a native informant who can serve as a conduit for information on tribal relations to non-natives gives her a means of entering non-native public discourse and for redirecting extant (racializing) portrayals of Indianness. These stories can be read as testing the possibilities for, in Bentley's terms quoted earlier, "post-diplomatic expressivity"—the potentials for depicting sustained and sustainable Native collectivities in the wake of the end of treaty making and the implementation of detribalization as the paradigmatic animating impulse of federal Indian law. The issue is not so much whether ethnographic idioms and imaginaries are better than other kinds of official and popular modes of representation at capturing the truth of Indigenous experience (Zitkala-Ša's or the Yanktons' more broadly), but rather how Zitkala-Ša inhabits and mobilizes the potentials in this kind of public presentation. She explores the capacities and limits (what we might call the affordances) of extant ethnographic strategies in their ability to create rhetorical space for addressing contemporary Indigenous socialities, territorialities, and responses to increasing settler intervention.[127] She experiments with and mediates the ethnographic as a form in

which to register the ongoing dynamics and complexities of Indigenous peoplehood. Attending to, in Piatote's terms, "the intimate domestic" of Native life
enables Zitkala-Ša to shift registers, moving away from a direct confrontation
with settler sovereignty toward an elaboration and celebration of Native strategies of survivance, tribal cohesion, and social reproduction. Such ethnographic
maneuvers, then, can be understood as providing an alternative means of gesturing toward Indigenous political orders in the absence of a public discourse
that would support articulations of Native sovereignty and in the presence of
prominent and intensifying efforts to cast peoplehood as an ensemble of racialized tribal proclivities out of which Indians need to be trained so that they can
become something better.

Yet, speaking for the Yanktons and for boarding school students in this way
takes shape within particular ways of characterizing Native people(s) that have
their own orientating frames and momentum that can pose problems for articulating Indigenous self-determination. Invoking non-native conceptions of
Indian wildness, for example, enables Zitkala-Ša to draw on interest in Wild
West shows as a way of valuing Native lifeways that do not fit the parameters
of Indian policy's civilizing imperative and that have been targeted by agents as
a drag on progress. Moreover, through this association, Native socialities can
appear invigorating and powerful, rather than destructive and/or pathological.
However, such images also can reinforce the sense of Native people(s) as backward and disappearing (their spectacular consumption driven by the notion of
their exoticism and ever-increasing scarcity), feeding back into an ethnological
narrative of Indianness as static if not outright regressive. In this way, the stories
employ the figure of the Fall in ways that subtly thematize such difficulties, the
dangers of being captured within settler notions of authentic Indianness sundered from questions of governance—the "culture" trap, as discussed earlier,
that predominates in contemporary non-native visions of Indianness.

What I want to highlight, though, is less the ultimate efficacy of Zitkala-Ša's
rhetorical strategies—both employing and problematizing an ethnographic
frame—than the stakes of those strategies and the intellectual and political
work they perform. Instead of centering textual access to tribal realness, or the
absence of it, this way of reading the stories underlines how Indigenous writings register shifts in dominant ways of representing Native peoplehood and
how they seek to engage such modes of representation in complex ways. In
this sense, as I have been arguing, a text's staging of its own representativity—
diplomatic, ethnographic, or otherwise—need not engender either an acceptance or an assessment of its claims so much as an investigation of how it
responds to extant conditions of possibility for signifying Native polities,

geographies, and self-determination. All of the writers discussed in this study are engaging with differently configured assemblages of law, policy, and popular perception, and each of them offers a version of representative speech in response. The ways they position themselves as speaking and standing for Native collectives engage the particular settler formations with which they are grappling, and these texts also are marked by specific, shifting, and contested contours of Indigenous worldmaking beyond the terms and imperatives of settler frameworks. In Zitkala-Ša's case, she's drawing on the rhetorical and conceptual resources of emergent ethnographic discourses as a way of providing an alternative to allotment-era depictions of the anarchonistic worthlessness of "tribal relations." However, such intellectual gambits are always contingent, responsive as they are to particular discursive and institutional configurations. The appeal to ethnographic form does not provide greater access to, in Vizenor's terms, the "tribal real," but more than that, over the course of the twentieth century this mode becomes adopted as part of federal policy in ways that constrain possibilities for signifying indigeneity to non-native authorities. Within the eras of both reorganization (starting in 1934) and self-determination (starting in 1970), which bookend the termination period, Native "culture" increasingly gets cast as something to preserve while also, as in Audra Simpson's concerns about Indian "difference" articulated earlier, implicitly being differentiated from questions of placemaking, landedness, and governance, which are expected to take liberal forms conducive to non-native jurisdiction. Further, the proper performance of forms of Indianness intelligible as such to non-natives (largely consisting of behaviors and activities that would be conceptualized as "culture"—such as dress, ritual, kinds of material culture and subsistence practices, language use) came to serve as a crucial way of proving Indianness both for the purposes of achieving federal recognition and in making claims for acknowledgment of various tribal rights. This development, however, does not mean that Zitkala-Ša's maneuvers should be understood as merely presaging or replicating these later developments, even as her texts raise questions about reading later writings through a quasi-ethnographic lens that somewhat unreflexively treats them as conduits to Indigenous being.

On Refusing the Ethnographic Imaginary,
or Reading for the Politics of Peoplehood

How might we conceptualize Indigenous resurgence as a project of reading?[1] The nineteenth-century texts I've been discussing seem far from contemporary situations and concerns, raising the question of what role they could play in how we understand current dynamics of recognition, refusal, and sovereignty. In addressing the contextual specificity of the circumstances in and out of which these authors wrote, I have sought to gesture toward resonances with the present, including the role of Native vanguards and elites, the absence of state acknowledgment, the construction of new categories of peoplehood, and the performance of cultural authenticity. More than offering parallels whose terms map directly onto situations now, though, the process of engaging with how each of these intellectuals negotiated settler networks and the politics of peoplehood draws on the tools of close reading to gesture toward an ethics of knowledge-production and develop an approach to thinking the form(s) of peoplehood that speaks to processes of enacting self-determination under continuing colonial occupation. In previous work, I've explored the potential political value of a conceptual pause, of recognizing kinds of unknowing as part of an open-ended ethics of relation.[2] Similarly, turning to nineteenth-century Native writings and investigating the dynamics of their claims to representativity creates a pause in trajectories of political analysis that posit a clear form for Indigenous peoplehood, a ready sense of how it relates to settler discourses, and a definite set of parameters for what the pursuit of self-determination entails. Reading for the ways intellectuals have mediated settler and Native networks and the situated possibilities as well as limits of their approaches offers a layered sense of the density of Indigenous political formations, including how they take shape amid particular kinds of colonial entanglements. In this way, resurgence appears less as the opposite of recognition than as part of a complex and shifting set of negotiations over the contours, character, and principles of Indigenous governance. This project of reading, however, depends on avoiding treating texts as expressions of ethnographic realness.

That kind of interpretation involves seeing texts as windows onto Indigenous socialities rather than as taking part in extant discussions and debates over Native politics, philosophies, and desirable forms of peoplehood. In the previous chapter, I addressed how the terms of Native representative speech changed at the end of the nineteenth century, moving from a diplomatic register to an anthropological one in which such speech indicated not so much political surrogation as cultural typification. Within that ethnographic imaginary, texts by Indigenous authors appear less as intellectual contributions to conversations about indigeneity, colonialism, collective identity, and governance than as a privileged entrée for non-natives into what is seen as Native cultural life. Writers function as native informants whose insider status grants them the ability to convey authentic accounts of everyday life and social patterns. While texts by Indigenous authors certainly extend beyond such (auto-)ethnographic representations, Native writers and writings continue to be read in the present in ways that are overdetermined by an implicitly ethnographic frame. As other scholars have noted, texts by writers of color often are seen as repositories of difference to which white readers can turn for forms of multicultural awareness and training in power-evasive kinds of pluralist tolerance. As Jodi Melamed demonstrates with regard to the work of literary studies in the late twentieth and early twenty-first centuries, it has been seen "as a privileged tool that white Americans can use to get to know difference": "The idea of culture as property owned by people of color functioned within a consumer economy" in which books have been attributed a capacity "to stand in for people" and in which "multicultural literature was presumed to be authentic, intimate, and representative." Melamed makes clear, though, "that literary texts themselves are not at issue here, rather literary studies" is as a set of institutionalized discourses and intellectual practices.[3] Similarly, Roderick Ferguson tracks how "the university arose as a prominent site of minority reconciliation" from the 1960s onward, not only "incorporating racial, gender, and ethnic minorities but also . . . giving the world a language for how to engage and tolerate the respective differences of those minorities"—dynamics in which "aesthetic culture" played a central role as a space of possibility through which to recognize and accommodate difference.[4] With regard to Native texts, we might see such patterns of reading for reified and consumable difference as an extension of a much longer history of ethnographic interpretive frames that sought to archive Indigenous cultures before they presumably disappeared.[5] The process of turning toward texts as vessels that contain and stand for extratextual formations of "culture" treats them as indexical, as simply pointing toward or reflecting kinds of collective identity and practice in ways that are "authentic, intimate, and representative," and the work of interpretation functions as a kind of extraction through which that content can be obtained and circulated. This sort of reading engages texts in a project of information retrieval, in Gayatri Spivak's terms, positioning these writings as containers whose supposed cultural substance can be mined and mobilized toward liberally inclusive ends.[6]

The vast majority of scholars working in Native literary studies repudiate those aims, emphasizing the ongoing violences of settler colonialism and the importance of analyzing such writings through the lens of Indigenous sovereignty and self-determination. However, even in doing so, certain ethnographic orientations can continue to influence the process of interpretation.[7] As I suggested in the introduction, to the extent that Native texts are understood as bearing the truth of Indigenous lives and histories, in contrast to settler erasures and falsifications, they largely conceptually function as intermediaries—as transporting, basically unchanged, content/information from elsewhere. When read in this implicitly indexical way, Indigenous writings operate as more or less faithful reproductions of an extratextual set of social configurations "on the ground," while such conditions themselves can be cast in somewhat singular terms (including when the conditions of peoplehood are presented as having altered and adapted over time but in ways that de facto are depicted as expressive of collective unanimity). If Native texts engage the "persistence of indigenous political systems, relationships, and epistemologies," those systems, relationships, and epistemologies are themselves multiple, changing, and sometimes at odds with each other, and more than solely illustrating such dynamics and potential conflicts, Indigenous writing can be read as actively mediating them.[8] Craig Womack observes, "We are not mere victims but active agents in history, innovators of new ways, of Indian ways, of thinking and being and speaking and authoring in this world created by colonial contact," indicating that the diversity of the "realities that constitute Indian identity" give rise to numerous "legitimate approaches in analyzing Native literary production."[9] In this vein, texts can be interpreted as themselves "active agents" in processes of navigating among varied understandings of Indigenous identity, placemaking, and governance; intellectually (re)framing such understandings; and developing new ones.

This manner of reading, which I've sought to stage in varied ways across the chapters, might be described as a refusal of the ethnographic imaginary in which Native self-representation is taken as necessarily encapsulating and mirroring an extratextual real whose holistic shape is presumed from the outset. More than emphasizing the intellectual labor that Native literature performs in constructing visions of peoplehood, though, I want to suggest that attending to that labor through this process of refusal, and the politics of reading it helps animate, opens toward ways of conceptualizing and engaging with the multidimensional and multivectored complexities of Indigenous governance—the situated wrangling with and over the practical, philosophical, and ethical densities of the political form(s) of peoplehood. I have focused on texts that in some fashion assert their own representativity, their ability to stand for a given (set of) people(s), and I have sought to trace in a somewhat granular fashion the strategic ways authors develop accounts of indigeneity that can engage and reorient extant settler frames of reference.

The interventions by such authors and texts, though, may look like recognition *rather than* refusal. In her articulation of refusal as an analytic and method for Indigenous studies, Audra Simpson observes, "There is a political alternative to 'recognition,' the much sought-after and presumed 'good' of multicultural politics. This alternative is 'refusal,'" adding, "Refusal comes with the requirement of having one's *political* sovereignty acknowledged and upheld." She further argues, "The impetus [is] to 'turn away' from the oppressor, to avert one's gaze and refuse the recognition itself," and later notes, "If a refusal to recognize also involves using one's territory in a manner that is historically and philosophically consistent with what one knows, then it is an incident of failed consent and *positive refusal*."[10] Refusal marks a *turning away* from the politics of recognition and the state's assertion of jurisdiction over Native peoples and territories. Moreover, such orientation away from the state involves embracing "what one knows." In this vein, the nineteenth-century writers I've discussed might be seen as, rather, turning *toward* non-native publics, and the dislocations between their formulations and countervailing Indigenous sociopolitical formations (such as Cherokee towns and clans, intertribal networks in southern New England largely maintained by Native women, or the geographies of Ghost Dancing and prophecy in the Great Basin) might be characterized as a failure to mark or engage Native refusals of settler mappings as well as the presence of alternative/subjugated knowledges.

Yet, there is also within Simpson's approach a sense of both the plurality of Native political visions and the relation between refusal and forcing settler acknowledgment on other terms. She suggests that Mohawk acts of opposition, such as in what has come to be called the Oka Crisis, "force us to ask how to define a citizenship for one's own people, according to one's political traditions while operating in the teeth of Empire, in the face of state aggression," and when speaking of "Iroquois' own space of recognition," she describes it as "a space shaped by political authority that does not derive solely from the state, but is drawn from their own traditions, their interpretations of that tradition, their shared archive of knowledge of each other, their genealogies, and their relationships with each other through time."[11] The struggle against "state aggression" affects the process by which peoplehood is conceptualized and lived, and collective knowledge of political traditions beyond those of the settler-state also gives rise to a range of "interpretations" of them and how they could and should be materialized in the present. From this perspective, refusal might be understood as highlighting dynamics of colonial entanglement while opening onto the complexities of Native social and political networks, including disagreements over how to shift state policies and what political traditions to employ in defining something like citizenship in the context of ongoing occupation and settler intervention. Thought in this way, refusal repudiates the legitimacy of the state's unilateral imposition of settler sovereignty and its political forms, and that repudiation makes space for attending to the multiple forms peoplehood can take, the conditions that shape the use of and movement among those forms, and the often overdetermined negotiations that occur "in the teeth of Empire." Approached as a project of interpretation, then, refusal entails setting aside an explicit or implicit sense of the inherent singularity or unanimity of peoplehood (in terms of its shape, scope, or character— what I've described as the ethnographic imaginary) in favor of emphasizing the open-endedness of processes of political meaning-making and collective decision-making with regard to political form.

Methodologically, the practices of close reading help underline the intellectual labor of producing political collectivity and the ways that work occurs within and is given shape by situated circumstances. In her discussion of comparative literature and the importance of engaging texts from the Global South in less reifying ways, Spivak argues that "we have to ask the question of the formation of collectivities without necessarily prefabricated contents," and she further notes, "In order to assume culture we must assume collectivity. Yet usually we assume collectivity on the basis of culture," adding, "I will call it begging the question, assuming culture at the origin begs the question of collectivity."[12] The contours and character of collectivity remain a question, rather than a presumptive whole whose coherence depends on an a priori attribution of a singular culture, the contents of which are always already known. What Spivak presents as question begging is what I've described as the ethnographic imaginary, in which Indigenous peoplehood—its organizing principles, practices, and structures—appears as a conceptually prefabricated unity. Instead, Spivak indicates that literary texts need to be read for their "surprising and unexpected maneuvers toward collectivity," and she emphasizes the ways their modes of figuration are "undecidable" in that they challenge "foregone conclusions" and "detach themselves from generalizations of collective identity."[13] While Spivak discusses attending to the work of figuration as a function of acknowledging the texts' "literariness," we might instead think of this wariness toward conceptual closure as a *literary* kind of interpretation, as a mode of reading in its broadest sense. This vision of the work of literary studies emphasizes its commitment to tracking how various kinds of figuration open possibilities for thinking collectivity and thinking it as in process, as continually open to refiguration in relation to changing circumstances. Spivak suggests, "What I am attempting is to force a reading. I would like to see if the text could possibly sustain the turning of identitarian monuments into documents for reconstellation."[14] Foregrounding processes of (re)figuration extends beyond (literary) texts per se, emphasizing a conceptual shift from searching for markers of identitarian confirmation—the carrying forward more or less unchanged of a political form of peoplehood already known as such—to attending to the dynamics of reconstellation—the mediations through which peoplehood is being (re)made and the ongoing (re)construction of the networks that constitute it. Practices of literary analysis, then, can offer models for highlighting the work performed by articulations and formulations of Indigenous governance in their multiplicity, negotiatedness, and participation within ever-evolving networks. In addressing the question of who can speak for Indigenous peoples and on what basis, the texts discussed across the chapters bring into focus the variability of Indigenous political form, the effects of colonial pressures on its articulation and circulation, the potential presence of nonidentical political formations, and the intellectual labor of managing and responding to those conjunctures.

Turning to these authors and writings from the past through a practice of reading focused on the undecidableness of Indigenous political form, then, provides some interpretive leverage on contemporary conditions by reframing the pursuit of recognition.[15] While the texts I've discussed primarily seek to engage non-native publics, they illustrate how the terms of collective identity remain unresolved, thereby presenting peoplehood as a dense site of political negotiation in which a range of principles, philosophies, and framings come into shifting relation. Their reorientations of settler templates (such as the popular accounts of King Philip, notions of tribal chieftainship, and Wild West topoi) show that colonial figurations are not unilateral in their meanings or effects and can themselves be reconstellated with visions of Indigenous sovereignty. Conversely, the texts' accounts of indigeneity also illustrate tensions between their formulations of governance and other processes at play among the people(s) in question. However, if one understands the navigation of and engagement within Native networks as also reliant on complex and shifting processes of figuration and as also generating tensions among divergent formulations of peoplehood, the scene of recognition is not utterly distinct from the scene of governance "on the ground." While refusing to conflate these scenes, one can see them as dialectically entangled, which allows discussion of the dynamics of recognition to complement conceptualizations of self-determination rather than serving as a foil for the latter.

When read as sites of Indigenous figuration, instead of either as capitulation to settler frames or reflection of extratextual truths, these writings themselves offer valuable stories about the process of political negotiation, the affordances and limits of particular conceptions of Indigenous governance, and the challenges of forging shared normative frameworks. As against the acceptance of state-sanctioned mappings of Native territoriality and jurisdiction, Mishuana Goeman asks, "How might our own stories become the mechanism in which we can critically (re)map the relationship between Native people and communities?" She further indicates the importance of "tak[ing] into account territories narrated through stories . . . that interrogate and complicate state-bounded territory by examining the social orders expressed and denied in its representations," earlier suggesting that the point of interrogating state accounts and engaging with Indigenous narratives of land and peoplehood is "not just about regaining that which was lost and returning to an original and pure point in history, but instead understanding the processes that have defined our current spatialities in order to sustain vibrant Native futures." Building on Goeman's analysis of Indigenous textual production as a form of storytelling, we can read nineteenth-century writings as engaged in processes of (re)mapping and in exploring the potential "social orders" enabled (and disavowed) through specific representations of political form. In addition, such texts not only can help highlight historical processes through which Indigenous spatialities were constructed and contested but can provide insight into negotiating among multiple conceptions of peoplehood, since, as Goeman suggests, "many histories and ways of seeing and mapping the world can occur at the same time."[16] In other words, these nineteenth-century texts can provide lessons about navigating political irresolution, difference, and conflict under conditions of intense colonial pressure.[17]

Such writings and the ways they engage the politics of peoplehood can form part of the past knowledge toward which contemporary thinkers turn in conceptualizing frames for the present and possibilities for further self-determination.

For example, Audra Simpson points to what she terms "backstreaming" as an Indigenous strategy of "viewing the present through periods and points of the past that are deemed relevant or especially meaningful," and Glen Coulthard argues that "a *resurgent* approach to Indigenous decolonization . . . builds on the value and insights of our past in our efforts to secure a noncolonial present and future."[18] To be clear, I'm not suggesting these older authors' formulations be taken as solutions, as ready answers to contemporary difficulties. Instead, with their emphasis on the character of representativity, these texts foreground problems, conflicts, and struggles over political form and collective identity. Those kinds of tensions can be understood not just as a function of the pursuit of recognition or of engagement with settler networks but as features of how Native networks (re)construct political meanings and formations. Scenes of recognition, then, themselves are part of the knowledges Indigenous people bring to the intellectual work of governance, and not simply as the inverse or negation of sovereignty or self-determination.

These texts also speak to the role of institutionalization in Indigenous governance. If critics of recognition have illustrated amply the dangers in accepting settler institutional frameworks, in terms of both seeking acknowledgment from them and aiming to model Native political practice on them, they have not necessarily addressed, in Ferguson's terms, "the desire for alternative institutionalities." How might we understand the investment in engaging with settler publics and their institutions and for creating Indigenous political apparatuses that are intelligible as such to non-natives as something other than necessarily expressive of some form of colonized subjectivity? How can we mark the specific forms of power and modes of differential access at play in particular, situated processes of institutionalization while still reading such processes without a "foregone conclusion" as to what they mean and do? Speaking of writings that often are treated as sources of multicultural extraction, Ferguson asks, "What happens if those texts are used to imagine how minoritized subjects and knowledge might inhabit institutional spaces in ways dominant institutions never intended?"[19] Similarly, nineteenth-century Native writings explore and register how Indigenous intellectuals have sought to redirect and reframe settler discourses and institutions in ways that would support expressions of and experiments with sovereignty and self-determination. Such efforts may be more or less successful on their own terms or in light of other normative concerns, more or less accountable to the Native publics they claim to serve, and more or less identified with the templates on which they draw. Yet, if these intellectual and political projects are not to be understood as inherently compromised (versus some set of principles seen as a priori more authentic/

liberatory), reading for their institutional imaginaries and attachments must be part of engaging the lessons they offer in the complexities of (re)producing Indigenous peoplehood and governance, especially in the midst of ongoing occupation. Within particular situated circumstances, what kinds of institutionalities help engender "sovereign landscapes" or increase the "future capacities" of Indigenous governance?[20]

I have argued for the value of turning to nineteenth-century writings as a way of highlighting the intellectual labor involved in (re)constructing Indigenous political form, the ways such form emerges through mediations of/in multiple (kinds of) networks, and the ways reading for processes of reconstellation further opens up consideration of the politics of peoplehood. Yet, that argument also comes with some significant caveats or concerns (the first two of which have been part of the analysis developed in the chapters): namely, the danger of losing track of the differential status of subaltern groups within dynamics of domination; the conflation of intellectual work with political process, or the substitution of the one for the other; and the reification of relations with settler publics and institutions. With regard to the first, while intellectual labor takes place at all levels among colonized peoples, there remains a need to mark the distinction between elite and subaltern classes. These groups may be intertwined in a range of ways, and what constitutes such "class" difference may be quite variable (possession of property or wealth in capitalist terms, access to colonial educational institutions, positions within state-sanctioned administrative networks, etc.). However, the need remains for analytical distinctions in terms of persons' and groups' ability to gain forms of relative privilege within colonial political economies and colonially recognized institutions. These differences include not only the ability to achieve visibility and broader circulation for one's intellectual work (such as through writing and publication) but also the kinds of political form and visions of peoplehood at play in that work. For example, as discussed in chapter 1, the sense of peoplehood articulated through Cherokee national institutions is not equivalent to the emphasis on clan and town affiliations that remained important to the majority who were not part of the English-literate and slaveholding elite, or, as addressed in chapter 3, the conception of "the Piute nation" for those close to the Winnemucca family does not map easily onto the Ghost Dance networks that organized much of Indigenous sociality across the Great Basin. The "domain of elite politics," in Ranajit Guha's terms, that arises around the institutional matrices and forms of colonial rule cannot broadly stand for colonized people's (and peoples') notions and practices of collectivity and governance.[21] Or, rather, to make that substitution is to confuse colonial grids of intelligibility for the terrain of politics as such. Even while displacing a sense of the proper authenticity of certain stagings of Indigenous collectivity (the portrait of ethnographic realness against which we might assess articulations of peoplehood), we still need a methodological commitment to reading for these classed distinctions and cleavages. In this way, those nineteenth-century intellectuals who were published authors are no less Indigenous by virtue of the fact of their publication than the ones who were not, but engaging their texts, as well as contemporary ones, involves attending to the kinds of privilege that make such circulation possible, less to evaluate the legitimacy of a given account than to consider the specific pressures, constraints, and frames to which it responds, how it does so, and what such mediations reveal about the conditions and potentials for living Indigenous peoplehood.

Reciprocally, intellectual labor is crucial to the work of politics, but intellectual production cannot replace processes of political decision-making. Texts may implicitly or explicitly argue for the need for a particular kind of political form, one that might be cast as consistent with the core "cultural" values and principles of a given (set of) people(s). Although the intellectual work of that portrayal certainly can contribute to deliberations and debates, the problem arises when that vision stages a claim to its own truth in ways that seek to delegitimize other visions and that vision is given further force by scholarly interpretive practices that treat that portrayal as expressive of the *real*. As Jean Dennison suggests, "American Indian culture is made to stand for all that is fundamental, pure, and noncolonized" in ways that can efface the effects of and circumstances created by "a destructive legacy of U.S. policies."[22] Moreover, depictions of the singularity of the form of peoplehood (its contours, organizing principles, the boundaries of belonging, etc.), whether articulated as "culture" or not, can efface the variety of perspectives held by those who would (or might) be understood as part of the people. In offering a sense of caution with regard to arguments to restore forms of Indigenous governance presented as expressive of a people's core principles or traditions, Robert Warrior notes, "It seems to me that such a clarion call to restore indigenous systems of governance would simultaneously prompt a need for a critical framework for working through crucial, contentious issues of difference, including differences between and among various indigenous traditions."[23] I have suggested that reading for the ways Native literature navigates the difficulties of recognition, including how texts stage their claims to representativity, might offer ideas and strategies for marking and engaging such differences in the (re)making of Indigenous governance. Learning from these stories about the challenges in (re)constructing Native networks of sovereignty and self-determination, though, depends on not treating them as if they could substitute for active popular negotiation over what principles, structures, and aims should shape such governance. We can read for how texts open up and point toward such political differences and difficulties, rather than turning to them for a kind of intellectual shortcut through those processes.

Finally, I have focused primarily on Indigenous-settler relations and the ways settler policies and publics influence both the portrayal of Indigenous governance and its enactment. However, that framing can overemphasize the settler-state as the orienting background of Indigenous political imagination and relation in ways that can efface dynamics of Native internationalism, transnationalism, and trans-indigeneity. As Nick Estes remarks of the struggle against the Dakota Access Pipeline (DAPL) at Standing Rock in 2016, "My Palestinian comrade Samia once called our sacrosanct duty at camp an 'intifada on the plains,' because she saw it as an uprising against the same occupier," later noting the relationships between the forces employed against water protectors and those employed to contain and discipline dissent elsewhere: "Local law enforcement and private security imagined themselves participating in a global counterinsurgency. . . . The tactics employed by TigerSwan, the murky mercenary security contractor hired by DAPL, were also confirmation that this was a global war. The security company had cut its teeth in the United States' never-ending 'war on terror,' in which it was deployed to run counterinsurgency operations against civilians in Iraq and Afghanistan."[24] More than connecting to anticolonial and anticapitalist movements elsewhere around the world, Native peoples' processes for developing their own modes of sovereignty and self-determination take place within networks of connection with other Indigenous peoples. Relations among Native peoples can be considered transnational by virtue of their existence as distinct nations.[25] Indeed, forging global networks has been a principal vehicle of Indigenous politics since at least the 1970s, including generating the UN Declaration on the Rights of Indigenous Peoples out of such matrices of diplomacy, accountability, and alliance.[26] Situating Native intellectual production and considerations of political form within these networks provides, perhaps, a more capacious approach than attending to the dialectics of engagement with the settler-state and non-native publics.[27] Moreover, as Chadwick Allen argues, trans-Indigenous methods of reading provide avenues beyond settler-oriented frames: "Not the frontier site of 'cultures in conflict,' not the colonial site of assimilation or conversion, not the postcolonial site of reaction or rejection, but rather a site of travel, exchange, and collaborative production explicitly marked as trans-Indigenous." He suggests, "Less attention has been paid, thus far, to how particular Indigenous literatures might educate—and delight or provoke—not only non-Indigenous readers but also readers from other Indigenous communities" through "the development of new networks of intellectual and artistic exchange."[28] This observation turns toward different kinds of networks, templates, and mediations than the ones I've addressed, on which Indigenous intellectuals draw and in which their work participates—ones that are vital to kinds of analysis not ultimately centered on settler agendas and ideologies.

While holding onto the decolonial potential of such alternative interpretive itineraries and frameworks, I still want to make a case for the significance of addressing and reconceptualizing the scene of recognition and for the value of the practices of reading it can engender. This study began with an effort to think about what nineteenth-century Native writings might bring to contemporary political theorizing and Indigenous movements for self-determination. My concern was that, from the vantage of current critiques of recognition, such intellectual work in its, arguably primary, engagement with non-native tropes, discourses, and audiences might seem at best irrelevant and at worst simply complicitous with settler institutionalities. Accepting the powerful and necessary insights of such critiques, I wanted to explore what it might mean to engage these writings as situated political and intellectual projects. Approaching the texts as beaters of Indigenous social and political formations "on the ground," as reflecting and conveying those realities, struck me as underemphasizing the work of representation (in both its senses)—the kinds of transpositions and translations to which critics of recognition point in Native engagements with settler institutional networks. Rather than conceptually seeking to bracket or bypass the difficulties of representation, such as by seeing the dynamics of negotiating non-native frameworks as more or less tactical maneuvers set against an already-known core of peoplehood that the author/text supports and seeks to protect, I wanted to underline and foreground those difficulties, attending to the labor of mediation and how that process—in various, contextually specific ways—(re)figured the form of peoplehood.

Thinking about peoplehood and Indigenous governance as a matter of *form* opens possibilities for addressing the multiplicity of ways of framing sovereignty, placemaking, and belonging, as well as the multidimensional dynamics of grappling with those differences, particularly under conditions of ongoing colonial occupation. Viewed from this perspective, the scene of recognition opens onto projects of resurgence, not as that which must be repudiated to achieve the latter but, instead, as potentially offering lessons about the plasticity and density of peoplehood and the challenges in moving among varied visions of what governance can/should entail. While particular texts may or may not be understood as engaged in processes of seeking recognition, foregrounding the ways they speak to such continuing tensions, unresolved issues, and the struggles involved in (re)shaping peoplehood positions Native literatures (past and present) as a vital resource for texturing accounts of Indigenous political imagination, including highlighting the complex negotiations that *are* the politics of peoplehood. That project of reading turns away from looking for the singular real that supposedly can ground analysis and toward a perhaps more sustained grappling with the open-ended unfinishedness of self-determination.

Notes

Introduction

1   On the process of federal acknowledgment for "Indian tribes," see Barker, *Native Acts*; Cramer, *Cash, Color, Colonialism*; Den Ouden and O'Brien, *Recognition*; Field, "Unacknowledged Tribes"; Klopotek, *Recognition Odysseys*; Miller, *Invisible Indigenes*; Miller, *Forgotten Tribes*. Congress also maintains the authority to extend acknowledgment to Native peoples on whatever basis it deems fit.

2   See 25 CFR 83 (consulted May 20, 2019).

3   States often can have their own criteria and processes for formally recognizing Native peoples as such, but such recognition does not translate into federal acknowledgment, whereas federal acknowledgment automatically includes acknowledgment by the states as well.

4   Barker, *Native Acts*, 22, 27.

5   When speaking of "networks," as well as a "template" that allows access to them, I am drawing on the work of Bruno Latour, whom I will engage more explicitly later in the introduction. See Latour, *Reassembling the Social*.

6   In the following, I am playing off of Gayatri Chakravorty Spivak's famous discussion of the relation between representation in its two senses, as proxy and portrait, first offered in "Can the Subaltern Speak?" See Spivak, *Critique of Postcolonial Reason*, 198–311. I will address this allusion more explicitly in the next section.

7   I am using the term "intellectuals" as something of a loose catchall to refer to people who were engaged in public activities that involved seeking to conceptualize the situations faced by Native peoples. Such work certainly did not happen only through writing in English or publication, even though such modes and activities are the ones I principally will be addressing. See Konkle, *Writing Indian Nations*; Martínez, *Dakota Philosopher*; Pexa, *Translated Nation*; Vigil, *Indigenous Intellectuals*; Warrior, *Tribal Secrets*.

8   See Barker, "Territory"; Estes, *Our History*; McCarthy, *Divided Unity*; Pasternak, *Grounded Authority*; Powell, *Landscapes of Power*; Simpson, "State Is a Man."

9   On ways of defining Indigenous literature and the issues at play in doing so, see Brooks, *Common Pot*; Calcaterra, *Literary Indians*; Cohen, *Networked Wilderness*; Goeman, *Mark My Words*; Justice, *Why Indigenous Literatures Matter*; Mignolo, *Darker Side*; Rasmussen, *Queequeg's Coffin*; Round, *Removable Type*; and Wyss, *English Letters*.

10 Brooks, *Common Pot*, xxi, 13, 219.

11 Brooks, *Common Pot*, xxxi. For another strong statement of such principles within Native literary studies, see also Womack, "Integrity."

12 See Cooke, "Indian Fields"; Deloria, *Indians in Unexpected Places*; Lyons, *X-marks*; O'Brien, *Firsting and Lasting*; Rifkin, *Beyond Settler Time*.

13 Justice, *Why Indigenous Literatures Matter*, xix, xx.

14 Justice, *Why Indigenous Literatures Matter*, 141.

15 On Indigenous "political orders," see Simpson, "State Is a Man."

16 Piatote, *Domestic Subjects*, 10. Similarly, Cheryl Suzack suggests, "Scholars have turned their attention to demonstrating how literary texts foreground Indigenous communities' social justice goals" (8), later arguing, "Literary texts enact justice-seeking objectives by telling stories to make explicit the limits of legal reasoning and to demonstrate the impact of settler-colonial dispossession on Indigenous communities by depicting accounts that open up a horizon for understanding injustice in other ways" (*Indigenous Women's Writing*, 87).

17 Konkle, *Writing Indian Nations*, 27, 29.

18 Turner, *Peace Pipe*, 81.

19 Brooks, *Common Pot*, xxxv.

20 Latour, *Reassembling the Social*, 39. My approach here, then, differs from Turner's way of discussing mediation, in which he suggests that "mediators" "engage the legal and political discourses of the state, guided by richer and more inclusive sets of assumptions about Aboriginal peoples, political sovereignty, and especially political recognition," and such "word warriors" draw on "the language of rights, sovereignty, and nationhood" in order to "explain our differences and in the process empower ourselves to actually change the state's legal and political practices." See Turner, *Peace Pipe*, 86, 92, 99, 101. What I'm describing here is not so much texts' effort to explain Indigenous social forms (modes of networking and mediation at play among Indigenous persons and in the operation of Native polities) as their effort to cast Indigenous peoplehood in frames and formats in use among non-natives, a portrayal that has consequences for what can signify as peoplehood.

21 While figured in quite different terms, my approach here is indebted to Craig Womack's description of art as about deviation and deviance, rather than a bearing forward of cultural norms, traditions, or singular visions of the nation/people. See Womack, *Art as Performance*.

22 Latour, *Reassembling the Social*, 108, 128.

23 Latour, *Reassembling the Social*, 53, 85.

24 Latour, *Reassembling the Social*, 222–223.

25 Latour, *Reassembling the Social*, 196.

26 Levine, *Forms*, 65, 85.

27 On the ways Black and Native formulations and assertions of "rights" sought to disorient white settler frames, and the ways articulations of "native"-ness took shape in the context of Anglo conceptions of positive and negative birthright, see Ben-zvi, *Native Land Talk*.

28 See Bowes, *Land Too Good*; Calloway, *Pen and Ink Witchcraft*; Cheyfitz, "Navajo-Hopi"; Jones, *License for Empire*; Prucha, *American Indian Treaties*; Rifkin, *Manifesting America*; Rockwell, *Indian Affairs*. For an alternative reading of the work of treaties, see Allen, "Postcolonial Theory"; Estes, *Our History*; Lyons, *X-marks*; and Williams, *Linking Arms*.

29 When addressing Native authors' mediations of what I am characterizing as settler templates, I do not mean to suggest that change operated in one direction, that non-natives were unaffected by ongoing engagements with Native peoples. For examples

of work within nineteenth-century literary studies that foregrounds the effects of Native presence, politics, and cultural production on non-native social forms and modes of self-understanding, see Bellin, *Demon of the Continent*; Bergland, *National Uncanny*; Calcaterra, *Literary Indians*; Cooke, "Indian Fields"; Maddox, *Removals*; Mielke, *Moving Encounters*; Scheckel, *Insistence*. My focus, though, lies on the contours, character, and labor of representing Indigenous collectivity and sovereignty to non-native publics and the complex relations between such textual accounts and extant geopolitical formations.

30 Vigil, *Indigenous Intellectuals*, 3–4, 6; Pexa, *Translated Nation*, 1, 148. See also Carpenter, *Seeing Red*; Greyser, *On Sympathetic Grounds*; Piatote, "Indian/Agent Aporia"; Powell, "Sarah Winnemucca Hopkins"; Wyss, *English Letters*.

31 Goeman, *Mark My Words*, 4, 15.

32 In *Tribal Secrets*, Robert Warrior develops the concept of Native intellectual sovereignty, in which he refuses an easy distinction between what can count as Native and what cannot. He argues, "If our struggle is anything, it is the struggle for sovereignty, and if sovereignty is anything, it is a way of life," adding, "It is a decision—a decision we make in our minds, in our hearts, and in our bodies—to be sovereign and to find out what that means in the process" (123). That "struggle for sovereignty," though, "is not a struggle to be free from the influence of anything outside ourselves, but a process of asserting the power we possess as communities and individuals to make decisions that affect our lives" (124). What I am suggesting, however, is that nineteenth-century Native writers' portrayals of peoplehood also navigate the context of non-native framings of indigeneity. While we might understand these writers as enacting intellectual sovereignty in that process, such sovereignty should be distinguished from (or, at least not treated as equivalent to or inherently continuous with) exertions and formations of political sovereignty in the sense of the dynamics of Indigenous governance.

In this way, I'm also departing from what has been termed Native literary nationalism. Within such approaches, texts are read as indicative of philosophies, principles, histories, and experiences that emanate from the author's people. Scholars working in this mode offer capacious understandings of what constitutes Native national identity, refusing reifying notions of what can count as such expression. For examples, see Justice, *Our Fire*; Kelsey, *Tribal Theory*; and Womack, *Red on Red*. While holding onto the importance of situating given texts in relation to their authors' peoples, I aim to explore how nineteenth-century writers, in particular, seek to engage with non-native publics in ways that affect how they stage depictions of political identity, sovereignty, and governance. Reciprocally, as I will suggest further in the next section, attending to that negotiation of settler templates draws attention back to the negotiation over political form happening within understandings of what constitutes peoplehood, governance, and placemaking "on the ground."

33 Latour observes that "framing things into some context is what actors constantly do. I am simply arguing that it is this very framing activity, this very activity of contextualizing, that should be brought into the foreground" (*Reassembling the Social*, 186). By "actors" Latour means mediators, rather than persons per se, and I am suggesting

that attending to the "framing activity" employed by Native texts (including their claims to representativity) speaks to the ways the process of addressing settler publics involves mediations with regard to political form, rather than simply expressing kinds of political form that are borne unmediated from elsewhere.

34 Piatote, *Domestic Subjects*, 173.

35 On the role of heteropatriarchal ideologies in formulations of Indigenous governance, see Barker, *Native Acts*; Denetdale, "Chairmen"; Goeman, *Mark My Words*; Kauanui, *Paradoxes*; Simpson, *As We Have Always Done*.

36 Spivak, *Critique of Postcolonial Reason*, 258, 259.

37 Spivak, *Critique of Postcolonial Reason*, 257, 260.

38 For an extended version of this argument, see Rifkin, *Manifesting America*. On the translation of Native collective placemaking into the terms of "property," see Barker, "Territory"; Cheyfitz, *Poetics*; Coulthard, *Red Skin, White Masks*; Goeman, *Mark My Words*; Nichols, *Theft Is Property!*; Pasternak, *Grounded Authority*.

39 Andersen, "From Difference to Density," 97.

40 On addressing forms in terms of their *affordances*, see Levine, *Forms*.

41 For discussion of the "Indian nation" as the way of figuring Indigenous modernity in the nineteenth century, refusing culturalizing and racializing narratives of Indian anachronism/incapacity, see Konkle, *Writing Indian Nations*; Lyons, *X-marks*; Womack, *Red on Red*. As I have argued elsewhere, though, presenting treaty-recognized Indigenous state forms in the nineteenth century as somewhat transparently expressive of Native popular will can efface the complexities of matters of class, consent, and colonial force. See Rifkin, *Manifesting America*.

42 For examples, see Barker, *Native Acts*; Denetdale, "Chairmen"; Coulthard, *Red Skin, White Masks*; Goeman, *Mark My Words*; Kauanui, *Paradoxes*; Klopotek, *Recognition Odysseys*; Million, *Therapeutic Nations*; Pasternak, *Grounded Authority*; Simpson, *Mohawk Interruptus*.

43 Coulthard, *Red Skin, White Masks*, 3, 30–31, 41.

44 Simpson, *As We Have Always Done*, 176; Simpson, *Mohawk Interruptus*, 11, 185. It should be noted that one of the most prominent state logics at play in matters of acknowledgment for Indian tribes in the United States is antiblackness. As Brian Klopotek observes, "Federal recognition, while in many ways a project intended to be supportive of indigeneity, carries white supremacist racial projects within it. First, it induces Indians to distance themselves from blacks by rewarding tribes that have maintained strict racial boundaries with peoples of African descent and punishing those that have not" (*Recognition Odysseys*, 267). See also Adams, *Who Belongs?*; Cramer, *Cash, Color, Colonialism*; Lowery, *Lumbee Indians*; Mandell, *Tribe, Race, History*.

45 Barker, *Native Acts*, 17, 28.

46 Spivak, *Critique of Postcolonial Reason*, 260. On the ways U.S. settler colonialism works through the production of such forms of legal subjectivity that confirm U.S. legal mappings and Native consent, see Rifkin, *Manifesting America*.

47 Coulthard, *Red Skin, White Masks*, 156, 16.

48 Berlant, *Cruel Optimism*, 1, 2, 49.

49 Coulthard, *Red Skin, White Masks*, 32, 39.

50 Barker, *Native Acts*, 217.

51 Barker, *Native Acts*, 223.

52 In this way, I'm distinguishing between identification (an affective investment in a particular form as expressive of ground-level self-understanding) and *mediation*, in Latour's sense discussed earlier. The relation I'm sketching also productively might be thought of through José Muñoz's articulation of "disidentification": a mode "that neither opts to assimilate within [dominant ideology] nor strictly opposes it; rather, disidentification is a strategy that works on and against dominant ideology"; disidentification is about "recycling and rethinking encoded meaning" in ways that "retain the problematic object [or term/concept] and tap into the energies that are produced by contradictions and ambivalences" (*Disidentifications*, 11, 31, 71). For discussion of contemporary modes of Indigenous–non-Indigenous alliance, although not necessarily conceptualized through figures of "recognition," see Grossman, *Unlikely Alliances*; Larsen and Johnson, *Being Together*; Mackey, *Unsettled Expectations*.

53 Spivak, *Critique of Postcolonial Reason*, 256.

54 Spivak, *Critique of Postcolonial Reason*, 261.

55 Simpson, *Dancing on Our Turtle's Back*, 16, 17–18.

56 Guha, "On Some Aspects," 39, 40. See also Beverley, *Subalternity and Representation*; Chatterjee, *Nation and Its Fragments*; Rodríguez, *Latin American Subaltern Studies*; Varadharajan, *Exotic Parodies*.

57 Allen, *Blood Narrative*, 18.

58 Latour, *Reassembling the Social*, 39.

59 On the ways settler sovereignty always remains within and beholden to Indigenous sovereignty, even if in often disavowed ways, see Cattelino, *High Stakes*; Cooke, "Indian Fields"; Karuka, "Prose of Counter-Sovereignty"; Nicoll, "Reconciliation"; Mackey, *Unsettled Expectations*; Pasternak, *Grounded Authority*; Stark, "Criminal Empire."

60 As Gerald Vizenor observes, "The tribal real is not an enterprise of resistance," but he also argues that efforts by Native intellectuals to enter into the "simulations" created by non-native discourses of Indianness, or potentially of Native collective identity, carry with them "shadows" that "tease and loosen the bonds of representation in stories" (*Manifest Manners*, 54, 72). As Amy Den Ouden and Jean O'Brien argue, "Recognition struggles raise questions about the efficacy of a purportedly inexorable logic of elimination, and bring attention to the instabilities of settler colonialism and its claims of mastery" (*Recognition*, 8), adding, "Indigenous struggles for recognition mark significant moments of refusal of the logic of elimination and potential disruption of the governmental discourses and strategies deployed to legitimize the nation-state's claim to power over indigenous peoples" (9).

61 Here I'm thinking of Kara Thompson's theorization of "the fold" and *convolution*. See Thompson, *Blanket*.

62 Dennison, *Colonial Entanglement*, 6, 8. This perspective resonates with John Borrows's argument that what is needed is "*akinoomaagewin*" or "physical philosophy," which is "derived from observation and practice" rather than "from identifying first principles and deducing conclusions from abstract propositions" (*Freedom and Indigenous Constitutionalism*, 10). He adds, "We must 'bob and weave' between what

would appear to be inconsistent alternatives, if we measured life by essentialized 'truths'"; "When we are free to act in complex, multifaceted, and variable ways, we more fully enrich our own and others' lives" (*Freedom and Indigenous Constitutionalism*, 18).

63 Carroll, *Roots of Our Renewal*, 17. As Carroll observes, though, the effort to indigenize the state form with respect to environmental policy also runs into existing processes "in which 'nation-building' strategies must be funneled through models designed for generating profits, increasing worker efficiency, and ensuring loyal customers, which, although they are potentially positive goals for some areas of tribal management, are incongruous with the goals of strengthening communities, enriching cultural identity, and maintaining sovereignty" (154).

64 Simpson, *Mohawk Interruptus*, 185, 109, 111.

65 On "orientation," see Ahmed, *Queer Phenomenology*. On the use of this concept to think about modes of settlement and indigeneity, see Rifkin, *Beyond Settler Time*; Rifkin, *Settler Common Sense*.

66 Goeman, *Mark My Words*, 12, 28–29.

67 Coulthard, *Red Skin, White Masks*, 13.

68 Simpson, *As We Have Always Done*, 8, 16, 23.

69 As Joanne Barker argues, when "tribal membership" comes to function as a kind of "property right," it can enact "exclusionary ideologies of race, gender, and sexuality," which stand in contrast to "Native customs and epistemologies" that involve "a generosity regarding intermarriage, adoption, and naturalization as well as alternative understandings of belonging and kinship that . . . [tie] members back to their lands and governments as citizens with multiple kinds of responsibilities" (*Native Acts*, 83, 94). In discussing the rearrangements of Hawaiian governance in the face of increased Euro-American presence, prior to annexation, J. Kēhaulani Kauanui observes, "We must note the intentional restructuring of Indigenous kinship in the quest to solidify Hawaiian sovereignty. Combating polygamy and polyandry, same-sex sexuality, and close consanguineous mating formed an overarching framework for restructuring the Indigenous polity in order to fend off encroachment. Hence the paradox: to fight that imperialism, Hawaiian chiefs enacted forms of colonial biopolitics in order to secure sovereign recognition" (*Paradoxes*, 159).

70 Simpson, *As We Have Always Done*, 53.

71 Carroll, *Roots of Our Renewal*, 173; Dennison, *Colonial Entanglement*, 10. See also Borrows, *Freedom and Indigenous Constitutionalism*; Pasternak, *Grounded Authority*; Richland, *Arguing with Tradition*; Turner, *Peace Pipe*.

Chapter 1. What's in a Nation?

1 On the history of the Treaty of New Echota, see Moulton, *John Ross*; McLoughlin, *Cherokee Renascence*; Wilkins, *Cherokee Tragedy*.

2 As Imani Perry argues, (hetero)patriarchy can be understood as collapsing "the wife and children of the patriarch . . . into his legal being" while producing racialized zones of "nonpersonhood," which involved "not simply exclusion from the rights and recognitions of legal personhood" but the systemic development of "particular

status[es] in intimate relation to" personhood secured "by means of laws"—such as the Cherokee Nation's institutionalization of chattel slavery (*Vexy Thing*, 24). As Circe Sturm observes, "Because ideas of race have persistently reinforced Euroamerican ideas of nation, Cherokees realized by the early 1800s that for their claims to nationhood to be considered legitimate within the Euroamerican context they would have to racially codify their distinct sense of peoplehood" (*Blood Politics*, 51).

3 For a fuller discussion of this process, see Rifkin, *Manifesting America*, 37–74. Some scholars, though, have misconstrued my previous argument as either reaffirming a distinction between mixed-bloods as progressives and full-bloods as traditionalists or suggesting that the U.S. government itself produced the Cherokee elite for its own purposes.

    For example, Joshua Nelson says of my previous work, "He argues that tribal nations are collective identities that in the final tally were engineered by the U.S. federal government as a means of consolidating its own power and creating a cohesive national narrative" and that "the most important subjectivity invented by U.S. influences for Cherokee people was that of an elite class" (*Progressive Traditions*, 150). In fact, what I argue is that a Cherokee elite organized a centralized, national government that drew on the terms of U.S. governance (including the forms of officially recognized Native voice within the treaty system) in order to challenge U.S. aims while also reorienting Cherokee governance to suit their own class principles—a line of analysis Nelson largely confirms and extends.

4 Guha, "On Some Aspects," 39.

5 The General Council passed numerous pieces of legislation designed to institute particular aspects of capitalist practice. These included the following: regulating ownership of turnpikes; nullifying all contracts with slaves not preapproved by their masters; authorizing marshals to collect debt; instituting a fifty cent poll tax on each "head of a family" and "single man" under sixty; setting up a registry for advertisements of "estray property"; outlawing "improvements within the distance of one-fourth of a mile of the field or plantation of another"; allowing the building of fences to demarcate ownership; classifying "improvements" as exclusively the possession of those who made them; and protecting contracts against a statute of limitations on seeking judicial relief for "contested claims." See Cherokee Nation, *Laws*, 6–19, 34–49. In addition, in the years leading up to the ratification of the Cherokee Constitution, the Cherokee legislature sought to consolidate forms of bourgeois domesticity in the following ways: making illegal marriages between "negro slaves" and Cherokees; written wills are made legally binding and the property of those who die intestate is to be "equally divided among his lawful and acknowledged children, allowing to the widow an equal share"; the children of Cherokee men and white women are to be "equally entitled to all the immunities and privileges enjoyed by the citizens descending from the Cherokee race, by the mother's side"; and polygamy is made illegal. See Cherokee Nation, *Laws*, 38, 53, 57.

6 Sometimes scholars will point to the holding of the land of the nation in common as a counter to such a claim, but land was fenced and houses and such were counted as "improvements" that themselves could be bought and sold. Theda Perdue refers to this dynamic as a "bifurcated system of property holding" (*Cherokee Women*,

136). Moreover, the provision in the Cherokee Constitution that the land was held in common by the nation had less to do with preventing private property claims per se than thwarting the effort of the federal government to have individual Cherokees enroll for emigration and then to treat the land they had occupied as transferrable, as private property, to the United States.

7 Guha, "On Some Aspects," 40.

8 As Partha Chatterjee argues with respect to India, "While the nationalist leadership sought to mobilize the peasantry as an anticolonial force in its project of establishing a nation-state, it was . . . careful to keep their participation limited to the forms of bourgeois representative politics in which peasants would be regarded as part of the nation but distanced from the institutions of the state," suggesting that such political norms provided "the foundations from which a positive content was supplied for the independent national state" (*Nation and Its Fragments*, 160, 203).

9 On conceptualizing Indigenous nationality as networks or webs of embodied relation, see Simpson, *As We Have Always Done*.

10 Simpson, *Dancing on Our Turtle's Back*, 16.

11 Given the prominence of slaveholding among the Cherokee elite and the role of Cherokee national governance in consolidating the terms of enslavement, my characterization of this formation as liberal political economy might seem rather odd. To the extent that liberalism refers to forms of wage work that historically have been juxtaposed with chattel slavery, this objection seems apt. However, work on the history of capitalism, particularly in the Americas, has illustrated the ways that conceptions of property and personhood within classic liberalism are not, in fact, opposed to slavery, that slavery provides one mode of enacting a racialized conception of property and personhood that is endemic to liberal political economy. See Arneil, *John Locke*; Kazanjian, *Colonizing Trick*; Lowe, *Intimacies of Four Continents*; Mehta, *Liberalism and Empire*; Perry, *Vexy Thing*; Tully, *Approach to Political Philosophy*.

12 For discussions of how Boudinot has been interpreted in these ways and the problems with such readings, see Cooke, "Indian Fields"; Konkle, *Writing Indian Nations*, 42–96; Nelson, *Progressive Traditions*, 167–197; Ross-Mulkey, "*Cherokee Phoenix*"; Schneider, "Boudinot's Change"; Smithers, *Cherokee Diaspora*, 84–91.

13 Guha, "On Some Aspects," 37.

14 Ahmed, *Queer Phenomenology*, 15, 38.

15 In their analysis of censuses of the eastern Cherokees in the early nineteenth century, especially the one taken in 1835, William McLoughlin and Walter H. Conser outline the existence of something of an aristocracy constituted by the forty-two richest families (out of approximately 2,600 families in the Cherokee Nation), as determined by the scope of their landholdings, production for the market, and slaveholding, and together this small group of families possessed the majority of the nation's wealth, conventionally defined ("Cherokee Censuses," 232–235). These families, which included that of John Ross, did play major roles in the operation of the Cherokee government, exercising a vastly disproportionate influence over the political affairs of the nation based on the size of this group relative to the population as a whole (less than 2 percent). However, Boudinot, for example, was not wealthy,

although he was related to those who were—including his uncle Major Ridge and cousin John Ridge. He was raised in Oothcaloga, a town known for residents' commitment to single-family homemaking, market-based agriculture, Christianity, and English literacy, and he was educated at Euro-American educational institutions—the Spring Place mission in the Cherokee Nation and the Cornwall School in Connecticut (run by the American Board of Commissioners for Foreign Missions). On Boudinot's biography, see Perdue, *Cherokee Editor*, 3–38; Peyer, *Tutor'd Mind*, 166–223; Wilkins, *Cherokee Tragedy*. Boudinot's investments in advocating for "civilization" and "progress" among the Cherokees cannot be understood merely as a function of personal class interests, suggesting further that what might be characterized as *elite orientations* should not be interpreted as simply a corollary of particular demographic indices (including measures of affluence).

16   On Cherokee geopolitics prior to the early nineteenth century, see Boulware, *Deconstructing the Cherokee Nation*; Driskill, *Asegi Stories*; Dunaway, "Rethinking Cherokee Acculturation"; Justice, *Our Fire*; McLoughlin, *Cherokee Renascence*; Perdue, *Cherokee Women*; Reid, *Better Kind of Hatchet*; Smithers, *Cherokee Diaspora*; Sweet, *American Georgics*, 122–152.

17   On developments in Cherokee governance from the early nineteenth century through the adoption of the Cherokee Constitution, see Cherokee Nation, *Laws*; McLoughlin, *Cherokee Renascence*; Nelson, *Progressive Traditions*; Perdue, *Cherokee Women*; Rifkin, *Manifesting America*, 37–74; Strickland, *Fire and the Spirits*; Wilkins, *Cherokee Tragedy*; Yarbrough, "Legislating Women's Sexuality." Often scholars present the Committee as having been created in 1817, when it first appears in the published Cherokee statutes (Cherokee Nation, *Laws*, 5), but it actually dates to 1809. See McLoughlin, *Cherokee Renascence*, 156–157; Wilkins, *Cherokee Tragedy*, 50–51.

18   Cherokee Nation, *Laws*, 11, 15, 31.

19   Between 1817 and 1824, the phrase "By order of the National Committee" appears on forty-five of sixty-two laws. See Cherokee Nation, *Laws*.

20   Boudinot, *Letters*, 175; text references are to pages in this edition. On the impeachment, see Garrison, *Legal Ideology of Removal*, 200–202, 206; Nelson, *Progressive Traditions*, 193; Wilkins, *Cherokee Tragedy*, 261–265.

21   See *Laws of the Colonial and State Governments*, 195–225. The discovery of gold in the Cherokee Nation in 1828 and the subsequent gold rush starting the next year significantly exacerbated white invasion onto Cherokee lands, even though the Georgia government in its annexation of Cherokee territory legislated that those who had illegally gone to prospect would receive none of the parcels of annexed land to be distributed by public lottery. These laws were contested by the Cherokee Nation in two U.S. Supreme Court cases: *Cherokee Nation v. Georgia* (1831), in which the Court finds that the Cherokees are a "domestic dependent nation" and, therefore, cannot file suit for original jurisdiction in the Supreme Court (not being a "foreign nation"); and *Worchester v. Georgia* (1832), which comes to the Court as an appeal from a Georgia state court and in which the Court finds that Georgia's laws with respect to the Cherokee Nation are in violation of the U.S. Constitution. See Ford, *Settler Sovereignty*; Garrison, *Legal Ideology of Removal*; McLoughlin, *Cherokee Renascence*; Moulton, *John Ross*; Norgren, *Cherokee Cases*; Pratt, "Violence."

22 On the "interpretive key," see Latour, *Inquiry*, 53–58.

23 For documents illustrating Boudinot's and John Ridge's shifts in perspective on removal, see Dale and Litton, *Cherokee Cavaliers*.

24 On Boudinot's invocation of the U.S. Constitution to argue for the legitimacy of Cherokee sovereignty, see Hudson, "Forked Justice."

25 For a particularly compelling argument on how Boudinot seeks to present the Cherokee case to the whites, see Cooke, "Indian Fields."

26 In this way, the question of belonging to the elite or commitment to elite principles is not a matter of relative "blood"-edness—a distinction between "progressive" mixed-bloods and "traditional" full-bloods. Instead, it consists of commitment to aspects of liberal political economy, including heterogendered modes of household and family formation. Censuses for the Cherokee Nation from 1820s and 1830s do suggest a statistical correlation between greater concentration of "full-bloods" in an area and less investment in production for the market and enslavement. See McLoughlin and Conser, "Cherokee Censuses." However, in practice among Cherokees in the period, the term "full-blood," as well as "mixed-blood," often was used to designate such orientations toward land, subsistence, and family rather than as an index of the racial composition of one's biological genealogy. Questions of racial genealogy, though, were of significant import with regard to persons of African descent (whether enslaved or not) in terms of both national policy and everyday modes of association, although those patterns also differed greatly among areas of the Cherokee Nation. On the question of blood in the period, see Justice, *Our Fire*; Miles, *Ties That Bind*; Nelson, *Progressive Traditions*; Perdue, "Clan and Court."

27 On these events, see Cherokee Nation, *Laws*, 67; McLoughlin, *Cherokee Renascence*, 168–185, 366–410; Parins, *Literacy and Intellectual Life*, 45–46. On the discourse of "improvements" in relation to the Cherokee Nation, see Sweet, *American Georgics*, 122–152. Toward the beginning of the speech, Boudinot notes, "I am aware of the difficulties which have ever existed to Indian civilization. I do not deny the almost insurmountable obstacles which we ourselves have thrown in the way of this improvement, nor do I say that difficulties no longer remain" (69–70), and while later suggesting that "Cherokees have advanced so far and so rapidly in civilization," he adds that "there are yet powerful obstacles, both within and without, to be surmounted," even as he also characterizes such resistance to "civilization" as a series of "individual failings" to be "passed over" ("Address to the Whites," 72).

28 Moulton, *John Ross*, 20, 32, 37.

29 For these various developments, see Cherokee Nation, *Laws*, 3, 9, 21, 29, 30–31, 34, 37, 38, 39, 44, 52–53, 57, 77, 79, 120–121, 128. On slavery in the Cherokee Nation, see Driskill, *Asegi Stories*; McLoughlin, *Cherokee Renascence*; Miles, *Ties That Bind*; Perdue, *Slavery*; Sturm, *Blood Politics*. For an account that seeks to place enslavement among the Five Tribes within a longer regional history of practices of captivity that predates European presence, see Snyder, *Slavery in Indian Country*.

30 The Cherokees were not the only Native people grappling with the dynamics of centralization, capitalization, enslavement, and heteropatriarchy. For example, on these issues and struggles in the Creek Nation in the same period, see Ethridge, *Creek Country*; Green, *Politics of Indian Removal*; Saunt, *Black, White, and Indian*.

31 Cherokee Nation, *Laws*, 45, 67, 73, 117.

32 There were two earlier periods of Cherokee history that have been described as removal crises—1808 to 1810 and 1817 to 1819—in which significant numbers of Cherokees were persuaded to remove west under federal pressure and with the threat of the liquidation of Cherokee national territory in the East. See Finger, *Tennessee Frontiers*, 275–314; McLoughlin, *Cherokee Renascence*, 128–167, 206–246; Wilkins, *Cherokee Tragedy*, 39–59.

33 Moulton, *Papers*, 157.

34 Moulton, *Papers*, 142.

35 Guha, "On Some Aspects," 39.

36 Moulton, *Papers*, 169.

37 Dunaway, "Rethinking Cherokee Acculturation," 170; Perdue, *Cherokee Women*, 144. See also Miles, "Circular Reasoning"; Miles, *Ties That Bind*; Reid, "Absolute and Unconditional Pardon"; Yarbrough, "Legislating Women's Sexuality."

38 Cherokee Nation, *Laws*, 121. This move was foreshadowed by the limitation of jury service to men in 1825 (Cherokee Nation, *Laws*, 44), as well as the increasing legal support for patriarchal and patrilineal modes of propertyholding and inheritance noted earlier. On this dynamic, see also Driskill, *Asegi Stories*; Miles, *Ties That Bind*.

39 Simpson, *As We Have Always Done*, 123.

40 Spivak, "Subaltern Studies," 4.

41 Carroll, *Roots of Our Renewal*, 17, 157, 168, 27.

42 As Jean Dennison suggests with regard to Osage leaders' views on contemporary constitutional process, "For [Chief] Gray, this moment was one of recognizing and acting upon the inherent sovereignty of the Osage, a sovereignty that was impotent if it did not have a powerful and well-crafted nation to actualize it" (*Colonial Entanglement*, 136). Also, as Jill Doerfler illustrates in *Those Who Belong*, her study of constitution making for White Earth, the tools of the state form can serve as a way of challenging institutionalized discourses of racialized Indianness. On this point, see also Konkle, *Writing Indian Nations*; Lyons, *X-marks*. On Native constitution making, see also Lemont, *American Indian Constitutional Reform*.

43 Latour, *Inquiry*, 18.

44 Joshua Nelson suggests that while "Boudinot's defense of the treaty party's actions in *Letters* does not hold up even on its own grounds," his critique of Cherokee officials' attempts to limit public debate "lines up with indigenist anarchist traditions that didn't just tolerate diversified views but built them into the very fabric of pluralist, participatory, noncoercive, democratic, consensus-based decision making" (*Progressive Traditions*, 195). However, Boudinot consistently preempts the possibility of public debate by asserting that he and other signatories to the treaty were the only ones among those who, due to their cultivation, "understood the situation of the Cherokees" that had the courage to act on their incontrovertible knowledge.

45 Schneider, "Boudinot's Change," 175.

46 Simpson, *As We Have Always Done*, 192, 8.

47 Simpson, *As We Have Always Done*, 50, 196–197. On Indigenous bodies as political orders, see also Simpson, "State Is a Man." On the violence of understanding Indigenous landedness only in terms of settler-state geographies, see Chang, *World*;

Goeman, *Mark My Words*; Povinelli, *Labor's Lot*; Ramirez, *Native Hubs*; Vizenor, *Fugitive Poses*.

48 While many scholars seek to challenge the distinction between "traditionals" and "progressives," especially given their reified and dichotomized quality and the ways those categories so often get attached to notions of bloodedness, I am suggesting that Boudinot himself is employing this dichotomy (although not in precisely these terms) as a way of seeking to discredit Ross and authorize the Treaty Party's actions.

49 Coulthard, *Red Skin, White Masks*, 13.

50 As Bernd Peyer observes, Boudinot's "conviction that his special qualifications gave him the right and responsibility to make decisions for the benefit of the entire Cherokee Nation appears to have been as much a characteristic of the Cherokee proto-elite as it was of the more conservative Old Light missionaries who influenced his life," adding, "Boudinot the 'traitor' was really not much farther away from or closer to Cherokee tradition than John Ross the 'patriot' at the moment he made his fatal decision" (*Tutor'd Mind*, 223).

51 See Dunaway, "Rethinking Cherokee Acculturation," 178–179; Finger, *Tennessee Frontiers*, 298, 300; Hill, *Weaving New Worlds*, 93; McLoughlin, *Cherokee Renascence*, 385–386; Perdue, *Cherokee Women*, 136, 144; Simpson Smith, "I Look on You"; Strickland, *Fire and the Spirits*, 79. Notably, John Ross himself suggests more than once that, in response to the Indian agent's call for removal, Cherokees should consult and hold meetings in their "respective neighborhoods" to canvas popular sentiment. See Moulton, *Papers*, 218, 306. Presumably, if he had been referring to the official districts of the nation, he would have said "districts," so the reference to "neighborhoods" seems to imply his recognition of the unofficial continuance of towns as meaningful units of Cherokee popular self-understanding.

52 Perdue, *Cherokee Women*, 151.

53 Dunaway, "Rethinking Cherokee Acculturation," 167–168. Dunaway largely draws on statistics from the Cherokee census of 1835. See McLoughlin and Conser, "Cherokee Censuses."

54 Sturm, *Blood Politics*, 11.

55 Quoted in Spivak, *Critique of Postcolonial Reason*, 271.

56 See Boulware, *Deconstructing the Cherokee Nation*; Dunaway, "Rethinking Cherokee Acculturation"; Perdue, *Cherokee Women*; Sweet, *American Georgics*, 122–152; Wilkins, *Cherokee Tragedy*.

57 Nelson, *Progressive Traditions*, 182. As Andrew Denson suggests, "Most members of the tribe did not embrace the ultimate goal of the civilizing mission, the complete remaking of the Cherokees in the European American image, but many took specific attractive elements of their neighbors' culture (in particular economic activities) and adapted them to Cherokee life" (*Demanding the Cherokee Nation*, 18).

58 As Nelson notes, "The central government became the product and producer of a nationalist consciousness that insisted on the subordination of local concerns to those of the larger body, effectively stifling public discourse in its promotion of acquiescence to the greater good, as defined by a concentrating, power-holding cadre" (*Progressive Traditions*, 147).

59 Simpson, *Mohawk Interruptus*, 109.

60 Moulton, *Papers*, 169.

61 On this presentation of the Cherokee leadership, which usually also involved charges that they were not *truly* Indian or representative of the Cherokee people due to their being of "mixed" blood, see Caison, *Red States*, 125–129; Garrison, *Legal Ideology of Removal*, 31, 128, 149; Moulton, *John Ross*, 43, 47.

62 Moulton, *Papers*, 156.

63 Moulton, *Papers*, 306.

64 Cherokee Nation, *Laws*, 4–5, 19, 24, 45, 118–119, 136.

65 Moulton, *Papers*, 257.

66 The petitions are reprinted in Kilcup, *Native American Women's Writing*, 29–30; all quotations are from this source. On Cherokee women's petitions in the pre-removal period, see Donaldson, "But We Are Your Mothers"; Justice, *Our Fire*, 39–42; Kilcup, *Fallen Forests*, 25–40; Miles, "Circular Reasoning." On white women's petitions against Cherokee removal, including the first petition sent by women to Congress on a matter of federal policy, see Portnoy, *Their Right to Speak*.

67 As Laura Donaldson notes, this "petition reminded those who wanted to sell the ancestral homelands and remove to Arkansas that the traditional basis for Cherokee sovereignty lay in recognizing the Cherokee's responsibilities to, rather than exercising power over, one another. And the originary basis for this recognition was their relationship with their mothers" ("But We Are Your Mothers," 53).

68 Simpson Smith, "I Look on You," 425. On removal as a severing of relations to non-human entities as well, see Carroll, *Roots of Our Renewal*.

69 See Moulton, *Papers*, 293, 295, 317, 390.

70 Not all Cherokees, though, endorsed remaining on the lands of the Cherokee Nation, as indicated by a number of previous migrations—especially in 1808–1810 and 1817–1819. These movements certainly are not unrelated to forms of U.S. federal pressure to remove, but the desire to live elsewhere cannot simply be reduced to colonial intervention. Cherokees had a long history of migration, and individuals' desire to move did not make them less Cherokee. On Cherokee diaspora, see Justice, *Our Fire*; Smithers, *Cherokee Diaspora*. In his futurist novel *Riding the Trail of Tears*, Cherokee author Blake Hausman also explores the ways that the notion of a singular Cherokee homeland can be understood as a back-formation from forced removal, as a replaying of what was lost, and the novel addresses how this vision of Cherokee history can generate a sense of tragic disappearance that resonates with settler stories of Indian vanishing, in ways that efface longer Cherokee histories and longstanding stories of migration as a part of Cherokee identity.

71 On Cherokee textual production prior to removal, see Justice, *Our Fire*; Nelson, *Progressive Traditions*; Parins, *Literacy and Intellectual Life*; Round, *Removable Type*, 123–149.

72 Spivak, *Critique of Postcolonial Reason*, 257.

73 See Gramsci, *Prison Notebooks*.

74 Denson, *Demanding the Cherokee Nation*, 39.

75 Moulton, *Papers*, 331–333. On the work performed by settler discourses of "faction" with regard to Indigenous polities, see McCarthy, *Divided Unity*; Pasternak, *Grounded Authority*.

76 Nelson, *Progressive Traditions*, 193.

77 Members of the Treaty Party also received special treatment by authorities in Georgia (who did not seize their lands), actively participated in the seizure of the nation's printing press, and requested that the Georgia Guard be sent out to find and imprison Ross supporters. See Moulton, *John Ross*, 62, 65; Parins, *Literacy and Intellectual Life*, 65–66; Wilkins, *Cherokee Tragedy*, 250, 271. Moreover, the then governor of Georgia had about four hundred copies of *Letters* printed and distributed, including sending copies to all the members of the U.S. Senate (Peyer, *Tutor'd Mind*, 218–219).

78 Schneider, "Boudinot's Change," 157. Schneider is responding to arguments such as Theda Perdue's that "the 'Nation' [Boudinot] gave his life to save simply did not exist" and that Boudinot's vision of the Cherokee Nation "had little basis in reality," further suggesting that Boudinot "was the product of colonization" (Perdue, Introduction, 32–33).

79 On the problems of discourses of Native "culture," see also Barker, *Native Acts*; Borrows, *Freedom and Indigenous Constitutionalism*; Dennison, *Colonial Entanglement*; Lyons, *X-marks*; Povinelli, *Cunning of Recognition*; Simpson, *Mohawk Interruptus*. As Dale Turner suggests with respect to notions of "tradition," "The first difficulty is to know how we ought to characterize the distinct forms of knowledge embedded in indigenous communities. Phrases like 'traditional knowledge' and 'indigenous ways of knowing' have become commonplace in both mainstream and indigenous cultures, yet we are not at all clear about what they mean *in relation to the legal and political discourses of the dominant culture*" (*Peace Pipe*, 98).

80 Schneider, "Boudinot's Change," 166.

81 Konkle, *Writing Indian Nations*, 96.

82 Warrior, "Native Critics," 180, 184, 204, 206.

83 Nelson, *Progressive Traditions*, 190, 191, 193, 197.

84 Nelson, *Progressive Traditions*, 195.

85 On the negotiations in Washington in the first half of 1835, see Dale and Litton, *Cherokee Cavaliers*, 10–15; Moulton, *Papers*, 317–333; Wilkins, *Cherokee Tragedy*, 267–270.

86 Konkle suggests that "what separates Boudinot from Ross . . . is that Boudinot assumes that he, as an educated, Christian man, knows what's best for the majority of the Cherokee population" (*Writing Indian Nations*, 95). This point, though, might be reframed: less a distinction between an elite belief that one knows what's best and a countervailing commitment to popular principles than the difference between a belief that such elite knowledge is sufficient in and of itself and an investment in some form of institutionalized engagement (however mediated) that can assent to elite-driven formulations. As Peyer suggests of the removal treaty, "The irony behind this tragic event is that Boudinot, the Ridges, and Ross essentially shared identical views concerning what they thought best for Cherokee development" (*Tutor'd Mind*, 213).

87 Latour, *Inquiry*, 107, 338, 341.

88 Moulton, *Papers*, 283, 288.

89 Moulton, *Papers*, 283.

90 As Ross states in that same appeal, "It is no more than reasonable and just, that ample time should be extended to the Cherokee people to prepare for so important a change of their political character, in their native land" (Moulton, *Papers*, 283).

91 Moulton, *Papers*, 318, 328, 332.

92 Moulton, *Papers*, 333.

93 Moulton, *Papers*, 337.

94 Konkle, *Writing Indian Nations*, 126.

95 Simpson, *Dancing on Our Turtle's Back*, 16.

Chapter 2. Experiments in Signifying Sovereignty

Parts of chapter 2 previously were published as "Shadows of Mashantucket: William Apess and the Representation of Pequot Place," *American Literature* 84, no. 4 (2012): 691–714.

1 On the operation of the federal treaty system, see Bruyneel, *Third Space of Sovereignty*; Calloway, *Pen and Ink Witchcraft*; Prucha, *American Indian Treaties*. On federal Indian policy in the late eighteenth and early nineteenth centuries, see also Ben-zvi, *Native Land Talk*; Hurt, *Indian Frontier*; Jones, *License for Empire*; Onuf, *Jefferson's Empire*; Rifkin, *Manifesting America*; Rockwell, *Indian Affairs*; Saler, *Settlers' Empire*. On Native-state relations in New England in the eighteenth and nineteenth centuries, see Brooks, *Common Pot*; Calloway, *After King Philip's War*; Den Ouden, *Beyond Conquest*; Mandell, *Behind the Frontier*; Mandell, *Tribe, Race, History*; O'Brien, *Dispossession by Degrees*; O'Connell, introduction to *On Our Own Ground*; Silverman, *Faith and Boundaries*; Silverman, "Impact of Indentured Servitude"; Sweet, *Bodies Politic*. For other considerations of the importance of attending to state law in this period, rather than thinking of Indian policy as solely a federal matter, see Garrison, *Legal Ideology of Removal*; Rosen, *American Indians and State Law*.

2 A version of this authority first is articulated in *U.S. v. Kagama*. I will discuss this change in chapter 4.

3 I should distinguish "metonymic" as I'm using it from Arnold Krupat's description of Native autobiography as illustrating a "synecdochic self" (Krupat, *Ethnocriticism*). I am talking not so much about Apess's presentation of himself and his life as part of a Pequot whole as about the ways Apess draws on various figures (including himself) that can stand for Native political identity in New England, so as to make such identity visible and graspable for non-natives. If synecdoche refers to using the part to represent the whole, metonymy refers to figuring one thing through another, offering a looser and more contingent sense of the relation between the tenor and the vehicle than in synecdoche.

4 On "unwitnessing," see Lopenzina, *Through an Indian's Looking-Glass*.

5 On the work of the background, see Ahmed, *Queer Phenomenology*.

6 Simpson, *Mohawk Interruptus*, 185, 11.

7 See Cramer, *Cash, Color, Colonialism*, 137–162; Den Ouden, "Altered State?"; Gould, "Nipmuc Nation"; Torres, "How You See Us."

8 Turner, *Peace Pipe*, 10, 30–31.

9   The records of the overseers for the Mashantucket reservation for the 1820s and 1830s suggest that those non-natives who were leased land on the reservation also routinely were paid by the overseers for goods provided to the Pequots, such that the cost of the lease largely was abated through the purchase of goods. Moreover, as tribes apparently did not receive any kind of regular funds from the state, the overseers were paid out of funds due to the tribe from land leasing and timber sales. Overseers would regularly record money due them for days spent on matters related to tribal affairs or for travel related to such matters. See New London County Court Files, Papers by Subject: Indians, box 2, Connecticut State Archives.

10   Latour, *Reassembling the Social*, 196.

11   On Indigenous density, see Andersen, "From Difference to Density." On the messiness of Indigenous socialities, see Barker, *Native Acts*.

12   Den Ouden and O'Brien, *Recognition*, 6.

13   Here, I am thinking of Gayatri Spivak's reminder that textual figuration and modes of reading beyond what she terms "information retrieval" call on us "to ask the question of the formation of collectivities without necessarily prefabricated contents" (*Death of a Discipline*, 26).

14   On the text as a temperance narrative, see Miller, "Mouth for God."

15   Critics have suggested as much, often contrasting *A Son of the Forest* to Apess's later work which is read as more "mature." For example, David Carlson suggests that Apess "manifests broad affinities with republican ideology and its liberal model of subjectivity" (*Sovereign Selves*, 96). For similar assessments, see Doolen, *Fugitive Empire*, 145–183; Konkle, *Writing Indian Nations*, 112; O'Connell, introduction to *On Our Own Ground*; Peyer, *Tutor'd Mind*, 152, 154; Sayre, "Defying Assimilation," 8; Warrior, *People and the Word*, 38.

16   Kucich, "William Apess's Nullifications," 11.

17   Unless otherwise explicitly noted, quotations from *A Son of the Forest* cited in text are from the 1831 edition, reprinted in Apess, *A Son of the Forest and Other Writings*.

18   See Miller, "Mouth for God," 236–237; Warrior, *People and the Word*, 23.

19   On racialization as a process of assemblage in which "flesh" marks both racial violence and the possibility for alternative social formations, see Weheliye, *Habeas Viscus*.

20   In particular, see Velikova, "Philip, King of the Pequots." However, the extensive genealogical connections among peoples in southern New England theoretically could allow for a Pequot woman to be descended from a Wampanoag sachem, even if Philip was not himself Pequot. See Bruchac, "Hill Town Touchstone," 726; Radus, "Apess's *Eulogy* on Tour," 98. The 1831 edition differs substantially from the 1829 one in the phrasing and order of the first few paragraphs, but it does reference King Philip, presents him as a leader of the "Pequods," and presents Apess's paternal grandmother as of the "royal family" descending from Philip (Apess, *Son of the Forest* [1829], 7–9).

21   See Simpson, "State Is a Man."

22   See Brooks, *Common Pot*, 175; Doolen, *Fugitive Empire*, 153–154.

23   On survivance, see Vizenor, *Manifest Manners*.

24   On this anecdote, see Bayers, "William Apess's Manhood," 128–129; Haynes, "Mark for Them All," 32; Murray, *Forked Tongues*, 59; O'Connell, introduction to

On Our Own Ground, xlviii–xlix; Sayre, "Defying Assimilation," 6; Wyss, *Writing Indians*, 158.

25   For readings of this passage, see O'Connell, introduction to *On Our Own Ground*, l–li; Stevens, "William Apess's Historical Self," 76–77; Wyss, *Writing Indians*, 158–159. The first edition makes reference to Apess having "frequently heard" stories from his paternal grandmother in his childhood, which could serve as the basis for the alternative account of Native history he offers. See Apess, *Son of the Forest* (1829), 8.

26   Brooks, *Common Pot*, 173. For a contrasting reading of Colrain and its place within geographies of trade and residency, see Bruchac, "Hill Town Touchstone."

27   Mandell, *Tribe, Race, History*, 29.

28   Den Ouden, *Beyond Conquest*, 168; Mandell, *Tribe, Race, History*, 18.

29   For overviews of Pequot history, see Campisi, "Emergence"; De Forest, *Indians of Connecticut*; Den Ouden, *Beyond Conquest*; Mandell, *Tribe, Race, History*; and McBride, "Historical Archaeology." The Mashantucket Pequots were federally recognized through congressional legislation in 1983 (O'Brien, *Firsting and Lasting*, 205). For discussion of the history and process of federal recognition for Mashantucket and other southern New England Native peoples, see Campisi, "New England Tribes"; Den Ouden and O'Brien, *Recognition*.

30   On the Pequot War and its immediate aftermath, see Cave, *Pequot War*; De Forest, *Indians of Connecticut*, 117–160; Fickes, "They Could Not Endure"; Salisbury, *Manitou and Providence*.

31   See Brooks, *Common Pot*; Den Ouden, *Beyond Conquest*; Mandell, *Tribe, Race, History*; O'Brien, *Dispossession by Degrees*; O'Connell, introduction to *On Our Own Ground*; Silverman, "Impact of Indentured Servitude."

32   On such accounts of Mashantucket in particular, see De Forest, *Indians of Connecticut*, 442–446; Mandell, *Tribe, Race, History*, 49. On kinship networks in Native New England prior to the eighteenth century, see Bragdon, *Southern New England*; Brooks, *Our Beloved Kin*; Den Ouden, *Beyond Conquest*; Plane, *Colonial Intimacies*.

33   For commentary on the representation of Apess's maternal grandmother in the text, see Konkle, *Writing Indian Nations*, 109; Murray, *Forked Tongues*, 60; O'Connell, introduction to *On Our Own Ground*, xxx–xxxi, l, lxv–lxvi, lxxvii; Peyer, *Tutor'd Mind*, 131; Sayre, "Defying Assimilation," 14–15; Tiro, "Denominated 'Savage,'" 655.

34   Hillhouse had served as an overseer to the Mashantucket Pequots. See Lopenzina, *Through an Indian's Looking-Glass*, 68.

35   On Native indenture in southern New England, see Mandell, *Tribe, Race, History*; O'Brien, *Dispossession by Degrees*; Silverman, "Impact of Indentured Servitude"; Sweet, *Bodies Politic*. In "The Emergence of the Mashantucket Pequot Tribe," Jack Campisi notes, by 1800, "of those who remained in Connecticut, a large number had moved off the reservation land and were indentured in white households or had moved onto white-owned farms, where they lived in virtual servitude" (125). On relations between Black and Indian racialization in colonial and early-national New England, including circumstances of labor and enslavement, see Sweet, *Bodies Politic*.

36   See Campisi, "Emergence," 123, 130; Connecticut State Archives: Indians, series 2, vol. 1, 121a; Connecticut State Archives: Indians, series 2, vol. 2, 39a; De Forest, *Indians of Connecticut*, 434–436; Mandell, *Tribe, Race, History*, 242n66. Drew

Lopenzina suggests that Williams would have been serving as overseer while Apess was living with him (*Through an Indian's Looking-Glass*, 73).

37 On the establishment of New London, see O'Brien, *Firsting and Lasting*, 156; Peyer, *Tutor'd Mind*, 127.

38 For examples, see Carlson, *Sovereign Selves*, 101; Doolen, *Fugitive Empire*, 149–150; Lopenzina, *Through an Indian's Looking-Glass*, 87–88; O'Connell, introduction to *On Our Own Ground*, xlvii–xlviii, lv; Peyer, *Tutor'd Mind*, 131–132, 163; Sayre, "Defying Assimilation," 6; Stevens, "William Apess's Historical Self," 69–72; Tiro, "Denominated '*Savage*,'" 656; Wyss, *Writing Indians*, 157. For exceptions that do consider the thematic importance of the Mashantucket reservation to Apess's work, although not at length, see Brooks, *Common Pot*, 173–176; Donaldson, "Making a Joyful Noise"; O'Connell, "Once More Let Us Consider"; Warrior, *People and the Word*, 8–15.

39 In the accounts of the Mashantucket Pequot overseers from the 1820s and 1830s, "Indian tribe in Groton," "Groton Indian Tribe," and "Pequot Tribe of Indians" are used interchangeably (New London County Court Files, Papers by Subject: Indians, RG 003, Judicial Department, box 2, Connecticut State Archives). See also De Forest, *Indians of Connecticut*, 421–446; Den Ouden, *Beyond Conquest*, 143–180; O'Brien, *Firsting and Lasting*, 170–171.

40 The mention in the first edition, removed in the second, of his having "frequently heard" stories from his paternal grandmother in his childhood also provides evidence of continuing contact with Pequots, especially his relatives on the reservation. See Apess, *Son of the Forest* (1829), 8.

41 Vizenor, *Manifest Manners*, 3, 72, 70–72.

42 For critical accounts that focus on Apess's Methodism in *A Son of the Forest*, see Donaldson, "Making a Joyful Noise"; Haynes, "Mark for Them All"; Miller, "Mouth for God"; O'Connell, introduction to *On Our Own Ground*; Tiro, "Denominated '*Savage*.'" Hilary Wyss suggests that, for Apess, "Methodism becomes the very structuring principle of his Nativeness" (*Writing Indians*, 160–161), but this claim seems to me to invert the relation between the two, with Methodism, instead, functioning as a means of making visible Indigenous collectivity and landedness. For an overview of the kinds of Christian revivalism and evangelicism that were popular in this period, and that came to be known as the Second Great Awakening, see Howe, *What Hath God Wrought*, 164–202.

43 On the relative openness of Methodism in this period to participation by nonelite persons, particularly people of color, see Bellin, *Demon of the Continent*, 88–97; Haynes, "Mark for Them All"; Tiro, "Denominated '*Savage*'"; Wyss, *Writing Indians*, 154–167. For further discussion by Apess of Aunt Sally George, see Apess, *Experiences of Five Christian Indians*, 88–91. Sally George was the sister of Apess's grandmother on his father's side, the grandmother who is mentioned in the 1829 edition as having spoken much with Apess when he was younger. While his grandmother might have lived with Apess's father in Colchester, the fact that Apess had a close link to his great-aunt, that grandmother's sister, when he comes to live at Mashantucket after returning from the war suggests that he might have spent time with Sally George, and also his grandmother, prior to running away from Williams's house.

44 In Connecticut, prior to 1821 overseers were appointed by the state legislature, and after 1821, when Indian affairs were put under the supervision of county courts, overseers were appointed by the court. See Mandell, *Tribe, Race, History*, 92. For Mashantucket, see Connecticut State Archives: Indians, series 2, vol. 1, 17a, 18, 21a; New London County Court Files, Papers by Subject: Indians, box 2.

45 Campisi, "Emergence," 127. In all of the petitions to the Connecticut General Assembly and, after 1821, the New London County Court with regard to the matter of the overseer, there are a number of women signatories (Connecticut State Archives: Indians, series 2, vol. 1, 21a; New London County Court Files, Papers by Subject: Indians, box 2). See also Lopenzina, *Through an Indian's Looking-Glass*, 139; Mandell, *Tribe, Race, History*, 93, 171.

46 Mandell, *Tribe, Race, History*, 40.

47 On Apess's use of temperance discourse to present himself taking part in appropriate forms of masculine uprightness and care, see Miller, "Mouth for God."

48 See Apess, *Experiences of Five Christian Indians*, 151–152. The petitions were in 1819, 1825, and 1831. See Connecticut State Archives: Indians, series 2, vol. 1, 21a; New London County Court Files, Papers by Subject: Indians, box 2.

49 There is a question of whether the person known as "King Philip" by the English continued to use the name "Metacom" or actually changed his name to "Philip" after receiving that name in negotiations with representatives of the Plymouth Colony. See Lepore, *Name of War*, xix–xx. I move back and forth between "Metacom" and "Philip," as a way of signaling the complexities of Apess's relation to the historical sachem and to non-native discourses about him.

50 Vogel, *Rewriting White*, 40.

51 On the commissioning of the play and its significance at the time, see Dillon, *New World Drama*, 233–240; Gaul, "Genuine Indian"; Grose, "Edwin Forrest"; Lepore, *Name of War*, 191–226; Martin, "Interpreting *Metamora*"; Rebhorn, "Edwin Forrest's Redding Up"; Sayre, "Melodramas of Rebellion"; Vogel, *Rewriting White*, 40–61.

52 In addition to stagings of *Metamora*, Metacom's prominence was secured also by the reprinting of Washington Irving's sketch "Philip of Pokanoket," the commemoration of the 150th anniversary of King Philip's War, the commemoration of the founding of Plymouth Colony, and various histories of New England that featured discussion of King Philip (including one for children by Lydia Maria Child). See Brooks, *Common Pot*, 199, 207; Conforti, *Imagining New England*, 181–186; Konkle, *Writing Indian Nations*, 132–135; Lopenzina, *Through an Indian's Looking-Glass*, 222; Mandell, *Tribe, Race, History*, 177–181; McWilliams, *New England's Crises*, 6–19; Peyer, *Tutor'd Mind*, 160; Sweet, *Bodies Politic*, 1–2; Velikova, "Philip, King of the Pequots."

53 As Lisa Brooks suggests, "The popularity of plays like *Metamora* opened up a space through which a Native orator like Apess might stage his own performance" (*Common Pot*, 199).

54 Wolfe, "Mourning, Melancholia," 3.

55 O'Brien, *Firsting and Lasting*, 184, 190.

56 Perhaps the most prominent among them are those by Catharine Maria Sedgwick and Lydia Maria Child. On this genre, see Burnham, *Captivity and Sentiment*;

Cooke, "Indian Fields"; Mielke, *Moving Encounters*; Rifkin, *When Did Indians Become Straight?*; Tawil, *Making of Racial Sentiment.*

57   On the remembrance of King Philip's War as part of ongoing "memoryscapes" in New England, see DeLucia, *Memory Lands.*

58   Apess, *Eulogy*, 105; text references are to this edition.

59   On Apess's citation of Metacom in ways that seek to reorient extant discourses of "Indian character," and to produce a different kind of history through doing so, see Cooke, "Indian Fields."

60   One cannot really overestimate the extent of Washington-worship among whites in the early-nineteenth-century United States. As Clayton Zuba suggests, "Just as George Washington served as more than an individual hero and president for nineteenth-century Americans, but also as an exemplary figure integral to U.S. identity, King Philip represents at once the highest ideal for native sovereignty and the plight of all Native Americans during the Indian Removal era" ("Apess's *Eulogy on King Philip*," 658). My argument, then, is that the analogy with Washington does not Americanize Apess but provides a frame to stage the separateness of Native nationhood, contra claims such as Todd Vogel's that "Apess transformed Philip into the republican forefather of George Washington and thereby became the cornerstone of the nation as his audience knew it" (*Rewriting White*, 50).

61   See Deloria, *Playing Indian*; Huston, *Land and Freedom*; Rifkin, *Settler Common Sense*; Taylor, *Liberty Men*. See also Caison, *Red States*, especially chap. 2.

62   Not only does Apess literally claim descent from Philip in *A Son of the Forest*, he does so in advertisements for the talk on which *Eulogy* is based. See Lopenzina, *Through an Indian's Looking-Glass*, 177.

63   Konkle, *Writing Indian Nations*, 105–106.

64   On the reversal of discourses of savagery in *Eulogy*, see Gussman, "O Savage, Where Art Thou?"

65   Konkle, *Writing Indian Nations*, 143.

66   O'Brien, *Firsting and Lasting*, 148, 186.

67   For an alternate reading of this passage and Apess's use of "we" in *Eulogy*, see Brooks, *Common Pot*, 204–209.

68   On patriarchy as not solely gendered power but as organizing a distinction between those who count as legal persons and those who do not (such as Black people and Indians), who are understood as properly subject to patriarchal control by full persons, see Perry, *Vexy Thing*. Apess's figuration of citizenship challenges such Indianization, but in *Eulogy*'s use of the figure of slavery to name conditions of anti-Indianness and antiblackness, it also contests the denial of personhood to people of color more broadly, even as the text reaffirms what can be understood as a heteropatriarchal conception of sovereignty and political order.

69   See Calloway, *After King Philip's War*; Mandell, *Tribe, Race, History*; Radus, "Apess's *Eulogy* on Tour."

70   On changing laws with regard to (white) women's ability to hold and inherit property in the nineteenth century, see Basch, *Eyes of the Law*; Cott, *Public Vows*, 24–55; and Isenberg, *Sex and Citizenship*, 155–190.

71   Simpson, *As We Have Always Done*, 51, 52.

72 Goeman, *Mark My Words*, 21, 12.

73 Brooks, *Our Beloved Kin*, 2, 168, 17, 19, 30. On Native patterns of kinship and leadership in southern New England prior to the late seventeenth century, see also Bragdon, *Southern New England*; DeLucia, *Memory Lands*; O'Brien, *Dispossession by Degrees*; Plane, *Colonial Intimacies*; Silverman, *Faith and Boundaries*.

74 Daniel Radus argues that *Eulogy* "transcends the nation as a category of indigenous affiliation" by "emphasizing instead the transnational networks that structured national belonging," thereby "echo[ing] and affirm[ing] the kinship bonds that strengthened articulations of indigenous nationhood in the nineteenth century" ("Apess's *Eulogy* on Tour," 95), but by contrast, I would suggest that the ways *Eulogy* routes contemporary Native political claims and struggles through Philip actually forecloses engagement with such networks and bonds, in terms of the seventeenth and nineteenth centuries.

75 On the ascendance of the heteronormative ideal of the nuclear family, see Boydston, *Home and Work*; Coontz, *Social Origins*; Cott, *Public Vows*; D'Emilio and Freedman, *Intimate Matters*; Merish, *Sentimental Materialism*; Rifkin, *When Did Indians Become Straight?*

76 O'Brien, *Dispossession by Degrees*, 143; Plane, *Colonial Intimacies*, 29.

77 See also Den Ouden, *Beyond Conquest*; Mandell, *Behind the Frontier*; Sweet, *Bodies Politic*, 44–54.

78 Mandell, *Tribe, Race, History*, 141.

79 Deborah Gussman suggests that *Eulogy* "positions Philip in relation to a family and a domestic economy, concerns that resonated with nineteenth-century audiences, particularly middle-class white women. Philip and his men are not just warriors or hunters but fathers, husbands, and brothers who are interested in providing for their wives, children, and sisters" ("O Savage, Where Art Thou?," 459).

80 In the nineteenth century, figurations of suitability for active citizenship (including voting rights, serving on juries, running for public office) still turned on notions of autonomy (as opposed to dependence and servility). While property qualifications were being removed in many states, white masculinity itself came to stand for such personal self-possession, in contrast to wives, children, slaves, and Indians. See Coviello, *Intimacy in America*; Keyssar, *Right to Vote*; Nelson, *National Manhood*; Welke, *Law and the Borders*.

81 Bird, Griswold, and Weekes, *Report of the Commissioners*, 26, 37–38; Campisi, *Mashpee Indians*, 105; Earle, *Report to the Governor*, 52; and Nielson, "Mashpee Indian Revolt," 416. The Mashpee, though, would not regain full use of their meetinghouse until 1840 and were not completely rid of Fish until 1846. See Campisi, *Mashpee Indians*, 107–108; Nielson, "Mashpee Indian Revolt," 417–418.

82 Apess, *Indian Nullification*, 166; text references are to pages in this edition.

83 As Lisa Brooks suggests, "The Mashpees firmly rejected the suggestion that Apess had been responsible for instigating the revolt and made clear that he was just a part of the village, not its leader" (*Common Pot*, 191).

84 Lopenzina, *Through an Indian's Looking-Glass*, 105–106.

85 On Mashpee history, see Campisi, *Mashpee Indians*; Mandell, *Behind the Frontier*; Mandell, *Tribe, Race, History*; Nielson, "Mashpee Indian Revolt"; Silverman, *Faith and Boundaries*.

86 Ellis, *Union at Risk*; Dahl, *Empire of the People*, 168. In order to use force against South Carolina in securing the supremacy of federal law, President Jackson needed the support of Northern congressmen, many of whom were sympathetic to the situation of the Cherokees. The decision in *Worchester v. Georgia* (1832) had found Georgia's attempts to annex Cherokee territory to be unconstitutional, but immense pressure was put on the missionaries in that case, including a resolution by the American Board of Commissioners for Foreign Missions (ABCFM) (their sponsoring institution), to accept the pardon offered by Georgia's governor Wilson Lumpkin before either the opening of the next Supreme Court session or the moment when federal action would become necessary in the nullification crisis. They accepted the pardons on January 14, 1833, thereby enabling a focus on South Carolina, which relented under federal threats.

87 Nielson, "Mashpee Indian Revolt," 401.

88 Konkle, *Writing Indian Nations*, 124; Dahl, *Empire of the People*, 174.

89 Bird, Griswold, and Weekes, *Report of the Commissioners*, 3, 15, 16, 19, 25.

90 On the limits of this report as a reliable document of Native history in Massachusetts, see Gould, "Nipmuc Nation."

91 Earle, *Report to the Governor*, 33, 121.

92 Earle, *Report to the Governor*, 62.

93 See Bowes, *Land Too Good*; Cooke, "Indian Fields."

94 In their official report on Indian affairs in Massachusetts in 1849, F. W. Bird, Whiting Griswold, and Cyrus Weekes observe, "The Marshpee Indians are not aliens. They are not a domestic nation, as the Cherokees are declared to be, by the supreme court of the United States. They have no rights secured by treaty, and no other rights than those of property and person, applying to them as to all other citizens" (*Report of the Commissioners*, 50).

95 On Northeastern protest against removal, see Andrew, *From Revivals to Removal*; Howe, *What Hath God Wrought*, 342–366; McLoughlin, *Cherokee Renascence*. For the ways white women's protests against Indian removal easily sat alongside commitments to colonizationist plans for removing freed people of color to Africa, see Portnoy, *Their Right to Speak*.

96 On sympathy as a discourse of place in the period, see Greyser, *On Sympathetic Grounds*.

97 Such autonomy also is suggested by the presentation of Native peoples in New England, including the Mashpee, as descendants of the lost tribes of Israel. See Zuck, "Lost Tribes."

98 Many Native people from southern New England, including numerous Mashpees, fought in the American Revolution on the side of the nascent United States. See Mandell, *Tribe, Race, History*; Sweet, *Bodies Politic*.

99 Carlson, *Sovereign Selves*, 117; Kucich, "William Apess's Nullifications," 5.

100 Apess, *Indian Nullification*, 187, 211, 217, 240.

101 Some scholars have suggested that Native articulations of sovereignty presume and extend the forms of nonpersonhood associated with blackness. See Sexton, "Vel of Slavery"; Wilderson, *Red, White, and Black*. Apess's gambit here, though, is less to distinguish Native and Black people (especially given their frequent genealogical

intermixing on reservations in southern New England) than to take up the more visible struggle for Black freedom as a vehicle through which to think a range of forms of state violence.

102 Doolen, *Fugitive Empire*, 148, 162.

103 Doolen, *Fugitive Empire*, 160, 162, 168.

104 See Bird, Griswold, and Weekes, *Report of the Commissioners*, 12, 14, 37; Den Ouden, *Beyond Conquest*; Earle, *Report to the Governor*, 131–132; Mandell, *Tribe, Race, History*; Plane and Button, "Massachusetts Indian Enfranchisement Act"; Rosen, *American Indians and State Law*, 155–179.

105 Mandell, *Tribe, Race, History*, 100.

106 Campisi, *Mashpee Indians*, 101; Mandell, *Tribe, Race, History*, 170.

107 See Latour, *Inquiry*.

108 As Latour suggests, "a form is simply something which allows something else to be transported from one site to another" (*Reassembling the Social*, 223).

109 In *The Experiences of Five Christians Indians of the Pequot Tribe* (1833), Apess does devote far more attention to Native women than he does in his other works. This text, though, largely replicates the kinds of focus women receive in his *A Son of the Forest*.

Chapter 3. Among Ghost Dances

Parts of chapter 3 previously were published as "Among Ghost Dances: Sarah Winnemucca and the Production of Tribal Identity," *Studies in American Indian Literatures* 31, nos. 1–2 (2019): 170–207.

1 On the Ghost Dances of 1870 and 1890, see DeMallie, "Lakota Ghost Dance"; Du Bois, *1870 Ghost Dance*; Hittman, "1870 Ghost Dance"; Hittman, *Wovoka*; Mooney, *Ghost-Dance Religion*; Ostler, *Plains Sioux*; Smoak, *Ghost Dances*; Warren, *God's Red Son*.

2 Smoak, *Ghost Dances*, 199, 204.

3 For brevity's sake, I will often use the term "Paiute," and in doing so, I am reflecting both Winnemucca's usage and that of critics who write about Winnemucca's life and *Life*. However, these references are only to the Northern Paiutes. The Southern Paiutes are a distinct (set of) group(s) whose language is quite different.

4 The charge of misrepresenting Paiute groups, though, has been made against Winnemucca by other Paiutes. See Carpenter, *Seeing Red*, 116–125; Scott, *Karnee*.

5 For examples, see Carpenter, *Seeing Red*; Kohler, "Send Word"; McClure, "Sarah Winnemucca"; Powell, "Sarah Winnemucca Hopkins"; Sorisio, "'I Nailed Those Lies.'"

6 Even when critical accounts note the existence of a range of Paiute bands that did not have a singular shared governing structure, they still tend to characterize the narrative as engaged in a struggle to better the situation of a unified political collectivity, sometimes referred to as "the Paiute tribe" or "the Paiute nation." For examples, see Carpenter, "Sarah Winnemucca"; Lape, "I Would Rather"; McClure, "Sarah Winnemucca"; Sneider, "Gender, Literacy, and Sovereignty"; Tisinger, "Textual Performance"; Walker, *Indian Nation*.

7 Powell, "Sarah Winnemucca Hopkins," 74.

8 Notably, critics almost entirely have avoided discussion of the relation between Winnemucca's narrative and the Ghost Dances.

9 Spivak, *Critique of Postcolonial Reason*, 258–259.

10 On processes of what elsewhere has been called "ethnogenesis," the creation of new peoples, see Andersen, *"Métis"*; Anderson, *Indian Southwest*; Fisher, *Shadow Tribe*; Lowery, *Lumbee Indians*; Shepherd, *Indian Nation*.

11 See Adams, *Who Belongs?*; Barker, *Native Acts*; Gunter, "Technology of Tribalism"; Klopotek, *Recognition Odysseys*; Lowery, *Lumbee Indians*; Tolley, *Quest for Tribal Acknowledgment*.

12 Goeman, *Mark My Words*, 12.

13 Estes, *Our History*, 185. See also Byrd, *Transit of Empire*; Saldaña-Portillo, *Indian Given*.

14 While focusing on how the narrative mediates extent discourses in Indian policy, this interpretation also builds on extant scholarship on *Life* that foregrounds Winnemucca's role as a mediator of one kind or another, including in her role as translator. For examples, see Carpenter, "Sarah Winnemucca"; Eves, "Finding Place to Speak"; Kohler, "Send Word"; Lape, "I Would Rather"; Powell, "Sarah Winnemucca Hopkins"; Sneider, "Gender, Literacy, and Sovereignty"; Sorisio, "Sarah Winnemucca"; Tisinger, "Textual Performance"; Walker, *Indian Nation*, 139–163.

15 Dennison, *Colonial Entanglement*, 5, 7.

16 Quoted in Carpenter and Sorisio, *Newspaper Warrior*, 161–162.

17 Carpenter and Sorisio, *Newspaper Warrior*, 163–164. On the relationship between Winnemucca and Elizabeth Peabody as well as Peabody's sister Mary Mann (who edited *Life among the Piutes*), see Hanrahan, "[W]orthy"; Sorisio, "'I Nailed Those Lies.'"

18 Winnemucca, *Life*, 2; text references are to pages in this edition.

19 Carpenter and Sorisio, *Newspaper Warrior*, 142.

20 In newspaper accounts from the 1860s onward, Winnemucca continually is referred to as a "princess" or "queen," and while sometimes such titles are used ironically when writers seek to disparate her and other Paiute people by depicting their "savage" actions, most often these terms are used as a straightforward way of indicating her status in what is cast as a single tribe. For examples, see Carpenter and Sorisio, *Newspaper Warrior*, 36, 44, 55, 63, 68, 113–114, 133, 149, 207.

21 Some authors seek to avoid confusion by referring to Sarah Winnemucca as "Sarah," so as not to have readers conflate her with her father. However, this gesture seems to me overfamiliarizing, unlike the way we refer to other authors. Instead, I will continue to refer to Sarah Winnemucca as "Winnemucca" and will refer to Sarah's father as "Chief Winnemucca," even as I explore the tensions at play in this designation.

22 The text at times suggests that Chief Winnemucca is Truckee's son and, at other times, that he's Truckee's son-in-law. See Winnemucca, *Life*, 14, 16, 30, 33, 37, 40, 41, 67, 120, 193. Scholars indicate that Truckee is Winnemucca's mother's father. See Carpenter and Sorisio, *Newspaper Warrior*, 4; Hittman, *Great Basin Indians*, 388; Senier, *Voices*, 76; Zanjani, *Sarah Winnemucca*, 21.

23 Zanjani, *Sarah Winnemucca*, 233–234.

24 On the text's mobilization of sentimental figurations, see Carpenter, "Sarah Winnemucca"; Carpenter and Sorisio, *Newspaper Warrior*, 1–30; Greyser, *On Sym-*

pathetic Grounds, 120–161; Hanrahan, "[W]orthy"; Kilcup, *Fallen Forests*, 270–288; Lape, "I Would Rather"; Powell, "Sarah Winnemucca Hopkins."

25 Canfield, *Sarah Winnemucca*, 177; Carpenter and Sorisio, *Newspaper Warrior*, 10, 26, 156; Powell, "Sarah Winnemucca Hopkins," 83.

26 On the establishment of the Malheur Reservation, see Annual Report of the Commissioner of Indian Affairs (hereafter cited as ARCIA) 1872, 453; Winnemucca, *Life*, 105; Zanjani, *Sarah Winnemucca*, 128.

27 On the history of the Pyramid Lake Reservation, see Knack and Stewart, *River Shall Run*. Congress disallowed the creation of any more executive order reservations in 1919 (McDonnell, *Dispossession*, 17).

28 At points, Egan refers to himself as "chief of the Snake River Piutes," rather than as a "sub-chief" (Winnemucca, *Life*, 144, 146).

29 In addition to those sources quoted, this portrait of Northern Paiute lifeways draws on Canfield, *Sarah Winnemucca*; Fowler and Liljeblad, "Northern Paiute"; Stowell, "Wada-Tika"; Zanjani, *Sarah Winnemucca*.

30 Knack and Stewart, *River Shall Run*, 14, 15.

31 Gualtieri, "Role of Moral Outrage," 22; Knack and Stewart, *River Shall Run*, 16; Zanjani, *Sarah Winnemucca*, 8.

32 Gualtieri, "Role of Moral Outrage," 23, 63. See also Knack and Stewart, *River Shall Run*, 25–26.

33 On similar problems in the emergence and use of the concept of the "tribe" to characterize Indigenous modes of relation, administratively and anthropologically, see Fisher, *Shadow Tribe*; Harmon, *Indians in the Making*; Harmon, *Power of Promises*.

34 Smoak, *Ghost Dances*, 18, 19.

35 Knack and Stewart observe, "If some members disagreed with the headman, they could leave, utilize their kinship ties to validate union with another band, and there follow another headman. If enough of the band lost faith in the abilities of an old headman, a new one emerged simply by the group's heeding his opinions and ignoring those of the elder. There were no strong political loyalties to chiefs" (*River Shall Run*, 27).

36 On puha, see Fowler and Liljeblad, "Northern Paiute"; Gualtieri, "Role of Moral Outrage"; Hittman, "1870 Ghost Dance"; Miller, *Prophetic Worlds*; Smoak, *Ghost Dances*.

37 Smoak suggests, "Power is essentially the opposite of sickness, and so the shaman's principal function was the healing rite" (*Ghost Dances*, 53).

38 Smoak, *Ghost Dances*, 57, 58.

39 See ARCIA 1871, 974; ARCIA 1872, 746; Howard, "Report," 211; Howard, *My Life*, 376.

40 As Gualtieri observes, "If a given population did not have its own antelope shaman, it had to travel to a neighboring group that did have such a shaman" ("Role of Moral Outrage," 76), adding, "This individual was also the fulcrum of a large amalgamation of people attending the annual, or even biennial antelope surrounds" (83).

41 Gualtieri, "Role of Moral Outrage," 85.

42 Zanjani, *Sarah Winnemucca*, 9.

43 See Hittman, "1870 Ghost Dance"; Gualtieri, "Role of Moral Outrage," 137, 141, 215–216; Smoak, *Ghost Dances*, 114–115. Canfield observes, "The 'pernicious' fandangos

for which Agent Rinehart had such contempt were held several times yearly. The numerous Paiute chiefs would agree upon a time and place, and often as many as three or four hundred people would assemble" (*Sarah Winnemucca*, 159). For mentions of Paiute "dancing" in the text, see Winnemucca, *Life*, 13, 40, 112.

44   See Howard, *Famous Indian Chiefs*, 265; Howard, *My Life*, 391–392; Smoak, *Ghost Dances*, 143; Stowell, "Wada-Tika," 151; Zanjani, *Sarah Winnemucca*, 132. On the use of the term "dreamer" in the period to refer to adherents of other prophet figures beyond Smohalla, including Wodziwob, see Canfield, *Sarah Winnemucca*, 273; Howard, *My Life*, 376, 418–419.

45   Quoted in Mooney, *Ghost-Dance Religion*, 711. On Smohalla, see Fisher, *Shadow Tribe*, 83–87; Miller, *Prophetic Worlds*, 118–121; Mooney, *Ghost-Dance Religion*, 708–731; Ruby and Brown, *Dreamer-Prophets*, 19–102; Trafzer and Beach, "Smoholla"; Walker and Schuster, "Religious Movements," 501, 505.

46   Zanjani, *Sarah Winnemucca*, 90. See also Carpenter and Sorisio, *Newspaper Warrior*, 18; Zanjani, *Sarah Winnemucca*, 284–286, 295.

47   Cheryl Walker suggests, "Perhaps it was the very amorphousness of Sarah Winnemucca's vision of the nation that kept it from being viable, however. The Paiutes themselves were decentralized . . . , spread out over a vast territory congregating around several different leaders" (*Indian Nation*, 163). However, we might approach the text's account of "the Piute nation" less as Winnemucca's vision than as a (set of) tactical maneuver(s) in relation to extent U.S. political discourses whose aim is to achieve particular aims.

48   The text here is referring to the Mud Lake Massacre in 1865 in which an army captain in search of cattle thieves had his men fire at a Paiute encampment, killing twenty-nine people including Winnemucca's mother and baby brother. See Canfield, *Sarah Winnemucca*, 44–45; Gualtieri, "Role of Moral Outrage," 316–318; Zanjani, *Sarah Winnemucca*, 78–79.

49   ARCIA 1878, 612; ARCIA 1879, 237; Canfield, *Sarah Winnemucca*, 115, 117; Stowell, "Wada-Tika," 188, 199; Zanjani, *Sarah Winnemucca*, 141.

50   Zanjani, *Sarah Winnemucca*, 43.

51   See Knack and Stewart, *River Shall Run*, 45, 134–137.

52   Carpenter and Sorisio, *Newspaper Warrior*, 33, 44, 36.

53   For examples, see Carpenter and Sorisio, *Newspaper Warrior*, 70, 114, 115. During that tour, which lasted through the summer of 1884, Winnemucca gave over three hundred lectures (Zanjani, *Sarah Winnemucca*, 244).

54   Canfield, *Sarah Winnemucca*, 17; ARCIA 1861, 718. See also ARCIA 1862, 359, 367; ARCIA 1864, 289; ARCIA 1870, 567; ARCIA 1873, 624.

55   I use "Yakima" since this is the spelling in the text, but the name the people and the reservation currently use is "Yakama."

56   Howard, *Famous Indian Chiefs*, 207–208, 217.

57   Canfield, *Sarah Winnemucca*, 48.

58   Gualtieri, "Role of Moral Outrage," 80. See also ARCIA 1866, 119; Canfield, *Sarah Winnemucca*, 3, 13, 18, 24, 27–28, 33, 263; Hittman, *Great Basin Indians*, 197; Howard, *Famous Indian Chiefs*, 226; Knack and Stewart, *River Shall Run*, 53. In an article in a Nevada newspaper published in September 1864, Chief Winnemucca

seeks to distance himself from Numaga: "Young Winnemucca is not my son; he says he is, but he is an imposter" (Carpenter and Sorisio, *Newspaper Warrior*, 34).

59 On the end of treaty making, see Bruyneel, *Third Space of Sovereignty*; Genetin-Pilawa, *Crooked Paths*; Prucha, *American Indian Treaties*. The effort by the House of Representatives to end treaty making was led by Henry Dawes, who later served as the sponsor of the General Allotment Act in the Senate (Washburn, *Assault on Indian Tribalism*, 25).

60 Bentley, *Frantic Panoramas*, 175.

61 Carpenter and Sorisio, *Newspaper Warrior*, 51, 64, 162.

62 Kohler, "Send Word," 61. On the text's broader negotiation of Euro-American assumptions about writing and practices of documentation, see also Carpenter, *Seeing Red*, 87–125; Lape, "I Would Rather"; Powell, "Sarah Winnemucca Hopkins"; Tisinger, "Textual Performance."

63 Zanjani, *Sarah Winnemucca*, 250.

64 Canfield, *Sarah Winnemucca*, 214.

65 Canfield, *Sarah Winnemucca*, 167. As Cari Carpenter notes in "Sarah Winnemucca Goes to Washington," "The Northern Paiutes who had been invited to DC by the US government had not been formally elected to represent their nation; Northern Paiute society traditionally consisted of bands, each with a headman, so that little centralized governance existed" (87).

66 Winnemucca, *Life*, 218, 219, 221.

67 Goeman, *Mark My Words*, 2.

68 Sorisio, "Sarah Winnemucca," 45.

69 Carpenter and Sorisio, *Newspaper Warrior*, 115.

70 Brooks, *Common Pot*, xxxv.

71 Powell, "Sarah Winnemucca Hopkins," 80.

72 Carpenter, *Seeing Red*, 108.

73 Howard, *Famous Indian Chiefs*, 208.

74 ARCIA 1864, 285–286; ARCIA 1866, 115.

75 ARCIA 1878, 599.

76 See Winnemucca, *Life*, 158, 160, 163, 170, 189. On Egan's leadership role, see ARCIA 1878, 616; ARCIA 1879, 235; Hittman, *Great Basin Indians*, 62–65; Howard, *Famous Indian Chiefs*, 259–277; Howard, *My Life*, 298–410; Smoak, *Ghost Dances*, 143–149; Zanjani, *Sarah Winnemucca*, 165, 186–187.

77 See Winnemucca, *Life*, 34, 37, 38, 41, 48, 70–72, 116, 244.

78 On the text's emphasis on the Paiutes' goodness, see McClure, "Sarah Winnemucca"; Powell, "Sarah Winnemucca Hopkins"; Sneider, "Gender, Literacy, and Sovereignty"; Walker, *Indian Nation*, 139–163.

79 Andrew Fisher characterizes the Columbia River Indians as a "shadow tribe," describing them as "a group whose boundaries are nebulous and whose members come from dozens of distinct communities" (*Shadow Tribe*, 6).

80 ARCIA 1870, 514. See also ARCIA 1872, 746.

81 ARCIA 1867, 63, 71–72; ARCIA 1871, 721.

82 Howard, "Report," 209.

83 Fisher, *Shadow Tribe*, 9, 63.

84 The disciplining of the peoples Winnemucca addresses tended not to be presented under the rubric of criminal justice. However, the criminalization of Native mobility, social and political orders, and warfare has been a prominent aspect of settler governance in both the United States and Canada. See Blee, *Framing Chief Leschi*; Martínez, "Remembering the Thirty-Eight"; Pasternak, *Grounded Authority*; Rand, *Kiowa Humanity*; Razack, *Dying from Improvement*; Simpson, *Mohawk Interruptus*; Stark, "Criminal Empire."

85 Smoak, *Ghost Dances*, 16, 21, 95–112.

86 ARCIA 1864, 229. See also ARCIA 1866, 114; ARCIA 1872, 447.

87 Stowell, "Wada-Tika," 90.

88 ARCIA 1867, 72–73. See also ARCIA 1863, 167; ARCIA 1864, 228; ARCIA 1872, 746; ARCIA 1875, 578; ARCIA 1877, 568–569; Fowler and Liljeblad, "Northern Paiute," 455–456; Hittman, *Great Basin Indians*, 60–62.

89 Simpson, *Mohawk Interruptus*, 11.

90 Goeman, *Mark My Words*, 12.

91 Estes, *Our History*, 185.

92 Simpson, *Mohawk Interruptus*, 158.

93 ARCIA 1862, 367.

94 See Gualtieri, "Role of Moral Outrage," 154, 180, 187.

95 See Hittman, *Great Basin Indians*, 227–228; Smoak, *Ghost Dances*, 75–78.

96 See ARCIA 1864, 289; Canfield, *Sarah Winnemucca*, 34; Gualtieri, "Role of Moral Outrage," 186, 294–296, 298.

97 In the wake of the Mud Lake Massacre, Chief Winnemucca left the Pyramid Lake region and took up residence in the area around Steens Mountain in southeastern Oregon. He also indicated his hostility toward the United States and may have participated in what has come to be known as the Snake War, a conflict that ran from 1864 to 1868 with a range of peoples in the vicinity of the Snake River. See Canfield, *Sarah Winnemucca*, 44–58; Gualtieri, "Role of Moral Outrage," 316–318; Zanjani, *Sarah Winnemucca*, 78–87.

98 Zanjani, *Sarah Winnemucca*, 112. See also Smoak, *Ghost Dances*, 124.

99 Canfield, *Sarah Winnemucca*, 69.

100 Canfield, *Sarah Winnemucca*, 159.

101 Howard, *My Life*, 376, 379.

102 Smoak, *Ghost Dances*, 118–130, 149.

103 Howard, "Report," 211; Rinehart quoted in Canfield, *Sarah Winnemucca*, 273.

104 Carpenter and Sorisio, *Newspaper Warrior*, 73; Zanjani, *Sarah Winnemucca*, 169.

105 See ARCIA 1879, 235–236; Canfield, *Sarah Winnemucca*, 150–157; Howard, "Report"; Stowell, "Wada-Tika," 232–244; Zanjani, *Sarah Winnemucca*, 186–190. One in five of those Paiutes relocated to Yakima died as a result of the removal (Carpenter and Sorisio, *Newspaper Warrior*, 6–7).

106 Carpenter and Sorisio, *Newspaper Warrior*, 85.

107 Howard, "Report," 214. For discussion of the ways Winnemucca's narrative draws on and revises Howard's official report, see Sorisio, "'I Nailed Those Lies.'"

108 Canfield, *Sarah Winnemucca*, 194. See also Stowell, "Wada-Tika," 244.

109 The letter from Schurz, reprinted in *Life*, includes the following: "The Pi-Utes, here-tofore entitled to live on the Malheur Reservation, their primeval home, are to have lands allotted to them in severalty, at the rate of one hundred and sixty acres to each head of a family"; "Those of the Pi-Utes, who in consequence of the Bannock war, went to the Yakima Reservation, and whoever may desire to rejoin their relatives, are at liberty to do so, without expense to the government for transportation. Those who desire to stay upon the Yakima Reservation and become permanently settled there will not be disturbed" (223–224). By 1884, when the remaining Paiutes at Yakima received official permission to leave, the Paiutes from Malheur largely had left and returned to the relative area from which they had been removed, with offi-cials largely turning a blind eye to this movement. See Canfield, *Sarah Winnemucca*, 214; Stowell, "Wada-Tika," 255; Zanjani, *Sarah Winnemucca*, 224.

110 McClure, "Sarah Winnemucca," 44. Similarly, Leah Sneider observes that Winnemucca "portrays her own people as already similar to idealized European Americans in their displays of civilized goodness; therefore, they should be left alone altogether" ("Gender, Literacy, and Sovereignty," 275).

111 I'm drawing on Chandan Reddy's formulation of "freedom through violence," which he uses to theorize the structural dynamic of contemporary U.S. (neo)liberalism.

112 Karen Kilcup argues for reading the text's mappings of rightful Paiute residence as an argument for environmental justice (*Fallen Forests*, 270–288).

113 On the ongoing seizure of reservation land at Pyramid Lake by whites over the course of the nineteenth century, as well as difficulties in getting official government recognition of the original boundaries of the reservation, see Knack and Stewart, *River Shall Run*.

114 On shifting understandings of the status of the Indian reservation from the mid-nineteenth century onward, see Bruyneel, *Third Space of Sovereignty*; Denetdale, *Re-claiming Diné History*; Fisher, *Shadow Tribe*; Genetin-Pilawa, *Crooked Paths*; Hoxie, *Final Promise*; Ostler, *Plains Sioux*; Piatote, "Indian/Agent Aporia"; Rand, *Kiowa Humanity*; Rockwell, *Indian Affairs*; Trennert, *Alternative to Extinction*; Warren, *God's Red Son*.

115 We might understand this claiming of the reservation as a late-nineteenth-century version of other strategies through which Native peoples have sought to challenge settler notions of Indians' "negative birthright." As Yael Ben-zvi suggests, English legal conceptions of landedness and belonging inherit from feudalism notions of "native"-ness that, in the eighteenth and nineteenth centuries, connote less an inher-ent relation to territory than an inherited status of lacking such standing, gaining ac-cess to place only by grant from a lord. Ideas of "native title," to which Winnemucca in some sense appeals, function less as a "positive birthright in favor of Indigenous peoples" than a particular Indian kind of "negative birthright." See Ben-zvi, *Native Land Talk*, 21–25, 67.

116 In a widely published letter written in 1870 to the commissioner of Indian Affairs, Winnemucca says of herself and her father that "he, myself and the most of the Humboldt and Queens River Indians were on the Truckee reservation at one time, but if we had stayed there it would have been only to starve," adding, "I think that if

they had received what they were entitled to from agents they would never have left there" (Carpenter and Sorisio, *Newspaper Warrior*, 38–39).

117   ARCIA 1869, 644; ARCIA 1870, 558.

118   The report further notes "the utter inadequacy of $15,000 in currency to provide for the Indian service in Nevada, where everything is bought and sold at coin rates." ARCIA 1872, 668–669.

119   ARCIA 1877, 572; ARCIA 1874, 588; ARCIA 1871, 960.

120   ARCIA 1878, 446–447.

121   ARCIA 1875, 852; ARCIA 1878, 613.

122   ARCIA 1875, 852; ARCIA 1879, 237. Attempts to live off reservation in longstanding areas of Native inhabitance were made increasingly difficult by the provisions of homestead laws that allowed for non-native land possession, such as the Oregon Donation Land Act of 1850 which made 320 acres available from the "public domain" to adult male citizens and 640 acres to married couples (Fisher, *Shadow Tribe*, 40).

123   Povinelli, *Labor's Lot*, 8. On pre-reservation Paiute patterns of sociospatiality in southeastern Oregon and Nevada, see Fowler and Liljeblad, "Northern Paiute"; Gualtieri, "Role of Moral Outrage"; Knack and Stewart, *River Shall Run*; Smoak, *Ghost Dances*; Stowell, "Wada-Tika."

124   ARCIA 1872, 453; ARCIA 1862, 397–398; ARCIA 1874, 589; ARCIA 1877, 546; Scott, *Karnee*, 72. As Knack and Stewart note, "The Central Pacific Railroad had granted Indians the privilege of riding ticketless on the roofs and flatbeds of the rail cars," and "Paiutes used the railroad to visit traditional hunting and gathering sites in season," "adapt[ing] the proffered new technology to their mobile lifestyle, which required the utilization of many widely spread resources each in season, much as they had in the old days" (*River Shall Run*, 103). On the crucial role of railroads in U.S. colonial capitalism, see Karuka, *Empire's Tracks*.

125   One Nevada agent complains, "The main difficulty encountered in carrying out the policy of the Government with the Indians of this superintendency is their lack of tribal organization. The Pah-Utes, numbering fully 5,000, are broken up into small bands of individuals, elected by themselves, called 'captains.' These bands act independently of each other. There is no authority to which the 'captains' hold themselves responsible, and through whom the Government can act. Each captain has to be dealt with separately and humored in his whims. These captains possess but little influence over their bands" (ARCIA 1870, 569).

126   Goeman, *Mark My Words*, 5, 36.

127   Pratt, "Wounded Knee."

128   Smoak, *Ghost Dances*, 3.

129   See Canfield, *Sarah Winnemucca*, 214, 256; Carpenter and Sorisio, *Newspaper Warrior*, 13, 207; Stowell, "Wada-Tika," 253–254.

130   Carpenter and Sorisio, *Newspaper Warrior*, 149.

131   Piatote, "Indian/Agent Aporia," 51.

132   ARCIA 1870, 570–571.

133   See Senier, *Voices*, 73–120.

134   Brooks, *Common Pot*, xlii.

Chapter 4. The Native Informant Speaks

1 On *U.S. v. Kagama* (118 U.S. 375 [1886]), see Harring, *Crow Dog's Case*, 142–174; Rifkin, "Indigenizing Agamben"; Wilkins, *American Indian Sovereignty*, 64–117. Although *Lone Wolf v. Hitchcock* (187 U.S. 553 [1903]) is the first case to articulate the notion that Congress exerts "plenary" authority in Indian affairs, the seeds of this doctrine of unlimited power are planted in *Kagama*.

2 *Kagama*, 376.

3 *Kagama*, 383. Here, the Court reformulates the notion of "domestic dependent nations" from *Cherokee Nation v. Georgia* (30 U.S. 1 [1831]). On *Cherokee Nation v. Georgia*, see Garrison, *Legal Ideology of Removal*, 125–150; Norgren, *Cherokee Cases*; Rifkin, *Manifesting America*, 48–53; Wilkins, *American Indian Sovereignty*, 19–63.

4 *Kagama*, 381–382.

5 John Wesley Powell, the first head of the U.S. Bureau of Ethnology (founded in 1879), often praised Morgan's work and made it required reading for people working in the Bureau (Darnell, *And Along Came Boas*, 89). On Morgan's significance and influence, see Ben-Zvi, "Where Did Red Go?"; Carr, *Inventing the American Primitive*, 157–165; Conn, *History's Shadow*; Fortes, *Kinship and Social Order*; Kuper, *Reinvention of Primitive Society*; Simpson, *Mohawk Interruptus*, 67–94; Trautmann, *Lewis Henry Morgan*.

6 Morgan, *Ancient Society*, 61, 104, 122–123, 65, vii.

7 See *Kagama*, 382. This representation of Native peoples' relation to the U.S. government also comes from *Cherokee Nation v. Georgia*.

8 Morgan, "Supplemental Report," 99, 98, 102.

9 On allotment and the boarding school system, see Adams, *Education for Extinction*; Cahill, *Federal Fathers and Mothers*; Child, *Boarding School Seasons*; Genetin-Pilawa, *Crooked Paths*; Hoxie, *Final Promise*; Katanski, *Learning to Write "Indian"*; McDonnell, *Dispossession*; Pfister, *Individuality Incorporated*; Piatote, *Domestic Subjects*; Ruppel, *Unearthing Indian Land*; Washburn, *Assault on Indian Tribalism*.

10 The concepts of "ethnology," "ethnography," and "anthropology" all overlap and intertwine in complex ways during the latter half of the nineteenth century and into the early twentieth century. See Baker, *Anthropology and Racial Politics*, 1–32; Carr, *Inventing the American Primitive*, 147–197; Conn, *History's Shadow*, 154–197; Darnell, *And Along Came Boas*; Gunn, *Ethnology and Empire*; Harvey, *Native Tongues*; Hinsley, *Smithsonian*; Mark, *Stranger*. My aim is less to suggest a clear distinction in the employment of the terms ethnology and ethnography in the period than to suggest the potential for differentiating between the ethnographic description of a contemporary *tribal* collective from the ethnological emplotment of that same group within a prefabricated teleology of human development in order to suggest how the former could be mobilized against the latter.

11 On the work of native informants in (proto-)anthropological projects from the mid-nineteenth through the mid-twentieth centuries, see Bruchac, *Savage Kin*; Cotera, *Native Speakers*; Fawcett, *Medicine Trail*; Mark, *Stranger*; Medicine, *Learning*; Michaelsen, *Limits of Multiculturalism*; Simpson, *Mohawk Interruptus*. In using the phrase "native informant," I'm also alluding to Gayatri Spivak's analysis of this

figure, which inspired much of the analysis here and to which I'll return. See Spivak, *Critique of Postcolonial Reason*.

12 On the emergence of the culture concept, see Baker, *Anthropology and Racial Politics*; Darnell, *And Along Came Boas*; Darnell, *Invisible Genealogies*; Elliott, *Culture Concept*; Evans, *Before Cultures*; Hegeman, *Patterns for America*; Simpson, "Why White People Love"; Visweswaran, *Un/common Cultures*.

13 She married Raymond Bonnin in 1902, but she continued to use the name Zitkala-Ša for her public and authorial persona. Given this choice, I will refer to her as Zitkala-Ša.

14 On "survivance," see Vizenor, *Manifest Manners*. This chapter focuses on Gertrude Simmons's earlier writings, but she continued to be a powerful presence in national discussions on "the Indian question" and in national Native organizations, particularly the Society of American Indians. In this way, she was part of a group of Native intellectuals in the early twentieth century who knew each other, all engaged similar issues, and took part in the same associations. On this cohort, see Ackley and Stanciu, *Laura Cornelius Kellogg*; Maddox, *Citizen Indians*; Vigil, *Indigenous Intellectuals*.

15 Some scholars have presented the autobiographical character of the stories as in contrast with a more genericizing account that would characterize ethnography. See Bernardin, "Sentimental Education," 221; Katanski, *Learning to Write "Indian*," 156–157; Spack, "Re-visioning Sioux Women." However, as I suggest below, her description of what are presented as commonplace events/dynamics in tribal life and her genericizing titles for the stories (use of "an Indian") speak to emergent ethnographic forms, and, in this way, her use of the first person suggests not separateness from ethnography but an authorized voice within it (as native informant).

16 For examples, see Barker, *Native Acts*; Engle, *Elusive Promise*; Lyons, *X-marks*; Povinelli, *Cunning of Recognition*; Simpson, *Mohawk Interruptus*.

17 I should note that in referring to them as "autobiographical stories," I'm less commenting on their genre than indicating that they clearly are patterned on the facts of Gertrude Simmons's life. On the implications of reading these texts as autobiography, see Bernardin, "Sentimental Education"; Carpenter, "Zitkala-Ša"; Cutter, "Zitakla-Sä's Autobiographical Writings"; Katanski, *Learning to Write "Indian*," 128–161; Kelsey, *Tribal Theory*, 62–75; Spack, "Re-visioning Sioux Women"; Totten, "Problem of Regionalism." I will return to the question of genre, specifically the implications of reading the texts as a form of ethnography, later in this section.

18 Macbain, "Cont(r)acting Whiteness," 55; Okker, "Native American Literatures," 90.

19 Burt, "Semblance of Civilization," 59.

20 Evans, *Before Cultures*, 43.

21 Lewandowski, *Red Bird, Red Power*, 37. On the other pieces that appeared alongside Zitkala-Ša's stories in the *Atlantic Monthly* and *Harper's*, see Burt, "Semblance of Civilization"; Chiarello, "Deflected Missives"; Hannon, "Commercial Magazine Apparatus"; Okker, "Native American Literatures"; Wilkinson, "Gertrude Bonnin's Rhetorical Strategies."

22 See Applegarth, *Rhetoric in American Anthropology*; Bentley, *Frantic Panoramas*; Bruchac, *Savage Kin*; Darnell, *And Along Came Boas*; Elliott, *Culture Concept*; Evans, *Before Cultures*; Simonsen, *Making Home Work*; Smith, *Reimagining Indians*.

María Cotera addresses the role of "storytelling practice" in texts authored by ethnographically trained women of color in the early twentieth century (Ella Deloria, Zora Neale Hurston, and Jovita González), noting that such practice "moves beyond the counterdiscursive rhetoric of their ethnographic work" (*Native Speakers*, 21). However, the generic difference between storytelling, as in the narrative style of fiction, and "ethnographic" writing proper does not emerge until the early twentieth century, such that earlier texts readily could function as both.

23 Simpson, *Mohawk Interruptus*, 101–102.Gayatri Spivak suggests, "In order to assume culture we must assume collectivity. Yet usually we assume collectivity on the basis of culture"; "I will call it begging the question, [since] assuming culture at the origin begs the question of collectivity" (*Death of a Discipline*, 27).

24 On the history of "culture" in Indian policy, see Barker, *Native Acts*; Benedict, *Patterns of Culture*; Biolsi, *Organizing the Lakota*; Collier, *Indians of the Americas*; Garroutte, *Real Indians*; Miller, *Forgotten Tribes*; Patterson, *Social History of Anthropology*; Pfister, *Individuality Incorporated*; Rifkin, "Around 1978."

25 Piatote, *Domestic Subjects*, 2.

26 The three stories have an unnamed narrator, and given the pen name of the author, readers likely would have assumed that the speaking subject was Zitkala-Ša herself. Moreover, the stories conform quite closely (although not exactly) to the details of Gertrude Simmons's life, licensing the reading of them as autobiographical. I will shift back and forth from referring to the speaking voice/consciousness of the stories as "the narrator" and as "Zitkala-Ša."

27 Zitkala-Ša, *American Indian Stories*, 68; text references are to pages in this edition.

28 A number of critics have commented on this scene, and I here build on their work. See Cutter, "Zitakla-Sä's Autobiographical Writings," 38; Macbain, "Cont(r)acting Whiteness," 56; Newmark, "Pluralism, Place," 335–336; Spack, "Re-visioning Sioux Women," 31; Totten, "Problem of Regionalism," 101; Wilkinson, "Gertrude Bonnin's Rhetorical Strategies," 45–46.

29 For discussion of why Native parents sought to place their children in boarding schools, see Child, *Boarding School Seasons*.

30 On Yankton history, see DeMallie, "Sioux until 1850" and "Yankton and Yantonai"; Estes, *Our History*; Hoover, *Yankton Sioux*; Lewandowski, *Red Bird, Red Power*; and Sansom-Flood, *Lessons from Chouteau Creek*.

31 In 1870, the Dakota Territory had about twice as many Native people as nonnatives, but by 1880, whites outnumbered Native people by about six to one (Hoxie, *Final Promise*, 43). The treaty, though, occurred long before Zitkala-Ša was born, and the dislocation referred to in the text most directly refers to the move by her mother—Taté I Yóhin Win—back to the vicinity of the Yankton agency in 1874 after the death of her husband, John Simmons (Lewandowski, *Red Bird, Red Power*, 18).

32 I am drawing on the annual reports of the agent to the Yankton Reservation from 1870 to 1900 contained in the Annual Report of the Commissioner of Indian Affairs (ARCIA).

33 ARCIA 1882, 109; ARCIA 1885, 285–286.

34 ARCIA 1885, 286.

35 See ARCIA 1872, 650; ARCIA 1877, 447; ARCIA 1886, 315–316; ARCIA 1888, 72.

36   See ARCIA 1893, 311; Sansom-Flood, *Lessons from Chouteau Creek*, 71–75. Between 1887 and 1900, Native peoples lost 28.5 million acres of reservation lands that had been deemed "surplus." During the whole of the allotment era (from 1887 to 1934), federally recognized Native lands went from 138 million acres to 52 million acres. See McDonnell, *Dispossession*, vii, 8.

37   On the separation of the "social" from the "political" within official interpretations of the scope and character of African American rights in the post-Reconstruction period, in ways that also treat racializing state determinations as if they were entirely extrajuridical qualities/identities, see Hartman, *Scenes of Subjection*.

38   Schuller, *Biopolitics of Feeling*, 7, 12, 21. As Schuller argues, contemporary celebrations of notions of malleability as the progressive opposite to ideas of racial fixity, then, not only do not recognize this earlier process of defining race in terms of impressibility and capacity for change but also overlook how judgments of relative malleability continue to bear within them racializing assumptions. On the ways "culture" as it emerged and circulated in the twentieth century continued to have racializing assumptions embedded within it, see Baker, *Anthropology and Racial Politics*; Barker, *Native Acts*; di Leonardo, *Exotics at Home*; Hegeman, *Patterns for America*; Visweswaran, *Un/common Cultures*; Weheliye, *Habeas Viscus*.

39   As Alexander Weheliye suggests in *Habeas Viscus*, "The differing elements articulated in an assemblage become components only in their relational connectivity with other factors" (46), further indicating, "Racializing assemblages articulate relational intensities between human physiology and flesh, producing racial categories, which are subsequently coded as natural substances" (50–51). Degrees of supposed Indian bloodedness were not used extensively at the federal level as a marker of legal competency or as a threshold for defining who counts as Native until the 1910s. See McDonnell, *Dispossession*; Spruhan, "Legal History"; Thorne, *World's Richest Indian*.

40   Barker, *Native Acts*, 20.

41   If patterns of what might be termed domesticity served largely as the basis for accounts of Indian raciality in the late nineteenth century, such understandings of race as enacted and reproduced through social patterns can be understood as building on earlier conceptions of Native languages as expressions and transmissions of Indian racial identity. See Bieder, *Science Encounters the Indian*; Gunn, *Ethnology and Empire*; Harvey, *Native Tongues*.

42   ARCIA 1881, 118–119; ARCIA 1886, 314.

43   In a letter in 1880, John Wesley Powell explains, "If we are to conduct our Indian affairs wisely and induct our barbaric tribes into the ways and institutions of civilization that the red man may become completely under our government and share in its benefits, the first step to be taken is to acquire a knowledge of the Indian tribal governments, religion, and sociology and industrial organization" (Darnell, *And Along Came Boas*, 37). Moreover, as Michael Elliott suggests, "East Coast based, mostly Protestant 'Friends of the Indian' made accurate observation the cornerstone of their efforts to solve the 'Indian question' and to integrate Native Americans into their version of American citizenship" (*Culture Concept*, 93).

44   The focus on such "domestic" scenes has led some critics to characterize the stories as participating within discourses of sentimentalism. See Bernardin, "Sentimental

Education"; Kelsey, *Tribal Theory*, 62–75; Wexler, "Tender Violence." As Schuller demonstrates, though, sentimentalism depended on notions of bodily affectability that were fundamentally Lamarckian in terms of its characterization of proper modes of sensation/impression, their intergenerational transmission, and attendant possibilities for producing durable social change. In the late nineteenth century, then, the ethnographic and the sentimental are adjacent and sometimes intersecting modes for addressing inheritance and heritability (Schuller, *Biopolitics of Feeling*). On the ways ethnographic accounts of Native peoples provided varied ways of addressing the "the woman question" in the period, see Carr, *Inventing the American Primitive*, 147–196; Simonsen, *Making Home Work*; Visweswaran, *Un/common Cultures*, 18–51.

45 One might read these stories as enacting what Christopher Pexa has termed "unheroic decolonization": "to seem utterly harmless to settler audiences while actually working to decolonize and rebuild Indigenous communities" (*Translated Nation*, 148).

46 While Zitkala-Ša likely would not have read the annual reports of the Yankton agent, I draw on them as a way of specifying the particular kinds of administrative discourses and frameworks at play on the Yankton Reservation, with which she would have been quite familiar, and these reports also express ideological tendencies and formulations at play in more widely circulated expressions of Indian policy.

47 ARCIA 1885, 283.

48 ARCIA 1885, 288. Native children's attendance at Anglo-run schools becomes legally mandated by congressional statute in 1891 (Child, *Boarding School Seasons*, 13).

49 ARCIA 1887, 143; ARCIA 1888, 65.

50 ARCIA 1891, 426.

51 ARCIA 1879, 157; ARCIA 1884, 106–107.

52 While a number of other Native writers in the early twentieth century also could be understood as working within an ethnographic idiom, broadly construed, including Charles Eastman and Luther Standing Bear, other Native intellectuals positioned themselves in the vein of Progressive reformers. See Ackley and Stanciu, *Laura Cornelius Kellogg*; Maddox, *Citizen Indians*; Porter, *To Be Indian*; Vigil, *Indigenous Intellectuals*.

53 Elliott, *Culture Concept*, 123.

54 La Flesche's memoir of his time in the boarding school on the Omaha Reservation, *The Middle Five*, also was published in 1900, but after Zitkala-Ša's stories in the *Atlantic Monthly*.

55 Bruchac, *Savage Kin*, 9, 17. Bruchac, though, powerfully illustrates how Native participants in anthropological projects "were not just naïve victims; they were arguably co-creators of the Americanist school of anthropology" (19), and her intensive archival work also reveals the numerous, unpublished texts generated by those who heretofore have been understood solely as "informants," rather than as writers in their own right. For an example, see also Fawcett, *Medicine Trail*.

56 See Carpenter, "Zitkala-Ša"; Cutter, "Zitakla-Sä's Autobiographical Writings"; Katanski, *Learning to Write "Indian*," 128–161; Lewandowski, *Red Bird, Red Power*, 40–42; Spack, "Re-visioning Sioux Women"; Totten, "Problem of Regionalism"; Velikova, "Troping"; Wexler, "Tender Violence."

57 Spivak, *Critique of Postcolonial Reason*, 118.

58 On the "tribal real," see Vizenor, *Manifest Manners*.

59 As Penelope Myrtle Kelsey argues, "by centering her narrative around domestic issues of home and family, Bonnin intentionally places her autobiography within a larger discussion about Dakota nationhood" (*Tribal Theory*, 66–67).

60 See Carpenter, "Zitkala-Ša"; Wilkinson, "Gertrude Bonnin's Rhetorical Strategies."

61 The tiospaye was the basis of Yankton, and other Dakota and Lakota, residency patterns. It comprised a shifting number of blood and other relatives. A variable number of tiospaye, themselves linked by more distant kinship ties, would combine to form a camp circle with its own council, whose rule for the most part was by persuasion rather than coercion. In this way, belonging to the camp circle as a geopolitical entity was defined by kinship. See Deloria, *Speaking of Indians*; DeMallie, "Kinship and Biology" and "Sioux until 1850"; Estes, *Our History*; Hoover, *Yankton Sioux*; Pexa, *Translated Nation*. On Zitkala-Ša's portrayal of the tiospaye, see Kelsey, *Tribal Theory*, 62–75.

62 ARCIA 1878, 544; ARCIA 1887, 138. The recurrent charges that Indians were lazy or that they did not want to do labor also had to do with agents' assumptions about the gendered division of labor. The expectation that men should be the principal ones engaging in agriculture did not fit with extant practices of subsistence for many peoples. Zitkala-Ša describes her mother and aunt's ordinary work in the fields in ways that would have been either invisible to white agents or characterized as a barbarous imposition of *drudgery* by Native men. See Zitkala-Ša, *American Indian Stories*, 81–82. As Ruth Spack suggests, "The women's farm work is described in idyllic terms" ("Re-visioning Sioux Women," 29).

63 ARCIA 1887, 140. As Herbert T. Hoover observes, "Federal officials were particularly eager to suppress giveaways because the sharing of property in this way was so contrary to the principles of capitalism that they were trying to instill in the Indians" (*Yankton Sioux*, 36), adding, "The decision to settle the Yanktons on scattered housing was a strategic ploy designed to isolate them from relatives and traditions. Families were separated, removed from village communities, and unable to participate in special events and religious ceremonies" (40).

64 Yankton agents also forbid travel to visit people on other reservations, except in rare circumstances, and they went so far as to punish those who did so without permission by denying them rations. See ARCIA 1877, 446; ARCIA 1886, 312.

65 ARCIA 1886, 317.

66 ARCIA 1887, 142.

67 Katanski, *Learning to Write "Indian,"* 94–95; Lewandowski, *Red Bird, Red Power*, 44.

68 Elliott, *Culture Concept*, 97, 131. As Steven Conn suggests, "History . . . vanished from the new ethnography," "just as individual natives stood for entire groups, in ethnographic writing a particular moment in time came to stand for an entire society's history" (*History's Shadow*, 164), and Elliott notes, "Several anthropologists—including [Frank Hamilton] Cushing, [John Wesley] Powell, and Alice Fletcher—openly supported the reformers' agenda of Americanization" (*Culture Concept*, 97), including the sense of a teleological process of human development culminating in Euro-American civilization. Moreover, Powell and particularly Fletcher directly participated in

advocating the adoption of the allotment policy and actively supported the boarding school system. See Carr, *Inventing the American Primitive*, 163–165, 174–185; Mark, *Stranger*, 70–101, 104–122, 194–195; Washburn, *Assault on Indian Tribalism*, 10–12.

69 Elliott, *Culture Concept*, 122. On determinations of authenticity in late-nineteenth-century ethnography, see Baker, *Anthropology and Racial Politics*, 66–116.

70 The development of what would come to known as the "culture concept" involved notions of historical diffusion, tracing how languages, stories, practices, forms of material culture, and beliefs moved among groups over time as they engaged with each other, but for Native peoples, (proto-)anthropologists approached diffusion largely in terms of pre–Euro-contact relations, with Euro-American social forms being understood as contamination or a fall from a more authentic tribal past. On the importance of diffusionism to notions of what would become "culture," see Darnell, *Invisible Genealogies*; Evans, *Before Cultures*; Hegeman, *Patterns for America*.

71 For examples, see Baker, *Anthropology and Racial Politics*, 68, 100–102; Elliott, *Culture Concept*, 98–99; Hoxie, *Final Promise*, 88–90; Kasson, *Buffalo Bill's Wild West*, 218.

72 On the relationship between an ethnographic imaginary (in which attending to details of everyday life reveal forms of group difference) and forms of mass spectacle in the late nineteenth century, see Baker, *Anthropology and Racial Politics*, 66–116; Bentley, *Frantic Panoramas*; Elliott, *Culture Concept*; Evans, *Before Cultures*; Hutchinson, *Indian Craze*; Trachtenberg, *Shades of Hiawatha*.

73 Quoted in Katanski, *Learning to Write "Indian,"* 98–99.

74 Carpenter, "Zitkala-Ša," 4.

75 On the ways Indianness circulated in ethnographic depictions as a commodity to be consumed, particularly within magazines with a national circulation, see Burt, "Semblance of Civilization"; Evans, *Before Cultures*, 24–50. On the broader "Indian craze" in the late nineteenth and early twentieth centuries, see Hutchinson, *Indian Craze*.

76 On Indianness as a means of figuring the antimodern, see Bederman, *Manliness and Civilization*; Carr, *Inventing the American Primitive*; Deloria, *Playing Indian*; Huhndorf, *Going Native*; Pfister, *Individuality Incorporated*; Smith, *Reimagining Indians*; Trachtenberg, *Shades of Hiawatha*.

77 Burt, "Semblance of Civilization," 63, 71. For discussion of Zitkala-Ša as playing Indian, see also Carpenter, "Detecting Indianness"; Vigil, *Indigenous Intellectuals*, 196–204.

78 Here I am drawing on Nancy Bentley's argument about post-diplomatic modes of Native speech. See Bentley, *Frantic Panoramas*, 151–187.

79 As Gary Totten suggests, "The first section of her autobiography epitomizes the freedom and self-determination she experiences on the plains" ("Problem of Regionalism," 100).

80 *Kagama*, 381; ARCIA 1886, 314.

81 Kasson, *Buffalo Bill's Wild West*, 5.

82 With respect to why Native people would be interested in participating in such shows, Kasson observes, "They found that touring as performers with the Wild West was an occupation at least as rewarding as the agency-enforced life in subsistence agriculture" (*Buffalo Bill's Wild West*, 184), later adding, "American Indians had complex motives for choosing to work for Buffalo Bill, including the desire to travel and earn money, the pleasures of riding and racing, the choice of a lesser evil as compared

to the grim life of the reservation or, in the case of the Wounded Knee prisoners, jail" as well as "preserving their culture, securing leadership and status, even perpetuating spiritual traditions" (211). See also Raibmon, *Authentic Indians*, 34–73.

83 Lewandowski, *Red Bird, Red Power*, 34. On Käsebier's photographs of Buffalo Bill's performers, see Hutchinson, *Indian Craze*, 131–170; Kasson, *Buffalo Bill's Wild West*, 203–209.

84 Lewandowski, *Red Bird, Red Power*, 37.

85 Baker, *Anthropology and Racial Politics*, 90; Kasson, *Buffalo Bill's Wild West*, 99.

86 Baker, *Anthropology and Racial Politics*, 93. Baker adds, "The fluidity of science and entertainment at the fair was not lost on some Lakota performers who apparently performed for both Putnam and Cody" (94).

87 Bentley, *Frantic Panoramas*, 81–82.

88 Elliott, *Culture Concept*, xxi.

89 Quoted in Baker, *Anthropology and Racial Politics*, 101–102. With respect to whether Indian agents should grant permission for Native performers to participate in such shows, Bentley notes, "For the commissioner [of Indian Affairs], the shows were a regressive retreat, a lapse into 'old ways' that allowed Indians to escape from the real 'battle of life'" (*Frantic Panoramas*, 178).

90 On these moments, see Bernardin, "Sentimental Education"; Hannon, "Commercial Magazine Apparatus"; Macbain, "Cont(r)acting Whiteness." On Native people working in the Indian Service, particularly in its schools, see Cahill, *Federal Fathers and Mothers*.

91 Bernardin, "Sentimental Education," 222. See also Spack, "Re-visioning Sioux Women," 25.

92 Lewandowski, *Red Bird, Red Power*, 40; Carpenter, "Zitkala-Ša," 9–10.

93 Bentley, *Frantic Panoramas*, 179–180.

94 As Elliott suggests, "If ethnography gave these authors a vocabulary for describing that experience to non-Native readers, it also forced them to become aware of how the culture concept more often treated Native Americans as scientific objects than as historical agents" (*Culture Concept*, 127).

95 Dawée is described as actually the narrator's "cousin," even though he "persisted in calling me his baby sister" (99), but he is patterned after Gertrude Simmons's brother David who attended Santee Normal Training School for a year and then Hampton Institute for three years, from 1877–1880 (Lewandowski, *Red Bird, Red Power*, 18).

96 Bentley, *Frantic Panoramas*, 151.

97 Baker, *Anthropology and Racial Politics*, 115.

98 As Scott Michaelsen suggests, however, an anthropological analytic, one based on the distinctness of different cultures, aims "to attend to the other according to its own terms—that is, to make a space for the other in the world, to record and account for its differences. And yet, anthropology inevitably domesticates alterity" (*Limits of Multiculturalism*, xxvii). It does so, he suggests, by creating the sense of "absolute gulfs" between cultural formations (87), especially those attributed to Euro-Americans and Natives, and in this way, difference hardens into a notion of insulated wholeness in which relations among "cultures" or possibilities for historical change become harder to imagine, particularly for nonwestern peoples.

99 Spivak, *Critique of Postcolonial Reason*, 259.

100 Spivak, *Critique of Postcolonial Reason*, 146.

101 Spivak, *Critique of Postcolonial Reason*, 238.

102 On this imagery, see Carpenter, "Zitkala-Ša," 8; Cutter, "Zitakla-Sä's Autobiographical Writings"; Katanski, *Learning to Write "Indian,"* 119; Kunce, "Fire of Eden"; Okker, "Native American Literatures," 95; Velikova, "Troping."

103 The reference to red apples, though, also can allude to the notion of being as "American as apple pie" and to the legend of Johnny Appleseed. Thanks to Beth Piatote for noting these connections.

104 Velikova, "Troping," 55.

105 Morgan, "Supplemental Report," 102.

106 As Amelia Katanski observes, "Zitkala-Ša never lived the 'before' picture, so crucial to the schools' construction of themselves as institutions of transformation," later adding, "Although she and her family have adapted elements of European American culture into their lives, they have not simultaneously discarded Yankton or 'Indian' cultural markers and values" (*Learning to Write "Indian,"* 116, 155).

107 Ron Carpenter notes the "economic goods that sustain Zitkala-Ša's family," including the coffee pot, the canvas from which her mother's wigwam is made, the log cabin into which her mother moves, curtains and tablecloths as well as the marbles Zitkala-Ša gets from a missionary ("Zitkala-Ša," 4–5). However, he characterizes such changes in Yankton material culture as a sign of becoming "bicultural" in ways that cast Yankton "culture" as static.

108 On this dynamic, see Baker, *Anthropology and Racial Politics*; Cotera, *Native Speakers*; Hinsley, *Smithsonian*; Simpson, "Why White People Love."

109 See Barker, *Native Acts*; Deloria, *Indians in Unexpected Places*; Engle, *Elusive Promise*; O'Brien, *Firsting and Lasting*; Raibmon, *Authentic Indians*; Simpson, *Mohawk Interruptus*.

110 See Kelsey, *Tribal Theory*, 69–70; Totten, "Problem of Regionalism," 104.

111 See ARCIA 1873, 605; ARCIA 1878, 544; ARCIA 1883, 111. Article 10 of the treaty of 1858, which determined the boundaries of the reservation, though, does state that the secretary of the interior has the authority to survey the reservation and apportion it as farms for individual families and single persons (Kappler, *Indian Affairs*, 2:779).

112 As Herbert T. Hoover notes, "Families that had prospered on assignments before 1887 refused to give up their cabins and improvements as agents assigned other names to their tracts of land. As a compromise, officials divided many allotments into two parcels of land: one consisting of a homestead in the valley, and the second of productive farmland without buildings up on the prairie" (*Yankton Sioux*, 39).

113 ARCIA 1891, 428. The allotment of the Yankton Reservation also involved the assignment of unusable lands in the hills, assignment of lands to those who were not legitimate claimants, and preferential assignments (in location and illegal amounts) to the wives and children of white men (McDonnell, *Dispossession*, 20).

114 ARCIA 1893, 311. Those "surplus" lands were actually opened for white settlement in 1895 (ARCIA 1895, 305).

115 ARCIA 1882, 109; ARCIA 1885, 285–286.

116 ARCIA 1874, 353; ARCIA 1875, 757.

117 For examples of such language, see ARCIA 1884, 104; ARCIA 1887, 140.

118 ARCIA 1887, 141.

119 ARCIA 1871, 933; ARCIA 1877, 446; ARCIA 1885, 288; ARCIA 1886, 312; ARCIA 1888, 70. The threat of starvation given the scope of government rations is so bad, that at one point, when speaking about mortality figures on the reservation, one of the agents notes, "Many Indians carefully conceal the deaths of their children, as when ascertained there is one less in the family to draw rations" (ARCIA 1884, 107).

120 Deloria, *Speaking of Indians*, 152–153.

121 As Laura Cornelius Kellogg (an Oneida intellectual and activist, a contemporary of Gertrude Bonnin's) argues in *Our Democracy and the American Indian* (1920), "The Carlisle point of view is to break up the Indian reservation—because of the environment. There is no reckoning made as to the loss in this step on the economic side": "The dismemberment of the Indian domain puts the Indian out into the labor world of the white man, landless" (Ackley and Stanciu, *Laura Cornelius Kellogg*, 85).

122 On survivance, see Vizenor, *Manifest Manners*.

123 ARCIA 1888, 69. See also ARCIA 1887, 141.

124 ARCIA 1890, 70; ARCIA 1897, 282.

125 ARCIA 1892, 191; ARCIA 1894, 303–304.

126 On Zitkala-Ša's use of silence in these stories, see Wilkinson, "Gertrude Bonnin's Rhetorical Strategies."

127 On the "affordances" of particular forms, see Levine, *Forms*.

Coda. On Refusing the Ethnographic Imaginary

1 The title draws on Audra Simpson's essay "On Ethnographic Refusal." When discussing her articulation of refusal as an analytic, though, I draw on her book *Mohawk Interruptus*, where the ideas and formulations from the essay have been revised and expanded.

2 See Rifkin, *Fictions of Land and Flesh*.

3 Melamed, *Represent and Destroy*, xvi, 15, 115, 15.

4 Ferguson, *Reorder of Things*, 189. For an excellent sociological discussion of how multiculturalism actually was implemented in English departments in the United States, see Bryson, *Making Multiculturalism*.

5 See Simpson, "Why White People Love." I should note, though, that when using the term "ethnographic" I'm talking about a particular mode of relating to and portraying Native peoples, rather than seeking to condemn tout court ethnographic methodologies used in the discipline of anthropology currently. For examples of excellent work by Indigenous ethnographers, on which I have drawn both in this study and elsewhere, see Carroll, *Roots of Our Renewal*; Dennison, *Colonial Entanglement*; Simpson, *Mohawk Interruptus*; Sturm, *Blood Politics*; TallBear, *Native American DNA*.

6 Spivak, *Critique of Postcolonial Reason*, 118.

7 Craig Womack warns of this tendency, in which "the supposed rationality of criticism has been associated with the act of ethnography itself, as if criticism were a synonym for anthropology" (*Art as Performance*, 50).

8   Brooks, *Common Pot*, xlii.

9   Womack, *Red on Red*, 6, 2.

10 Simpson, *Mohawk Interruptus*, 11, 24, 128.

11 Simpson, *Mohawk Interruptus*, 158, 159.

12 Spivak, *Death of a Discipline*, 26, 27.

13 Spivak, *Death of a Discipline*, 58, 70.

14 Spivak, *Death of a Discipline*, 91.

15 To clarify, by "undecidable" I do not mean that Indigenous political form can *never* be known or that it is inherently amorphous, but rather suggest it should not be posited beforehand outside of the contexts of its articulation, negotiation, and materialization in specific practices and formations. For a similar discussion of the concept of "sovereignty," see Barker, "For Whom Sovereignty Matters."

16 Goeman, *Mark My Words*, 12, 34, 3, 6.

17 Here, I'm also thinking of Craig Womack's reminder that "we might tell stories about the stories," particularly in terms of tensions and difficulties within Native nations (*Art as Performance*, 99).

18 Simpson, *Mohawk Interruptus*, 72; Coulthard, *Red Skin, White Masks*, 149. Similarly, as Nick Estes suggests, "By drawing upon earlier struggles and incorporating elements of them into their own experience, each generation continues to build dynamic and vital traditions of resistance. Such collective experiences build up over time and are grounded in specific Indigenous territories and nations" (*Our History*, 21).

19 Ferguson, *Reorder of Things*, 108, 230.

20 Carroll, *Roots of Our Renewal*, 173; Dennison, *Colonial Entanglement*, 10. Here, I'm also thinking of the ways Shiri Pasternak's work refigures the meanings of "jurisdiction" in order to open up possibilities for envisioning Indigenous governance (as well as marking the ways settler governance seeks to erode and replace Indigenous political forms). See Pasternak, *Grounded Authority*.

21 Guha, "On Some Aspects," 39. Here we might also note Spivak's running caution about confusing the perspectives/frames of postcolonial migrants with the situated understandings and analyses of subaltern populations in the countries from which migrants have emigrated. For sustained consideration of this difference as it works out in contemporary political mappings and representations, see Spivak, *Other Asias*.

22 Dennison, *Colonial Entanglement*, 89.

23 Warrior, "Native Critics," 209.

24 Estes, *Our History*, 6, 251.

25 See Goeman, *Mark My Words*; Huhndorf, *Mapping the Americas*.

26 See Allen, *Blood Narrative*; Anaya, *Indigenous Peoples*; Charters and Stavenhagen, *Making the Declaration Work*; Clech Lâm, *Edge of the State*; Engle, *Elusive Promise*; Estes, *Our History*; Niezen, *Origins of Indigenism*. On Indigenous internationalism and/or transnationalism, see also Lyons, *The World*; McGlennen, *Creative Alliances*.

27 For discussions of various anticolonial (re)framings of internationalism in the twentieth and twenty-first centuries, see also Bonilla, *Non-Sovereign Futures*; Getachew, *Worldmaking after Empire*; Manela, *Wilsonian Moment*; Wilder, *Freedom Time*.

28 Allen, *Trans-Indigenous*, xxvii, 136.

Bibliography

Ackley, Kristina, and Cristina Stanciu, eds. *Laura Cornelius Kellogg:* Our Democracy and the American Indian *and Other Works.* Syracuse, NY: Syracuse University Press, 2015.

Adams, David Wallace. *Education for Extinction: American Indians and the Boarding School Experience, 1875–1928.* Lawrence: University Press of Kansas, 1995.

Adams, Mikaëla M. *Who Belongs? Race, Resources, and Tribal Citizenship in the Native South.* New York: Oxford University Press, 2016.

Adorno, Theodor W. *Negative Dialectics* (1966). Translated by E. B. Ashton (1973). New York: Continuum, 1987.

Ahmed, Sara. *Queer Phenomenology: Orientations, Objects, Others.* Durham, NC: Duke University Press, 2006.

Allen, Chadwick. *Blood Narrative: Indigenous Identity in American Indian and Maori Literary and Activist Texts.* Durham, NC: Duke University Press, 2002.

Allen, Chadwick. "Postcolonial Theory and the Discourse of Treaties." *American Quarterly* 52, no. 1 (2000): 59–89.

Allen, Chadwick. *Trans-Indigenous: Methodologies for Global Native Literary Studies.* Minneapolis: University of Minnesota Press, 2012.

Anaya, S. James. *Indigenous Peoples in International Law.* New York: Oxford University Press, 1996.

Andersen, Chris. "From Difference to Density." *Cultural Studies Review* 15, no. 2 (2009): 80–100.

Andersen, Chris. *"Métis": Race, Recognition, and the Struggle for Indigenous Peoplehood.* Vancouver: University of British Columbia Press, 2014.

Anderson, Gary Clayton. *The Indian Southwest, 1580–1830: Ethnogenesis and Reinvention.* Norman: University of Oklahoma Press, 1999.

Andrew, John A., III. *From Revivals to Removal: Jeremiah Evarts, the Cherokee Nation, and the Search for the Soul of America.* Athens: University of Georgia Press, 1992.

Annual Report of the Commissioner of Indian Affairs. 1117 S.exdoc. Washington, DC: Government Printing Office, 1861.

Annual Report of the Commissioner of Indian Affairs. 1157 H.exdoc. Washington, DC: Government Printing Office, 1862.

Annual Report of the Commissioner of Indian Affairs. 1182 H.exdoc. Washington, DC: Government Printing Office, 1863.

Annual Report of the Commissioner of Indian Affairs. 1220 H.exdoc. Washington, DC: Government Printing Office, 1864.

Annual Report of the Commissioner of Indian Affairs. 1284 H.exdoc. Washington, DC: Government Printing Office, 1866.

Annual Report of the Commissioner of Indian Affairs. 1326 H.exdoc. Washington, DC: Government Printing Office, 1867.

Annual Report of the Commissioner of Indian Affairs. 1414 H.exdoc. Washington, DC: Government Printing Office, 1869.

Annual Report of the Commissioner of Indian Affairs. 1449 H.exdoc. Washington, DC: Government Printing Office, 1870.

Annual Report of the Commissioner of Indian Affairs. 1505 H.exdoc. Washington, DC: Government Printing Office, 1871.

Annual Report of the Commissioner of Indian Affairs. 1560 H.exdoc. Washington, DC: Government Printing Office, 1872.

Annual Report of the Commissioner of Indian Affairs. 1601 H.exdoc. Washington, DC: Government Printing Office, 1873.

Annual Report of the Commissioner of Indian Affairs. 1639 H.exdoc. Washington, DC: Government Printing Office, 1874.

Annual Report of the Commissioner of Indian Affairs. 1680 H.exdoc. Washington, DC: Government Printing Office, 1875.

Annual Report of the Commissioner of Indian Affairs. 1800 H.exdoc. Washington, DC: Government Printing Office, 1877.

Annual Report of the Commissioner of Indian Affairs. 1850 H.exdoc. Washington, DC: Government Printing Office, 1878.

Annual Report of the Commissioner of Indian Affairs. 1910 H.exdoc. Washington, DC: Government Printing Office, 1879.

Annual Report of the Commissioner of Indian Affairs. 2018 H.exdoc. Washington, DC: Government Printing Office, 1881.

Annual Report of the Commissioner of Indian Affairs. 2100 H.exdoc. Washington, DC: Government Printing Office, 1882.

Annual Report of the Commissioner of Indian Affairs. 2191 H.exdoc. Washington, DC: Government Printing Office, 1883.

Annual Report of the Commissioner of Indian Affairs. 2287 H.exdoc. Washington, DC: Government Printing Office, 1884.

Annual Report of the Commissioner of Indian Affairs. 2379 H.exdoc. Washington, DC: Government Printing Office, 1885.

Annual Report of the Commissioner of Indian Affairs. 2467 H.exdoc. Washington, DC: Government Printing Office, 1886.

Annual Report of the Commissioner of Indian Affairs. 2542 H.exdoc. Washington, DC: Government Printing Office, 1887.

Annual Report of the Commissioner of Indian Affairs. 2637 H.exdoc. Washington, DC: Government Printing Office, 1888.

Annual Report of the Commissioner of Indian Affairs. 2841 H.exdoc. Washington, DC: Government Printing Office, 1890.

Annual Report of the Commissioner of Indian Affairs. 2934 H.exdoc. Washington, DC: Government Printing Office, 1891.

Annual Report of the Commissioner of Indian Affairs. 3088 H.exdoc. Washington, DC: Government Printing Office, 1892.

Annual Report of the Commissioner of Indian Affairs. 3210 H.exdoc. Washington, DC: Government Printing Office, 1893.

Annual Report of the Commissioner of Indian Affairs. 3306 H.exdoc. Washington, DC: Government Printing Office, 1894.

Annual Report of the Commissioner of Indian Affairs. 3382 H.doc. Washington, DC: Government Printing Office, 1895.

Annual Report of the Commissioner of Indian Affairs. 3641 H.doc. Washington, DC: Government Printing Office, 1897.

Apess, William. *Eulogy on King Philip, as Pronounced at the Odeon, in Federal Street, Boston* (1836). In *A Son of the Forest and Other Writings*, edited by Barry O'Connell, 103–138. Amherst: University of Massachusetts Press, 1997.

Apess, William. *The Experiences of Five Christian Indians of the Pequot Tribe* (1833). In *A Son of the Forest and Other Writings*, edited by Barry O'Connell, 57–102. Amherst: University of Massachusetts Press, 1997.

Apess, William. *Indian Nullification of the Unconstitutional Laws of Massachusetts Relative to the Marshpee Tribe; or, The Pretended Riot Explained* (1835). In *On Our Own Ground: The Complete Writings of William Apess, a Pequot*, edited by Barry O'Connell, 163–274. Amherst: University of Massachusetts Press, 1992.

Apess, William. *A Son of the Forest* (1831). In *A Son of the Forest and Other Writings*, edited by Barry O'Connell, 1–56. Amherst: University of Massachusetts Press, 1997.

Apess, William. *A Son of the Forest: The Experience of William Apes, A Native of the Forest, Comprising a Notice of the Pequod Tribe of Indians. Written by Himself.* New York: published by author, 1829.

Applegarth, Risa. *Rhetoric in American Anthropology: Gender, Genre, and Science.* Pittsburgh: University of Pittsburgh Press, 2014.

Arneil, Barbara. *John Locke and America: The Defence of English Colonialism.* Oxford: Clarendon Press, 1996.

Baker, Lee D. *Anthropology and the Racial Politics of Culture.* Durham, NC: Duke University Press, 2010.

Barker, Joanne. "For Whom Sovereignty Matters." In *Sovereignty Matters: Locations of Contestation and Possibility in Indigenous Struggles for Self-Determination*, edited by Joanne Barker, 1–32. Lincoln: University of Nebraska Press, 2005.

Barker, Joanne. *Native Acts: Law, Recognition, and Cultural Authenticity.* Durham, NC: Duke University Press, 2011.

Barker, Joanne. "Territory as Analytic: The Dispossession of Lenapehoking and the Subprime Crisis." *Social Text* 36, no. 2 (2018): 19–39.

Basch, Norma. *In the Eyes of the Law: Women, Marriage, and Property in Nineteenth-Century New York.* Ithaca, NY: Cornell University Press, 1982.

Bayers, Peter L. "William Apess's Manhood and the Native Resistance in Jacksonian America." *MELUS* 31, no. 1 (2006): 123–146.

Bederman, Gail. *Manliness and Civilization: A Cultural History of Gender and Race in the United States, 1880–1917.* Chicago: University of Chicago Press, 1995.

Bellin, Joshua David. *Demon of the Continent: Indians and the Shaping of American Literature.* Philadelphia: University of Pennsylvania Press, 2001.

Benedict, Ruth. *Patterns of Culture* (1934). Boston: Houghton Mifflin Company, 2005.

Bentley, Nancy. *Frantic Panoramas: American Literature and Mass Culture, 1870–1920*. Philadelphia: University of Pennsylvania Press, 2009.

Ben-zvi, Yael. *Native Land Talk: Colliding Birthrights in Early US Culture*. Lebanon, NH: University Press of New England, 2018.

Ben-zvi, Yael. "Where Did Red Go? Lewis Henry Morgan's Evolutionary Inheritance and U.S. Racial Imagination." *CR: The New Centennial Review* 7, no. 2 (2007): 201–229.

Bergland, Renée L. *The National Uncanny: Indian Ghosts and American Subjects*. Hanover, NH: University Press of New England, 2000.

Berlant, Lauren. *Cruel Optimism*. Durham, NC: Duke University Press, 2011.

Bernardin, Susan. "The Lessons of a Sentimental Education: Zitkala-Ša's Autobiographical Narratives." *Western American Literature* 32, no. 3 (1997): 213–238.

Beverley, John. *Subalternity and Representation: Arguments in Cultural Theory*. Durham, NC: Duke University Press, 1999.

Bieder, Robert E. *Science Encounters the Indian, 1820–1880: The Early Years of American Ethnology*. Norman: University of Oklahoma Press, 1986.

Biolsi, Thomas. *Organizing the Lakota: The Political Economy of the New Deal on the Pine Ridge and Rosebud Reservations*. Tucson: University of Arizona Press, 1992.

Bird, F. W., Whiting Griswold, and Cyrus Weekes. *Report of the Commissioners Relating to the Conditions of the Indians in Massachusetts*. Boston: Massachusetts General Court, 1849.

Blee, Lisa. *Framing Chief Leschi: Narratives and the Politics of Historical Justice*. Chapel Hill: University of North Carolina Press, 2013.

Bonilla, Yarimar. *Non-Sovereign Futures: French Caribbean Politics in the Wake of Disenchantment*. Chicago: University of Chicago Press, 2015.

Borrows, John. *Freedom and Indigenous Constitutionalism*. Toronto: University of Toronto Press, 2016.

Boudinot, Elias. "An Address to the Whites." In *Cherokee Editor: The Writings of Elias Boudinot*, edited by Theda Perdue, 65–84. Athens: University of Georgia Press, 1996.

Boudinot, Elias. *Letters and Other Papers Relating to Cherokee Affairs: Being a Reply to Sundry Publications Authorized by John Ross* (1837). In *Cherokee Editor: The Writings of Elias Boudinot*, edited by Theda Perdue, 155–234. Athens: University of Georgia Press, 1996.

Boulware, Tyler. *Deconstructing the Cherokee Nation: Town, Region, and Nation among Eighteenth-Century Cherokees*. Gainesville: University Press of Florida, 2011.

Bowes, John P. *Land Too Good for Indians: Northern Indian Removal*. Norman: University of Oklahoma Press, 2016.

Boydston, Jeanne. *Home and Work: Housework, Wages, and the Ideology of Labor in the Early Republic*. New York: Oxford University Press, 1990.

Bragdon, Kathleen J. *Native People of Southern New England, 1500–1650*. Norman: University of Oklahoma Press, 1996.

Brooks, Lisa. *The Common Pot: The Recovery of Native Space in the Northeast*. Minneapolis: University of Minnesota Press, 2008.

Brooks, Lisa. *Our Beloved Kin: A New History of King Philip's War*. New Haven, CT: Yale University Press, 2018.

Bruchac, Margaret M. "Hill Town Touchstone: Reconsidering William Apess and Colrain, Massachusetts." *Early American Studies* 14, no. 4 (2016): 712–748.

Bruchac, Margaret M. *Savage Kin: Indigenous Informants and American Anthropologists.* Tucson: University of Arizona Press, 2018.

Bruyneel, Kevin. *The Third Space of Sovereignty: The Postcolonial Politics of U.S.- Indigenous Relations.* Minneapolis: University of Minnesota Press, 1997.

Bryson, Bethany. *Making Multiculturalism: Boundaries and Meaning in U.S. English Departments.* Stanford, CA: Stanford University Press, 2005.

Burnham, Michelle. *Captivity and Sentiment: Cultural Exchange in American Literature, 1682–1861.* Hanover, NH: Dartmouth College, 1997.

Burt, Ryan. "'Death Beneath this Semblance of Civilization': Reading Zitkala-Sa and the Imperial Imagination of the Romantic Revival." *Arizona Quarterly* 66, no. 2 (2010): 59–88.

Byrd, Jodi. *The Transit of Empire: Indigenous Critiques of Colonialism.* Minneapolis: University of Minnesota Press, 2011.

Cahill, Cathleen D. *Federal Fathers and Mothers: A Social History of the United States Indian Service, 1869–1933.* Chapel Hill: University of North Carolina Press, 2011.

Caison, Gina. *Red States: Indigeneity, Settler Colonialism, and Southern Studies.* Athens: University of Georgia Press, 2018.

Calcaterra, Angela. *Literary Indians: Aesthetics and Encounter in American Literature to 1920.* Chapel Hill: University of North Carolina Press, 2018.

Calloway, Colin G., ed. *After King Philip's War: Presence and Persistence in Indian New England.* Hanover, NH: University Press of New England, 1997.

Calloway, Colin G. *Pen and Ink Witchcraft: Treaties and Treaty Making in American Indian History.* New York: Oxford University Press, 2013.

Campisi, Jack. "The Emergence of the Mashantucket Pequot Tribe, 1637–1975." In *The Pequots in Southern New England: The Fall and Rise of an American Indian Nation*, edited by Laurence M. Hauptman and James D. Wherry, 117–140. Norman: University of Oklahoma Press, 1990.

Campisi, Jack. *The Mashpee Indians: Tribe on Trial.* Syracuse, NY: Syracuse University Press, 1991.

Campisi, Jack. "The New England Tribes and Their Quest for Justice." In *The Pequots in Southern New England: The Fall and Rise of an American Indian Nation*, edited by Laurence M. Hauptman and James D. Wherry, 179–193. Norman: University of Oklahoma Press, 1990.

Canfield, Gae Whitney. *Sarah Winnemucca of the Northern Paiutes.* Norman: University of Oklahoma Press, 1983.

Carlson, David J. *Sovereign Selves: American Indian Autobiography and the Law.* Urbana: University of Illinois Press, 2006.

Carpenter, Cari M. "Detecting Indianness: Gertrude Bonnin's Investigation of Native American Identity." *Wicazo Sa Review* 20, no. 1 (2005): 139–159.

Carpenter, Cari M. "Sarah Winnemucca Goes to Washington: Rhetoric and Resistance in the Capital City." *American Indian Quarterly* 40, no. 2 (2016): 87–108.

Carpenter, Cari M. *Seeing Red: Anger, Sentimentality, and American Indians.* Columbus: Ohio State University Press, 2008.

Carpenter, Cari M., and Carolyn Sorisio, eds. *The Newspaper Warrior: Sarah Winnemucca Hopkins's Campaign for American Indian Rights, 1864–1891.* Lincoln: University of Nebraska Press, 2015.

Carpenter, Ron. "Zitkala-Ša and Bicultural Subjectivity." *Studies in American Indian Literatures* 16, no. 3 (2004): 1–28.

Carr, Helen. *Inventing the American Primitive: Politics, Gender, and the Representation of Native American Literary Traditions, 1789–1936.* New York: New York University Press, 1996.

Carroll, Clint. *Roots of Our Renewal: Ethnobotany and Cherokee Environmental Governance.* Minneapolis: University of Minnesota Press, 2015.

Cattelino, Jessica. *High Stakes: Florida Seminole Gaming and Sovereignty.* Durham, NC: Duke University Press, 2008.

Cave, Alfred A. *The Pequot War.* Amherst: University of Massachusetts Press, 1996.

Chang, David A. *The World and All the Things upon It: Native Hawaiian Geographies of Exploration.* Minneapolis: University of Minnesota Press, 2016.

Charters, Clare, and Rodolfo Stavenhagen, eds. *Making the Declaration Work: The United Nations Declaration on the Rights of Indigenous Peoples.* Copenhagen: International Work Group for Indigenous Affairs, 2009.

Chatterjee, Partha. *The Nation and Its Fragments: Colonial and Postcolonial Histories.* Princeton, NJ: Princeton University Press, 1993.

Cherokee Nation. *Laws of the Cherokee Nation: Adopted by the Council at Various Periods* (1852). Wilmington, DE: Scholarly Resources, 1973.

Cheyfitz, Eric. "The Navajo-Hopi Land Dispute: A Brief History." *Interventions* 2, no. 2 (2000): 248–275.

Cheyfitz, Eric. *The Poetics of Imperialism: Translation and Colonization from* The Tempest *to* Tarzan. Rev. ed. Philadelphia: University of Pennsylvania Press, 1997.

Chiarello, Barbara. "Deflected Missives: Zitkala-Ša's Resistance and Its (Un)Containment." *Studies in American Indian Literatures* 17, no. 3 (2005): 1–26.

Child, Brenda J. *Boarding School Seasons: American Indian Families, 1900–1940.* Rev. ed. Lincoln: University of Nebraska Press, 2012.

Clech Lâm, Maivân. *At the Edge of the State: Indigenous Peoples and Self-Determination.* Ardsley, NY: Transnational Publishers, 2000.

Cohen, Matt. *The Networked Wilderness: Communicating in Early New England.* Minneapolis: University of Minnesota Press, 2009.

Collier, John. *Indians of the Americas* (1947). New York: Mentor and Plume Books.

Conforti, Joseph A. *Imagining New England: Explorations of Regional Identity from the Pilgrims to the Mid-Twentieth Century.* Chapel Hill: University of North Carolina Press, 2001.

Conn, Steven. *History's Shadow: Native Americans and Historical Consciousness in the Nineteenth Century.* Chicago: University of Chicago Press, 2004.

Cooke, Jason Scott. "Indian Fields: Historicizing Native Space and Sovereignty in the Era of Removal." PhD diss., University of North Carolina Greensboro, 2017.

Coontz, Stephanie. *The Social Origins of Private Life: A History of American Families, 1600–1900.* New York: Verso, 1988.

Cotera, María Eugenia. *Native Speakers: Ella Deloria, Zora Neale Hurston, Jovita González, and the Poetics of Culture.* Austin: University of Texas Press, 2008.

Cott, Nancy F. *Public Vows: A History of Marriage and the Nation.* Cambridge, MA: Harvard University Press, 2000.

Coulthard, Glen Sean. *Red Skin, White Masks: Rejecting the Colonial Politics of Recognition*. Minneapolis: University of Minnesota Press, 2014.

Coviello, Peter. *Intimacy in America: Dreams of Affiliation in Antebellum Literature*. Minneapolis: University of Minnesota Press, 2005.

Cramer, Renée Ann. *Cash, Color, Colonialism: The Politics of Tribal Acknowledgment*. Norman: University of Oklahoma Press, 2005.

Cutter, Martha J. "Zitkala-Sä's Autobiographical Writings: The Problems of a Canonical Search for Language and Identity." *MELUS* 19, no. 1 (1994): 31–44.

Dahl, Adam. *Empire of the People: Settler Colonialism and the Foundations of Modern Democratic Thought*. Lawrence: University Press of Kansas, 2018.

Dale, Edward Everett, and Gaston Litton, eds. *Cherokee Cavaliers: Forty Years of Cherokee History as Told in the Correspondence of the Ridge-Watie-Boudinot Family* (1939). Norman: University of Oklahoma Press, 1995.

Darnell, Regna. *And Along Came Boas: Continuity and Revolution in Americanist Anthropology*. Philadelphia: John Benjamins, 1998.

Darnell, Regna. *Invisible Genealogies: A History of Americanist Anthropology*. Lincoln: University of Nebraska Press, 2001.

De Forest, John W. *History of the Indians of Connecticut: From the Earliest Known Period to 1850* (1851). Whitefish, MT: Kessinger, 2007.

Deloria, Ella. *Speaking of Indians* (1944). Lincoln: University of Nebraska Press, 1998.

Deloria, Philip J. *Indians in Unexpected Places*. Lawrence: University Press of Kansas, 2004.

Deloria, Philip J. *Playing Indian*. New Haven, CT: Yale University Press, 1998.

DeLucia, Christine M. *Memory Lands: King Philip's War and the Place of Violence in the Northeast*. New Haven, CT: Yale University Press, 2018.

DeMallie, Raymond J. "Kinship and Biology in Sioux Culture." In *North American Indian Anthropology: Essays on Society and Culture*, edited by Raymond J. DeMallie and Alfonso Ortiz, 125–146. Norman: University of Oklahoma Press, 1994.

DeMallie, Raymond J. "The Lakota Ghost Dance: An Ethnohistorical Account." *Pacific Historical Review* 51, no. 4 (1982): 385–405.

DeMallie, Raymond J. "Sioux until 1850." In *Handbook of North American Indians*, vol. 13.2, *Plains*, edited by Raymond J. DeMallie, 718–760. Washington, DC: Smithsonian Institution Press, 2001.

DeMallie, Raymond J. "Yankton and Yanktonai." In *Handbook of North American Indians*, vol. 13.2, *Plains*, edited by Raymond J. DeMallie, 777–793. Washington, DC: Smithsonian Institution Press, 2001.

D'Emilio, John, and Estelle B. Freedman. *Intimate Matters: A History of Sexuality in America*. 2nd ed. Chicago: University of Chicago Press, 1997.

Denetdale, Jennifer Nez. "Chairmen, Presidents, and Princesses: The Navajo Nation, Gender, and the Politics of Tradition." *Wicazo Sa Review* 21, no. 1 (2006): 9–28.

Denetdale, Jennifer Nez. *Reclaiming Diné History: The Legacies of Navajo Chief Manuelito and Juanita*. Tucson: University of Arizona Press, 2007.

Dennison, Jean. *Colonial Entanglement: Constituting a Twenty-First-Century Osage Nation*. Chapel Hill: University of North Carolina Press, 2012.

Den Ouden, Amy E. "Altered State? Indian Policy Narratives, Federal Recognition, and the 'New' War on Native Rights in Connecticut." In *Recognition, Sovereignty Struggles*, and Indigenous Rights in the United States: A Sourcebook, edited by Amy E. Den Ouden and Jean M. O'Brien, 169–194. Chapel Hill: University of North Carolina Press, 2013.

Den Ouden, Amy E. Beyond Conquest: Native Peoples and the Struggle for History in New England. Lincoln: University of Nebraska Press, 2005.

Den Ouden, Amy E., and Jean O'Brien, eds. Recognition, Sovereignty Struggles, and Indigenous Rights in the United States: A Sourcebook. Chapel Hill: University of North Carolina Press, 2013.

Denson, Andrew. Demanding the Cherokee Nation: Indian Autonomy and American Culture, 1830–1900. Lincoln: University of Nebraska Press, 2004.

Di Leonardo, Micaela. Exotics at Home: Anthropologies, Others, American Modernity. Chicago: University of Chicago Press, 1998.

Dillon, Elizabeth Maddock. New World Drama: The Performative Commons in the Atlantic World, 1649–1849. Durham, NC: Duke University Press, 2014.

Doerfler, Jill. Those Who Belong: Identity, Family, Blood, and Citizenship among the White Earth Anishinaabeg. East Lansing: Michigan State University Press, 2015.

Donaldson, Laura E. "'But We Are Your Mothers, You Are Our Sons': Gender, Sovereignty, and the Nation in Early Cherokee Women's Writing." In Indigenous Women and Feminism: Politics, Activism, Culture, edited by Cheryl Suzack, Shari M. Hunhdorf, Jeanne Perreault, and Jean Barman, 43–55. Vancouver: University of British Columbia Press, 2010.

Donaldson, Laura E. "Making a Joyful Noise: William Apess and the Search for Postcolonial Method(ism)." In Messy Beginnings: Postcoloniality and Early American Studies, edited by Malini Johar Schueller and Edward Watts, 29–44. New Brunswick, NJ: Rutgers University Press, 2003.

Doolen, Andy. Fugitive Empire: Locating Early American Imperialism. Minneapolis: University of Minnesota Press, 2005.

Driskill, Qwo-Li. Asegi Stories: Cherokee Queer and Two-Spirit Memory. Tucson: University of Arizona Press, 2016.

Du Bois, Cora. The 1870 Ghost Dance (1938). Lincoln: University of Nebraska Press, 2007.

Dunaway, Wilma. "Rethinking Cherokee Acculturation: Agrarian Capitalism and Women's Resistance to the Cult of Domesticity, 1800–1838." American Indian Culture and Research Journal 21, no. 1 (1997): 155–192.

Earle, John Milton. Report to the Governor and Council, Concerning the Indians of the Commonwealth, under the Act of April 6, 1859. Boston: William White, 1861.

Elliott, Michael A. The Culture Concept: Writing and Difference in the Age of Realism. Minneapolis: University of Minnesota Press, 2002.

Ellis, Richard E. The Union at Risk: Jacksonian Democracy, States' Rights, and the Nullification Crisis. New York: Oxford University Press, 1987.

Engle, Karen. The Elusive Promise of Indigenous Development: Rights, Culture, Strategy. Durham, NC: Duke University Press, 2010.

Estes, Nick. Our History Is the Future: Standing Rock versus the Dakota Access Pipeline and the Long Tradition of Indigenous Resistance. New York: Verso, 2019.

Ethridge, Robbie. Creek Country: The Creek Indians and Their World. Chapel Hill: University of North Carolina Press, 2003.

Evans, Brad. *Before Cultures: The Ethnographic Imagination in American Literature, 1865–1920*. Chicago: University of Chicago Press, 2005.

Eves, Rosalyn Collings. "Finding Place to Speak: Sarah Winnemucca's Rhetorical Practices in Disciplinary Spaces." *Legacy: A Journal of American Women Writings* 31, no. 1 (2014): 1–22.

Fawcett, Melissa Jayne. *Medicine Trail: The Life and Lessons of Gladys Tantaquidgeon*. Tucson: University of Arizona Press, 2000.

Ferguson, Roderick A. *The Reorder of Things: The University and Its Pedagogies of Minority Difference*. Minneapolis: University of Minnesota Press, 2012.

Fickes, Michael L. "'They Could Not Endure That Yoke': The Captivity of Pequot Women and Children after the War of 1637." *New England Quarterly* 73, no. 1 (2000): 58–81.

Field, Les W., with the Muwekma Ohlone Tribe. "Unacknowledged Tribes, Dangerous Knowledge: The Muwekma Ohlone and How Identities Are 'Known.'" *Wicazo Sa Review* 18, no. 2 (2003): 79–94.

Finger, John R. *Tennessee Frontiers: Three Regions in Transition*. Bloomington: Indiana University Press, 2001.

Fisher, Andrew H. *Shadow Tribe: The Making of Columbia River Indian Identity*. Seattle: University of Washington Press, 2010.

Ford, Lisa. *Settler Sovereignty: Jurisdiction and Indigenous People in America and Australia, 1788–1836*. Cambridge, MA: Harvard University Press, 2010.

Fortes, Meyer. *Kinship and the Social Order: The Legacy of Lewis Henry Morgan* (1969). New Brunswick, NJ: Aldine Transaction Publishers, 2006.

Fowler, Katherine S., and Sven Liljeblad. "Northern Paiute." In *Handbook of the North American Indians*, vol. 11, *Great Basin*, edited by Warren L. D'Azevedo and William C. Sturtevant, 435–465. Washington, DC: Smithsonian Institution Press, 1986.

Garrison, Tim Alan. *The Legal Ideology of Removal: The Southern Judiciary and the Sovereignty of Native American Nations*. Athens: University of Georgia Press, 2002.

Garroutte, Eva Marie. *Real Indians: Identity and the Survival of Native America*. Berkeley: University of California Press, 2003.

Gaul, Theresa Strouth. "'The Genuine Indian Who Was Brought Upon the Stage': Edwin Forrest's *Metamora* and White Audiences." *Arizona Quarterly* 56, no. 1 (2000): 1–27.

Genetin-Pilawa, C. Joseph. *Crooked Paths to Allotment: The Fight over Federal Indian Policy after the Civil War*. Chapel Hill: University of North Carolina Press, 2012.

Getachew, Adom. *Worldmaking after Empire: The Rise and Fall of Self-Determination*. Princeton, NJ: Princeton University Press, 2019.

Goeman, Mishuana. *Mark My Words: Native Women Mapping Our Nations*. Minneapolis: University of Minnesota Press, 2013.

Gould, Rae. "The Nipmuc Nation, Federal Acknowledgment, and a Case of Mistaken Identity." In *Recognition, Sovereignty Struggles, and Indigenous Rights in the United States: A Sourcebook*, edited by Amy E. Den Ouden and Jean M. O'Brien, 213–236. Chapel Hill: University of North Carolina Press, 2013.

Gramsci, Antonio. *Selections from the Prison Notebooks*. Edited and translated by Quintin Hoare and Geoffrey Nowell Smith. New York: International Publishers, 1971.

Green, Michael D. *The Politics of Indian Removal: Creek Government and Society in Crisis.* Lincoln: University of Nebraska Press, 1982.

Greyser, Naomi. *On Sympathetic Grounds: Race, Gender, and Affective Geographies in Nineteenth-Century North America.* New York: Oxford University Press, 2018.

Grose, B. Donald. "Edwin Forrest, *Metamora*, and the Indian Removal Act of 1830." *Theatre Journal* 37, no. 2 (1985): 181–191.

Grossman, Zoltán. *Unlikely Alliances: Native Nations and White Communities Join to Defend Rural Lands.* Seattle: University of Washington Press, 2017.

Gualtieri, Michael Allen. "The Role of Moral Outrage in the Northern Paiute Wars of the Mid-19th Century." PhD diss., University of Oregon, 2006.

Guha, Ranajit. *Dominance without Hegemony: History and Power in Colonial India.* Cambridge, MA: Harvard University Press, 1997.

Guha, Ranajit. "On Some Aspects of the Historiography of Colonial India." In *Selected Subaltern Studies*, edited by Ranajit Guha and Gayatri Chakravorty Spivak, 37–44. New York: Oxford University Press, 1988.

Gunn, Robert Lawrence. *Ethnology and Empire: Languages, Literature, and the Making of the North American Borderlands.* New York: New York University Press, 2015.

Gunter, Dan. "The Technology of Tribalism: The Lemhi Indians, Federal Recognition, and the Creation of Tribal Identity." *Idaho Law Review* 35 (1998): 85–123.

Gussman, Deborah. "'O Savage, Where Art Thou?': Rhetorics of Reform in William Apess's *Eulogy on King Philip*." *New England Quarterly* 77, no. 3 (2004): 451–477.

Hannon, Charles. "Zitkala-Sä and the Commercial Magazine Apparatus." In *The Only Efficient Instrument: American Women Writers and the Periodical*, edited by Aleta Feinsod Cane and Susan Alves, 179–201. Iowa City: University of Iowa Press, 2005.

Hanrahan, Heidi M. "'[W]orthy the Imitation of the Whites': Sarah Winnemucca and Mary Peabody Mann's Collaboration." *MELUS* 38, no. 1 (2013): 119–136.

Harmon, Alexandra. *Indians in the Making: Ethnic Relations and Indian Identities around Puget Sound.* Berkeley: University of California Press, 1998.

Harmon, Alexandra, ed. *The Power of Promises: Rethinking Indian Treaties in the Pacific Northwest.* Seattle: University of Washington Press, 2008.

Harring, Sidney L. *Crow Dog's Case: American Indian Sovereignty, Tribal Law, and United States Law in the Nineteenth Century.* New York: Cambridge University Press, 1994.

Hartman, Saidiya V. *Scenes of Subjection: Terror, Slavery, and Self-Making in Nineteenth-Century America.* New York: Oxford University Press, 1997.

Harvey, Sean P. *Native Tongues: Colonialism and Race from Encounter to the Reservation.* Cambridge, MA: Harvard University Press, 2015.

Hausman, Blake M. *Riding the Trail of Tears.* Lincoln: University of Nebraska Press, 2011.

Haynes, Carolyn. "'A Mark for Them All to . . . Hiss At': The Formation of Methodist and Pequot Identity in the Conversion Narrative of William Apess." *Early American Literature* 31, no. 1 (1996): 25–44.

Hegeman, Susan. *Patterns for America: Modernism and the Concept of Culture.* Princeton, NJ: Princeton University Press, 1999.

Hill, Sarah H. *Weaving New Worlds: Southeastern Cherokee Women and Their Basketry.* Chapel Hill: University of North Carolina Press, 1997.

Hinsley, Curtis M. *The Smithsonian and the American Indian: Making Moral Anthropology in Victorian America*. Washington, DC: Smithsonian Institution Press, 1981.

Hittman, Michael. "The 1870 Ghost Dance at the Walker River Reservation: A Reconstruction." *Ethnohistory* 20, no. 3 (1973): 247–278.

Hittman, Michael. *Great Basin Indians: An Encyclopedic History*. Reno: University of Nevada Press, 2013.

Hittman, Michael. *Wovoka and the Ghost Dance*. Rev. ed. Lincoln: University of Nebraska Press, 1990.

Hoover, Hebert T., in collaboration with Leonard R. Bruguier. *The Yankton Sioux*. New York: Chelsea House, 1988.

Howard, O. O. *Famous Indian Chiefs I Have Known*. New York: Century Company, 1908.

Howard, O. O. *My Life and Experiences among Our Hostile Indians: A Record of Personal Observations, Adventures, and Campaigns among the Indians of the Great West, with Some Account of Their Life, Habits, Traits, Religion, Ceremonies, Dress, Savage Instincts, and Customs of Peace and War*. Hartford, CT: A. D. Worthington, 1907.

Howard, O. O. "Report of Brigadier-General O. O. Howard." *Report of the Secretary of the War*. House Ex. Doc. 1, Part 2. 45th Cong, 3rd Sess. Washington, DC: Government Printing Office, 1878, 207–236.

Howe, Daniel Walker. *What Hath God Wrought: The Transformation of America, 1815–1848*. New York: Oxford University Press, 2007.

Hoxie, Frederick E. *A Final Promise: The Campaign to Assimilate the Indians, 1880–1920* (1984). Cambridge: Cambridge University Press, 1992.

Hudson, Angela Pulley. "'Forked Justice': Elias Boudinot, the U.S. Constitution, and Cherokee Removal." In *American Indian Rhetorics of Survivance: Word Medicine, Word Magic*, edited by Ernest Stromberg, 50–65. Pittsburgh: University of Pittsburgh Press, 2006.

Huhndorf, Shari M. *Going Native: Indians in the American Cultural Imagination*. Ithaca, NY: Cornell University Press, 2001.

Huhndorf, Shari M. *Mapping the Americas: The Transnational Politics of Contemporary Native Culture*. Ithaca, NY: Cornell University Press, 2009.

Hurt, R. Douglas. *The Indian Frontier, 1763–1846*. Albuquerque: University of New Mexico Press, 2002.

Huston, Reeve. *Land and Freedom: Rural Society, Popular Protest, and Party Politics in Antebellum New York*. New York: Oxford University Press, 2000.

Hutchinson, Elizabeth. *The Indian Craze: Primitivism, Modernism, and Transculturation in American Art, 1890–1915*. Durham, NC: Duke University Press, 2009.

Isenberg, Nancy. *Sex and Citizenship in Antebellum America*. Chapel Hill: University of North Carolina Press, 1998.

Jones, Dorothy V. *License for Empire: Colonialism by Treaty in Early America*. Chicago: University of Chicago Press, 1982.

Justice, Daniel Heath. *Our Fire Survives the Storm: A Cherokee Literary History*. Minneapolis: University of Minnesota Press, 2006.

Justice, Daniel Heath. *Why Indigenous Literatures Matter*. Waterloo, ON: Wilfrid Laurier University Press, 2018.

Kappler, Charles J. *Indian Affairs: Laws and Treaties*. 5 vols. Washington, DC: Government Printing Office, 1913.

Karuka, Manu. *Empire's Tracks: Indigenous Nations, Chinese Workers, and the Transcontinental Railroad*. Oakland: University of California Press, 2019.

Karuka, Manu. "The Prose of Counter-Sovereignty." In *Formations of United States Colonialism*, edited by Alyosha Goldstein, 87–109. Durham, NC: Duke University Press, 2014.

Kasson, Joy S. *Buffalo Bill's Wild West: Celebrity, Memory, and Popular History*. New York: Hill and Wang, 2000.

Katanski, Amelia V. *Learning to Write "Indian": The Boarding-School Experience and American Indian Literature*. Norman: University of Oklahoma Press, 2005.

Kauanui, J. Kēhaulani. *Paradoxes of Hawaiian Sovereignty: Land, Sex, and the Colonial Politics of State Nationalism*. Durham, NC: Duke University Press, 2018.

Kazanjian, David. *The Colonizing Trick: National Culture and Imperial Citizenship in Early America*. Minneapolis: University of Minnesota Press, 2003.

Kelsey, Penelope Myrtle. *Tribal Theory in Native American Literature: Dakota and Haudenosaunee Writing and Indigenous Worldviews*. Lincoln: University of Nebraska Press, 2008.

Keyssar, Alexander. *The Right to Vote: The Contested History of Democracy in the United States*. Rev. ed. New York: Basic Books, 2009.

Kilcup, Karen. *Fallen Forests: Emotion, Embodiment, and Ethics in American Women's Environmental Writing, 1781–1924*. Athens: University of Georgia Press, 2013.

Kilcup, Karen, ed. *Native American Women's Writing, 1800–1924: An Anthology*. Malden, MA: Blackwell, 2000.

Klopotek, Brian. *Recognition Odysseys: Indigeneity, Race, and Federal Tribal Recognition Policy in Three Louisiana Indian Communities*. Durham, NC: Duke University Press, 2011.

Knack, Martha C., and Omer C. Stewart. *As Long as the River Shall Run: An Ethnohistory of Pyramid Lake Indian Reservation*. Rev. ed. Reno: University of Nevada Press, 1999.

Kohler, Michelle. "Send Word: Sarah Winnemucca and the Violence of Writing." *Arizona Quarterly* 69, no. 3 (2013): 49–76.

Konkle, Maureen. *Writing Indian Nations: Native Intellectuals and the Politics of Historiography, 1827–1863*. Chapel Hill: University of North Carolina Press, 2004.

Krupat, Arnold. *Ethnocriticism: Ethnography, History, Literature*. Berkeley: University of California Press, 1992.

Kucich, John J. "William Apess's Nullifications: Sovereignty, Identity, and the Mashpee Revolt." In *Sovereignty, Separatism, and Survivance: Ideological Encounters in the Literature of Native North America*, edited by Benjamin D. Carson, 1–16. Newcastle upon Tyne, UK: Cambridge Scholars, 2009.

Kunce, Catherine. "Fire of Eden: Zitkala-Ša's Bitter Apple." *Studies in American Indian Literatures* 18, no. 1 (2006): 73–82.

Kuper, Adam. *The Reinvention of Primitive Society: Transformations of a Myth* (1988). London: Routledge, 1997.

Lape, Noreen Groover. "'I Would Rather Be with My People, but Not to Live with Them as They Live': Cultural Liminality and Double Consciousness in Sarah Winnemucca

Hopkins's *Life among the Piutes: Their Wrongs and Claims.*" *American Indian Quarterly* 22, no. 3 (1998): 259–279.

Larsen, Soren C., and Jay T. Johnson. *Being Together in Place: Indigenous Coexistence in a More Than Human World.* Minneapolis: University of Minnesota Press, 2017.

Latour, Bruno. *An Inquiry into Modes of Existence: An Anthropology of the Moderns.* Translated by Catherine Porter (2013). Cambridge, MA: Harvard University Press, 2013.

Latour, Bruno. *Reassembling the Social: An Introduction to Actor-Network Theory.* New York: Oxford University Press, 2017.

Laws of the Colonial and State Governments, Relating to Indians and Indian Affairs, from 1633 to 1831 Inclusive. Stanfordville, NY: Earl E. Coleman, 1979.

Lemont, Eric D., ed. *American Indian Constitutional Reform and the Rebuilding of Native Nations.* Austin: University of Texas Press, 2006.

Lepore, Jill. *The Name of War: King Philip's War and the Origins of American Identity.* New York: Vintage Books, 1998.

Levine, Caroline. *Forms: Whole, Rhythm, Hierarchy, Network.* Princeton, NJ: Princeton University Press, 2015.

Lewandowski, Tadeusz. *Red Bird, Red Power: The Life and Legacy of Zitkala-Ša.* Norman: University of Oklahoma Press, 2016.

Lopenzina, Drew. *Through an Indian's Looking-Glass: A Cultural Biography of William Apess, Pequot.* Amherst: University of Massachusetts Press, 2017.

Lowe, Lisa. *The Intimacies of Four Continents.* Durham, NC: Duke University Press, 2015.

Lowery, Malinda Maynor. *Lumbee Indians in the Jim Crow South: Race, Identity, and the Making of a Nation.* Chapel Hill: University of North Carolina Press, 2010.

Lyons, Scott Richard, ed. *The World, the Text, and the Indian.* Albany: State University of New York Press, 2017.

Lyons, Scott Richard. *X-marks: Native Signatures of Assent.* Minneapolis: University of Minnesota Press, 2010.

Macbain, Tiffany Aldrich. "Cont(r)acting Whiteness: The Language of Contagion in the Autobiographical Essays of Zitkala-Ša." *Arizona Quarterly* 68, no. 3 (2012): 55–69.

Mackey, Eva. *Unsettled Expectations: Uncertainty, Land and Settler Decolonization.* Halifax, NS: Fernwood, 2016.

Maddox, Lucy. *Citizen Indians: Native American Intellectuals, Race, and Reform.* Ithaca, NY: Cornell University Press, 2005.

Maddox, Lucy. *Removals: Nineteenth-Century American Literature and the Politics of Indian Affairs.* New York: Oxford University Press, 1991.

Mandell, Daniel R. *Behind the Frontier: Indians in Eighteenth-Century Massachusetts.* Lincoln: University of Nebraska Press, 1996.

Mandell, Daniel R. *Tribe, Race, History: Native Americans in Southern New England, 1780–1880.* Baltimore: Johns Hopkins University Press, 2008.

Manela, Erez. *The Wilsonian Moment: Self-Determination and the International Origins of Anticolonial Nationalism.* New York: Oxford University Press, 2007.

Mark, Joan. *A Stranger in Her Native Land: Alice Fletcher and the American Indians.* Lincoln: University of Nebraska Press, 1988.

Martin, Scott C. "Interpreting *Metamora*: Nationalism, Theater, and Jacksonian Indian Policy." *Journal of the Early Republic* 19, no. 1 (1999): 73–101.

Martínez, David. *Dakota Philosopher: Charles Eastman and American Indian Thought.* Minneapolis: Minnesota Historical Society Press, 2009.

Martínez, David. "Remembering the Thirty-Eight: Abraham Lincoln, the Dakota, and the U.S. War on Barbarism." *Wicazo Sa Review* 28, no. 2 (2013): 5–29.

McBride, Kevin A. "The Historical Archaeology of the Mashantucket Pequots, 1637–1900: A Preliminary Analysis." In *The Pequots in Southern New England: The Fall and Rise of an American Indian Nation*, edited by Laurence M. Hauptman and James D. Wherry, 96–116. Norman: University of Oklahoma Press, 1990.

McCarthy, Theresa. *In Divided Unity: Haudenosaunee Reclamation at Grand River.* Tucson: University of Arizona Press, 2016.

McClure, Andrew S. "Sarah Winnemucca: [Post]Indian Princess and Voice of the Paiutes." *MELUS* 24, no. 2 (1999): 29–51.

McDonnell, Janet A. *The Dispossession of the American Indian, 1887–1934.* Bloomington: Indiana University Press, 1991.

McGlennen, Molly. *Creative Alliances: The Transnational Designs of Indigenous Women's Poetry.* Norman: University of Oklahoma Press, 2014.

McLoughlin, William G. *Cherokee Renascence in the New Republic.* Princeton, NJ: Princeton University Press, 1986.

McLoughlin, William G., and Walter H. Conser Jr. "The Cherokee Censuses of 1809, 1825, and 1835." In *The Cherokee Ghost Dance: Essays on the Southeastern Indians, 1789–1861*, edited by William McLoughlin, 215–250. Macon, GA: Mercer University Press, 1984.

McWilliams, John. *New England's Crises and Cultural Memory: Literature, Politics, History, Religion, 1620–1860.* New York: Cambridge University Press, 2004.

Medicine, Beatrice. *Learning to Be an Anthropologist and Remaining "Native."* Urbana: University of Illinois Press, 2001.

Mehta, Uday Singh. *Liberalism and Empire: A Study in Nineteenth-Century British Liberal Thought.* Chicago: University of Chicago Press, 1999.

Melamed, Jodi. *Represent and Destroy: Rationalizing Violence in the New Racial Capitalism.* Minneapolis: University of Minnesota Press, 2011.

Merish, Lori. *Sentimental Materialism: Gender, Commodity Culture, and Nineteenth-Century American Literature.* Durham, NC: Duke University Press, 2002.

Michaelsen, Scott. *The Limits of Multiculturalism: Interrogating the Origins of American Anthropology.* Minneapolis: University of Minnesota Press, 1999.

Mielke, Laura L. *Moving Encounters: Sympathy and the Indian Question in Antebellum Literature.* Amherst: University of Massachusetts Press, 2008.

Mignolo, Walter D. *The Darker Side of the Renaissance: Literacy, Territoriality, and Colonization.* Ann Arbor: University of Michigan Press, 1995.

Miles, Tiya. "'Circular Reasoning': Recentering Cherokee Women in the Antiremoval Campaign." *American Quarterly* 61, no. 2 (2009): 221–243.

Miles, Tiya. *Ties That Bind: The Story of an Afro-Cherokee Family in Slavery and Freedom.* Berkeley: University of California Press, 2005.

Miller, Bruce Granville. *Invisible Indigenes: The Politics of Nonrecognition.* Lincoln: University of Nebraska Press, 2003.

Miller, Christopher L. *Prophetic Worlds: Indians and Whites on the Columbia Plateau* (1985). Seattle: University of Washington Press, 2003.

Miller, Mark Edwin. *Forgotten Tribes: Unrecognized Indians and the Federal Acknowledgment Process*. Lincoln: University of Nebraska Press, 2004.

Miller, Mark J. "'Mouth for God': Temperate Labor, Race, and Methodist Reform in William Apess's *A Son of the Forest*." *Journal of the Early Republic* 30, no. 2 (2010): 225–251.

Million, Dian. *Therapeutic Nations: Healing in an Age of Indigenous Human Rights*. Tucson: University of Arizona Press, 2013.

Mooney, James. *The Ghost-Dance Religion and the Sioux Outbreak of 1890* (1896). Lincoln: University of Nebraska Press, 1991.

Morgan, Lewis Henry. *Ancient Society, or Researches in the Lines of Human Progress from Savagery through Barbarism to Civilization* (1877). New York: Gordon Press, 1977.

Morgan, Thomas J. "Supplemental Report on Indian Education." In *Annual Report of the Commissioner of Indian Affairs to the Secretary of the Interior*, 93–114. Washington, DC: Government Printing Office, 1890.

Moulton, Gary E. *John Ross: Cherokee Chief*. Athens: University of Georgia Press, 1978.

Moulton, Gary E., ed. *The Papers of Chief John Ross*. Vol. 1, *1807–1839*. Norman: University of Oklahoma Press, 1985.

Muñoz, José Esteban. *Disidentifications: Queers of Color and the Performance of Politics*. Minneapolis: University of Minnesota Press, 1999.

Murray, David. *Forked Tongues: Speech, Writing, and Representation in North American Indian Texts*. Bloomington: Indiana University Press, 1991.

Nelson, Dana. *National Manhood: Capitalist Citizenship and the Imagined Fraternity of White Men*. Durham, NC: Duke University Press, 1998.

Nelson, Joshua B. *Progressive Traditions: Identity in Cherokee Literature and Culture*. Norman: University of Oklahoma Press, 2014.

Newmark, Julianne. "Pluralism, Place, and Gertrude Bonnin's Counternativism from Utah to Washington, DC." *American Indian Quarterly* 36, no. 3 (2012): 318–347.

Nichols, Robert. *Theft Is Property! Dispossession and Critical Theory*. Durham, NC: Duke University Press, 2019.

Nicoll, Fiona. "Reconciliation in and out of Perspective: White Knowing, Seeing, Curating, and Being at Home in and against Indigenous Sovereignty." In *Whitening Race: Essays in Social and Cultural Criticism*, edited by Aileen Moreton-Robinson, 17–31. Canberra: Aboriginal Studies Press, 2004.

Nielson, Donald M. "The Mashpee Indian Revolt of 1833." *New England Quarterly* 58, no. 3 (1985): 400–420.

Niezen, Ronald. *The Origins of Indigenism: Human Rights and the Politics of Identity*. Berkeley: University of California Press, 2003.

Norgren, Jill. *The Cherokee Cases: The Confrontation of Law and Politics*. New York: McGraw Hill, 1996.

O'Brien, Jean. *Dispossession by Degrees: Indian Land and Identity in Natick, Massachusetts, 1650–1790*. New York: Cambridge University Press, 1997.

O'Brien, Jean. *Firsting and Lasting: Writing Indians Out of Existence in New England*. Minneapolis: University of Minnesota Press, 2010.

O'Connell, Barry. Introduction to *On Our Own Ground: The Complete Writings of William Apess, a Pequot*, edited by Barry O'Connell, xiii–lxxxi. Amherst: University of Massachusetts Press, 1992.

O'Connell, Barry. "'Once More Let Us Consider': William Apess in the Writing of New England Native American History." In *After King Philip's War: Presence and Persistence in Indian New England*, edited by Colin G. Calloway, 162–177. Hanover, NH: University Press of New England, 1997.

Okker, Patricia. "Native American Literatures and the Canon: The Case of Zitkala-Ša." In *American Realism and the Canon*, edited by Tom Quirk and Gary Scharnhorst, 87–101. Newark: University of Delaware Press, 1994.

Onuf, Peter S. *Jefferson's Empire: The Language of American Nationhood*. Charlottesville: University Press of Virginia, 2000.

Ostler, Jeffrey. *The Plains Sioux and U.S. Colonialism from Lewis and Clark to Wounded Knee*. New York: Cambridge University Press, 2004.

Parins, James W. *Literacy and Intellectual Life in the Cherokee Nation, 1820–1906*. Norman: University of Oklahoma Press, 2013.

Pasternak, Shiri. *Grounded Authority: The Algonquins of Barriere Lake against the State*. Minneapolis: University of Minnesota Press, 2017.

Patterson, Thomas C. *A Social History of Anthropology in the United States*. New York: Berg, 2001.

Perdue, Theda. *Cherokee Women: Gender and Cultural Change, 1700–1835*. Lincoln: University of Nebraska Press, 1998.

Perdue, Theda. "Clan and Court: Another Look at the Early Cherokee Republic." *American Indian Quarterly* 24, no. 4 (2000): 562–569.

Perdue, Theda. Introduction to *Cherokee Editor: The Writings of Elias Boudinot*, 3–38. Athens: University of Georgia Press, 1996.

Perdue, Theda. *Slavery and the Evolution of Cherokee Society, 1540–1866*. Knoxville: University of Tennessee Press, 1979.

Perry, Imani. *Vexy Thing: On Gender and Liberation*. Durham, NC: Duke University Press, 2018.

Pexa, Christopher. *Translated Nation: Rewriting the Dakota Oyáte*. Minneapolis: University of Minnesota Press, 2019.

Peyer, Bernd C. *The Tutor'd Mind: Indian Missionary-Writers in Antebellum America*. Amherst: University of Massachusetts Press, 1997.

Pfister, Joel. *Individuality Incorporated: Indians and the Multicultural Modern*. Durham, NC: Duke University Press, 2004.

Piatote, Beth H. *Domestic Subjects: Gender, Citizenship, and Law in Native American Literature*. New Haven, CT: Yale University Press, 2013.

Piatote, Beth H. "The Indian/Agent Aporia." *American Indian Quarterly* 37, no. 3 (2013): 45–62.

Plane, Ann Marie. *Colonial Intimacies: Indian Marriage in Early New England*. Ithaca, NY: Cornell University Press, 2000.

Plane, Ann Marie, and Gregory Button. "The Massachusetts Indian Enfranchisement Act: Ethnic Contest in Historical Context, 1849–1869." In *After King Philip's War:*

Presence and Persistence in Indian New England, edited by Colin G. Calloway, 178–206. Hanover, NH: University Press of New England, 1997.

Porter, Joy. *To Be Indian: The Life of Iroquois-Seneca Arthur Caswell Parker*. Norman: University of Oklahoma Press, 2001.

Portnoy, Alisse. *Their Right to Speak: Women's Activism in the Indian and Slave Debates*. Cambridge, MA: Harvard University Press, 2005.

Povinelli, Elizabeth A. *The Cunning of Recognition: Indigenous Alterities and the Making of Australian Multiculturalism*. Durham, NC: Duke University Press, 2002.

Povinelli, Elizabeth A. *Labor's Lot: The Power, History, and Culture of Aboriginal Action*. Chicago: University of Chicago Press, 1993.

Powell, Dana. *Landscapes of Power: Politics of Energy in the Navajo Nation*. Durham, NC: Duke University Press, 2018.

Powell, Malea D. "Sarah Winnemucca Hopkins: Her Wrongs and Claims." In *American Indian Rhetorics of Survivance: Word Medicine, Word Magic*, edited by Ernest Stromberg, 69–94. Pittsburgh: University of Pittsburgh Press, 2006.

Pratt, Adam J. "Violence and the Competition for Sovereignty in Cherokee Country, 1829–1835." *American Nineteenth-Century History* 17, no. 2 (2016): 181–197.

Pratt, Scott L. "Wounded Knee and the Prospect of Pluralism." *Journal of Speculative Philosophy* 19, no. 2 (2005): 150–166.

Prucha, Francis Paul. *American Indian Treaties: The History of a Political Anomaly*. Berkeley: University of California Press, 1994.

Radus, Daniel. "Apess's *Eulogy* on Tour: Kinship and the Transnational History of Native New England." *Studies in American Indian Literatures* 28, no. 3 (2016): 81–110.

Raibmon, Paige. *Authentic Indians: Episodes of Encounter from the Late-Nineteenth-Century Northwest Coast*. Durham, NC: Duke University Press, 2005.

Ramirez, Renya K. *Native Hubs: Culture, Community, and Belonging in Silicon Valley and Beyond*. Durham, NC: Duke University Press, 2007.

Rand, Jacki Thompson. *Kiowa Humanity and the Invasion of the State*. Lincoln: University of Nebraska Press, 2008.

Rasmussen, Birgit Brander. *Queequeg's Coffin: Indigenous Literacies and Early American Literature*. Durham, NC: Duke University Press, 2012.

Razack, Sherene H. *Dying from Improvement: Inquests and Inquiries into Indigenous Deaths in Custody*. Toronto: University of Toronto Press, 2015.

Rebhorn, Matthew. "Edwin Forrest's Redding Up: Elocution, Theater, and the Performance of the Frontier." *Comparative Drama* 40, no. 4 (2006): 455–481.

Reddy, Chandan. *Freedom with Violence: Race, Sexuality, and the US State*. Durham, NC: Duke University Press, 2011.

Reid, John Phillip. *A Better Kind of Hatchet: Law, Trade, and Diplomacy in the Cherokee Nation during the Early Years of European Contact*. University Park: Pennsylvania State University Press, 1976.

Reid, Julie L. "An Absolute and Unconditional Pardon: Nineteenth-Century Cherokee Indigenous Justice." In *The Native South: New Histories and Enduring Legacies*, edited by Tim Alan Garrison and Greg O'Brien, 126–143. Lincoln: University of Nebraska Press, 2017.

Richland, Justin. *Arguing with Tradition: The Language of Law in Hopi Tribal Court.* Chicago: University of Chicago Press, 2008.

Rifkin, Mark. "Around 1978: Family, Culture, and Race in the Federal Production of Indianness." In *Critically Sovereign: Indigenous Gender, Sexuality, and Feminist Studies,* edited by Joanne Barker, 169–206. Durham, NC: Duke University Press, 2017.

Rifkin, Mark. *Beyond Settler Time: Temporal Sovereignty and Indigenous Self-Determination.* Durham, NC: Duke University Press, 2017.

Rifkin, Mark. *Erotics of Sovereignty: Queer Native Writing in the Era of Self-Determination.* Minneapolis: University of Minnesota Press, 2012.

Rifkin, Mark. *Fictions of Land and Flesh: Blackness, Indigeneity, Speculation.* Durham, NC: Duke University Press, 2019.

Rifkin, Mark. "Indigenizing Agamben: Rethinking Sovereignty in Light of the 'Peculiar' Status of Native Peoples." *Cultural Critique* 72 (Fall 2009): 88–124.

Rifkin, Mark. *Manifesting America: The Imperial Construction of U.S. National Space.* New York: Oxford University Press, 2009.

Rifkin, Mark. *Settler Common Sense: Queerness and Everyday Colonialism in the American Renaissance.* Minneapolis: University of Minnesota Press, 2014.

Rifkin, Mark. *When Did Indians Become Straight? Kinship, the History of Sexuality, and Native Sovereignty.* New York: Oxford University Press, 2011.

Rockwell, Stephen J. *Indian Affairs and the Administrative State in the Nineteenth Century.* New York: Cambridge University Press, 2010.

Rodríguez, Ileana. *The Latin American Subaltern Studies Reader.* Durham, NC: Duke University Press, 2001.

Rosen, Deborah A. *American Indians and State Law: Sovereignty, Race, and Citizenship, 1790–1880.* Lincoln: University of Nebraska Press, 2007.

Ross-Mulkey, Mikhelle Lynn. "*The Cherokee Phoenix*: Resistance and Accommodation." *Native South* 5 (2012): 123–148.

Round, Philip H. *Removable Type: Histories of the Book in Indian Country, 1663–1880.* Chapel Hill: University of North Carolina Press, 2010.

Ruby, Robert H., and John A. Brown. *Dreamer-Prophets of the Columbian Plateau: Smoholla and Skolaskin.* Norman: University of Oklahoma Press, 1989.

Ruppel, Kristin T. *Unearthing Indian Land: Living with the Legacies of Allotment.* Tucson: University of Arizona Press, 2008.

Saldaña-Portillo, María Josefina. *Indian Given: Racial Geographies across Mexico and the United States.* Durham, NC: Duke University Press, 2016.

Saler, Bethel. *The Settlers' Empire: Colonialism and State Formation in America's Old Northwest.* Philadelphia: University of Pennsylvania Press, 2015.

Salisbury, Neal. *Manitou and Providence: Indians, Europeans, and the Making of New England, 1500–1643.* New York: Oxford University Press, 1982.

Sansom-Flood, Renée. *Lessons from Chouteau Creek: Yankton Memories of Dakota Territorial Intrigue.* Sioux Falls, SD: Center for Western Studies, 1986.

Saunt, Claudio. *Black, White, and Indian: Race and the Unmaking of an American Family.* New York: Oxford University Press, 2005.

Sayre, Gordon. "Defying Assimilation, Confounding Authority: The Case of William Apess." *A/B: Autobiography Studies* 11, no. 1 (1996): 1–18.

Sayre, Gordon. "Melodramas of Rebellion: *Metamora* and the Literary Historiography of King Philip's War in the 1820s." *Arizona Quarterly* 60, no. 2 (2004): 1–32.

Scheckel, Susan. *The Insistence of the Indian: Race and Nationalism in Nineteenth-Century American Culture.* Princeton, NJ: Princeton University Press, 1998.

Schneider, Bethany. "Boudinot's Change: Boudinot, Emerson, and Ross on Cherokee Removal." *ELH* 75, no. 1 (2008): 151–177.

Schuller, Kyla. *The Biopolitics of Feeling: Race, Sex, and Science in the Nineteenth Century.* Durham, NC: Duke University Press, 2018.

Scott, Lalla. *Karnee: A Paiute Narrative.* Reno: University of Nevada Press, 1966.

Senier, Siobhan. *Voices of American Indian Assimilation and Resistance: Helen Hunt Jackson, Sarah Winnemucca, and Victoria Howard.* Norman: University of Oklahoma Press, 2001.

Sexton, Jared. "The Vel of Slavery: Tracking the Figure of the Unsovereign." *Critical Sociology* (December 2014): 1–15.

Shepherd, Jeffrey P. *We Are an Indian Nation: A History of the Hualapai People.* Tucson: University of Arizona Press, 2010.

Shorter, David Delgado. *We Will Dance Our Truth: Yaqui History in Yoeme Performances.* Lincoln: University of Nebraska Press, 2014.

Silverman, David J. *Faith and Boundaries: Colonists, Christianity, and Community among the Wampanoag Indians of Martha's Vineyard, 1600–1871.* New York: Cambridge University Press, 2005.

Silverman, David J. "The Impact of Indentured Servitude on the Society and Culture of Southern New England Indians, 1680–1810." *New England Quarterly* 74, no. 4 (2001): 622–666.

Simonsen, Jane E. *Making Home Work: Domesticity and Native American Assimilation in the American West, 1860–1919.* Chapel Hill: University of North Carolina Press, 2006.

Simpson, Audra. *Mohawk Interruptus: Political Life across the Borders of Settler States.* Durham, NC: Duke University Press, 2014.

Simpson, Audra. "On Ethnographic Refusal: Indigeneity, 'Voice' and Colonial Citizenship." *Junctures* 9 (2007): 67–80.

Simpson, Audra. "The State Is a Man: Theresa Spence, Loretta Saunders and the Gender of Settler Sovereignty." *Theory and Event* 19, no. 4 (2016).

Simpson, Audra. "Why White People Love Franz Boas; or, The Grammar of Indigenous Dispossession." In *Indigenous Visions: Rediscovering the World of Franz Boas,* edited by Ned Blackhawk and Isaiah Lorado Wilner, 166–181. New Haven, CT: Yale University Press, 2018.

Simpson, Leanne Betasamosake. *As We Have Always Done: Indigenous Freedom through Radical Resistance.* Minneapolis: University of Minnesota Press, 2017.

Simpson, Leanne Betasamosake. *Dancing on Our Turtle's Back: Stories of Nishnaabeg Re-Creation, Resurgence, and a New Emergence.* Winnipeg: Arbeiter Ring, 2011.

Simpson Smith, Katy. "'I Look on You . . . As My Children': Persistence and Change in Cherokee Motherhood, 1750–1835." *North Carolina Historical Review* 87, no. 4 (2010): 403–430.

Smith, Sherry L. *Reimagining Indians: Native Americans through Anglo Eyes, 1880–1940.* New York: Oxford University Press, 2000.

Smithers, Gregory D. *The Cherokee Diaspora: An Indigenous History of Migration, Resettlement, and Identity*. New Haven, CT: Yale University Press, 2015.

Smoak, Gregory E. *Ghost Dances and Identity: Prophetic Religion and American Indian Ethnogenesis in the Nineteenth Century*. Berkeley: University of California Press, 2006.

Sneider, Leah. "Gender, Literacy, and Sovereignty in Winnemucca's *Life among the Piutes*." *American Indian Quarterly* 36, no. 3 (2012): 257–287.

Snyder, Christina. *Slavery in Indian Country: The Changing Face of Captivity in Early America*. Cambridge, MA: Harvard University Press, 2010.

Sorisio, Carolyn. "'I Nailed Those Lies': Sarah Winnemucca Hopkins, Print Culture, and Collaboration." *J19: The Journal of Nineteenth-Century Americanists* 5, no. 1 (2017): 79–106.

Sorisio, Carolyn. "Sarah Winnemucca, Translation, and US Colonialism and Imperialism." *MELUS* 37, no. 1 (2012): 35–60.

Spack, Ruth. "Re-visioning Sioux Women: Zitkala-Sa's Revolutionary *American Indian Stories*." *Legacy* 14, no. 1 (1997): 25–42.

Spivak, Gayatri Chakravorty. *A Critique of Postcolonial Reason: Toward a History of the Vanishing Present*. Cambridge, MA: Harvard University Press, 1999.

Spivak, Gayatri Chakravorty. *Death of a Discipline*. New York: Columbia University Press, 2003.

Spivak, Gayatri Chakravorty. *Other Asias*. Oxford: Wiley-Blackwell, 2008.

Spivak, Gayatri Chakravorty. "Subaltern Studies: Deconstructing Historiography." In *Selected Subaltern Studies*, edited by Ranajit Guha and Gayatri Chakravorty Spivak, 3–32. New York: Oxford University Press, 1988.

Spruhan, Paul. "A Legal History of Blood Quantum in Federal Indian Law to 1935." *South Dakota Law Review* 51, no. 1 (2006): 1–50.

Stark, Heidi Kiiwetinepinesilk. "Criminal Empire: The Making of the Savage in a Lawless Land." *Theory and Event* 19, no. 4 (2016).

Stevens, Scott Manning. "William Apess's Historical Self." *Northwest Review* 35, no. 3 (1997): 67–84.

Stowell, Susan Jane. "The Wada-Tika of the Former Malheur Indian Reservation." PhD diss., University of California, Davis, 2008.

Strickland, Rennard. *Fire and the Spirits: Cherokee Law from Clan to Court*. Norman: University of Oklahoma Press, 1975.

Sturm, Circe. *Blood Politics: Race, Culture, and Identity in the Cherokee Nation of Oklahoma*. Berkeley: University of California Press, 2002.

Suzack, Cheryl. *Indigenous Women's Writing and the Cultural Study of Law*. Toronto: University of Toronto Press, 2017.

Sweet, John Wood. *Bodies Politic: Negotiating Race in the American North, 1730–1830*. Philadelphia: University of Pennsylvania Press, 2003.

Sweet, Timothy. *American Georgics: Economy and Environment in American Literature, 1580–1864*. Philadelphia: University of Pennsylvania Press, 2002.

TallBear, Kimberly. *Native American DNA: Tribal Belonging and the False Promise of Genetic Science*. Minneapolis: University of Minnesota Press, 2013.

Tawil, Ezra F. *The Making of Racial Sentiment: Slavery and the Birth of the Frontier Romance*. New York: Cambridge University Press, 2008.

Taylor, Alan. *Liberty Men and Great Proprietors: The Revolutionary Settlement on the Maine Frontier, 1760–1820*. Chapel Hill: University of North Carolina Press, 1990.

Thompson, Kara. *Blanket*. New York: Bloomsbury Academic, 2018.

Thorne, Tanis C. *The World's Richest Indian: The Scandal over Jackson Barnett's Oil Fortune*. New York: Oxford University Press, 2003.

Tiro, Karim M. "Denominated '*Savage*': Methodism, Writing, and Identity in the Works of William Apess, a Pequot." *American Quarterly* 48, no. 4 (1996): 653–679.

Tisinger, Danielle. "Textual Performance and the Western Frontier: Sarah Winnemucca Hopkins's *Life among the Piutes: Their Wrongs and Claims*." *Western American Literature* 37, no. 2 (2002): 170–194.

Tolley, Sara-Larus. *Quest for Tribal Acknowledgment: California's Honey Lake Maidus*. Norman: University of Oklahoma Press, 2006.

Torres, Ruth Garby. "How You See Us, Why You Don't: Connecticut's Public Policy to Terminate the Schaghticoke Indians." In *Recognition, Sovereignty Struggles, and Indigenous Rights in the United States: A Sourcebook*, edited by Amy E. Den Ouden and Jean M. O'Brien, 195–212. Chapel Hill: University of North Carolina Press, 2013.

Totten, Gary. "Zitkala-Ša and the Problem of Regionalism: Nations, Narratives, and Critical Traditions." *American Indian Quarterly* 29, nos. 1–2 (2005): 84–123.

Trachtenberg, Alan. *Shades of Hiawatha: Staging Indians, Making Americans, 1880–1930*. New York: Hill and Wang, 2004.

Trafzer, Clifford E., and Margery Ann Beach. "Smoholla, the Washani, and Religion as a Factor in Northwestern Indian History." *American Indian Quarterly* 9, no. 3 (1985): 309–324.

Trautmann, Thomas R. *Lewis Henry Morgan and the Invention of Kinship*. Berkeley: University of California Press, 1987.

Trennert, Robert A., Jr. *Alternative to Extinction: Federal Indian Policy and the Beginnings of the Reservation System, 1846–51*. Philadelphia: Temple University Press, 1975.

Tully, James. *An Approach to Political Philosophy: Locke in Contexts*. New York: Cambridge University Press, 1993.

Turner, Dale. *This Is Not a Peace Pipe: Towards a Critical Indigenous Philosophy*. Toronto: University of Toronto Press, 2006.

Varadharajan, Asha. *Exotic Parodies: Subjectivity in Adorno, Said, and Spivak*. Minneapolis: University of Minnesota Press, 1995.

Velikova, Roumiana. "'Philip, King of the Pequots': History of an Error." *Early American Literature* 37, no. 2 (2002): 311–335.

Velikova, Roumiana. "Troping in Zitkala-Sa's Autobiographical Writings, 1900–1921." *Arizona Quarterly* 56, no. 1 (2000): 49–64.

Vigil, Kiara M. *Indigenous Intellectuals: Sovereignty, Citizenship, and the American Imagination, 1880–1930*. New York: Cambridge University Press, 2015.

Visweswaran, Kamala. *Un/common Cultures: Racism and the Rearticulation of Cultural Difference*. Durham, NC: Duke University Press, 2010.

Vizenor, Gerald. *Fugitive Poses: Native American Indian Scenes of Absence and Presence*. Lincoln: University of Nebraska Press, 1998.

Vizenor, Gerald. *Manifest Manners: Postindian Warriors of Survivance*. Hanover, NH: Wesleyan University Press, 1994.

Vogel, Todd. *Rewriting White: Race, Class, and Cultural Capital in Nineteenth-Century America*. New Brunswick, NJ: Rutgers University Press, 2004.

Walker, Cheryl. *Indian Nation: Native American Literature and Nineteenth-Century Nationalisms*. Durham, NC: Duke University Press, 1997.

Walker, Deward E., and Helen H. Schuster. "Religious Movements." In *Handbook of North American Indians*, vol. 12, *Plateau*, edited by Deward E. Walker Jr., 499–514. Washington, DC: Smithsonian Institution Press, 1998.

Warren, Louis S. *God's Red Son: The Ghost Dance Religion and the Making of Modern America*. Basic Books: New York, 2017.

Warrior, Robert. "Native Critics in the World: Edward Said and Nationalism." In *American Indian Literary Nationalism*, edited by Jace Weaver, Craig S. Womack, and Robert Warrior, 179–224. Albuquerque: University of New Mexico Press, 2006.

Warrior, Robert. *The People and the Word: Reading Native Non-Fiction*. Minneapolis: University of Minnesota Press, 2005.

Warrior, Robert. *Tribal Secrets: Recovering American Indian Intellectual Traditions*. Minneapolis: University of Minnesota Press, 1995.

Washburn, Wilcomb E. *The Assault on Indian Tribalism: The General Allotment Law (Dawes Act) of 1887* (1975). Malabar, FL: Robert E. Krieger, 1986.

Weheliye, Alexander G. *Habeas Viscus: Racializing Assemblages, Biopolitics, and Black Feminist Theories of the Human*. Durham, NC: Duke University Press, 2014.

Welke, Barbara Young. *Law and the Borders of Belonging in the Long Nineteenth-Century United States*. New York: Cambridge University Press, 2010.

Wexler, Laura. "Tender Violence: Literary Eavesdropping, Domestic Fiction, and Educational Reform." In *The Culture of Sentiment: Race, Gender, and Sentimentality in Nineteenth-Century America*, edited by Shirley Samuels, 9–38. New York: Oxford University Press, 1992.

Wilder, Gary. *Freedom Time: Negritude, Decolonization, and the Future of the World*. Durham, NC: Duke University Press, 2015.

Wilderson, Frank B., III. *Red, White, and Black: Cinema and the Structure of U.S. Antagonisms*. Durham, NC: Duke University Press, 2010.

Wilkins, David E. *American Indian Sovereignty and the U.S. Supreme Court: The Masking of Justice*. Austin: University of Texas Press, 1997.

Wilkins, Thurman. *Cherokee Tragedy: The Ridge Family and the Decimation of a People*. 2nd ed. Norman: University of Oklahoma Press, 1986.

Wilkinson, Elizabeth. "Gertrude Bonnin's Rhetorical Strategies of Silence." *Studies in American Indian Literatures* 25, no. 3 (2013): 33–56.

Williams, Robert A. *Linking Arms Together: American Indian Treaty Visions of Law and Peace, 1600–1800*. New York: Oxford University Press, 1997.

Winnemucca Hopkins, Sarah. *Life among the Piutes* (1883). Reno: University of Nevada Press, 1994.

Wolfe, Eric A. "Mourning, Melancholia, and Rhetorical Sovereignty in William Apess's *Eulogy on King Philip*." *Studies in American Indian Literatures* 20, no. 4 (2008): 1–23.

Womack, Craig. *Art as Performance, Story as Criticism: Reflections on Native Literary Aesthetics*. Norman: University of Oklahoma Press, 2009.

Womack, Craig. "The Integrity of American Indian Claims; or, How I Learned to Stop Worrying and Love My Hybridity." In *American Indian Literary Nationalism*, by Jace Weaver, Craig S. Womack, and Robert Warrior, 91–178. Albuquerque: University of New Mexico Press, 2006.

Womack, Craig. *Red on Red: Native American Literary Separatism*. Minneapolis: University of Minnesota Press, 1999.

Wyss, Hilary E. *English Letters and Indian Literacies: Reading, Writing, and New England Missionary Schools, 1750–1830*. Philadelphia: University of Pennsylvania Press, 2012.

Wyss, Hilary E. *Writing Indians: Literacy, Christianity, and Native Community in Early America*. Amherst: University of Massachusetts Press, 2000.

Yarbrough, Fay. "Legislating Women's Sexuality: Cherokee Marriage Laws in the Nineteenth Century." *Journal of Social History* 38, no. 2 (2004): 385–406.

Zanjani, Sally. *Sarah Winnemucca*. Lincoln: University of Nebraska Press, 2001.

Zitkala-Ša. *American Indian Stories, Legends, and Other Writings*. Edited by Cathy N. Davidson and Ada Norris. New York: Penguin Books, 2003.

Zuba, Clayton. "Apess's *Eulogy on King Philip* and the Politics of Native Visualcy." *Early American Literature* 52, no. 3 (2017): 651–677.

Zuck, Rochelle Raineri. "William Apess, the 'Lost Tribes,' and Indigenous Survivance." *Studies in American Indian Literatures* 25, no. 1 (2013): 1–26.

Ghost Dances: Chief Winnemucca and, 133; collective identification through, 174–75; dissemination of, 140–41; emergence of, 32–33, 127–28, 139; geographies and networks of, 150, 157–61, 259n43; non-native characterizations of, 171–74; origin of, 140; Winnemucca's nonengagement with, 130–32, 149, 159–61

Goeman, Mishuana: on mediation of settler colonialism, 130, 170; on Native governance, 27; on recognition, 148, 156; on representativity, 13; on territoriality, 227; on women and governance, 107–8

governance (Native): Boudinot's discussion of, 36, 46–52; in Cherokee Nation, 40–52, 69–76; colonial alteration of, 39–40; federal oversight of, 185–95; in *Indian Nullification* (Apess), 112; Indigenous norms of authority and, 17; Mashpee self-governance declaration, 114–16; Metacom as symbol of Indigeneity and, 97–111; Native framing of, 27–28; non-native recognition of, 16–28; representativity linked to, 68–76; in Zitkala-Ša's work, 181, 185–95

governmentality, settler colonialism and, 18–19

Griswold, Whiting, 117

grounded normativity, Coulthard's concept of, 57–58

Gualtieri, Michael Allen, 137, 139–40, 145

guardian system (non-native superintendents): anomalous characterization of Indigenous status as justification for, 118; Apess's rejection of, 103; land appropriation under, 250n9; Mashpee resistance to, 123; over New England indigenous communities, 77–79, 94–96; refusal in Apess's texts of, 80; state control of, 253n44; suppression of Native self-governance and, 115–16

Guha, Ranajit, 22, 36–37, 40, 58

Gussman, Deborah, 255n79

Hallett, Benjamin F., 112–13, 120

Harper's magazine, 181

Hausman, Blake, 247n70

"Have We Failed the Indian?" (Dawes), 181

Haworth, J. M., 147

heteropatriarchy: Apess's Metacom as symbol of, 97–98, 106–11, 126; in Cherokee Nation, 36, 58–62, 240n2; in Zitkala-Ša's work, 181

Hillhouse, William, 89

history, Apess's King Philip narrative and framing of, 98–111

homestead law, reservation land dispossession and, 116n122

Howard, O. O. (Gen), 144, 151, 154, 158–59, 168

Humboldt Register, 144

Idaho Statesman, 158

"Impressions of an Indian Childhood" (Zitkala-Ša), 181–95

improvement, Cherokee politics and rhetoric of, 63–76

incapacity, settler configurations of, 199–206

indenture of Indigenous peoples, Apess's depiction of, 88–90

India, colonial rule and nationalism in, 22, 36–37, 242n8

"An Indian Teacher among Indians" (Zitkala-Ša), 181–95

Indian courts, establishment of, 185

Indian education: Indigenous pedagogy and, 194–95; Indigenous resistance to, 188–95; settler colonial projects for, 178; Zitkala-Ša's account of, 180, 183–84

Indian Nullification of the Unconstitutional Laws of Massachusetts Relative to the Marshpee Tribe; or, The Pretended Riot Explained (Apess), 31–32; negative space of nullification in, 111–26; sovereignty and self-determination in, 78–79, 82, 125–26

"Indian/Agent Aporia, The" (Piatote), 172

Indigenous identity: Apess on perceptions of, 83–85, 92–96; densities of, 212; dignity and pride in, 214–15; federal government assault on, 182–95; Metacom as dominant symbol of, 97–111; non-native perceptions of, 177–79, 185–95; resurgence of, 221–33; separation from settler state and, 55–62; settler recognition of, 1–3; spectacularization of, 200–206; wildness characterization of, 195–206; in Winnemucca's Paiute narrative, 128–32; in Zitkala-Ša's work, 191–95

information retrieval, Spivak's concept of, 223, 250n13

Inquiry into Modes of Existence, An (Latour), 70–71

institutional norms: Cherokee adoption of, 37, 241n6; Indigenous politics and, 18–28, 73–76, 228–29

intellectual labor, 66–67; Indigenous politics and, 228–33

intermarriage, Indigenous women with non-natives, 87–88, 110–11

intermediaries, texts as, 10, 16, 236n20

intracommunity recognition, 26

Irving, Washington, 253n52

Jackson, Andrew, 42–43, 256n86

Justice, Daniel Heath, 8

Käsebier, Gertrude, 206

Kasson, Joy, 200, 271n82

Katanski, Amelia, 273n106

King Philip, 21; adoption of name by, 253n49; Apess's narrative of, 79, 96–111, 125–26; as family and domestic figure, 255n79; Indigenous political claims and struggles and, 255n74; lineage of, 84, 250n20; Washington identified with, 99–101, 107, 254n60. *See also* Metacom (King Philip, Wampanoag sachem)

King Philip's War, 96–111; as mutual destruction for settlers and Natives, 105–6; women's role in, 108–9

kinship networks: Cherokee governance and, 31; geopolitics and, 150, 270n61; intermarriage and, 87; Native women and development of, 32, 94, 96, 106, 109, 126; non-native perceptions of, 159, 169; Paiute bands and, 137–38; of southern New England tribes, 10, 255n74; tribal identity and, 157, 240n69; Yankton tiospaye, 21, 270n61; in Zitkala-Ša's work, 192–95

Klopotek, Brian, 238n44

Knack, Martha C., 136, 259n35

Kohler, Michelle, 146

Konkle, Maureen, 8, 65–66, 73, 102, 116, 248n86

Krupat, Arnold, 249n3

Kucich, John J., 82, 121

La Flesche, Francis, 190, 196–97

land rights and land seizure: absence of recognition and, 80; allotment policy and, 172–73, 178–79, 199, 213–20; Cherokee concepts of, 41–42, 53–62, 241n6; Cherokee migration history and, 247n70; dispossession of Indigenous New England tribes and, 86–91; grounded normativity concept of, 57–58; Metacom narrative in context of, 105–11; railroad infringement on, 143, 264n125; on reservations, 165–74, 268n38; tribal identity and, 199–206; Winnemucca's advocacy for, 171–74, 263n115; in Zitkala-Ša's writing, 183–95

Latour, Bruno, 10–11, 52, 70–71, 124, 178, 237n33

Leggins (Paiute leader), 160, 164

Letters and Other Papers Relating to Cherokee Affairs (Boudinot), 30–31: absence of non-elite perspectives in, 42; Cherokee formation of peoplehood in, 52–62; Cherokee identity in, 47–52; elite orientation and, 39–52; intellectual perspective *vs.* collective deliberation in, 62–76; publication of, 35–39; representativity as collective identity in, 53–62

Levine, Caroline, 11

Lewandowski, Tadeusz, 181, 203

liberalism, Cherokee governance and, 37–38, 242n11

Life among the Piutes (Winnemucca), 32, 127–75; biographical elements in, 132–34; Congressional and public appearances in, 147–48; diplomatic engagement in, 145–49; disaggregation of Native space in, 150–61; federal agents in, 168–74; non-native audience for, 130–32, 147–48; Paiute identity in, 149–61; reservation politics in, 162–74; unification narrative in, 131–32

lineage-based power, Winnemucca's characterization of, 133–37

Lopenzina, Drew, 79

Major Crimes Act, 176

Malheur Reservation: non-native characterizations of, 146–47, 153; Paiute governance on, 140, 142, 144; prophet movement and, 158–61; in Winnemucca's narrative, 134, 162–75, 263n109

Mandell, Daniel, 86, 95

Manifest Manners (Vizenor), 91

Mann, Mary, 132

marriage forms, Indigenous rituals and practices and, 110

Mashantucket Pequots, 31–32: acknowledgment/erasure cycle and, 86–87; Apess relations with, 79–80, 82–96, 124–25; dispossession of, 88–89; politics and governance of, 95–96; settler land expropriation from, 89–90, 251n13

Mashpee, 32, 79; Apess as representative for, 111–26; self-governance declaration by, 114–26

Massosoit (sachem), 108

matrilinearity: Cherokee marginalization of, 49–50; in Cherokee Nation governance, 58–62, 246n67

McLoughlin, William, 242n15

mediation: identification and, 239n52; Indigenous writing as, 223–33; Native representation and, 62–76; texts as, 10, 16, 236n20; in Winnemucca's narrative, 130–32, 147–49; Zitkala-Ša's work as, 192–95

medicine men *See* shamanism

Melmed, Jodi, 222

memory and commemoration, Apess's King Philip narrative and, 98–111

Metacom (King Philip, Wampanoag sachem), 31–32; Apess's narrative of, 78–79, 96–111, 125–26; as family and domestic figure, 255n79; Indigenous political claims and struggles and, 255n74; origin of name, 253n49; Washington identified with, 99–101, 107, 254n60. *See also* King Philip; King Philip's War

Metamora (play), 96–97, 100–101, 106, 111, 125, 253n52

Methodism, Apess's characterization of, 93–95, 252n42

metonymic substitution: Apess on Indigenous self-determination and, 78–79, 119–26; in *Eulogy* (Apess), 105–11; Apess's Native experiences and, 94–96; Native wildness and, 84–85; terminology for, 249n3

Michaelsen, Scott, 272n98

Middle Five, The (La Flesche), 196–97

migration, Indigenous patterns of: Cherokee Nation history and, 247n70; Winnemucca's link to danger and disorder and, 130–32

missionization, impact on Native identity of, 212–20

mixed-race intermarriages: Cherokee bloodedness and, 241n3, 244n26, 246n8; Indigenous women in southern New England and, 87–88

Mohawk Interruptus (Simpson), 182

monarchical language: in *Eulogy* (Apess), 101–2, 105–11; in Winnemuca's narrative, 130–37

Morgan, Lewis Henry, 177–78, 195

Morgan, Thomas J., 178

Mud Lake Massacre, 260n48, 262n97

My Life and Experiences (Howard), 158

Namumpun *See* Weetaamoo (Namumpum) (saunkskwa)

Natchez (Paiute leader), 138, 141–42, 150

National Council (Cherokee Nation). *See* General Council

nationalism: Cherokee concepts of, 36, 240n3; criticism as remedy for excess in, 66; elite orientation framework for, 40; in Native writing, 237n32; peoplehood linked to, 54–62

nationhood: absence of, for southern New England tribes, 88–89, 124–26; in *Eulogy* (Apess), 105–11; Cherokee concepts of, 55–62, 119–20; Metacom as figure of, 99; non-native perceptions of, 178–79, 185–95; Paiute identity and, 149–61; U.S. jurisdiction *vs.* tribal authority and, 176–77; in Winnemucca's narrative, 128–37

Native Acts (Barker), 1, 18, 20, 186, 240n69

"Native Critics in the World" (Warrior), 66

native informant, Zitkala-Ša as, 198–220

Native intellectuals: Cherokee governance and, 62–66; definition of, 235n7; dissent in nationalist discourse of, 66; engagement with settler colonialism and, 80–81; non-native focus on, 91, 194–95; popular will and, 72–76; portrayal of Indigenous political collectivity and, 124–26; transnational Indigenous relations and, 231–33

Native internationalism, transnationalism and trans-indigeneity, 231–33

Native networks, political form in, 53–62

Native writing: in English, 8; ethnographic research in, 190–95; form in, 11; indigeneity representation in, 6–9; resurgence and role of, 222–33

Nelson, Joshua, 59, 241n3, 245n44

networks: of Ghost Dances and prophet movements, 150; Native writing and role of, 15; Paiute, Columbia Rivier Indian and Bannock differentiation and, 156–57; on reservations, 192–95; in southern New England reservations, 94–96, 106–7

New England: national origin mythology and role of, 98–99; state jurisdiction over Natives in, 31–32

Newe peoples, 137

New York Times, 143

Nielson, Donald, 115

non-natives: Appess's relations with, 83–96; Boudinot's appeal to, 61–62; Cherokee elites' orientation toward, 67–76, 246n58; engagement in Winnemucca's narrative with, 130–32, 141–42, 146–49; ethnographic perspectives of, 182; governance of southern New England Indigenous peoples by, 77–126; Indigenous development and impact of, 195–206; Indigenous New England intermarriage with, 87–88, 109–10; Indigenous self-expression and, 214; King Philip as representative Indian for, 101–11; mimicking of Indigenous peoples by, 100; Native intellectuals' interaction with, 65–76; Native writing for, 9–10, 13, 125–26, 148; nullification narrative of, 115–16; Winnemucca's narrative and engagement with, 141–48, 150–61; Zitkala-Ša's engagement with, 181, 190–95

Northern Paiute people, Winnemucca's writing on, 127–75

Numaga (Paiute leader), 145

O'Brien, Jean, 81–82, 103–4, 111

Oceti Sakowin (Seven Council Fires), 184

Office of Indian Affairs, World's Columbian Exposition and, 202

Oka Crisis, 224–25

"On Some Aspects of the Historiography of Colonial India" (Guha), 36–37, 40

Oregon Donation Land Act (1850), 116n122

Osage constitutional reform, 25, 245n42

Our Beloved Kin (Brooks), 108–9

Outlook magazine, 194

Oytes (Paiute leader), 127, 135–36, 139–41, 149, 152–53, 160–61

pacifism, Winnemucca's characterization of Paiutes and, 152–61

Paiutes: Bannocks and, 158–61; Ghost Dances and, 32–33; non-native condensation of leadership of, 143–45; political process and structure in, 133–37, 143–44; reservation politics and, 162–74; self-contained identity of, 149–61; tribal divisions within, 257n3, 257n6; Winnemucca's claim as spokesman for, 128–32, 136

Parrish, Samuel, 135–36, 140, 152, 164, 166

Pasheco (prophet figure), 157

Pasternak, Shiri, 275n20

patriarchal leadership. *See* heteropatriarchy

patriotism: Boudinot's framing of, 53–57, 61–62, 66; of King Philip (Metacom), 101, 105–11

Peabody, Elizabeth, 132, 146

peoplehood: Apess's depiction of, 82–83, 92–96; Boudinot's vision of, 46, 52–62; Cherokee concepts of, 36, 48–49, 119–20, 240n2; Cherokee formation of, 52–62; culture and, 230–33; difference and, 15; Ghost Dance movements and forms of, 128–32; Metacom as symbol of Indigeneity and, 97–111; in Native writing, 9, 23–24, 27–28, 237n32; Paiute concepts of, 145; prophet movement rejections of, 162; reading for politics of, 221–33; recognition of, 1–5; reservations and delineation of, 162; textual accounts of, 4–5; in Winnemucca's narrative, 128–32; in Zitkala-Ša's work, 191–95; in Zitkala-Ša's writing, 182–95

Pequot War, 86–87

Perdue, Theda, 50, 58

performance: of wildness, in Wild West Shows, 200–206; Zitkala-Ša's stories as, 198–99, 207–20

Pexa, Christopher, 13

Peyer, Bernd, 245n50

"Philip of Pokanoket" (Irving), 253n52

Piatote, Beth, 8, 14, 172, 182, 190, 219

Plane, Ann Marie, 110

political economy: Cherokee governance and, 39–52; southern New England Indigenous exploitation and, 88–89

politics and political process: in *Eulogy* (Apess), 102–11; in *Indian Nullification* (Apess), 119–26; Cherokee vision of, 41–42; elite orientation and, 39–40; form and subjectivity of, 26–28; Indigenous concepts of, 9, 55–62; Indigenous nationhood and, 177–78; Native writing and representation of, 13–14, 25–28; non-native expectations of Indigenous forms of, 156, 177–78; Paiute processes and formation of, 133–46; of peoplehood, 63–76; of recognition, 17–18; refusal and, 224–25, 275n15

popular consent, Cherokee governance and role of, 69–76

popular entertainment, wildness trope of Indigenous identity and, 200–206

Povinelli, Elizabeth, 169

Powell, John Wesley, 268n43, 270n68

Powell, Malea, 128, 151

Pratt, Richard Henry, 202

Pratt, Scott L., 171

primitive, non-native yearning for, 198–206

property rights, Cherokee concepts of, 41–42, 241n6

prophet movements: emergence of, 139–41; geographies and networks of, 150, 157–61; Ghost Dances and, 127–28, 139; rejection of reservations by, 162–74; reservation refusal and, 170–74; Winnemucca's disregard of, 149

puha, 139–41, 161, 174

Pyramid Lake Reservation: government land seizures in, 164–72; political structure of, 136–38, 145–46; railroad infringement on, 143; treaty negotiations and, 146; US government creation of, 138–39; in Winnemucca's narrative, 134, 147, 162, 164, 173–74

Pyramid Lake War of 1860, 145

racism: Apess on experiences with, 84–87; in Cherokee Nation, 36, 244n26; Native sovereignty linked to, 116–17, 256n101; non-native perceptions of Indigeneity and, 185–86, 216–20, 268n41

recognition: Apess on nullification and, 118–26; in *Eulogy* (Apess), 105–11; Native writing and critiques of, 16–28, 232–33; politics of, 17–20; racism and, 238n44; resurgence and, 221–33; settler colonial refusal of, 79–80; in Winnemucca's narrative, 131–32, 148–49

Red Man and Helper (newspaper), 196

Reed, J., 113–14

refusal: as alternative to recognition, 18, 26–28; Apess on nullification and, 118–26; Cherokee identity and politics of, 59–62, 69–76; of ethnographic imaginary, 221–33, 275n20; of recognition, 79–80, 156; of reservation life, 168–74, 215–20, 273nn111–12; Simpson's articulation of, 79–80, 103, 156, 224–25

removal: Boudinot's endorsement of, 63–76; Cherokee identity and politics of, 35–39, 44–52, 61–62, 67–76, 245n32; federal agents' recommendations for, 185; of Paiutes, 144; Treaty Party negotiations over, 64–65

representation and representativity: Apess on exemplarity and, 79–111; collective voice and, 75–76; colonial alteration of, 39–40; exemplarity and, 79; Metacom as symbol of Indigeneity, 97–111; in Native writing, 5, 8–9; non-native ethnography and, 179; participatory deliberation separated from, 68–76; politics of, 13–14, 21–22, 59–62; resurgence and, 222–33; of tribal relations, 33; in Winnemucca's narrative, 128–32, 135–37; in Zitkala-Ša's work, 180–81, 193–95, 198–206

"Representative Indian, The" (*Outlook*), 194–95

reservations: dispossession of Paiutes on, 162–74, 263n115, 264n122; federal agents' administration of, 184–85, 192–95; land seizure in, 77–126, 172–79, 199, 213–20, 273nn111–12; mortality rates on, 189, 274n119; Native resistance to, 154; in southern New England, 94–96, 106–7; in Winnemucca's narrative, 130–32, 134, 136–39, 143, 145–48; in Zitkala-Ša's work, 185–95, 203–6

Ridge, John, 35, 41, 242n15; impeachment of, 65

Ridge, Major, 35, 41, 242n15; impeachment of, 65

Riding the Trail of Tears (Hausman), 247n70

Rinehart, W. V., 134, 140, 142, 158, 159, 163, 165–69

Ross, John: Boudinot's criticism of, 35, 38, 40–44, 58; Cherokee governance and, 47–49, 53, 59–60, 68–76; elite status of, 242n15; firing of Boudinot by, 64; on refusal, 70–71; resistance to land loss by, 56–57; Treaty Party negotiations and, 64–65, 71–72

Round Dance, Paiute ritual of, 140

Said, Edward, 66

Salem Gazette, 132

"Sarah Winnemucca, Translation, and US Colonialism and Imperialism" (Sorisio), 148

savagery, Winnemucca's narrative and figuration of, 151

scalping, in Winnemucca's narrative, 150–51

Schneider, Bethany, 54, 65

"The School Days of an Indian Girl" (Zitkala-Ša'), 181–95

Schuller, Kyla, 185–86, 268n38

Schurz, Carl, 160–61

Seeing Red (Carpenter), 151

self-determination: Apess on nullification of, 114; in Apess's writing, 78–111; Indigenous sovereignty and, 18, 81, 103–4, 221, 223, 227–33

self-governance: Apess's conceptualization of, 79–111; in Zitkala-Ša's work, 192–95

sentimentalism, characterization of Zitkala-Ša's work as, 268n44

settler colonialism: in Apess's biography, 88; Apess's nullification rhetoric and, 119–26; categorization of tribes in, 156–61; Cherokee governance and, 36–41; Cherokee identity as separate from, 52–62; elite orientation and, 40; Indigenous governance and, 231–33; jurisdiction over Indigenous sovereignty and, 178; Metacom narrative and illegitimacy of, 101; Native writing and, 12, 34, 226–33; prophet movement disruption of, 157–62; southern New England Indigenous peoples and regime of, 77–126; subjectivity of Indigenous governance and, 17; tribal recognition and, 2–3; Winnemucca narrative and influence of, 130–32, 143–49, 163–74; in Zitkala-Ša's writing, 182–95, 207–20

settler networks: Apess's Metacom narrative and, 98–111; Boudinot on engagement with, 63–76; Cherokee representativity and, 76; Indigenous recognition and, 4

Seven Years' War, Native participation and mortality in, 87

shamanism: geographies and networks of, 157–61; prophet movements and, 127–28, 138–40, 149

Simmons, Gertrude. *See* Zitkala-Ša

Simpson, Audra, 18, 26, 59; on backstreaming, 228; on non-native perceptions of culture, 182; on refusal of recognition, 79–80, 103, 156, 224

Simpson, Leanne, 18, 22–24, 27–28, 50, 55, 107

Sitting Bull, 200

slavery: in *Eulogy* (Apess), 254n68; in *Indian Nullification* (Apess), 121–22; in Cherokee Nation, 37–38, 242n11

Smith, Katy Simpson, 60–61

Smoak, Gregory, 127–28, 137, 139, 154

Smohalla (Indigenous prophet), 140–41, 153, 158–59

Snake tribes, white trapper characterization of, 155

Snake War, 262n84

Society of American Indians, 266n14

sociopolitical formations: non-native perceptions of, 178–79; of Paiutes, 134–38, 140–42; resurgence and, 221–33; static ethnographic framing of, 195–206; tribal identity and, 200–206; as wildness, 198–206; in Winnemucca's narrative, 128–32, 149; in Zitkala-Ša's work, 186–95

Son of the Forest, A (Apess), 31–32, 78; critical analysis of, 250n15; geopolitics and exploitation in, 82–96, 124–26; peoplehood vision in, 97

Sorisio, Carolyn, 148

southern New England, Apess on Indigenous politics in, 77–126

sovereignty: in Apess's writing, 79–81, 92–96, 119–20, 122–26; Carroll's concept of, 27–28; Cherokee concepts of, 49, 66–76, 119–20; Indigenous governance and, 4–5; Metacom as symbol of, 97, 103–11; self-determination and, 81; state nullification in New England of, 116, 119–26; in Zitkala-Ša's writing, 183–95

vision complexes: Indigenous kinship patterns and rituals and, 159–61; Native resistance linked to, 153–54; prophet movements and, 127–28, 138–39

Vizenor, Gerald, 91, 239n60

Walker, Cheryl, 260n47

Walker Reservation, 141

Wampanoags: Mashpee and, 114–15; resistance to settler colonialism and, 108–9

Wampy, Anne, 95–96

Warrior, Robert, 66–67, 230, 237n32

Washington, George: Metacom identified with, 99–101, 107; white reverence for, 21, 254n60

Washington Post, 143, 148–49

Watson, Irene, 156

Weekes, Cyrus, 117

Weetamoo (Namumpum) (saunkskwa), 108–11

Weheliye, Alexander, 268n39

White Path's Rebellion, 47–48, 69

White's Manual Institute (Indian boarding school), 180, 193

wildness: settler tropes of Natives and, 84–86; in Zitkala-Ša's stories, 196–206

Williams, William, 89–90, 93

Winnemucca (Paiute chief), 127–30; Congressional testimony of, 147; dreams of, 137–39; Ghost Dance movement and, 158–61; news accounts of, 143–44; non-native characterizations of, 143–46; Paiute identity reflected through, 157–61; Pasheco and, 157; reservation policies and, 167; shamanistic powers, 140; US relations with, 141–43, 150–51; Winnemucca (S) as descendant of, 132–34; in Winnemucca (Sarah)'s narrative, 134–42

Winnemucca, Sarah, 2, 24; avoidance of Ghost Dances by, 130–32, 149, 159–61; on Columbia River Indians, 152–61; Congressional petitions and testimony by, 147, 159–61, 171, 261n65; genealogical heritage and status of, 132–34, 148–49, 258n20; lecture tour by,

143; on Native mobility and prophecy, 32; on Paiute governance and politics, 134–41; Paiute identity characterized by, 149–61; as Paiute representative, 128–32, 147–49, 171–74; promiscuity accusations against, 134; reservation policies in narrative of, 162–74

Wodziwob (Paiute prophet), 127–28, 139–41, 158

Wolfe, Eric, 98

Womack, Craig, 223

women: in Cherokee Nation political structure, 40, 49–50, 58–62; displacement in New England tribes of, 87–88, 94–96, 107–8; governance on New England reservations by, 106–7; Paiute limits on succession of, 132; saunkswa (female Algonquian leaders), 108–11

Worcester v. Georgia, 43, 256n86

World's Columbian Exposition (Chicago, 1893), 200–202

Wounded Knee massacre, 200

Wovoka (Paiute prophet), 127–28

Wyss, Hilary, 252n42

Yakima Reservation: Paiute removal to, 144, 146–47, 152, 159–61; in Winnemucca's narrative, 162–74, 263n109

Yankton Reservation: land seizure in, 213–20; Zitkala-Ša's life in, 180, 183–95

Yankton tiospaye, 21, 270n61

Zanjani, Sally, 140, 141, 143

Zitkala-Ša, 2, 24; ethnographic subjectivity in stories of, 176–220; national activism of, 266n14; Native life in writings of, 181–95; peoplehood and sovereignty in work of, 179–81; performance as native informant, 207–20; on reservations and boarding schools, 33; wildness in fiction of, 196–206; influence of Wild West Shows in writings by, 200–206

Zuba, Clayton, 254n60